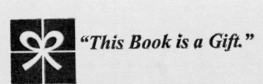

COLUMBUS

COLUMBUS

The Four Voyages

LAURENCE BERGREEN

VIKING

VIKING
Published by the Penguin Group
Penguin Group (USA) Inc., 375 Hudson Street, New York, New York 10014, U.S.A. • Penguin Group (Canada), 90 Eglinton Avenue East, Suite 700, Toronto, Ontario, Canada M4P 2Y3 (a division of Pearson Penguin Canada Inc.) • Penguin Books Ltd, 80 Strand, London WC2R 0RL, England • Penguin Ireland, 25 St Stephen's Green, Dublin 2, Ireland (a division of Penguin Books Ltd) • Penguin Books Australia Ltd, 250 Camberwell Road, Camberwell, Victoria 3124, Australia (a division of Pearson Australia Group Pty Ltd) • Penguin Books India Pvt Ltd, 11 Community Centre, Panchsheel Park, New Delhi – 110 017, India • Penguin Group (NZ), 67 Apollo Drive, Rosedale, Auckland 0632, New Zealand (a division of Pearson New Zealand Ltd) • Penguin Books (South Africa) (Pty) Ltd, 24 Sturdee Avenue, Rosebank, Johannesburg 2196, South Africa • Penguin Books Ltd, Registered Offices: 80 Strand, London WC2R 0RL, England

First published in 2011 by Viking Penguin, a member of Penguin Group (USA) Inc.

10   9   8   7   6   5   4   3   2   1

Copyright © Laurence Bergreen, 2011
All rights reserved

Illustration credits begin on page 421.

LIBRARY OF CONGRESS CATALOGING-IN-PUBLICATION DATA
Bergreen, Laurence.
    Columbus : the four voyages / Laurence Bergreen.
    p. cm.
    Includes bibliographical references and index.
    ISBN 978-0-670-02301-1 (hardback)
    1. Columbus, Christopher—Travel—America. 2. America—Discovery and exploration—Spanish. 3. Explorers—America—Biography. 4. Explorers—Spain—Biography. I. Title.
    E118.B47 2011
    970.01'5092—dc22   2011013900

Printed in the United States of America
Designed by Carla Bolte
Maps by Jeffery L. Ward

TO MY MOTHER

and

IN MEMORY OF MY FATHER AND BROTHER

A BATTER'D, wreck'd old man,
Thrown on this savage shore, far, far from home,
Pent by the sea, and dark rebellious brows, twelve dreary months,
Sore, stiff with many toils, sicken'd, and nigh to death,
I take my way along the island's edge,
Venting a heavy heart. . . .

Steersman unseen! henceforth the helms are Thine;
Take Thou command—(what to my petty skill Thy navigation?)
My hands, my limbs grow nerveless;
My brain feels rack'd, bewilder'd; Let the old timbers part—I will not
    part!
I will cling fast to Thee, O God, though the waves buffet me;
Thee, Thee, at least, I know.

Is it the prophet's thought I speak, or am I raving?
What do I know of life? what of myself?
I know not even my own work, past or present;
Dim, ever-shifting guesses of it spread before me,
Of newer, better worlds, their mighty parturition,
Mocking, perplexing me.

And these things I see suddenly—what mean they?
As if some miracle, some hand divine unseal'd my eyes,
Shadowy, vast shapes, smile through the air and sky,
And on the distant waves sail countless ships,
And anthems in new tongues I hear saluting me.

—from "Prayer of Columbus," Walt Whitman, 1871

 CONTENTS

🐚 DRAMATIS PERSONAE 🐚

Christopher Columbus, Admiral of the Ocean Sea
Bartholomew Columbus, his brother, the Adelantado ("Advancer")
Diego Columbus, his brother
Felipa Moñiz, his wife

Diego Columbus, his son with Felipa Moñiz
Ferdinand Columbus, his son with Beatriz de Arana

Ferdinand II of Aragon, king of Castile
Isabella I of Castile
Juan Rodríguez de Fonseca, bishop and chaplain to Isabella

João II of Portugal, the "Perfect Prince"
Manuel I of Portugal

Vicente Yáñez Pinzón, sailor of Palos, Spain
Martín Alonso Pinzón, brother of Vicente
Francisco Martín Pinzón, brother of Vicente
Diego Alvarez Chanca, physician, friend of Columbus
Juan de la Cosa, cartographer
Father Ramon Pané, priest, emissary to the Taínos
Antonio de Torres, associate of Columbus

Luis de Torres, translator on the first voyage

Guacanagarí, Taíno cacique

Guarionex, cacique

Caonabó, Carib cacique

Anacaona, Caonabó's wife, executed by the Spanish

The Quibián, cacique

Alonso de Ojeda, Columbus's lieutenant and rival

Amerigo Vespucci, Florentine bureaucrat and explorer

Francisco Roldán, mutineer on the third voyage

Francisco de Bobadilla, judicial investigator

Nicolás de Ovando, governor of Hispaniola

Francisco Porras, mutineer on the fourth voyage

Diego Méndez, leader of rescue mission on the fourth voyage

Bartolomé de Las Casas, soldier, friar, chronicler

LIST OF MAPS

COLUMBUS

October 1492

"I sailed to the West southwest, and we took more water aboard than at any other time on the voyage," wrote Christopher Columbus in his logbook on Thursday, October 11, 1492, on the verge of the defining moment of discovery. It occurred not a moment too soon, because the fearful and unruly crews of his three ships were about to mutiny. Overcome with doubt himself, he had tried to remind the rebels of their sworn duty, "telling them that, for better or worse, they must complete the enterprise on which the Catholic Sovereigns"—Isabella of Castile and Ferdinand of Aragon, who jointly ruled Spain—"had sent them." He could not risk offending his royal patrons, whom he lobbied for ten years to obtain this commission, and so he insisted, "I started out to find the Indies and will continue until I have accomplished that mission, with the help of Our Lord." And they had better follow his lead or risk a cruel punishment.

Suddenly it seemed as if his prayers had been answered: "I saw several things that were indications of land." For one thing, "A large flock of sea birds flew overhead." And for another, a slender reed floated past his flagship, *Santa María*, and it was green, indicating it had grown nearby. *Pinta*'s crew noticed the same thing, as well as a "manmade" plank, carved by an unknown hand, perhaps with an "iron tool." Those aboard *Niña* spotted a stick, equally indicative that they were approaching land. He encouraged the crew to give thanks rather than mutiny at this critical moment, doubled the number of lookouts, and promised a generous reward to the first sailor to spot terra firma.

And then, for hours, nothing.

Around ten o'clock that night, Columbus anxiously patrolled the highest deck, the stern castle. In the gloom, he thought he saw something resembling "a little wax candle bobbing up and down." Perhaps it was a torch belonging to fishermen abroad at night, or perhaps it belonged to someone on land, "going from house to house." Perhaps it was nothing more than a phantom sighting, common at sea, even for expert eyes. He summoned a couple of officers; one agreed with his assessment, the other scoffed. No one else saw anything, and Columbus did not trust his own instincts. As he knew from experience, life at sea often presented stark choices. If he succeeded in his quest to discover the basis of a Spanish empire thousands of miles from home, he would be on his way to fulfilling his pledge to his royal sponsors and attaining heroic status and unimaginable wealth. After all the doubts and trials he had endured, his accomplishment would be vindication of the headiest sort. But if he failed, he would face mutiny by his obstreperous crew, permanent disgrace, and the prospect of death in a lonely patch of ocean far from home.

Throughout the first voyage, Columbus kept a detailed record of his thoughts and actions, in which he sought to justify himself to his Sovereigns, to his Lord, and to himself. He believed that history would be listening. In his record, he began by explaining the premise of the voyage in terms of Reconquista, the reclaiming of the Iberian Peninsula from Muslims who had occupied it for centuries. For Columbus, the success of this military campaign made his voyage possible, and, given his mystical bent, inevitable.

Addressing the "most Christian and very Exalted, Excellent and mighty Princes, King and Queen of the Spains and of the Islands of the Sea, our Lord and Lady, in the present year 1492"—his Sovereigns, Ferdinand and Isabella, in other words—he reminisced about their war against the Moors (Muslims), especially their memorable retaking of the "the very great City of Granada"—the former Moorish stronghold. Columbus was there, or so he claimed. He "saw the Royal Standards of Your Highnesses" appear on the "towers of Alhambra," the former seat of Moorish rule. He even saw "the Moorish King come forth to the gates of the city and kiss the Royal Hands of Your Highnesses." Even then, Columbus reminded them, he was thinking of his grand design to establish trade with the fabled "Grand Khan" in the east, the "King of Kings." And it so happened, according to his epic recitation of events, that the Sovereigns, avowed enemies of "all idolatries and heresies," resolved to send him—Christopher Columbus—to India in order to convert those in distant lands to "our Holy Faith"—the *only* faith. Recasting events slightly to flatter Ferdinand and Isabella, he claimed that they "ordained that I should not go by land"—why, as a mariner, would he?—but "by the route of the Occident," in other words, by water.

In reciting this very recent history, Columbus made sure to incorporate the expulsion of the Jews from Spain, accomplished by a royal decree dated March 31, 1492, which he welcomed as the final impetus for his voyage. "After all the Jews had been exiled from your realms and dominions in the same month of January Your Highnesses commanded me that with a sufficient fleet I should go to India, and for this granted me many graces." And what graces they were. They "ennobled me so that henceforth I might call myself 'Don' and be 'Grand Admiral of the Ocean Sea and Viceroy and Perpetual Governor' of all the islands and mainland that I should discover and win." Not only that, "My eldest son should succeed me, and thus from rank to rank for ever." His preening revealed that hereditary titles and wealth had inspired him to go as much as anything else.

Thereafter, his tone became more practical and objective.

"I departed from the city of Granada on the 12th day of the month of May of the same year 1492, on a Saturday, and came to the town of Palos, which is a seaport, where I fitted for the sea three vessels"—*Niña*, *Pinta*, and his flagship, *Santa María*—"well suited for such an enterprise, and I departed well furnished with very many provisions and many seamen on the third day of the month of August on a Friday, at half an hour before sunrise, and took the route for the Canary Islands of Your Highnesses . . . that I might thence take my course and sail until I should reach the Indies, and give the letters of Your Highnesses to those princes, and thus comply with what you had commanded."

That was the plan, in all its grandeur and simplicity.

His journal was to form an important part of the enterprise, and he explained his purpose: "I thought to write down upon this voyage in great detail from day to day all that I should do and see, and encounter." Like all such journals, it had its share of unconscious distortions, intentional omissions, which occurred whenever he deemed it necessary to conceal his route from rivals, or when the reality of his exploration strayed from his expectations. For all its lacunae, it remains the best guide to both his deeds and deceptions. With it, he planned to "make a new chart of navigation, upon which I shall place the whole sea and lands of the Ocean Sea in their proper positions under their bearings, and, further, to compose a book, and set down everything as in a real picture." He knew that keeping this record, in addi-

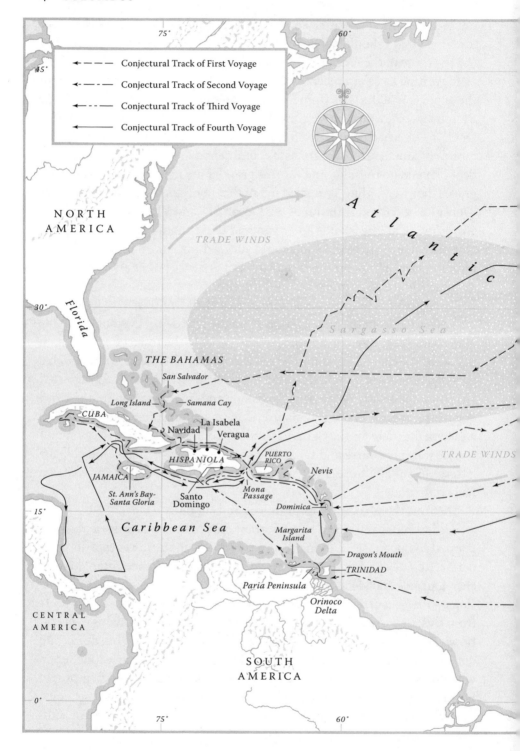

Conjectural Track of First Voyage
Conjectural Track of Second Voyage
Conjectural Track of Third Voyage
Conjectural Track of Fourth Voyage

NORTH AMERICA

TRADE WINDS

Florida

Atlantic

Sargasso Sea

THE BAHAMAS

San Salvador

Long Island — — Samana Cay

CUBA

Navidad   La Isabela
          Veragua

HISPANIOLA

PUERTO RICO

Nevis

TRADE WINDS

JAMAICA

St. Ann's Bay-
Santa Gloria

Santo
Domingo

Mona
Passage

Dominica

Caribbean Sea

Margarita
Island

Dragon's Mouth

TRINIDAD

Paria Peninsula

Orinoco
Delta

CENTRAL
AMERICA

SOUTH
AMERICA

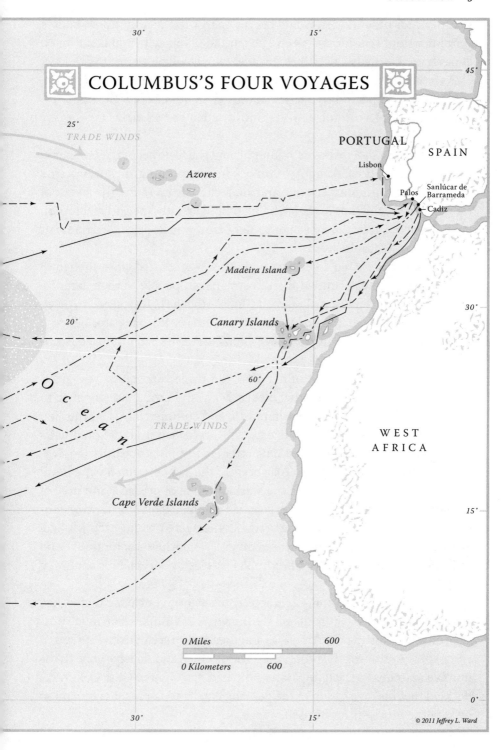

COLUMBUS'S FOUR VOYAGES

25°
TRADE WINDS

PORTUGAL

SPAIN

Azores

Lisbon

Palos

Sanlúcar de
Barrameda

Cadiz

Madeira Island

20°

Canary Islands

60°

TRADE WINDS

**WEST
AFRICA**

Cape Verde Islands

15°

0 Miles   600

0 Kilometers   600

30°

15°

© 2011 Jeffrey L. Ward

tion to all his other duties, would tax his energy to the hilt. "Above all it is very important that I forget sleep," he reminded himself, "and labor much at navigation, because it is necessary, and which will be a great task."

As he embarked on this task, something happened on that October night, something unexpected, appearing sooner than anticipated: the light, if it was a light, from a distant shore, telling him that he had arrived.

The moon rose shortly before midnight, and the little fleet sailed on, making about nine knots. About two o'clock in the morning, a cannon's roar shattered the calm, startling one and all. It came from *Pinta*, the fastest of the three ships, and thus in the lead. Columbus instantly knew what it meant: land. "I learned that the first man to sight land was Rodrigo de Triana." It lay just six miles to the west.

As Columbus passed a sleepless night, the fleet coasted close enough to the shore for his disgruntled men to spy "naked people" rather than the sophisticated and handsomely garbed Chinese that he had expected to meet. Based on his naive reading of Marco Polo's *Travels*, the navigator believed he had arrived at the eastern shore of China just as he had promised Ferdinand and Isabella he would.

He would spend the rest of his life—and three subsequent voyages—attempting to make good on that pledge. Many in Europe were inclined to dismiss Polo's account, by turns fantastic and commercial, as a beguiling fantasy, while others, Columbus especially, regarded it as the pragmatic travel guide that Polo intended. His attempt to find a maritime equivalent to Marco Polo's journey to Asia bridged the gap between the medieval world of magic and might, and the stark universe of predator and prey of the Renaissance. Although Marco Polo had completed his journey two hundred years earlier, Columbus nevertheless expected to find the Mongol empire intact, and Kublai Khan, or another Grand Khan like him, alive and well and ready to do business. But Kublai was long gone, and his empire in ruins.

Protected by his delusion, Columbus conveniently concluded that he had reached an island or peninsula on the outskirts of China, a leap made possible only by omitting the Americas and the Pacific Ocean from his skewed geography. And as for the promised reward, which should have gone to the humble seaman, Rodrigo de Triana, who had first sighted land, Columbus decided that his own vision of the glowing candle took precedence, and so he kept the proceeds for himself.

* * *

Does it matter anymore? As an explorer, the Admiral of the Ocean Sea is widely seen as an opportunist who made his great discovery without ever acknowledging it for what it was, and proceeded to enslave the populace he found, encourage genocide, and pollute relations between peoples who were previously unknown to each other. He was even assumed to have carried syphilis back to Europe with him to torment Europe for centuries thereafter. He excused his behavior, and his legacy, by saying that he merely acted as God's instrument, even as he beseeched his Sovereigns, Ferdinand and Isabella of Spain, to enrich him and his family. Historians have long argued that Columbus merely rediscovered the Americas, that the Vikings, the Celts, and American Indians arrived in the "New World" long before his cautious landfall. But Columbus's voyages to the New World differed from all the earlier events in the scope of its human drama and ecological impact. Before him, the Old World and the New remained separate and distinct continents, ecosystems, and societies; ever since, their fates have been bound together, for better or worse.

To the end of his days, Columbus remained convinced that he sailed for, and eventually arrived at, the outskirts of Asia. His unshakeable Chinese delusion motivated his entire subsequent career in exploration. No comparable figure in the age of discovery was so mistaken as to his whereabouts. Had Columbus been the one to name his discovery, he might well have called it "Asia" rather than "America."

Obsessed with his God-given task of finding Asia, Columbus undertook four voyages within the span of a decade, each very different, each designed to demonstrate that he could sail to China within a matter of weeks and convert those he found there to Christianity. But as the voyages grew in complexity and sophistication, and as Columbus failed to reconcile his often violent experiences as a captain and provincial governor with the demands of his faith, he became progressively less rational and more extreme, until it seemed as if he lived more in his glorious illusions than in the grueling reality his voyages laid bare. If the first voyage illustrates the rewards of exploration, the subsequent three voyages illustrate the costs—political, moral, and economic.

The celebrated first voyage (1492–93) illustrated the discovery of a New World and all its promise, and portended much trouble to come. After this triumph, matters darkened considerably during the hastily assembled second voyage (1493–96). Columbus intended to solidify his navigational accomplishments of the previous year, colonize the New World, and locate

China once and for all. But because of his inability to control the men of this vastly expanded fleet, and his inability to solve the China puzzle, he came close to squandering everything he had attained.

The grim third voyage (1498–1500) was entirely different in character, taking Columbus farther south than ever before. Although he kept up a brave pretense of finding China, he was forced to acknowledge that he might have stumbled across a separate and distinct "new world." Meanwhile, his management of the fledgling Spanish empire, and his quest for gold, devolved into cruel mistreatment of the Indians. The master of navigation became the victim on land of his lack of administrative ability.

As the voyage proceeded, Columbus became increasingly detached from reality, losing himself in extended mystical reveries. At one point, he persuaded himself he had located the entrance to paradise. Throughout his quest, the rational, in the form of maritime expertise, and the mystical occasionally blended into harmonious action, but more often were at odds, resulting in conflicts extending from the natural world to the supernatural. Despite his web of delusions, Columbus discovered so many lands that if he had succeeded in retaining control of all he had explored, with the right to pass on his titles to his heirs—as Ferdinand and Isabella had once promised—he and his new dynasty would have ruled over a kingdom larger and more powerful than Spain itself. So Ferdinand and Isabella decided to replace him with a lesser official, but, playing to his vanity, they permitted him to retain empty titles such as admiral and viceroy.

Ever resilient, Columbus beseeched his Sovereigns for the means to make one more voyage to the New World. His wish was soon granted, and why not? It was more convenient to send Columbus away than to keep him at home.

The wild fourth voyage (1502–4), often called the High Voyage, was a family enterprise, and Columbus included his young son Ferdinand to help secure the family legacy. Ferdinand's account of his father's life is an often overlooked trove of information and observations about Columbus, not as history has judged him, but as his intimates saw him—the story of a father and son caught in the grip of imperial ambition. What began as a journey of personal vindication of his honor ended as a Robinson Crusoe–like adventure of shipwreck and rescue imperiling the lives of all who participated. No wonder it was Columbus's favorite of his four voyages.

At close range, Columbus's accomplishments seem anything but foreordained or clear-cut. An aura of chaos hovers over his entire life and adventures, against which he tries to impose his remarkably serene will. But as his son Ferdinand makes clear, his father is always vulnerable—to the whims of monarchs, to tides and storms, and to the moods of the sailors serving under him. He emerges as a hostage to fortune in the high-stakes game of European expansion; time and again, his exploits could have gone one way or another, were it not for his singular vision. ❧

A NOTE ON DISTANCES AND DATES

Nautical mile: approximately 6,080 feet
Fathom: traditionally the distance between the fingertips of a person's outstretched arms, or six feet
League: approximately three nautical miles

With minor exceptions, dates are given in the Julian calendar, which had been in effect since 45 BC, and was the calendar Columbus used.

In 1582, Pope Gregory XIII initiated a new calendar, still in use today, to compensate for accumulated errors in the Julian calendar. Ten days were omitted, so October 5, 1582, became October 15.

Thus, the eclipse Columbus experienced in Jamaica on February 29, 1504, corresponds to March 10, 1504, in the Gregorian calendar.

PART ONE

Discovery

CHAPTER 1

Thirty-three Days

On Friday morning, October 12, Columbus ventured ashore, followed by the Pinzón brothers: Martín Alonso, *Pinta*'s captain, and Vicente Yáñez, *Niña*'s captain. Only hours before, these two contentious brothers had been ready to mutiny against Columbus, believing that he was leading them to certain destruction; now they were walking on land inhabited by well-meaning people. It was the moment of first contact.

Soon the two parties from separate hemispheres were engrossed in the most basic of rites, trade. The tawny-skinned inhabitants offered squawking, blinking parrots and skeins of cotton thread, for which they received tiny hawk's bells, used to track birds in falconry, and glass beads from the pallid visitors. The officers unfurled the royal standard, while Columbus, seeking to validate his discovery, summoned the fleet's secretary and comptroller to "witness that I was taking possession of this Island for the King and Queen." In so doing, he claimed a modest coral island in the Bahamas, now generally assumed to be San Salvador.

The people of the island visited by Columbus were the Taínos, a widely distributed ethnic group, skilled at cultivating corn and yams, and making pottery. Despite their peaceful manner, they could be fierce warriors, but they had met their match. The arrival of the Spaniards in the New World heralded the extinction of the Taíno culture, but for now, the tribe possessed a blend of sophistication and innocence that Columbus tried to capture in his diary:

All that I saw were young men, none of them more than 30 years old, very well built, of very handsome bodies and very fine faces; their hair coarse, almost like the hair of a horse's tail, and short, the hair they wear over their eyebrows, except for a hank behind that they wear long and never cut. Some of them paint themselves black (and they are of the color of the Canary Islanders, neither black nor white), and others paint themselves white, and some red, and others with what they find. And some paint their faces, others the body, some the eyes only, others only the nose. They bear no arms, nor know thereof; for I showed them swords and they grasped them by the blade and cut themselves through ignorance. They have no iron. Their darts are a kind of rod without iron, and some have at the end a fish's tooth and other things.

The Spaniards had come all this way, across the Ocean Sea, expecting to confront a superior civilization. How disconcerting to be confronted with "naked people" who were "very poor in everything." Columbus and his men would have to be careful not to hurt them, rather than the other way around. "I saw some who had marks of wounds on their bodies, and made signs to them to ask what it was, and they showed me that people of other islands which are near came there and wished to capture them, and they defended themselves. And I believe that people do come here from the mainland to take them as slaves."

Slaves. The idea instantly struck Columbus as plausible, even desirable. "They ought to be good servants," he continued, "and of good skill, for I see they repeat very quickly whatever was said to them." And, in the same breath, he judged that "they would easily be made Christians, because it seemed to me that they belonged to no religion." He planned to present six of these nameless, naked individuals to his royal sponsors, Ferdinand and Isabella, "that they may learn to speak."

In the morning, masses of Indians crowded the beach to gape at the three ships from afar. Others arrived by dugout ("fashioned like a long boat from the trunk of a tree") carrying forty or fifty men, who propelled themselves with a curious object that the European sailors, despite their lifelong acquaintance with the ocean, had never before seen. Having no word for it, Columbus called it a "thing like a baker's peel," a broad, mostly flat blade attached to a long handle. We know it as a canoe paddle.

They brought additional gifts for Columbus, who dismissed them as "trifles too tedious to describe." It was gold that he—and Spain—wanted, not trinkets or parrots. He glimpsed tiny amounts in the form of jewelry piercing their noses, and immediately began asking for the source of this precious metal. If his instincts were correct, the gold came from Çipango—Japan. "I intend to go and see if I can find the Island of Çipango," he emphasized. He was confident that the gentle people in their dugout canoes would direct him to the island.

After this first encounter, Columbus's fleet skirted the coast of San Salvador. Wherever they went, excitement erupted onshore. Some of the startled inhabitants offered food and drink, and others, both men and women, hastened into their boats shouting, "Come and see the men who come from the sky!" It seemed to Columbus that those ashore were giving thanks to God as they threw themselves on the ground.

He would have made other landfalls, but his nautical instinct warned him away from a "great reef of rocks which surrounded the whole of this island." Infuriatingly, "inside this reef there are some shoal spots, but the sea moves no more than within a well," and so he sailed on, and on, overwhelmed by the splendor of the Caribbean, its cobalt waters, cottony clouds, and periwinkle skies. To flatter Ferdinand and Isabella, he compared the spectacle to the countryside around Seville in the months of April and May, but in fact the pellucid ocean in which he found himself was even more gorgeous and beguiling. Columbus said that he "saw so many islands that I could not decide where to go first; and those men whom I had captured made signs to me that they were so many that they could not be counted, and called by their names more than a hundred." He eventually decided to make for the largest landmass, estimating that it lay five leagues from the island he designated San Salvador.

Exhilarated and distracted, he did not linger at his new anchorage. "When from this island I saw another bigger one to the West, I made sail to navigate all that day until nightfall because otherwise I would not have been able to reach the western cape." He called it Santa María de la Concepción, and dropped anchor there at sunset. The island is often assumed to be Rum Cay, to use its more mundane modern name, and one hardly befitting Columbus's exalted sense of mission.

Driven by the search for gold, he had allowed his wily captives to lead him to this spot because those who dwelled there "wore very big bracelets of gold on their legs and arms." When the ships approached the shore, the hostages escaped one by one, and Columbus belatedly realized he had been deceived. Irritated, he would have sailed on, but, he stated, "it was my wish to bypass no island without taking possession," and so he did in the name of Castile, even though "having taken one you can claim all." Such were the rules of exploration and empire as he understood them.

He dispatched several seamen in hot pursuit of the fugitives, chasing

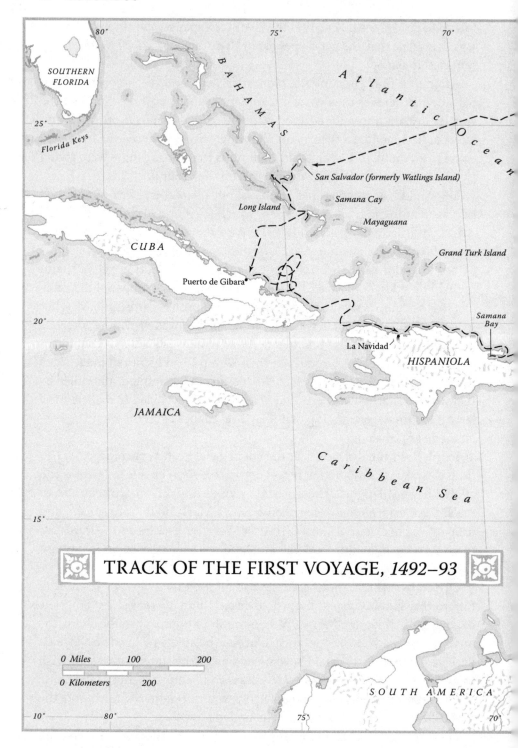

SOUTHERN
FLORIDA

Florida Keys

BAHAMAS

Atlantic Ocean

San Salvador (formerly Watlings Island)

Long Island

Samana Cay

Mayaguana

CUBA

Grand Turk Island

Puerto de Gibara

Samana
Bay

La Navidad

HISPANIOLA

JAMAICA

Caribbean Sea

TRACK OF THE FIRST VOYAGE, 1492–93

0 Miles   100   200
0 Kilometers   200

SOUTH AMERICA

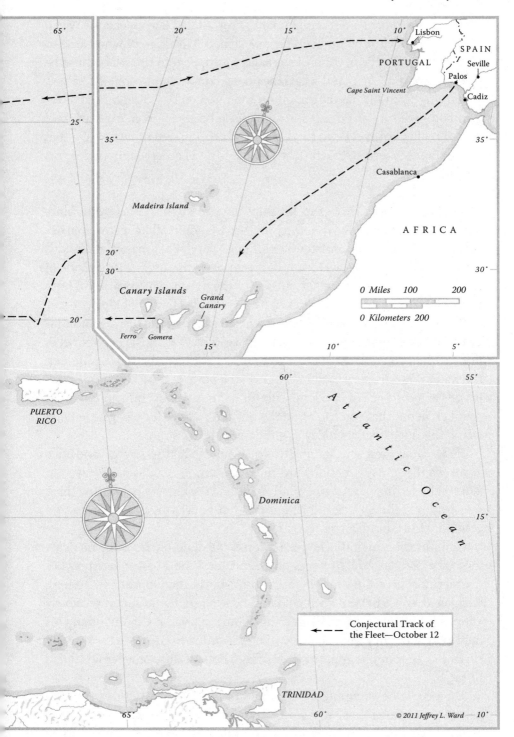

65°   20°   15°   10° Lisbon

SPAIN

PORTUGAL   Seville

Palos

Cape Saint Vincent   Cadiz

25°

35°   35°

Casablanca

AFRICA

Madeira Island

20°

30°   30°

Canary Islands   Grand
Canary

0 Miles   100   200

0 Kilometers 200

20°   Ferro Gomera   15°   10°   5°

PUERTO
RICO   60°   55°

A t l a n t i c   O c e a n

15°

Dominica

TRINIDAD

← ─ ─   Conjectural Track of
the Fleet—October 12

65°   60°   © 2011 Jeffrey L. Ward   10°

them ashore, but, as he ruefully noted, "they all fled like chickens." When another dugout canoe innocently approached "with a man who came to trade a skein of cotton, some of the sailors jumped into the sea because he wouldn't come aboard," and seized the poor fellow as a replacement detainee. Observing from his vantage point on the poop deck, Columbus "sent for him and gave him a red cap and some little beads of green glass which I placed on his arm, and two hawk's bells which I placed on his ears"—that is, the standard-issue trinkets of little value—"and I ordered him back to his dugout."

Later, on Monday, October 15, his ships urged on by a southeasterly wind, Columbus cautiously navigated to another island, in all its features as described by Columbus consistent with Long Island, Bahamas. The island is eighty miles long and only four miles wide, and appears as a jagged pile of sand and rock rising above the surface of the ocean, which varies in hues from lush aubergine to sparkling white surrounded by a light blue corona.

Columbus kept his head about him as he gaped at the display and diligently recorded instructions for future navigators: "You must keep your eyes peeled when you wish to anchor, and not anchor near the shore, although the water is always very clear and you see the bottom. And among all these islands at a distance of two lombard—or cannon—shots off-shore there is so much depth that you can't find the bottom": advice for navigating Long Island that holds as true today as it did five centuries ago.

He was now almost as far north as he would go on this voyage, and once again his thoughts turned toward India. Columbus would have stayed to admire the setting—"very green and fertile and the air very balmy, and there may be many things that I don't know"—but he was on a mission "to find gold" and the Grand Khan.

Complicating his task, he had entered into one of the most intricate mazes of islands and isthmuses on the planet. From the vantage point of the thermosphere, hundreds of miles above, the islands appear as scattered, burnished leaves flecked with gold and floating on liquid sapphire, slowly churning, blossoming, and fluorescing. From sea level, as Columbus and his men saw them, they were no less striking, seeming to rise from the heaving surface of the sea like apparitions, or fragments of stars or asteroids fallen to earth.

The people he encountered appeared to be participating in a timeless pageant, and Columbus, ever curious, jotted down his impressions. In the channel running between Santa María and Long Island, he came upon a man alone in a dugout canoe, paddling from one island to the other. "He carried a bit of his bread that would be about the size of your fist, and a calabash of water, and a lump of bright red earth powdered and then kneaded, and some dry leaves which must be something much valued among them, since they offered me some . . . as a gift." The dry leaves happened to be among the oldest crops known to humanity, yet it was virtually unknown in Europe. Apparently, the leaves had been cured, and their pungent scent lingered in the air and imbued the pores of every one who handled it and inhaled its smoke. The leaves belonged to genus *Nicotiana*: the tobacco plant.

The man came alongside *Santa María* and gestured that he wished to come aboard. Columbus granted the request and "had his dugout hoisted on deck, and all he brought guarded, and ordered him to be given bread and honey and drink." The Admiral vowed to "give him back all his stuff, that he may give a good account of us" and report that he was given all he needed by the emissary of the beneficent Sovereigns of Spain.

Late on October 16, Columbus's modest altruistic gesture paid generous dividends. The fleet happened to be in search of anchorage, frustrated by the inability of soft coral reefs to provide a reliable stay against the agitation of the sea. The man whom he had given water, nourishment, and transport noticed the situation. "He had given such a good account of us that all this night aboard the ship [that] there was no want of dugouts, which brought us water and what they had. I ordered each to be given something, if only a few beads, 10 or 12 glass ones on a thread, and some brass jingles, such as are worth in Castile a maravedí each"—a Spanish coin worth about twelve cents.

Overcoming his reluctance to disembark, Columbus went ashore on Long Island, and was pleasantly surprised by the inhabitants, "a somewhat more domestic people, and tractable, and more subtle, because I observe that in bringing cotton to the ship and other things, they know better how to drive a bargain than the others." To his relief, the islanders wore clothing, which seemed to reflect their sophistication and civility. "I saw clothes of cotton made like short cloaks, and the people are better disposed, and the women wear in front of their bodies a small piece of cotton which barely covers their genitals."

Lush, dark vegetation blanketed the island. Impenetrable mangroves overhung ledges, casting dismal shadows. Spiky beach plums obstructed the way to the island's interior. Those able to hack a path through the brush might come upon a basin of murky water swaying within a deep blue hole.

In another part of the island, caves tempted the bravest or most foolhardy to explore their depths. It was all strange and different from anything the men had ever witnessed. "I saw many trees very unlike ours," Columbus marveled, "and many of them have their branches of different kinds, and all on one trunk, and one twig is of one kind and another of another, and so unlike that it is the greatest wonder of the world. How great is the diversity of one kind from the other!" He had stumbled across flora following a separate evolutionary path from its European counterparts. Catching his breath, he resumed, "For instance, one branch has leaves like a cane, others like mastic; and thus on one tree five or six kinds, and all so different." How could this be? They were not grafted by human hands, "for one can say the grafting is spontaneous." No matter what plant Columbus was describing, his astonishment was apparent. The same wild proliferation could be found among fish—"so unlike ours that it is marvelous; they have some like dories, of the brightest colors in the world, blue, yellow, red, and of all colors, and others painted in a thousand ways; and the colors are so bright, that there is no man would not marvel and would not take great delight in seeing them; also there are whales." Sheer surprise and enchantment hijacked his grandiose agenda. Or were the snares of this world leading him fatally astray?

Columbus, normally so purposeful, wandered through the Bahamas for a full week, as if through a dreamscape. "I discovered a very wonderful harbor with one mouth, or rather one might say two mouths, for it has an island in the middle, and both are very narrow, and within it is wide enough for 100 ships, if it were deep and clean," he recorded on October 17 as he approached Cape Santa María. "During this time I walked among some trees which were the most beautiful thing that I had ever seen, viewing as much verdure in so great development as in the month of May in Andalusia, and all the trees were as different from ours as day from night." He was charmed and baffled by the spectacle. "Nobody could say what they were, nor compare them to others of Castile." The sights of so many unidentifiable trees and plants and flowers caused him "great grief," almost as if he were blind or speechless.

Only gold roused him from his reveries. The moment he spotted a man "who had in his nose a gold stud" engraved with characters, he urgently tried to strike a deal, "and they answered me that never had anyone dared to barter for it." If his intuition proved correct, the gold stud bore Chinese or perhaps Japanese inscriptions, but he was unable to examine it.

The next day "[t]here came so fair and sweet a smell of flowers and trees from the land, that it was the sweetest thing in the world." And ahead, a smaller island, and another, so many that he despaired of exploring them all "because I couldn't do it in fifty years, for I wish to see and discover the most that I can before returning to Your Highnesses (Our Lord willing) in April." *Fifty years*: he was just beginning to appreciate the enormity and incomprehensibility of the lands he had found. Everything was strange and different—the vegetation, the people, the musky odor of flowers wafting from a nearby island. It was only October, the New World only a week old in his awareness. More than six months remained until he was due back in Spain, and anything could happen in this unexplored world.

As the entries in his diary increased, he related his experiences at sea with confidence and eloquence. On its surface, the diary is meant to convey the startling drama and novelty of his voyage, in which everything was a discovery, every experience and sensation was being registered for the first time by the European sensibility, and with European sensitivity—more specifically, the regal Castilian sensibility that Columbus longed to emulate. He tried to blend imperiousness and intelligence, as if holding the world at arm's length to study it. For Columbus, an expatriate from Genoa, a merchant sailor and self-taught navigator, the aristocratic tone was a carefully crafted impersonation notable for what he omitted or downplayed or misunderstood as much as the startling discoveries he recorded.

As his voyage proceeded, the diary subtly transformed itself into a manifesto of discovery, and beyond that, a mirror into which he could not stop looking as it came to reflect his vision, his ambition, his will to greatness, himself. In his own mind, his experiences and observations were so persuasive that they interfered with his ability to respond to the ever-changing reality of exploration. Instead, he was confined by his rigid expectations.

To complicate matters, students of his remarkable diary must rely on a transcription of the original journal of the first voyage, which has been lost. It comes down through two main sources. The first is Columbus's natural, or illegitimate, son Ferdinand, a sailor turned historian; the second is Bartolomé de Las Casas, the friar and chronicler. Ferdinand naturally sought to burnish his father's tarnished reputation, while Las Casas sought a deep enough circle in hell in which to cast the explorer. But Las Casas's attitude toward Columbus is more nuanced than that of a single-minded critic. He was aware of the complexity of the undertaking, to which he was an eyewitness and participant, yet also capable of seeing events in a larger historical context, living both in the moment and out of it. He lacked a holograph—the handwritten version—of the journal; instead, he worked from a flawed version about which he registered occasional scholarly complaints. In addition to routine copying errors, the unknown scribe on whom Las Casas relied had a troubling tendency to confuse "miles" with "leagues," and even "east" with "west." Such mistakes made it difficult to retrace Columbus's route precisely.

As a champion of the dignity and human rights of the Indians, Las Casas included numerous passages in which Columbus admired his hosts. Las Casas switches frequently between direct quotation of the copy before him, in which Columbus speaks in the first person, and detailed summaries in which the Admiral is referred to in the third person, giving the impression that Columbus, like Caesar, referred to himself in that manner. (The scrupulous Las Casas distinguishes between the two by using quotation marks for direct quotations.)

Columbus's vague, occasionally deceptive reports of tides, harbors, shoals, and sailing tactics complicated matters further. These descriptions were destined to cause centuries of chroniclers and would-be explorers to gnash their teeth over the absence of precise and useful navigational information— which was Columbus's intention. Divulging his navigational theories and practices ran counter to his ingrained Genoese instincts as a pilot and mariner. It was more dangerous to reveal than conceal; if he was not careful, he might find himself marooned in Seville, or Lisbon, watching copycat missions exploit his discoveries. So he fell back on generic descriptions of beaches, harbors, tides, and shoals in an effort to cover his wake even as he wrote with an eye on posterity.

Alternately puzzled and overconfident, he wrestled with the most basic problem of exploration: his location. His subject was his discovery of "India," but his principal concern remained himself, his travails, and his sense of heroism. Whenever Columbus stood outside the momentous events of explorations and calmly retold his account, the unfolding of God's will became an important theme; when he was in the service of the Lord, there were no accidents, only degrees of devotion. In the service of the Lord, he saw himself as a priest of exploration.

But when Columbus's convictions outran reality, or when his vanity and anxiety got the better of him, he succumbed to his darker instincts. He seemed oblivious to the well-being of others, and alarmingly ready to sacrifice all for an exalted, unattainable goal, whether it was the discovery of the Grand Khan's empire or the liberation of Jerusalem. In these dramas, he saw himself as a tormented, heroic figure. The greater his fantasies, the more inhuman he became. His journal, in part a record of his passionate instability, records some of his suffering from a sense of dread and oppression, relieved mainly by intimations of glory and omnipotence. He was more than a discoverer, he was an intensifier of both his voyages and his inner struggles. This penchant for self-dramatization is part of the reason Columbus's exploits are so memorable; he insisted on making them so.

As the journal gathered substance, it became an important record of the voyage, the rudder of the Admiral's psyche, a stay against both actual and psychic storms. It was not, however, a source of comfort to Columbus. In place of the expected sense of vindication, the Admiral often sounds ever more frantic and embattled by his discoveries and their challenges. He becomes aware that he is entering into a lasting struggle in which every triumph seems to be accompanied by a misstep, unforeseen consequences, or even a potential crime. Paradoxically, as his power and prominence (in his own mind) increase, so does his vulnerability—to Indians, to rivals such as the Pinzón brothers, to a dimly perceived sense that the stakes of the voyage are higher and more ambiguous than those he originally formulated. Rather than finding a nautical analogue to Marco Polo's travels, and a path to personal wealth, he had blundered into an "other world," as he came to call it, where there were no maps to guide him. He was lost and misguided for all practical purposes, yet he could not admit that possibility to himself and the others on the voyage; it was much better to insist that he had not yet found what they sought, but that conviction alone did not offer much comfort. The more he found, the more frantic he became, as the empire he sought revealed itself to be greater and more varied than he had imagined.

As Columbus went island-hopping, marveling at the "singing of the little birds" and the "grass like April in Andalusia," while he looked for gold, he heard from a cacique about a "large island" that the explorer reflexively decided "must be Japan." And visiting that island nation, he was "determined to go to the mainland," that is, China, "and to the city of Quinsay," Marco Polo's antique term for the Song dynasty capital, now known as Hangzhou, the richest and largest city in the medieval world. In this magnificent setting, Columbus imagined himself presenting "Your Highnesses' letters to the Grand Khan, and to beg a reply and come home with it."

Although he was situated in the midst of the Bahamas, he remained convinced that he had arrived at the doorstep of Asia. In reality, Quinsay lay more than eight thousand miles west of his position in the Caribbean, but these dimensions contradicted his firmly held assumptions about the size of the globe and the placement of continents—not that other navigators or cosmographers in Europe had a more accurate notion of these things. The precise globes that Columbus studied are not known, but one of the most influential representations of the day, by Martin Behaim, a German mapmaker in the service of Portugal, did indicate that Çipango was at hand. Columbus could not admit the possibility that these globes and all their assumptions might be spectacularly wrong.

When not contemplating his China delusion, Columbus returned to his other chimera: gold.

He spent a night and the following day, October 22, "waiting to see if the king here or other people would bring gold or anything substantial." Many came to observe, some naked, others painted red, black, or white, offering cotton or other local items in exchange for simple European utensils. The only gold in evidence took the form of jewelry that some of the Indians wore "hanging from the nose." They were willing to exchange these items for hawk's bells, but upon examining the haul, he complained, "There's so little that it is nothing at all."

From gold, his mind swung back to Asia. He reckoned he was but a day's sail from Japan, or Çipango, not the eight thousand miles separating him from his improbable destination. On October 23, he wrote of blithely departing for Cuba, "which I believe should be Çipango," to look for gold. "On the globes that I saw," he reminded himself, "it is in this region." So stated Martin Behaim.

At midnight, Columbus weighed anchor and shaped a course for Cuba, but by nightfall he had nothing to show for his brave effort, as the wind "blew up brisk and I didn't know how far it was to the island of Cuba." Accordingly, he lowered sail, except for the forecourse, until rain caused him to furl that sail as well. So it went for four days, "and how it rained!"

On Sunday, October 28, he entered a deep, unobstructed river—perhaps Bahía Bariay in Cuba—and anchored within its protective embrace, where he beheld "trees all along the river, beautiful and green, and different from ours." He labored over his descriptions of flora and fauna with extreme care, as if the natural bounty could substitute or distract from the wonders he had failed to find so far—gold, spices, and tangible evidence of the Grand Khan, whom he had crossed an ocean to see, without realizing that two oceans, and two centuries, separated them.

Instead, he wrote of flowers and singing birds and a barkless dog, probably domesticated by local "fishermen who had fled in fear." Within their huts, he found an eerie sight: "nets of palm fiber and ropes and fish-hooks of horn, and bone harpoons, and other fishing tackle, and many fireplaces within." But where were the inhabitants of this Arcadia? With stifled breathing and hesitant footfalls, his men warily crept through the timeless village.

Ordering that nothing be disturbed, he returned to his ship and resumed his voyage upriver, groping for superlatives to describe Cuba: "The most beautiful that eyes have ever seen: full of very good harbors and deep rivers." Indians, when he encountered them, spoke of ten great rivers, and, he wrote, "one cannot circumnavigate it with their canoes in 20 days." He refused to entertain the implication that Cuba was an island. If he had not arrived on Asia's doorstep, where was he? It was a question that haunted the entire premise of the voyage.

He persuaded himself that the inhabitants, or Indians, mentioned "mines of gold and pearls," and claimed he caught a glimpse of "mussel shells" that might contain pearls, and on the basis of this misunderstanding, concluded that the "ships of the Grand Khan, great ones," had preceded him.

Baffled, curious, predatory, he made his way inland, admiring grander dwellings, which he struggled to describe in the idiom he understood: "They were made in the manner of Moorish tents, very large, and looking like tents in an encampment, without regularity of streets, but one here and another there; and inside well swept and clean, and their furnishings well made . . . of very fair palm branches." Here and there masks, some masculine, others feminine, adorned the walls, but he could not ascertain "whether these are for beauty or to be worshipped." Again, he emphasized, "they didn't touch a thing."

On Tuesday, October 30, the fleet was under way again, *Pinta* carrying Indian guides, and Columbus still planning to happen upon the Grand Khan. By November 1, he went ashore near Puerto de Gibara, on Cuba's northeastern shore, deploying his Indian passengers as scouts and emissaries. They were engaged as before in a fruitless search for gold. On this occasion, he observed "a piece of worked silver hanging from the nose" of an Indian, a detail that sparked his curiosity. His men engaged in communicating by sign language with the locals, taking a tribal conflict for full-blown war between the islanders and the Grand Khan. "It is certain," he proclaimed, "that this is the mainland," and that Quinsay lay only one hundred leagues distant. It was time to prepare a scouting party to reach the legendary Chinese capital.

Columbus dispatched "two Spanish men: the one was called Rodrigo de

Xerez, who lived in Ayamonte, and the other was one Luis de Torres . . . of Murcia and had been born a Jew, and knew, it is said, Hebrew and Aramaic and also some Arabic." Two Indians accompanied the scouts, and carried "strings of beads to buy food with." They had their orders to find the island's king, present their credentials, exchange gifts, and discover their actual location. They had six days to complete their mission.

As Columbus was at pains to explain, Luis de Torres was a recent *converso*, or convert, to Christianity, and probably an unwilling one. His original name is believed to have been Yosef Ben Ha Levy Haivri, "Joseph the Son of Levy the Hebrew," and he would become the first person of Jewish origin to settle in the New World. Columbus had brought Torres on the voyage both for his political skills and his linguistic abilities. They might have dealings with Arab traders, and in the event they encountered descendants of the Lost Tribes of Israel, Torres was expected to communicate with them. Columbus was, in reality, wholly unprepared for speaking with the "Indians" in their actual tongue and resorted to improvised sign language, a modus operandi that generated ambiguity and confusion that he took as confirmation of his fantastic ideas about the Grand Khan.

On the morning of November 3, Columbus went aboard the ship's launch to await the scouting party and survey a "very remarkable harbor, very deep and clear of rocks," with a beach well suited to careening, or repairing the hulls of ships.

A few days later, on November 4, Martín Alonso Pinzón, who considered himself the expedition's virtual co-leader, went ashore and made a highly promising find, "two pieces of cinnamon," actually *Canella winterana*, or wild cinnamon blossoms, giving off their smoky-sweet odor. He was eager to trade this desirable commodity, and would have done so, were it not for the "penalty the admiral had imposed." There were even cinnamon groves nearby, according to *Pinta*'s boatswain, but on inspection, Columbus decided that was not the case. The Spanish explorers listened intently to tales of gold and pearls "in an infinite amount." The more they listened, the more credulous they became, until Columbus was registering reports of men with the heads of dogs "who ate men and that in killing one they beheaded him and drank his blood and cut off his genitals." Grotesque stories such as these sounded similar to tales recounted by Sir John Mandeville, whose fanciful tales were at least as popular in western Europe as Marco Polo's. Such things could not happen here—or could they?

* * *

The scouts, Rodrigo de Xerez and Luis de Torres, returned to describe their reconnoitering on Tuesday, November 6. Within twelve leagues, they said, they had found a "village" with fifty tents and a thousand inhabitants, who received the visitors "with great solemnity." They were pleased to report that the inhabitants "touched them and kissed their hands and feet, marveling and believing that they came from the sky." They were offered chairs, while their hosts squatted at their feet, as one of their Indian companions explained to the throng that as Christians, their visitors "were good people." A respectful frenzy ensued. "The men went out and the women entered, and squatted in the same fashion around them, kissing their hands and feet, feeling them to ascertain if they were of flesh and bones like themselves; begging them to stay at least five days." The visitors responded in a calculatingly commercial vein, displaying samples of spices they sought, cinnamon and pepper and the like, and inquiring where they could be found, receiving only vague directions ("around there, to the southeast") by way of reply. They found no Chinese, no Arabs, no descendants of the Lost Tribes of Israel, and no trace of the Grand Khan. But they had made friends and potential allies. Five hundred men and women wished to accompany them on their return "to the sky," as they imagined. They allowed only a handful the privilege of their company.

Returning to the ships, "the two Christians met on the way many people who were going to their towns, women and men, with a firebrand in the hand, [and] herbs to drink the smoke thereof." This brief observation referred to tobacco, a new and strange practice to the Spanish, who observed the Indians making cigars and setting fire to *tobacos*, the fumes of which they inhaled deeply. But spices remained the ultimate cash crop for Columbus, who, for the time being, remained oblivious to the commercial value and addictive attributes of this aromatic leaf.

After hearing the report, Columbus, rather than dwelling on the failure of the expedition to meet its objectives, offered Ferdinand and Isabella a considered and nuanced appraisal of the "Indians" surrounding him, as he tried to come to terms with their obvious humanity and potential for conversion to Christianity:

They are a people very guileless and unwarlike . . . but they are very modest, and not very dark, less so than the Canary Islanders. I maintain, Most Serene Princes, that if they had access to devout religious persons knowing the language, they would all turn Christian, and so I hope in Our Lord that Your

Highnesses will . . . convert them as you have destroyed those who would not seek to confess the Father, Son and Holy Ghost.

Having expressed this sincere hope, Columbus predicted that if Ferdinand and Isabella followed this path, they would be "well received before the eternal Creator" when the time came for them to "leave your realms." With that inspirational flourish, he prepared the fleet for departure. Within a day, a robust wind blew up to carry the ships away.

The next two weeks found Columbus increasingly exasperated by the flaws in his navigational techniques and maps, and stubbornly pursuing the civilized grandeur of the East even as the brilliance of the Caribbean seduced him. He eventually returned to Cuba to resume his patient exploration, river by river, musing on "the cities of the Grand Khan, which will doubtless be discovered."

He lost count of the harbors he visited, the palm trees, and all the other trees and bushes and wildlife that he could not recognize or name, and mountains so high that it seemed to him that there were none higher in all the world, "nor any so beautiful and clear, without clouds or snow." The islands, too numerous to count, he took to be "those found on the world maps at the end of the Far East." He speculated that there were "immense riches and precious stones and spiceries in them, and that they extend much further to the south, and spread out in every direction." At all this, Columbus "marveled greatly."

Wherever he went, both "islands and lands," Columbus made a practice of erecting a cross, an arduous project. He wrote of fashioning crosses from trees, proclaiming, "It is said that a carpenter could not have made [it] better proportioned." Once the cross was in place, he and his men solemnly prayed before it, pilgrims in search of an elusive Jerusalem.

Cuba, he came to realize, was heavily populated with gregarious Indians. On Sunday, November 10, a dugout canoe arrived with six men and five women to pay their respects. Columbus returned their hospitality by "detaining" them in expectation of returning to Spain with them. He bolstered their number with seven additional women and three boys. He explained his thinking this way: "I did this because the men would behave better in Spain with women of their country than without them."

His decision, he said, was based on his experiences "detaining" the inhabitants of Africa's west coast to Portugal. "Many times I happened to take men of Guinea that they might learn the language in Portugal, and after they returned it was expected to make some use of them in their own country, owing to the good company that they had enjoyed and gifts they had received," but matters never turned out as hoped. The problem, he decided, was that without their women the men would not cooperate. This time, the result would be different. His latest captives, "having their women, will find it good business to do what they are told, and these women would teach our people their language," which, he assumed, "is the same in all these islands of India."

As if to prove his point, he recorded a vignette that remained fresh in his memory: "This night there came aboard in a dugout the husband of . . . two women and father of three children, a boy and two girls, and said he wished to come with them, and begged me hard." Columbus allowed the supplicant to join the expedition. "They all now remained consoled with him," the Admiral noted, but he was disappointed to report that his newest ally was "more than 45 years," too old for vigorous labor.

Columbus noted on November 11 that the inhabitants of Cuba appeared to practice "no religion," but at least they were not "idolaters," and, he decided, "very gentle and without knowledge of what is evil, neither murder nor theft; and they are without arms and so timid that a hundred of them flee before one person of ours, although they may be playing the fool with them." His recommendation: "Your Highnesses ought to resolve to make them Christians, for I believe that if you began, in a short time you would achieve the conversion to our holy faith of a multitude of folk, and would acquire great lordships and riches and all their inhabitants for Spain." And why was that? "Because without doubt there is in these countries a tremendous quantity of gold." The Indians, he pointed out, busy themselves mining gold "and wear it on their necks, ears, arms and legs, and the bracelets are very large." God and gold: what better reasons to found an empire across an ocean?

Shortly before sunset that evening Columbus raised sail and proceeded east by south to a promontory he named the Cape of Cuba.

Of all the days he had endured at sea thus far, November 21, a Wednesday, proved to be the most treacherous, and not just because he committed a spiraling series of navigational misjudgments. Based on the hasty, elliptical comments in his diary, it appears that he was attempting to use his quadrant to fix his location. The quadrant readings placed him at a latitude of 42 degrees, but "it seemed to him that he could not be so far distant [from the equator]." His assumption was correct. The 42nd parallel passes through the border between New York and Pennsylvania; he was, in fact, at 21 degrees of latitude. At least he knew that something was seriously awry, it being "manifest that in latitude 42 degrees in no part of the earth is there believed to be heat, unless it be for some accidental reason." Infuriated, he complained that the quadrant must be at fault and in need of repair.

Had Columbus relied on celestial navigation alone, he would have wandered off course, but he possessed another asset that made all the difference: an inborn sense of the sea, of wind and weather. Like other navigators of the day, Columbus did not refer to "true north" (the geographic north pole) or to the "north magnetic pole" (where the earth's magnetic field suddenly points downward). Instead, he set his course, or direction, with reference to the winds, eight in all, each bearing a traditional Italian name. Tramontana indicated north, Greco northeast, Levante east, Sirocco southeast, Ostro or Auster south, Libeccio or Africo southwest, Ponente west, and Maestro northwest. Because these names referred to the familiar geography of the Mediterranean, Columbus and other navigators simplified this system into eight cardinal points—N, NE, E, SE, S, SW, W, and NW. As additional refinement, he included eight intermediate points—*los medios vientos*—or half winds. These were NNE, ENE, ESE, SSE, SSW, WSW, WNW, and NNW. There was a further subdivision as well, each point equivalent to 11¼ degrees, or one compass point.

Columbus remained silent concerning his truly remarkable gift: dead reckoning, that is, sailing by the seat of his pants, estimating time and distances with simple devices such as a rope or buoy or landmark. He was an intuitive master of the most ancient form of navigation. All his maps and charts and painfully acquired formal education—so impressive, yet so misleading—were of little use to him. He relied on his instincts and experience concerning tides and wind; the color of the sea and composition of clouds mattered more to him than the mathematical calculations of the era's leading cosmographers. They had never gone to sea, but Columbus had. His dead reckoning proved so accurate that he had already sailed from Spain to the New World without incident the very first time, and, incredibly, with no loss of life. And each time after that, he improved his course based on experience rather than theory.

The onset of a crisis on November 22 startled him out of the mathematical maze into which he had blundered: "This day Martín Alonso Pinzón"—his chief rival for glory on the voyage—"departed with the caravel *Pinta* without the permission or desire of the Admiral." Columbus had no idea why; the weather was fine. Perhaps Pinzón had located a source of gold and wished to keep it secret. Striking an ominous note, Columbus added that he was already building a case against the rebellious captain, noting, "Many other things he had done and said to me."

Martín Alonso Pinzón's unauthorized flight was troubling because the voyage had benefited from a professional collaboration between the two captains. A portrait of *Pinta*'s captain (on display in Madrid's Museo Naval) shows a studious young man who looks more like a scholar or an aide-de-camp than a sea dog or mutineer. His melancholy gaze suggests that he is lost in contemplation or looking at a distant object. He had been born in Palos, which is to say, born to the sea, in 1441 and was now over fifty, experienced, even old for a captain.

As recently as September 25, Columbus had written approvingly in his logbook about a chart "on which it seems the Admiral had depicted certain islands on that sea." Martín Alonso expressed the opinion that the islands were nearby, and Columbus agreed, and the fleet's inability to locate them could be attributed to the "currents which set the ships all the while to the NE." Assuming this to be the case, Columbus asked Pinzón to return the chart for further study "with his pilot and mariners."

At sunset, "Martín Alonso came up on the poop of his ship, and with much joy shouted to the Admiral, claiming largesse"—a reward—"for sighting land." What land? Columbus deliberately kept the name and location of the island vague so that his rivals would not be able to take advantage of the discovery.

Before paying up, he "went down on his knees to give thanks to Our Lord, and Martín Alonso said the *Gloria in excelsis Deo* with his people." Soon *Niña*'s rigging groaned with the weight of sailors, who had scaled it to catch sight of land, only twenty-five leagues distant, by Columbus's reckoning. He was wrong. The fleet sailed on that day, and the next, and a week later, the ships were still in search of land. In his journal, Columbus revealed that he had tinkered with the distances to reassure the crew that their goal was slowly but surely approaching, but he might have manufactured this excuse to disguise his miscalculation.

If Martín Alonso Pinzón took exception to this strategy, or suffered doubts about the wisdom of their navigational choices, Columbus did not record it. The challenge lent a sense of drama to a voyage that was in danger of losing its raison d'être, and it offered a chance to prove his mettle. He gravitated toward the crisis as if it were a manifestation of divine will. He had made a career thus far out of proving others wrong, not because he had better theories or answers, but because he was more resilient. He was confident that he could put the renegade captain in his place. But first, Columbus had to catch him.

In fact, he faced challenges from all three Pinzón brothers.

The first was Vicente Yáñez Pinzón, a part owner of both *Niña* and *Pinta*, both caravels—ships combining Western rigging with an Eastern, or lateen, sail for better maneuverability. Columbus's flagship, *Santa María*, was known simply by the generic term *nao*; it was round, stable, broad-beamed, and most likely built according to time-honored methods by Basque shipwrights. Juan de la Cosa, who also served as the ship's master, owned her. And the second brother was Francisco Martín Pinzón, who served as captain of *Niña*.

So Columbus was surrounded by Pinzón brothers, whose support had been critical in his overcoming skepticism for the voyage from the seamen of Palos, from which the fleet had sailed, and from nearby Huelva and Moguer. To the practical seamen, Columbus appeared as a wild-eyed dreamer and foreigner who spoke of crossing a sea that no one to their knowledge had succeeded in crossing before—Mar Tenebroso, it was sometimes called, "Dark Sea," practically synonymous with death itself—to reach fantastic kingdoms such as China and Japan that might not exist, except in the minds of dreamers and scholars, and now Columbus was asking them to trust him with their lives in his unlikely quest. He met with stiff resistance, until Martín Alonso Pinzón urged them to join with these words: "Friends, come away with us on this voyage. You are living here in misery. Come with us on this voyage, and to my certain knowledge we shall find houses roofed with gold and all of you will return prosperous and happy." Pinzón's words and reputation and example won the seamen over to Columbus's side. "It was because of this assurance of prosperity and the general trust in him that so many agreed to go with him," said one of his listeners.

Actually, he had done even more than that for Columbus. According to his son, Arias Pérez Pinzón, his father happened to have a friend, a cosmographer, or celestial mapmaker, who worked in the Vatican Library and who passed on a copy of a chart showing that one could sail westward across the Atlantic to Japan. (Without knowledge of the New World and the Pacific Ocean, such speculation ran rampant.) Martín Alonso, his son said, decided to mount a voyage of his own, but met with rebuffs in Portugal and Spain. In search of safe haven, spiritual support, and scholarly advice, Columbus retreated to the Monasterio de Santa María de la Rábida, a dramatically situated Franciscan friary in the town of Palos de la Frontera. There he encountered Martín Alonso Pinzón, who displayed a copy of the chart. Columbus was on the verge of abandoning Spain for France in his search for backing, but once equipped with this crucial document, he was finally able to win the support of the Spanish Sovereigns.

So the sudden, unexplained disappearance of Martín Alonso Pinzón on November 22 signified more than an ordinary act of insubordination. And because Pinzón was a part owner of the fleet, Columbus could not treat him as he might an ordinary seaman and punish him for disloyalty; the most he could do was outwait and outwit him, and eventually prove him wrong. Yet there was reason for hope. It might be expected that Pinzón's two brothers would follow suit, but they remained loyal to Columbus rather than to their brother. Columbus could not guess what their behavior implied about the fitness of Martín Alonso Pinzón, but he was bolstered by their loyalty; in fact, he expected no less.

For his part, Martín Alonso Pinzón believed he was just as responsible for the voyage as Columbus. Yet it was Columbus, not Pinzón, who had negotiated the terms of the voyage with Ferdinand and Isabella, including the detailed and explicit series of capitulations, or agreements, about his obligations and entitlements. Lacking comparable credentials, Pinzón behaved as though he had been forced into a partnership with a hotheaded Genoese mystic named Christopher Columbus who was out to claim the glory for himself, if he did not get them all killed in encounters with storms, sea monsters, reefs, or starvation.

So far, he had managed an unprecedented feat in the history of exploration, sailing across the Atlantic without loss of life. In contrast, Martín Alonso Pinzón became ever more erratic.

"This night Martín Alonso followed the course to the East," Columbus recorded on November 22 as he headed toward an island called Vaneque, lured by the promise of gold, or so the Indians said. Columbus passed the night sailing toward the island, and then, to his surprise, it seemed that Pinzón had changed course and was "coming toward him; and the night was very clear and the light wind favorable for coming to him, had he so wished." Through weary eyes, the Admiral gradually realized that he had been mistaken; perhaps Pinzón had maneuvered toward the flagship but had changed his mind. The mystery of his motives and plans bedeviled Columbus as he shaped a course for the island he called Bohío, about which the Indians conveyed a familiar set of rumors concerning "people who had one eye in the forehead" and fearsome cannibals. When the Indians realized the course chosen by Columbus would lead to Bohío, he wrote, "they were speechless." Columbus did not dismiss the rumors of cannibals entirely, remarking that he believed "there is something in this." Bohío would have to wait.

In the predawn darkness of Sunday, November 25, Columbus went ashore at Cayo Moa Grande, located on Cuba's northeastern coast. It was unusual to begin an expedition on the Lord's Day, but he was operating on an instinct "that there should be a good river there." His hunch seemed to pay off when he "went to the river and saw some stones shining in it, with some veins in them of the color of gold"—actually, they were iron pyrites, or fool's gold—but Columbus convinced himself that he had discovered the genuine article. "He ordered some of these stones to be collected to bring to the Sovereigns."

This investigation quickly led him to something less precious than gold, but of greater practical value: wood to repair and strengthen the ships. "Being there, the ship's boys sang out that they saw pine trees; he looked toward the sierra and saw many great and such marvelous ones, that he could not exaggerate their height and straightness, like spindles, thick and elongated, when he realized that ships could be had, and planks without number, and masts for the best ships of Spain. He saw oaks and arbutus" or, rather, trees closely resembling them, "and a good river, and the means to build sawmills. He saw on the beach many other stones of the color of iron, and others that some said were from silver mines; all of which the river brought down. There he cut a lateen-yard and mast for the mizzen of the caravel *Niña*." The neighboring cape was so capacious that "100 ships could lie without any cable or anchors." He envisioned a large, productive shipyard busily engaged in harvesting sturdy pine trees to construct "as many ships as were wanted," all sealed with readily available pitch. The possibilities for a permanent outpost in this newly discovered land provoked Columbus to paroxysms of ecstasy and overstatement. It seemed that the prospects for settlement steadily improved with every landfall; the air became sweeter, the prospect more pleasing to the eye, and nowhere more than here, in Cuba. Anyone seeing this land, he maintained, would be "full of wonder." And, of course, China lay just over the horizon.

Columbus continued to praise his newly discovered land, evoking "nine very remarkable harbors which all seamen considered wonders, and five great rivers . . . very high and beautiful mountains . . . the most beautiful valleys . . . thick with high and leafy trees, which were glorious to see." The one gnawing concern in this paradise was "tremendous fear" of cannibals, rumored to launch raiding parties in which they captured the land's timid inhabitants. The Indians he had brought on board as passenger-captives were horrified when they realized he was headed for their domain, "lest they make a meal of them, nor could he quiet their fears." Instead, they babbled about the cannibals' single eyes and "dogs' faces." Columbus chose to deal with the rumors thus: "The Admiral believed they were lying, and thought that those who had captured them must be under the sovereignty of the Grand Khan."

On November 27, from Baracoa, near the easternmost end of Cuba, he composed his most comprehensive summary yet. He revised his estimate of his findings upward, always upward, partly because he was convinced of the region's strategic value, even if it was not China, and partly to distract the Sovereigns from the embarrassing circumstance that he had not accomplished what he had promised to do. "A thousand tongues would not suffice, nor his hand to write, for it appeared that it was enchanted," he wrote of Cuba and its neighbors. Did anyone doubt the truth of his observations? "It is certain, Lord Princes, that when there are such lands there should be profitable things without number; but I tarried not in any harbor." His justification for sailing across the Atlantic at great risk and expense, only to pass over exactly what he sought, was not entirely convincing: "I sought to see the most countries that I could, to give the story of them to Your Highnesses," adding in passing, "and I do not know the language, and the people of the lands do not understand me nor I them, nor does anyone on board."

This observation did not square with the many conversations with Indians that he had already recorded in his diary, in which he described how Indians told him about gold, or trees, or harbors. Even allowing for significant misunderstanding, some inevitable, and some willful, between the two parties, there was no doubt that Columbus and his men had been carrying on multiple dialogues with their Indian hosts about trading, religion, Christianity, and local geography ever since the fleet's first landfall on October 12. Each party confirmed the other's mystical and religious prophecies and fantasies. The Indians thought Columbus's fleet fulfilled the longstanding, widely held belief that divine or divinely inspired creatures like them would visit the islands, and Columbus believed that whatever he encountered was intended by God, even though the Taínos were not exactly what he had in mind. Mutual recognition vied with mutual confusion. But the unspoken potential behind the discovery varied greatly for each party. For the Indians, it meant a visitation from above, and implied being uplifted rather than degraded. For Columbus, it implied the possibility of exploitation and enslavement, and the acquisition of limitless personal wealth.

To communicate with the Indians, he relied on his translator, Luis de Torres, but it quickly became apparent that he lacked the languages necessary to communicate in these islands. In his stead, Columbus enticed Indians aboard ship to act as guides and interpreters, only to realize that "these Indians whom I took along I often misunderstood, taking one thing for the opposite, and I don't trust them much"—not because he failed to understand them, but because "they have tried to flee." Columbus contradicted himself once more, writing that he was, after all, learning the Indian language "little by little," and "I will have this language taught to people of my household." And then he revealed, "I see that all so far have one language," implying that he had some familiarity with their tongue.

The "one language" about which he wrote was Arawak, now classed as a member of the Maipurean linguistic family, widely spoken across the Caribbean and South America. In his haphazard yet thorough exploration of the Caribbean Basin, he probably encountered two regional Arawakan dialects, Cuban and Bahamian.

Indian culture, even agriculture, scarcely interested Columbus. In a letter to Ferdinand and Isabella, he spoke of the lands he explored as a spiritual and economic tabula rasa on which his Sovereigns would leave a lasting imprint of empire. "Your Highnesses will command a city and fortress to be built in these parts," he predicted, "and these countries converted; and I certify"—a term with the force of an oath—"to Your Highnesses that it seems to me that there could never be under the sun [lands] superior in fertility, in mildness of cold and heat, in abundance of good and pure water; and the rivers are not like those of Guinea, which are all pestilential," he noted as an afterthought. And as everyone at court knew, Guinea fell squarely within Portugal's sphere of influence.

To prevent the Portuguese and other meddlesome outsiders such as the French or Arab pirates from poaching on this newly discovered paradise, Columbus urged Ferdinand and Isabella "not to consent that any foreigner does business or sets foot here, except Christian Catholics, since was the end and the beginning of the enterprise," a sentiment with which the Sovereigns and generations of clerics would find themselves in solemn agreement. It would remain his last chance but also his most persuasive argument: no matter what else went wrong, or whatever else he failed to accomplish on his voyage, he was bringing Christianity to the Indians before anyone else.

Assessing his accomplishments thus far, Columbus was on firmer ground concerning the health of his men. He boasted that "nobody has even had a headache or taken to his bed through sickness; except one old man with pain of gravel, from which he has suffered all his life, and he was well at the end of two days." That happy circumstance "applies to all three vessels." It was a remarkable piece of good fortune, given the unprecedented nature of the voyage, Columbus's distorted view of geography, his unreliable celestial navigation, and their primitive, unsanitary ships.

No sooner had Columbus informed the Sovereigns of his grand vision than he heard an alarming account from some of his crew. While reconnoitering, they told him, "they found in a house a cake of wax," a fetish object that he found intriguing enough to bring home with him to Spain to display to the Sovereigns. Also, "the seamen found in a house a man's head in a basket, covered with another basket and hanging to a post." According to their description, these dried heads were festooned about the settlement, forming a gruesome tableau. Columbus assumed that the object "must be those of some ancestors of the family; because those houses were of a kind where many persons live in one, and they should be relations descended from only one."

Despite his shockproof tone, he urgently wanted to seek the relative safety of open water, but just then heavy rain, dark clouds, and a southwest wind dead astern blew in and made navigation all but impossible. The rain was so intense his men could practically inhale it, and it went in cycles, replaced by shifting veils of mist. An hour later, the rain would descend and commence weeping over the same sodden scene. The next day, November 30, the damp wind shifted to the east, contrary to his course.

Unable to put to sea, he dispatched a scouting party of eight seamen and two Indians (as translators and guides) to assess the region and its settlements. "They went to many houses, and found nobody nor anything, for all had fled": a New World hauntingly devoid of people. Finally they spied "four young men who were digging in their fields," but the moment the Indians saw the intruders, "they turned to flee; couldn't catch them." The fearful inhabitants left behind impressive signs of civilization, "many villages, and very fertile land all cultivated, and great rivers of water, and near one they saw a dugout or canoe of 95 palms' length, of a single log, very handsome, and 150 people could find room in it and navigate," that is, if there were any people, but there were none.

The ships rode uneasily at anchor, poised to head out to sea. With rain increasing day by day, the seamen fretted that a storm would blow up and destroy the ships, but Columbus believed that a large rock at the mouth of the harbor would protect them from the worst of the weather, or so he said. But their situation was more precarious than he believed, or let on to the others. If the wind shifted, the rock would be no help at all.

At last, he saw people, even if they refused to stay put. It was Monday, December 3, and Columbus, venturing onto land and following a winding creek, had just come upon "five very great dugouts, . . . very handsome and well worked." Appraising the canoes as a navigator, he declared them a gratifying mixture of form and function. As he walked on, he came across a "boathouse very well ordered and covered, so that neither sun nor water could do [the dugouts] damage." Within, protected by the structure, he examined a "canoe made of a single log like the others," comparable to a large rowboat or barge "of 16 thwarts." The artistry that went into the vessel impressed him deeply. "It was a pleasure to see their workmanship and fine appearance." A pleasure for him, that is, but not for Spanish bureaucrats, who had dispatched him to save souls, forge trade with the Grand Khan, and, in the process, outfox the wily Portuguese. Examples of indigenous handicrafts were of scant interest to Spanish officialdom; gold was what they wanted, gold and power.

Leaving the boathouse, Columbus "climbed a mountain" and from the summit surveyed broad fields "planted with many things of the country." A man of the sea, Columbus was unfamiliar with the names of the fruits and vegetables he encountered; some he took to be gourds, or *calabazas*, among the first plant species to be cultivated.

Suddenly "the people of the village" appeared. The moment they saw the strange figure on the mountain, they took flight. He dispatched his Indian guides to reassure them, and bestow gifts of hawk's bells, brass rings, and green and yellow glass beads. Concerning the skittish Indians, Columbus "assured the Sovereigns that 10 men could put to flight 10,000, so cowardly and timid are they." It was true that they were armed with simple spears, but on examination, they proved to be nothing more than reeds with fire-hardened tips. Wanting them for himself, Columbus employed "a good ruse, bartering in such manner that they gave them all." And so the timid Indians were deprived of their rudimentary weapons by the cunning Admiral, whom they had come to fear and revere.

Just when Columbus believed he had charmed and disarmed the populace, the Indians raised their arms skyward and shouted. Suddenly he saw the face of one Indian "become as yellow as wax" as he frantically gestured to Columbus that people—the Caribs, in all likelihood—were coming. The Indian pointed to a loaded crossbow held by one of the Spaniards, indicating that "they would all be killed" by this unseen menace. To emphasize his point, the Indian grabbed a scabbard and withdrew a sword, brandishing it.

The Indians fled, with Columbus calmly following. When he caught up with them, they were readying for battle. "There were very many, all painted red and naked as their mothers bore them, and some of them with feathers on the head and other plumes, all with their bundles of darts." Columbus proceeded to disarm them by means of bribery and distraction. "I went up to them and gave them some piece of bread and demanded their spears, for which I gave them a hawk's bell, to others a brass ring, to others some beads, so that all were pleased." The Indians offered their precious spears in return, because "they think that we have come from the sky." If only they had the gold and spices he sought, how easy it would be to acquire these precious items from them.

The day ended with Columbus entering "a beautiful house" with "marvelous work" hanging from the ceilings; he did not know how to describe what he beheld, most likely intricately woven mats adorned with shells, so striking that he thought he had stumbled into a temple. With sign language, he asked the Indians if they said their prayers here, and "they said no; and one of them climbed up and gave me all that was there."

The morning of December 4 brought a light wind, and Columbus was finally able to set forth from the harbor he had taken to calling Puerto Santo. He ran along the coast, passing a landmark he named Cape Lindo, often identified as Punta Fraile, Cuba.

He spied a "great bay" that just might be a strait or passageway leading to the empire of the Grand Khan and sailed throughout the night "in order to see the land which went to the E," but eventually he yielded in his ambition on the advice of Indian guides. The coast he was now exploring, with its intimations of the Eastern kingdom, actually belonged to Cuba, "which up to then he had considered mainland by reason of its extent, for he had easily gone about 120 leagues along it."

By considering the possibility that Cuba was an island—not a promontory of the Asian mainland—Columbus seemed to abandon one of the most cherished hopes of his voyage. He had not, as yet, found Asia, nor the Grand Khan, yet he could not bring himself to acknowledge that he had found some other land. Unable to solve this geographic puzzle, he lost himself in the act of sailing, heading back once more to the island of Hispaniola, ceaselessly exploring, for what, he could not say.

As night was coming on, Columbus sent *Niña* ahead to "sight the harbor by daylight, because she was speedy; and arriving at the mouth of the harbor"—on the coast of modern-day Haiti—"which was like the Bay of Cadiz, and because it was already night, she sent in her barge to sound the harbor, and which showed the light of a candle" to indicate the way. Columbus approached, "hoping that barge would show signals to enter the harbor," but just then "the light on the barge went out." As a consequence, *Niña* "ran off shore and showed a light to the Admiral, and coming up to her, they told him what had happened. At this point, the men on the barge showed another light; the caravel went to it, and the Admiral could not, and stayed all that night beating about."

After this intricate dance of wind and current and flickering torchlight, the new day, December 6, dawned, and Columbus "found himself 4 leagues from the harbor." He caught glimpses of onshore fires, their columns of smoke "like beacons," perhaps warning of a tribal war on land, from which he felt characteristically exempt.

"At the hour of vespers, he entered the harbor, and gave it the name Puerto de San Nicolas, because it was the feast of St. Nicholas, for his honor," Columbus wrote, extolling its "beauty and graciousness." He considered it his right and responsibility to confer names wherever he went, regardless of the site's traditional designation, and in many instances, the name has stuck, erasing history in the process. There was a power in naming, almost as if he were converting his surroundings to Christendom; naming was claiming.

Considering it superior to all other harbors he had visited on his voyage, Columbus explored its perimeter, sounded its depths, searched for hazards, and was pleased to declare, "There does not seem to be a single shoal." Its length could comfortably accommodate "a thousand carracks," a heavy hint to his Sovereigns about the region's potential. "The whole harbor is very breezy and uninhabited, clear of trees," he commented. The majestic sweep extended as far as the eye could see, an emerald set in shimmering sapphire. "The land is very high, and all open country or clear." In another direction, he saw "a beautiful plain," large villages, and dugouts that were fifteen thwarts long, fleeing rather than approaching his ships. The Indians accompanying suddenly announced they had "great desire to go to their own country," but he had his suspicions about their motives, and they, no doubt, about his.

At seven the following morning, the commencement of the dawn watch, Columbus spread sail, and put Port St. Nicolas to stern.

The approaching rain portended three solid days of cloudbursts and downpours. "Blew hard from the NE," he noted laconically, hard enough, in fact, to force the ships to drag their anchors, "at which the Admiral was surprised." Again, his scouts saw signs of human habitation, but by the time they went ashore, the inhabitants had disappeared into the tropical forest. The image of a bewildered Columbus both entreating and frightening the indigenous people of the Caribbean is at odds with the storehouse of conventionally heroic images of the Admiral as divinely inspired, supremely confident, bringing Christianity and Spanish rule to untutored peoples. And it is at odds with the argument that he planned to exploit, enslave, degrade, or slaughter the timid, mostly unarmed Indians whose language he tried to learn, and whose seamanship he admired. At this juncture, he was neither a bringer of laws nor a spreader of disease, as centuries of commentators and portrait painters have represented him, but rather an earnest, fearless, and misguided navigator (and self-serving chronicler) who had difficulty impressing his sense of mission and self-importance on others, beginning with his own crew. Only the Indians who had never before seen his like were impressed, and they responded by taking flight. The more familiar they became with him and his men, the more they gravitated toward the explorer, partly because he deftly bribed them with trinkets, and partly because of an unspoken sense of a shared potential destiny between these two disparate groups. Their behavior, the way they clung to him like iron filings to a magnet, suggests that despite his confusion about where he was and his indecisiveness, his sense of high purpose communicated itself to his hosts. At the same time, he was also the cunning merchant of Genoa, looking for resources to trade and exploit.

Further exploration of Hispaniola and neighboring islands—it is not clear exactly which, owing to Columbus's often disjointed syntax—brought him into contact with more Taínos and their preoccupation with the marauding and man-eating Caribs. "All these islands live in great fear of those Caniba," he lamented. "And so I repeat what I have said, that Caniba is nothing else than the people of the Grand Khan, which should be very near and own ships, and they come to capture them, and since they don't return they suppose that they've been eaten." Oblivious to the irony of his observation,

Columbus remarked, "Every day we understand these Indians better, and they us, although at many times they have understood one thing for another." Who was more misguided, the Indians or Columbus himself, who clung to the belief that he had arrived in Asia, on the doorstep of the Grand Khan?

The next day, December 12, provided additional proof of Columbus's contradictory impulses. It began with the seamen raising a "great cross at the entrance of the harbor." Once this deed had been accomplished, three seamen walked inland, supposedly to "see the trees and plants," only to confront a "great crowd of people," all of them naked, and all of whom fled at the sight of the intruders. This time, under orders from Columbus, they captured a woman, who happened to be "young and beautiful," and brought her, in all her innocence and nakedness, before the Admiral, who "had her clothed and gave her glass beads and hawk's bells and brass rings; and he sent her ashore very honorably, according to his custom."

Columbus claimed that the young woman preferred to stay with the other female detainees, whom he planned to hand over to Ferdinand and Isabella as exotic gifts. Of greater interest, "This woman wore on her nose a little piece of gold, which was a sign that there was gold in that island." For Columbus, this sign, no matter how insignificant, was more than a mere indication or clue, it was a manifestation of the latent wealth and power of these islands, and so it was sufficient to inspire him to continue his quest.

Columbus dispatched another party, who came upon a large village with "1,000 houses and more than 3,000 men," all fleeing the approaching Christians and their Indian guide, who shouted that they need not fear, "that the Christians were not from Caniba but from the sky, and that they gave many things to all those whom they met." Most of those fleeing heeded the Indian, turned, and "came up to the Christians and placed their hands on their heads, which was a sign of great respect and friendship." Despite the reassurances, "they were all trembling."

Once the fear abated, the Taínos invited the Christians into their homes and offered them the "roots"—tubers, specifically—"like great carrots that they grow and plant in all these countries." Tubers come in two varieties, stem tubers, such as potatoes, and root tubers. This homely brown root tuber, with its skimpy, gnarled reddish shoots, formed the staple of the Indian diet: the starchy, sturdy cassava plant. (It sometimes goes by the names yucca and manioc.) Columbus's men found that Taíno agriculture surpassed the slash-and-burn techniques of other tropical societies. To cultivate cassava, the Taínos laboriously fashioned rows of small, mounded fields, about three feet by nine feet, called *conucos*, designed to resist erosion, to facilitate water drainage during the rainy season, and to store cassava tubers for as long as three years against the possibility of famine. With the cassava, "they make bread of it, and cook and roast it, and it has the flavor proper to chestnuts." In time, the Spanish came to call this homely brown tuber the "bread of the Indies."

Cassava is rich in calories, if little else, and until cooked, nearly tasteless. But raw cassava requires careful preparation; it contains trace quantities of cyanide (cyanogenic glucoside) that must be leached away by scraping and fermenting; ingesting unprocessed cassava causes painful chronic pancreatitis, or inflammation of the pancreas. Only forty milligrams of cassava cyanide can kill a cow. To make cassava fit for consumption, the Indian women grated the tubers and mixed the dried flour with water to form a paste, which they spread in a thin layer over a basket. The treatment, lasting five hours, broke down most of the toxic cyanogenic glucosides in the cassava, and the resulting hydrogen cyanide, also extremely toxic, escaped into the air. Only then did cassava flour become safe for human consumption.

The cassava was but one of many plants unknown to Columbus and his men—unknown across Europe, in fact. The Admiral, the fleet's physician Dr. Chanca, and his men wondered at the sight of strange peppers, beans, peanuts, and *batatas*, or sweet potatoes, growing in the rich Caribbean soil. Even more enticing were dozens of new and unusual varieties of fruit new to European palates. The Spanish visitors had their first sight and taste of papaya, mango, guava, star apple, mammee apple, and passion fruit. And there were the *piñas*, or pineapples, "produced on plants like thistles in the manner of aloes with many pulpy leaves," a fascinated visitor noted, trying to compare them to more familiar European plants. This fruit had scales and bark "about the thickness of a melon," and took a year or so to mature. It was said to smell "better than peaches," and one or two of them would suffuse the interior of a dwelling with their sweet perfume.

There was more. When the Indians learned that Columbus desired a parrot, they brought as many of the tropical birds as he and his men wished, without asking anything in return. They were gorgeous, iridescent creatures of scarlet, cobalt, and yellow, accented with black-and-white markings around the head; as long as a man's arm, they were watchful and animated. When not cracking seeds in their powerful mandibles, they mimicked human speech and even seemed to comprehend it. Of all the non-human creatures Columbus's men encountered on the island, they were the most intelligent and sociable.

The parrots did not distract Columbus from the singular beauty of the women arrayed before them; where he previously gaped at their near nakedness and lack of modesty, he now recorded reports of "two wenches as white as they can be in Spain," who inhabited a region whose "lands were cultivated and . . . down the center of the valley a very wide and great river which could irrigate all the lands. All the trees were green and full of fruit, and the plants all flowery and very tall, the paths very broad and good." From this point forward, Columbus bursts the bounds of conventional logbook discourse, for a time leaving behind all mention of tides and winds and sail for rapturous and visionary description. "The air," he wrote, "was like April in Castile," reverberating with intoxicating sounds that struck him as "the greatest delight in the world," with all of nature in harmony. "At night some little birds sang sweetly, the crickets and frogs made themselves heard, the fishes were as in Spain; they say much mastic and aloes and cotton trees"—but, he had to add, jarred from his reverie, "gold they found not." The spell broken, he busied himself trying to measure the length of the night and day with hourglasses, but without the expected result, and he was forced to admit, "there could be some mistake because either they didn't turn them so promptly, or the sand failed to pass through." His grumbling at the impasse is palpable. It was apparent that his imagination and instincts remained more finely attuned and far-reaching than his clumsy handling of his flawed instruments.

The next day, he departed Puerto de la Concepción—now Moustique Bay, Haiti—and made his way toward a craggy, mountainous island that reminded the crew of the humped back of a turtle, and so it came to be called Turtle or Tortoise Island, best known by its Spanish name, Tortuga. He beheld "a very high land but not mountainous, and it is very beautiful and very populous." He resolved to try for Tortuga again the following day, December 15, this time anchoring "half a league to leeward off a beach, good, clean holding ground."

Columbus dropped abundant hints that he was becoming melancholy and disoriented in paradise. He had arrived, and he was still lost. He yearned to find the gold he had promised his Sovereigns, and himself, and beyond that, a larger sense of purpose. Over his journal hovers the sense that, having failed thus far to make contact with the Grand Khan or other powerful and wealthy rulers, his ambitious voyage lacked redeeming purpose. He had witnessed what had befallen Bartolomeu Dias, the Portuguese explorer, on his return to Lisbon from the Cape of Good Hope four years earlier. Dias had spent two years of struggle and deprivation to reach this goal, risking his life and those of his crew, only to receive a lukewarm reception from the vain and volatile king of Portugal. Two years later, in 1490, still trying to win his sovereign's favor, and his share of glory, Dias embarked on another expedition and perished.

The tragic career of this noble mariner stood as a cautionary tale, one that Columbus did not intend to repeat in the fertile paradise he had discovered. His psyche required a greater destiny.

CHAPTER 2

Son of Genoa

No matter where he went, or who he became, Columbus remained a son of Genoa, the Ligurian seaport where bold maritime exploration was a way of life.

In 1291, the Vivaldi brothers of Genoa, Ugolino and Vadino, assembled a carefully planned and well-capitalized ocean voyage to India. Relying on a drastically oversimplified idea of the earth's geography and size, they believed they could reach their destination by sailing west, or perhaps by circumnavigating Africa. They had access to maps and portolan charts, showing the coast in detail, and they sailed in galleys similar to those employed by Genoese mariners since the 1270s. Had they reached their destination, history might have celebrated Vivaldi Day rather than Columbus Day. But the brothers' lumbering galleys proved no match for the high seas, and the brave fleet disappeared without a trace.

In 1336, Lanzarotto Malocello navigated his way to the Canary Islands, bestowing the name Lanzarote on one of them. Only five years later Nicoloso da Recco arrived at the Azores. Ever more ambitious voyages by sea came to seem inevitable. Many daring Genoese voyagers formed partnerships with the kingdom of Portugal, and in 1317 a Genoese led the emerging Portuguese navy. The plague and political instability slowed but did not halt the pace of discovery; by 1441, when António de Noli reached the Cape Verde Islands, the idea of additional islands beckoning across the Atlantic to the south and west became a powerful attraction for Columbus and other ambitious Italian navigators.

Tragic events at sea formed an essential part of Genoa's culture, and that of the surrounding Ligurian region, the setting for some of Europe's most ancient human settlements. The steep, rocky Ligurian coast offered rich and fertile soil, but in limited quantities. The meager amount of arable land forced farmers to carve narrow terraces into mountainsides. The most reliable crop happened to be Savona wine, produced west of Genoa. These restrictions spurred Ligurians to look to the sea for sustenance and survival. Of necessity, Ligurian sailors and pilots, rowers and riggers, emerged as the best and the bravest in Italy, or perhaps the most foolhardy. A Ligurian proverb warned, *"O mare o l'è male"*: The sea is evil.

A necessary evil, however.

All along its length, the region, known as the Ligurian Riviera, sheltered harbors and ports for sailors venturing into the sea for their livelihood. The port of Genoa, with its generous harbor, reigned over all, a semicircle jutting out from the hills of Sarzana, highlighted by a pier. Ships sought the port's *mandraccio*, or shelter. "The harbor curves around in an arc here and, lest the fury of the sea damage the ships, comes protected by a jetty, which, it is said, would have cost only a little more had it been made of silver," wrote Enea Silvio Piccolomini (later Pope Pius II) of Columbus's home port in 1423.

It was here that Columbus was born in 1451. Questions and alternative theories about Columbus's origins have long located his birth and upbringing in places as varied as Portugal, Spain, and northern Africa, but the evidence, including 453 legal and commercial documents, overwhelmingly places him in Genoa, the son of Domenico Columbus, a weaver, tavern keeper, and local politician.

Bartolomé de Las Casas, later a remorseless critic of the explorer, plainly states that "Christopher was universally acknowledged to be Genoese by birth." Stories about his ancestors insist that "his forebears were people of rank and had once been wealthy," as if to suggest that Columbus sought to restore the status of his family, who "appear to have lost their fortune during the wars and internecine squabbles that one finds at every turn throughout the history of Lombardy," the dominant region of northern Italy.

Concerning the name Columbus, Las Casas relates that in antiquity it had been "Colonus," but he "elected to style himself Colón," a transformation Las Casas ascribed to the "will of the Lord, who had chosen him to carry out the task conveyed by the name Christopher Colón." Following his subject's interpretation of his name, "he was named Christopher, that is to say, *Christum ferens*, which is Latin for the bearer or carrier of Christ."

Columbus took to signing his name with elaborate flourishes to underscore his reputation as the man "adjudged worthy above all others to bring these numberless peoples who had lain in oblivion throughout so many centuries to the knowledge and worship of Christ." Las Casas explained that

Colón meant "new settler," which he judged a "fitting title for a man whose industry and whose labors led to the discovery of numberless souls."

The adult Columbus appeared in Genoese records in October 1470 in connection with a commercial transaction. "In the name of our Lord," it begins, "Christopher Columbus, son of Domenico, more than nineteen years of age, and in the presence of, and by the authority, advice and consent of Domenico, his father, present and authorizing, voluntarily . . . confessed and in truth publicly recognized, that he must give and pay to Pietro Belesio of Porto Maurizio, son of Francesco, present, forty-eight lire, thirteen soldi and six denari di genovini, and this is for the remainder owed for wine sold and consigned to the same Christopher and Domenico by Pietro." Domenico promised to guarantee his son's obligation in the presence of several witnesses including Raffaele of Bisagno, a baker.

Domenico's trade as a wool weaver and carder signified to his fellow Genoese that, given wool's prestige, he was a presence in Genoa's commercial scene. Wool weavers maintained their own guild. More than a trade union, a guild offered its members a way of life. There were over eighty at the time of Columbus's childhood in La Superba, as Genoa called itself. They settled trade disputes, represented their members before the doge, administered exams to those seeking to gain entry, and organized weddings and funerals for their members, including gifts and the specifics of religious observance.

They educated their members' children, and it was under the guild's auspices that Christopher studied arithmetic, geography, and navigation. The schools offered two curricula. Those who studied Latin, the Latinantes, paid ten soldi for the privilege; all others paid five. Latin was employed for documents, scientific papers, and other formal utterances; otherwise, the Genoese dialect with its mellifluous French inflection prevailed. "*Son zeneize, rizo ræo, strenzo i denti e parlo ciæo*" runs a popular regional expression. "I'm Genoese, I seldom laugh, I grind my teeth, and I say what I mean": attitudes Columbus epitomized. By the time he left Genoa, he knew at least two languages, Genoese and Latin, and he later acquired Portuguese and Spanish.

Columbus's mother, Susanna Fontanarossa, belonged to a prosperous landowning family in Quezzi, a village of the valley of Bisagno, near Genoa. Her father was Jacobi di Fontanarubea, or, as he came to be known, Giacomo Fontanarossa. Susanna was a popular name in the region, and associated with the church of Santa Susanna in Rome. She was born about 1425, and upon her marriage brought a dowry consisting of a house and land, both of which were subsequently sold. She and her husband Domenico, Columbus's father, bore at least five children: Giovanni Pelegrino, Bartholomew, Diego, Bianchinetta, and the infant who would be called Christopher Columbus. She died about 1480, little known to the world at large, though she had influenced it greatly through her children.

Maritime trade was vital to Genoa's existence, and local authorities managed it with great care. At the top of the regulatory pyramid, the Office of the Sea had final say over the harbor and shore, and the Office of the Commune Fathers oversaw the docks and piers, as well as the excavation of the harbor necessary for the ships' safety. Equally critical, the Office of Health worked strenuously to prevent ships from returning with the plague and similar diseases. No one aboard an arriving ship was permitted to set foot on terra firma without obtaining a permit, available for a fee from the Office of Health's representative on Genoa's Spinola Bridge. If a ship's crew might have been exposed to plague in their travels, they were subjected to a strict quarantine. Beggars, if caught, were subjected to a penalty of three lashings, and lepers were forbidden to enter the city, nor was anyone allowed to feed or shelter them. Despite these regulations, the plague was a frequent and dreaded visitor in Genoa, worse in summer, milder in winter. In self-defense, households burned clothes and other goods thought to be contaminated.

The Genoese bureaucracy extended beyond the entrance to the harbor, keeping track of ships as they traveled to and from their destinations across the Mediterranean. Vessels departing from Genoa were generally observed by sentries at the Lanterna, and by other sentries posted along the shore. If they spied an unusual occurrence—a dangerous-looking craft or an accident at sea—they reported their suspicions to the Lanterna by means of smoke signals during the day or fires at night.

In 1490, smoke signals alerted Genoa to an attack by corsairs from Nice. The city mounted a rapid retaliation, catching the aggressors by surprise, rescuing its own men, in the process contributing to the city-state's fierce reputation. Genoa punished its enemies, and took care of its own. It posted consuls to strategically important cities, and they regularly communicated by ship-borne letter, or, when urgent, by smoke signals. This intelligence network gave Genoa military and strategic advantage over its rivals, who took out their frustrations and grievances with reprisals, and, when possible, by capturing Genoese galleys and imprisoning all those on board. (Marco Polo of Venice was one of thousands of enemies of the Republic of Genoa who were subjected to this treatment.) Genoa responded to the increased threats by ordering ships to travel in convoys, heavily armed, and prepared to respond to attack. Genoese pirates earned a reputation for savagery, as well as for slave trading. They constantly did battle with Catalans and with the French, who gradually overtook the Genoese Republic by force, and by marriage. Gradually the republic lost its influence, as newer, larger powers emerged. The spices, especially pepper, and gems that had formerly arrived by ship in Genoa now went to Lisbon and later to Madrid as the commercial center of gravity drifted from the Mediterranean to the Iberian Peninsula. In its shrunken universe, Genoa focused on trade with North African ports, which could be extremely profitable, as well as extremely dangerous, and on currency exchange, an arena in which its bankers became known as swift and hard negotiators.

This was the tumultuous era into which Christopher Columbus was born, and in which he came of age.

In the year of Christopher Columbus's birth, 1451, western Europe was slowly advancing, inspired by ideas and art disseminated from Italy, but Genoa succumbed to waves of political instability. Two years later, the city suffered a commercial blow with the fall of Constantinople, bringing with it a steady decline in Mediterranean commerce. During Columbus's earliest years, the French fortunes revived, and in 1458, when Christopher was seven years old, the Genoese doge ceded Genoa to King Charles VII of France, reaping a personal fortune from the sale of his kingdom to its enemies. This outrageous turn of events came about because the rival Genoese factions preferred to invite a foreign power—the French—to rule rather than one side or the other. For once, Genoa hovered on the brink of peace.

After this victory, which could have led to political unification, the two main Genoese factions, the Fregoso and the Adorno, resumed battling each other. There were riots and assassinations, and civil strife that fed on itself and festered on the doorstep of the Columbus household.

In the fall of 1459, when Columbus was about to turn eight years old, he lived about fifty yards from Genoa's Porta di Sant'Andrea, the scene of a violent confrontation. At that moment, the doge, Pietro Fregoso, after losing round after round of battles with the French, and further undercut by the rival Adornos, found himself cornered within the city walls, with only three knights for protection, the remnant of a once-formidable army. Galloping from one gate to another in search of freedom, he was confronted by his pursuers. One of them, Giovanni Cosa, caught up with him and struck him twice on the head with a deadly iron mace; Pietro, the doge, escaped this attack, only to confront a barrage of stones hurled at him from the rooftops.

Unable to flee the city, the wounded leader rode uncertainly to his palace, where he collapsed and died within hours. Soon after, his body was returned to the street, where his political enemies gathered to dismember his corpse. Meanwhile, his troops, along with his brother Massimo, also tried to flee, only to meet with similarly appalling executions.

One hundred yards from the spot where the corpse of the doge Pietro was mutilated lived the Columbus family, in Vico Dritto di Ponticello, in a house owned by Domenico. It was possible that the young boy witnessed the gruesome event—stoning, the mutilation—and heard the shouts of the bloodthirsty victors. And if he was aware of the outrage, he would have had reason to tremble with dread, because his father, Domenico, was allied with the Fregoso faction, and his fortunes declined with theirs.

Then a way out of the deadly rivalry presented itself.

Milan's ruler, Francesco Sforza, with the support of Genoese citizens who had sickened of the internecine political warfare, won appointment in 1463 as lord of the city. Compared with the ceaseless strife that had preceded it, Sforza's regime was a great success, a time of relative peace and prosperity. Yet the Sforza clan demonstrated little appreciation of Genoa's distinguishing feature: its maritime trade. Neglected, Genoese shipping withered, and the few colonies the city had acquired were lost; the Genoese empire, always tentative and fragile, dwindled until even Corsica's surpassed it. The prospects for ambitious navigators and explorers such as Christopher Columbus vanished.

Coming of age as an outcast in his hometown, and taking to the sea at an early age, Columbus devoted the rest of his life struggling to replace this lost empire. At first personal, the search turned political, and drove Columbus farther than he ever imagined, beyond Italy and Europe, beyond the Mediterranean, England, and Iceland, beyond the Canaries, all the way to the New World. Only an epic quest could match his ambition; nothing less would suffice. What began as recovery would end as discovery.

In Columbus's youth, Genoa was in the throes of a rapid transformation. Shops, warehouses, stables, and markets piled atop each other in raucous and foul-smelling confusion. The wooden houses characteristic of the medieval era gave way to stone dwellings with tiled floors, massive fireplaces, and loggias arrayed along the narrow, winding streets called *carrugi*. The newer homes contained bathrooms with washbasins, bowls, and jugs with water, and soap in ivory boxes from Savona. In Columbus's time, sailors aboard ships in the *mandraccio* gazed upward to the west to the somber gray stone palaces highlighted with towers of reddish brown and vertiginous battlements.

It was one of the largest cities in western Europe, with a population approaching 75,000, the equal of London, Paris, or Venice. In prosperous times, the port churned with ships and travelers from Genoa's most popular destinations, instantly distinguishable by their garb and dialect. Lombards stood apart from Tuscans and from Levantines in billowing breeches. Turks in their turbans clustered in small groups, as did Greeks, recognizable from their short pleated blouses known as *fustanellas*. Catalans were readily identified by the *barretinas* they wore on their heads; Sardinians in black breeches and hood, and a loose white shirt, easily stood out.

Clothing worn by the Genoese was strictly regulated by the Office of Virtue, beginning in 1439. The Office enforced a series of sumptuary laws to regulate morality by curbing luxury and excess, as well as prostitution. These laws limited the amount of money Genoese could spend on luxury items, and even on weddings, limited to fifty guests. They regulated the days on which prostitutes, a staple of Genoese nightlife, could roam the streets. They measured their time with clients by the half hour, marked by a flickering candle. "Girls with a candle," as the prostitutes were known, were forbidden to enter a cemetery or approach a church, and had to wear insignia indicating their profession. If caught out of bounds, the prostitutes were punished by having their noses amputated, and their livelihood ruined.

The same Office of Virtue governing matters of dress and prostitution also regulated marital transactions; romance rarely entered into the equation. Married women were meant to maintain their homes; they were supposed to be as somber as their husbands. Given half a chance, the Genoese could be lavish spenders, especially when it came to weddings, but ultimately rules and regulations prevailed, down to the smallest details.

Sumptuary laws dictated that men wore sober gray attire. Red and purple were out of bounds. The value of jewelry and dresses owned by women was sharply limited, and if it exceeded the prescribed limit, the owners were fined. Fines extended to personal conduct, as well. A woman who committed adultery was fined thirty lire; if she failed to pay, she was beheaded. A husband who put his wife out on the street to make room for a lover was fined twenty-five lire. Marriages occurred when women—girls, actually— reached age fifteen, the bargain sealed with a handshake, and the bride not present, only the family representatives, notary, and matchmaker. In Genoa, a deal was a deal, whether for love or money.

Slavery was deeply woven into the fabric of the Genoese economy, especially traffic in girls who were only thirteen or fourteen years old. Every Genoese household, even modest ones, had one or two female slaves. Although Christianity prohibited bondage, an exception was made for these non-Christian slaves; they were Russian, Arab, Mongol, Bulgarian, Bosnian, Albanian, and Chinese. Slave traders and pirates sold them on a regular basis to Genoa; occasionally their wide net included a Christian girl, whom they kidnapped and would return for a high ransom. The transactions were formal, notarized and deeded. Most slaves were sold "as is." If others, whose health had been guaranteed, developed epilepsy or other health problems, the owner demanded an annulment of the contract. Some cautious buyers kept the girl of their choice on a trial basis to judge whether she would remain charming and adapt to a life of slavery in Genoa. Once acquired by a Genoese master, girls became mere property, bound to gratify his sexual wants, as well as those of his friends. Merchants able to afford a concubine, and many in this prosperous city could, maintained them in households separate from their families. The master of the house specified the terms of the arrangement with the local notary public, especially concerning sensitive matters such as inheritance rights for children born out of wedlock.

Not all slaves were obedient, and occasionally one attempted to escape, or even poison her master. If caught, she would be subjected to prolonged torture until she confessed her crimes, and in addition, confessed to witchcraft and heresy. She was then subjected to the "penance of fire," that is, burned at the stake. Less serious infractions committed by the slaves met with frequent lashings in private. This was the slavery with which Christopher Columbus was familiar.

Merchants gathered around the Piazza Banchi, Genoa's commercial center, dotted with the *scagni*, or stalls, of bankers, money changers, and moneylenders, who did business with customers at a counter using a scale for weighing gold and silver. Heavily laden mules trudged through narrow winding streets, with large bales of goods strapped tightly to their backs. Some mules bore sacks of woven jute—*zerbini*—on either flank, similar to saddlebags, as they made their way between impossibly tall houses, the monotonous shade occasionally broken by sunlight pouring down from a garden or a flower-bedecked sundeck. In hot weather and in cold, the constricted streets sent up a stench consisting of dung, spices, tar employed in caulking the leaky ships, and the grease used by tanners to preserve and soften stiff hides. Amid the reek, *bastagi*, or porters, loaded and unloaded the wares carried by the mules off and on the ships. Their racket reverberated off the stones of Genoa, a cacophony composed of hammers beating hot iron on cool anvil, of the softer thud of mallets on barrel hoops, of piercing commands delivered to the ships' crews, and of sailors chanting as they rowed or coiled ropes. Peddlers sang odes to their fish, their cloth, their fruit, anything they hoped to turn into money, and behind them, shopkeepers patiently waited for seagoing customers. Guilds for sailmakers, caulkers, coopers, carpenters, lantern makers, welders of anchors and cannon, and other trades associated with shipbuilding and maintenance clustered around the base of the docks.

The city's mind and heart, no less than its economy, focused on the sea. "The Genoese, while loving the family above himself, was always ready to leave it behind to cross the seas to foreign countries," the Genoese historian Emilio Pandiani has written. "He was a trader and navigator first."

In the cramped harbor, the ships, the focus of Genoa's pride and commercial frenzy, jostled for space and attention. They consisted mostly of traditional galleys distinguished by a row of oars on either side, each oar powered by five or six oarsmen. More than a hundred oarsmen were at the ready if the wind died, under the command of the pilot, or *comito*. When necessary, they crowded on deck with body-length shields bearing brilliant coats of arms, to form a human shield against attack. Others carried bows and arrows, and catapults for throwing "Greek fire"—probably blazing petroleum—along with devices for grappling and boarding other craft in battle. On the forecastle, near the prow, engines of war known as mangonels stood ready. These were giant slingshots capable of bombarding an enemy with a lethal array of objects, including stones and firebombs.

Galleys extended to well over one hundred feet in length, and at the widest part ranged from twelve to fifteen feet. Their keels and decks were usually fashioned from oak. They sported two tall, slender masts, seventy-five feet high, both rigged with triangular sails at an angle to the mast. The distinctive, highly maneuverable lateen, or Latin, sail is believed to have originated with Roman vessels as early as the third century AD, although they have long been identified with daring Arab sailors, especially pirates raiding vulnerable European or African coastlines. The principal types of galleys with which Columbus was familiar were the narrow, maneuverable galley known as the *zenzil*, and the bastard galley, distinguished by a round stern and greater width. The former were generally used for battle and the latter for transport and trade.

Personnel consisted of the captain, or *patrono*; the pilot; a ship's clerk; a gunsmith, or *insegnator*; carpenters and caulkers to maintain the ship; a barber who doubled as a surgeon; a barrel keeper to mind the precious stores of water; a waiter and many other servants; a cook; twenty jack-of-all-trades sailors; weapons specialists; and several ship's boys. In Columbus's youth, most oarsmen were freemen, later supplanted with slaves or prisoners condemned to hard labor. Under this grim regimen, oarsmen-slaves were chained to rowing benches and tortured by an overseer's stinging whip while a whistle marked time. It was aboard such ships that Genoese navigators such as Columbus learned their harsh trade.

As an apprentice seaman, Columbus likely participated in maritime expeditions along the Ligurian Riviera, extending as far west along the sparkling cobalt Mediterranean Sea as Nice, as far east as the town of Porto Venere in the province of La Spezia, and as far south as Corsica, the fourth-largest island in the Mediterranean and a prized colony of Genoa.

He later sailed a thousand miles to the Greek island of Chios in the Aegean Sea. Despite its distance from Liguria, Chios was tightly controlled by the Genoese. Although outnumbered ten to one, the commercial invaders retained their hold by allowing religious freedom for the inhabitants while exploiting the island for its economic potential by means of a financial organization known as a *maona*, overseen by a chief magistrate, or *podestá*, appointed by Genoa. With this system, the Genoese established trading posts and warehouses for profitable commodities such as salt and pitch. They also traded in "Chios tears," the ivory-colored resin that dripped from the mastic trees (*Pistacia lentiscus*) dotting the hillsides. (With its smoky, astringent taste, mastic is still used for chewing gum.)

By the time Columbus returned from Chios, his father had moved the family residence from Vico Dritto di Ponticello to the nearby hills of Savona, perhaps because he was allied with the losing faction in Genoa's political strife, or, just as likely, for the sake of a safer environment.

Columbus was soon aboard the ship *Bechalla*, carrying a cargo of mastic from Chios, bound for Portugal, Flanders, and England. It was May 1476, and he was almost twenty-five years old. Military conflict embroiled many of the Mediterranean states; in response, Genoa dispatched ships in convoys. The one in which he found himself included three galleys, a battleship, and *Bechalla*, with a crew from Liguria. Despite his age, he probably shipped out as an ordinary seaman.

August 13 found the convoy off the coast of Portugal when a massive fleet of French and Portuguese ships under the command of Guillaume de Casenove, a daring privateer (or naval mercenary), suddenly struck. In theory, Genoa and France were at peace, and Casenove had no cause for attack, but he could always find a technicality to justify his aggression. Although outnumbered, the Genoese bravely grappled with the enemy, that is, they harnessed themselves to their attackers, and attempted to defeat them in hand-to-hand combat. At day's end, three Genoese and four enemy ships had been sunk in battle, with a loss of life in the hundreds. The surviving craft fled for safe harbors. *Bechalla* was not among them.

When Columbus's ship sank, he jumped into the sea. Few sailors prided themselves on their swimming ability at that time, and his best hope was rescue, or, failing that, grabbing onto some buoyant piece of shipwreck. This Columbus did. At times he pushed it as he swam to shore, and when he was too tired to swim, he climbed atop it to rest. He was wounded, exactly how and where is not clear, and the injury deepened his exhaustion and desperation. Eventually he covered six miles, perhaps the longest six miles he would ever travel, to the shore and the ancient town of Lagos, at the extreme southeastern edge of Portugal, not far from the city of Sagres, originally the "Sacrum Promontorium" in Latin, or Holy Promontory, that offered refuge to sailors about to round Cape St. Vincent, the most westerly point of the Iberian Peninsula. It was here, at Sagres, that Prince Henry the Navigator had gathered an eclectic group of followers—mariners, cosmologists, and shipbuilders—a generation earlier. It is difficult to imagine the castaway Columbus, grasping the lumber of his lost ship, washing up on a more propitious location than this narrow, windswept plateau reaching into the Atlantic. Accustomed to studying natural phenomena for signs and premonitions, sailors are by nature superstitious, and Columbus was no exception. It seemed as if fate, in the form of the shipwreck, was lifting the ambitious young mariner out of Genoa and positioning him at the brink of the unknown.

The inhabitants of Lagos treated shipwrecked sailors such as Columbus humanely, and when he recovered from his ordeal, he traveled to Lisbon, where he found refuge in the city's Genoese colony.

The following year he undertook an even more hazardous journey, this time to the north. "I sailed in the year 1477, in the month of February, a hundred leagues beyond the island of Tile"—mostly likely "Thule," or Iceland, which maintained trade with Lisbon—"and to this island, which is as big as England, come English with their merchandise, especially those from Bristol. And at the season when I was there, the sea was not frozen, but the tides were so great that in some places they rose 26 *braccia*"—about fifty feet, in his estimation—"and fell as much in depths." It is unlikely that Columbus experienced anything like a fifty-foot tide, unless he confronted a giant tsunami triggered by one of the frequent volcanic eruptions in the vicinity of Iceland. On this or another voyage he traveled to Ireland, where he encountered "men of Cathay," that is, China. In Galway, he reported seeing "a man and a woman of extraordinary appearance in two boats adrift." Who were they? Where had they originated? Were they Asian, or some other unknown people?

In the spring of 1477, Portugal was heavily committed to exploration, and, with its critical shortage of labor, desperate for new worlds, and their inhabitants, to conquer and exploit. Portuguese expeditions had already settled the Azores, off Africa's west coast, as early as 1439, and were heading farther south. The age of exploration was under way.

The capital city, and Portugal's chief seaport, was approaching its zenith. Alfonso V had ceded power to his son, João II, in 1476, and the transition ushered in an era of expansion unlike anything in the country's history. In sumptuous Lisbon, Columbus observed the distinctive caravels that became the chief vessel of exploration, a hybrid of square- and lateen-rigged sails, developed decades before under the patronage of Prince Henry the Navigator. These sturdy, maneuverable ships were able to sail into the wind, and so withstand storms, and tides, and they carried Portuguese explorers far and wide. Near the docks, he could overhear familiar languages as varied as Icelandic, English, Spanish, Genoese, Flemish, as well as African idioms new to his ear. At any given moment, ships of a dozen lands unloaded their cargo of fragrant spices and took on provisions for their next voyage. In the background, Italian, Portuguese, and Jewish financiers bankrolled the enterprises, as João II, ensconced in his palace nearby, looked on with an approving, if covetous, gaze.

Accustomed to the rigors of Genoa and the hazards of the Mediterranean, Columbus could have been excused for believing he had arrived in a kind of exploration heaven. Unlike the relatively confined ports to which he was accustomed, Lisbon was located at the mouth of the river Tagus, where it emptied into the Atlantic. A favorable wind carried ships over a sandbar and into the vastness of the open ocean. To the north, Iceland and England; to the south, the Azores and Africa. No one knew what lay to the west, but across Europe, theories promoted by kings and clergy and cosmologists argued that a fleet sailing west would eventually reach the distant lands visited by Marco Polo two centuries before: China, Asia, India. The first

European country to do so would have an enormous strategic and economic advantage over all its rivals.

By the time he ascended to the Portuguese throne in 1481, King João was twenty-six years old (four years younger than Columbus), and prepared to rule. His father had bequeathed to him a consolidated but virtually bankrupt state, which the young king proposed to expand into an empire. Even before he came to power, he had worked alongside his father, familiarizing himself with the throne's expanding interests in Africa, and leading the rapidly expanding Junta dos Mathemáticos, charged with coordinating the kingdom's exploration on land and sea. He reformed taxation, restored solvency to the Portuguese crown, and, emulating his great-uncle Prince Henry the Navigator, revived the expansion of the Portuguese empire.

He is remembered as the "Perfect Prince" by historians and students of the Portuguese monarchy, after Niccolò Machiavelli's ruthless prescription for the exercise of power. More tellingly, João II earned the sobriquet "The Tyrant," a violent despot who was despised and envied by his nobles. To cite but a few instances of his arbitrary exercise of power, he ordered all those with castles to submit their titles to the crown for confirmation, which could be granted or withheld. He dispatched representatives of the crown to supervise the nobles' administration of their estates. And he presided over the abolition of bureaucratic offices that gave the nobility jurisdiction over the legal affairs of their districts. That was just the beginning. He gutted two of the most powerful Portuguese dynasties, the house of Viseu and the house of Braganza. The Braganzas were the largest landowners in all of Portugal, and Fernando II, the Duke of Braganza, controlled a private army of ten thousand men and three thousand horses. The Duke of Viseu was, among his many other titles, estates, and offices, the lord of Portugal's newly established offshore outposts of Madeira Island and the Azores, and as such posed an obstacle to the crown's imperial aspirations.

In the first instance, João II rocked his kingdom by executing a potential rival for the throne, Fernando II of Braganza. In this case, letters had come to light showing a subversive liaison between Fernando II and the sovereigns of Spain, Ferdinand and Isabella. The Duke of Braganza was quickly seized, put on trial for treason, and after the inevitable guilty verdict, beheaded. Later, the Braganza estates were confiscated, and the surviving members of the dynasty fled to the kingdom of Castile for safety. Soon after, João II turned his attention to another perceived enemy, concluding that his cousin, Infante Diogo, Duke of Viseu, planned to overthrow him. In this case, he dispensed with a trial and personally stabbed him to death. What made the death all the more shocking was that their families were related; João II's wife was Leonor of Viseu.

This was the lethal milieu into which Columbus stumbled. Although he had begun to master the sea, and proved himself fearless in command of a ship, he had a lot to learn about people, power, and politics. He could plot a course with ease, but lacked the ability to flatter a king. The title of a chapter chosen by his son Ferdinand for a biography of the Admiral reflected Columbus's self-centered approach: "How the Admiral Grew Angry with the King of Portugal, to Whom He Had Offered to Discover the Indies." To anyone familiar with the Portuguese court, to say nothing of navigation, this statement was outrageous. One did not dare to grow angry with this king, who was prone to sudden violence. Nor did one offer to "discover the Indies," as if that were a straightforward demand. One humbly petitioned for backing to attempt a voyage of exploration in the king's name. And of course Columbus never did fulfill his proposed objective. As deft and decisive on the water as he was clumsy and awkward on land, he urged the king to see things his way, to approve a sea route to Asia, but João stubbornly looked to other explorers and to the east rather than the west. Diogo Cáo won his backing to explore central Africa in 1482, and five years later, Bartolomeu Dias rounded the Cape of Good Hope in the name of Portugal.

Columbus spent eight years in Lisbon trying to make his vision of exploration a reality, and records of his time there are sketchy, when they exist at all. The Lisbon earthquake of November 1, 1755, destroyed records and other priceless artifacts pertaining both to him and to much of Lisbon's history. A few particulars survive, however. The first was his allusion—in the pages of the diary of the first voyage—to his participation in the thriving Portuguese slave trade. The Portuguese were the first Europeans to arrive on Africa's west coast, Guinea, and the explorer Antão Gonçalves became the first Portuguese to buy slaves there. The Portuguese considered themselves entitled to own slaves by papal decree. In 1452, Pope Nicholas V authorized the Portuguese king, Alfonso V, to enslave "Saracens"—that is, Muslims—"pagans and any other unbelievers," an entitlement he confirmed in a papal bull three years later, in case there was any lingering question about his intentions.

The early Portuguese slave trade assumed several forms, from inherited slavery to indentured servitude: forced labor for a fixed period of time, occasionally with modest wages. This was the form of slavery with which Columbus was familiar. He briefly wrote about his experimenting with importing entire families from Guinea to Portugal, not just men, and his disappointment that the experiment did not ensure greater loyalty or co-operation among the slaves. The problem, as Columbus saw it, was the Babel of tongues spoken in Guinea. His experience with the Portuguese slave trade prepared him to look on the Indians he encountered as potential slaves. Were they energetic? Cooperative? Strong enough to endure crossing the Atlantic and colder climates? Were they more valuable as slaves or as Christian converts?

During his years in Lisbon, Columbus was joined by his brother Bartholomew, ten years his junior. An acquaintance, Andrés Bernáldez, formerly of Seville, characterized Bartholomew at this time as a "hawker of printed books, who carried on his trade in this land of Andalusia," as well as a "man of great intelligence though with little book learning, very skilled in the art of cosmography and the mapping of the world."

A knowledgeable dealer in maps, Bartholomew set up business in Lisbon and made Christopher a partner. It is likely that conversations between the two helped him to refine his theories about sailing to China, without clearing up the fundamental misconceptions bequeathed to Renaissance Europe by Paolo dal Pozzo Toscanelli, whose map, lacking both the Pacific Ocean and the Americas, gained credibility partly because it portrayed the world as Europeans of the time—not just Columbus—wanted to see it, smaller and more manageable than it actually was, with India, its spices, and the Grand Khan all within reach. Had Columbus, along with the rest of western Europe, known of the true dimensions of the globe, it is doubtful that he would have proposed sailing halfway around it to India, or that any monarch would have backed the enterprise.

In partnership with Bartholomew, Christopher moved among Lisbon's small but influential Genoese colony, regarded as tough and capable in business. Genoese expatriates and opportunists had long exploited routes into other societies. They intermarried, they changed their names, they learned the local languages, they served local authorities—whatever it took to gain status and respect.

One Sunday, Columbus attended Mass at Lisbon's Convento dos Santos, the Convent of All Saints, where he noticed a young woman of about nineteen—or, as it is recorded in more sentimental accounts of their meeting, she noticed *his* devotion. Her name was Felipa Moñiz, the daughter of a wellborn Italian, Bartolomeo Perestrello, who had been active in the colonization of Madeira Island, and his wife Caterina Visconti. Circumstances suggest that Columbus was in search of a wellborn wife at the time. The Convento dos Santos was maintained by nuns charged with providing for the wives and daughters of those fighting in distant lands. Here he might have a chance to meet a woman who answered to his ambition in one of the few approved places for bachelors to encounter eligible young women. Scant details of the courtship survive, and his son Ferdinand offers only conventional reassurances about his father's conduct: "Inasmuch as he behaved very honorably, and was a man of such fine presence, and withal so honest, that she held such conversation with him and enjoyed such friendship with him that she became his wife."

She beheld, according to a description written much later by his son Ferdinand, a "well built man of more than medium stature, long visaged with cheeks somewhat high, but neither fat nor thin. He had an aquiline nose and his eyes were light in color; his complexion too was light, but kindling to a vivid red. In his youth his hair was blond"—or, in some accounts, reddish in hue—"but when it came to his thirtieth year it all turned white. In eating and drinking and the adornment of his person he was always continent and modest. Among strangers his conversation was affable, and with members of his household very pleasant, but with modest and pleasing dignity."

He was, as his son took pains to note, extremely pious. "In matters of religion he was so strict that for fasting and saying all the canonical offices he might have been taken for a member of a religious order. And he was so great an enemy to cursing and swearing, that I never heard him utter any other oath than, 'By San Fernando!'" If true, Columbus's aversion to foul language made him an absolute rarity among men of the sea. "When he was angry with anyone, his reprimand was to say, 'May God take you!' for doing or saying that. And when he had to write anything, he would not try the pen without first writing these words, *Jesus cum Maria sit nobis in via*, and in such fair letters that he might have gained his bread by them alone." This is one of the most detailed and accurate physical descriptions of Columbus to survive, idealized by filial piety, yet perceptive.

It was, for Columbus, a strikingly advantageous match. The son of a weaver, tavern keeper, and local politician allied with the losing faction in Genoese politics suddenly enjoyed promising connections and standing in the exclusive world of Portuguese nobility and exploration. Although Genoa was known for being antiroyalist, he let stand the mistaken impression that he was somehow allied with Genoese nobility. (Eventually his air of mystery would lead to speculative fantasies about his origins: Portuguese, or Jewish, or Catalan. It would be left to his son Ferdinand—his earliest biographer—to offer corrections, later confirmed by historians.)

Felipa had more authentic connections to nobility. On her mother's side, she traced a relationship to the Portuguese royal family from the twelfth century. Her grandfather Gil Ayres Moñiz had ruled a wealthy estate in the Algarve region of Portugal, a prize wrested with difficulty from Arabs who had controlled it, and he had fought alongside Prince Henry the Navigator in the Battle of Ceuta in 1415. The Genoese navigator with the red or blond hair appeared capable of taking his place in their midst, bold and capable of bringing new wealth from somewhere—Greece? Asia? Africa?—to the family and taking his place beside his wife's distinguished ancestors. With royal patronage assured by his marriage into the Portuguese elite, Columbus could be forgiven for thinking that the way was clear: discovery, acquiring distant lands and glorious titles, and the dutiful creation of a large family to inherit them and perpetuate his name.

On her father's side, Felipa brought even more interesting, if complex, credentials. The Perestrellos were known as much for their indiscretions and illegitimate children as they were for their political and ecclesiastic connections. Bartolomeo married several times, and Felipa was the product of his second or, according to some accounts, third union. Her siblings consisted of Bartolomeo junior and a sister, Violante, with whom Columbus was said to have enjoyed cordial relations. According to well-established legend, Columbus's father-in-law had been granted rights to tiny Porto Santo, lying thirty miles northeast of Madeira Island, by Prince Henry the Navigator. Bartolomé de Las Casas, who was personally acquainted with—and deeply conflicted about—the subject of his scholarly inquiries, surmises that Perestrello possessed instruments, maps, and charts of his realm that eventually came into Columbus's possession, and "from seeing and reading which, he received much pleasure." Perestrello was not known to have any experience or ability with seafaring, and even if this account is highly embellished, it does appear that Prince Henry gave Perestrello hereditary control of tiny Porto Santo as a result of manipulation rather than bold exploration. It is possible that Columbus considered Porto Santo a staging area from which to launch his own expedition when the time was right. Here was a paradigm in miniature for his own, more grandiose ambitions: find an island, claim it for king and country, and exploit it for personal and dynastic benefit.

* * *

After the nuptials, Columbus and Felipa moved into the house of his prominent in-laws. Felipa became all but invisible to posterity, and there is no evidence to suggest that theirs was an affair of the heart. But the other Perestrellos endowed Columbus, a rough-and-ready sailor from Genoa, with a new context in which to pursue his career, thanks to his mother-in-law, who, Las Casas recounted, "realized that Columbus had a passion for the sea and for cosmography, as men who are possessed of a passion for something talk about it night and day." So she told him how "her husband Perestrello had a great passion for things of the sea and how he had voyaged, at the request of Prince Henry [the Navigator] and in the company of two other knights, to settle the island of Porto Santo, discovered but a few days previously." Porto Santo became the founding of Perestrello's fortune and renown: an object lesson for the newly married Columbus.

His mother-in-law gave her late husband's "instruments, documents, and navigation charts" to Columbus as if passing a scepter from one generation to another, and eventually he found himself living on his father-in-law's demesne, Porto Santo, where Columbus's wife gave birth to their firstborn son, Diego.

On Porto Santo and its newly discovered neighbor, Madeira Island, "there were a great many vessels bringing settlers and much talk of fresh discoveries that were being made every day." Las Casas relates that Columbus talked with seamen returning from the "western seas" who had "visited the Azores and Madeira and other islands." One in particular, a man named Martin, "a pilot in the service of the Portuguese crown," told an intriguing tale. When 450 leagues west of Cape Vincent, "he sighted a piece of wood floating near his ship, and, fishing it out of the sea, discovered it was ingeniously carved, though not, as far as he could judge, with iron implements. Since the wind had for several days been blowing from the west he supposed that the piece of wood originated from some island or islands that lay to the west."

Tantalizing sightings of exotic lands abounded. A "one-eyed sailor" claimed that during a voyage to Ireland he had caught a glimpse of the "Tartary," or central Asia, "as it curved around to the west, but foul weather prevented them from reaching it." Whatever that one-eyed sailor thought he saw, it was probably not central Asia, but it did not yet exist on European maps. And then there was the "seaman from Galicia called Pedro de Velasco who, in a conversation he had with Christopher Columbus in Murcia"—a city in southern Spain—"mentioned a voyage to Ireland on which he had sailed and which went so far to the northwest that they came across land to the west of Ireland." Perhaps Iceland, or Nova Scotia, or some imaginary continent that existed somewhere between geography and mythology. An expedition was needed to decide which it was. Columbus learned of a wealthy merchant of Genoa, Luca di Cazana, who was badgered by a Portuguese pilot, Vicente Dias, into backing three or four expeditions in search of a mysterious island, "sailing over a hundred leagues and finding nothing." After such failures, both pilot and sponsor gave up hope of "finding the land in question." And two other expeditions with the same avowed goal both disappeared, "leaving behind not a trace."

Another seaman, Pedro Correa, married to the sister of Columbus's wife, corroborated Martin the pilot's story. He swore, says Las Casas, that "he also came across a piece of wood that had been carried there by the winds from the same quarter and that it, too, had been carved in a similar fashion." Not only that, but he had seen "canes so thick that one joint of such a cane could hold over six liters of water or of wine." Columbus said that he heard the same story from the king of Portugal. It seemed to Columbus that King João "was persuaded that these canes had come from some island or islands not far off to the west, or that they had been carried by the wind and the current all the way from India itself, for they were quite unlike anything that was known in Europe." He also heard about pine trees washing ashore on islands in the Atlantic, "although no pine trees grow anymore throughout the Azores." Still more tantalizing, there was a story in circulation about the bodies of two men washed up in the Azores, who had "very broad faces and features quite different from those of Christians."

Add to that enticing tale reports of rafts, described as "Indian canoes with houses on board," and the entire world seemed to invite discovery and speculation. These random floating objects were as strange and enigmatic as meteorites from distant worlds touching down to earth. Something strange was out there. "All such tales certainly fanned the flames of Christopher Columbus's interest in the whole business," Las Casas remarked, "and they show God nudging him along in the same direction." It took one incident in particular, the "clinching factor," as Las Casas put it, and forever after the subject of controversy, to crystallize in Columbus's mind. It began with a vessel from Spain bound for Flanders or possibly England, being violently blown off course, as if in a fairy tale or in a nightmare, and discovering an island.

The crew barely survived the ordeal, only to perish on the way home to Spain. "Most of them died of hunger and disease brought on by overwork and the few that survived as far as the island of Madeira were ill when they arrived and all soon died there." Columbus "got wind of the whole incident from the poor wretches who made it back to Madeira or from the pilot himself." The story goes that he might have invited the pilot to stay with him, and be debriefed, until he expired within the walls of Columbus's dwelling. Before the end, the pilot supposedly gave his host a "detailed account of everything that had happened and left him a written record of the bearings the vessel had followed, the route they had taken, the distances they had covered, the degrees of longitude and latitude involved, and the exact place they had found the island." Given the impossibility of determining longitude at the time, the "exact place" of the island was highly questionable.

One of the most persuasive accounts of distant lands came from the pen of "Master Paolo," a Florentine physician, who maintained an extensive network of correspondence with informed sources in the Portuguese court. Learning of these bulletins, Columbus cultivated the physician by sending a globe through a Florentine intermediary, Lorenzo Girardi, who lived in Lisbon. After passing along this tangible symbol of exploration, Columbus announced his own grand scheme for exploration and trade in precious items such as spices. Impressed, Master Paolo replied in Latin with a summary of his knowledge of China and its riches, which advanced Columbus's understanding of the fabled land from an emerging global perspective. "Do not marvel at my characterizing the region as 'the West,'" he counseled Columbus, "when these lands are commonly known as 'the East,' for any man who sails westward will always find these lands to the west, just as he who sets out overland to the east will find them in the east." And he included a chart illustrating what he meant.

Master Paolo expounded on China and its numerous merchants. "There are as many ships, seamen, and merchants in the area as in any other part of the world." In the city of "Zaiton," by which he probably meant Hangzhou, the wealthy capital of southern China, "every year a hundred large ships load and unload their cargoes of pepper, not to mention the many others that carry spices of other lands." He also informed Columbus of a "sovereign known as the Grand Khan, a name which in our own tongue"—Italian—"means king of kings." The ancestors of this Khan, Paolo recounted, "greatly desired to have contact and dealings with Christians, and, some two hundred years ago, sent an embassy to the Holy Father asking him to send them a large number of learned and wise men who might instruct them in our faith, but those who were sent were forced to return home because of difficulties they encountered along the way." As Paolo continued his tale, it became apparent that he relied heavily on Marco Polo's popular account, which concerned the Venetian's adventures in Asia from 1279 to 1295, and on the stories of a Chinese ambassador. In the physician's telling, the events of two centuries before seemed to be happening in the present as he wove the two eras into a tapestry of royal palaces, rivers of great length and breadth, "vast numbers of cities" dotting their banks (in one case, two hundred cities along the length of a single river), "broad bridges made entirely of marble and adorned with marble pillars" over which flowed spices, precious stones, gold, silver, and many other "things of great value."

How to get there? Simple, according to Master Paolo the physician: "From the city, in a line directly to the west, there are twenty-six spaces marked on the map, each representing two hundred and fifty miles, before you arrive at the most noble city of Quinsay"—Marco Polo's distinctive name for the capital city of Hangzhou, and a dead giveaway of Master Paolo's source—"which is a hundred miles in circumference," and, in the same breath, of "Çipango," Marco Polo's name for Japan. "This island is most rich in gold and pearls and precious stones, and you should know that the temples and royal palaces are covered in solid gold." Once again, getting there posed no problem to the initiated. "Because the route is unknown, all these things are hidden from us, even though one can voyage there without danger or difficulty."

Columbus responded that he could find this extraordinary realm by sailing along a route indicated on a map supplied by Master Paolo, who was, it bears repeating, no navigator. Elated by the endorsement, he replied, "I am gratified to find my map so well understood and to learn that such a voyage is not only theoretically possible but will now become a fact and a source of honor and estimable gain and the greatest fame among all Christian men." As if he were dispatching Columbus himself, he promised a voyage of "powerful kingdoms and noble cities and the richest of provinces abounding in all manner of goods that are much in demand," not to mention spices and gems, rulers even more eager to have contact with the West than the West was to have contact with them, to exchange wisdom, knowledge, and religion. "I do not wonder that you, as a man of great courage," Master Paolo wrote to Columbus, "should find your heart inflamed with the desire to put this enterprise into effect."

Columbus enlarged upon these clues of undiscovered western islands with scholarly efforts of his own. He studied Ptolemy's influential *Geography*, which had reached Europe from Constantinople in about AD 1400. In 1406–1409, Jacopo Angeli da Scarperia translated the text into Latin. It became the first book to be printed with engraved illustrations, in an edition published in Bologna dating from 1477, and was subsequently translated into several European languages. Ptolemy's cartography was both inspiring and greatly misleading. Ptolemy, who lived in the second century AD, underestimated the size of the world by one-sixth. He did not know of the existence of the American continent, or of the Pacific Ocean, the largest body of water on the planet. The problem of determining longitude had yet to be solved, and would not be until the late eighteenth century. For all these reasons, relying on Ptolemy's *Geography* proved as deceptive as it was inspirational.

Somewhere, at the confluence of Ptolemy's flawed cartography, the legends of antiquity, Marco Polo's account, and sailors' anecdotes lay clues of a great prize waiting to be discovered. Columbus had his plan, and now he needed the backing of a powerful royal sponsor, and money.

Living in Portugal with his well-connected Portuguese wife, Columbus naturally presented his proposal to the Portuguese king. By this time, Columbus considered himself all but Portuguese, although the Portuguese themselves preferred to regard him as an upstart Genoese mariner who had settled in Lisbon, one of the largest expatriate colonies of Genoese to be found anywhere. They remained suspicious of the outsiders like him flourishing in their midst.

Heedless of these considerations, and fired by the accounts he had gathered, Columbus pressed on, requesting that the king equip three caravels for the voyage, including chests filled with goods for barter such as cloth from Flanders, hawk's bells, brass basins, sheet brass, strings of glass beads of several different colors, small mirrors, scissors, knives, needles, pins, canvas shirts, coarse-colored cloth, red caps—tools and trinkets for conquering the lands and peoples hiding in plain sight somewhere in the Western Sea.

These practical matters were easily accomplished. The personal demands that Columbus made of King João were far more onerous, and unrealistic. He wanted a title, preferably "Knight of the Golden Spurs," that would permit him and his descendants to style themselves "Don." He also wished for himself the grandest title he could think of: Admiral of the Ocean Sea, "with all the privileges of rank, prerogatives, rights, revenue, and immunities enjoyed by the admirals of Castile."

Even to Portuguese ears, accustomed to overstatement, this description verged on the absurd. A tireless conversationalist and self-promoter, Columbus never knew when to stop, and he demanded appointment as "viceroy and governor in perpetuity of all the islands and terra firma discovered either personally by him or as a result of his voyage." And he planned to award himself one-tenth of "all the moneys accruing to the crown in respect of gold, silver, pearls, gems, metals, spices, and all other articles of value and merchandise of whatever kind, nature, or variety, that should be purchased, bartered, discovered, or won in battle throughout the length and breadth of the lands under his jurisdiction." It was clear that Columbus considered himself a partner of the crown's exploration program, and potential ruler of a kingdom—moreover, a kingdom larger and wealthier than Portugal itself.

His megalomania did not go over well in the small, gossip-ridden Portuguese court. João de Barros, a court historian, portrayed the would-be Admiral of the Ocean Sea "as a big talker and boastful, full of fancy and imagination," and so, "the king lent little credit to what he had to say." Yet João II subsequently consulted three experts about Columbus's claims: Dr. Calzadilla, Master Rodrigo, and Master Josepe, "the latter a Jew," in Las Casas's words. "The king placed great trust in these men when it came to questions of exploration and cosmography and they, according to our writer, regarded Columbus's words as sheer vanity." It would seem that an automatic refusal was inevitable. Instead, the king appeared to hesitate, and caused Columbus to wait for an answer.

The three experts consulted by the Portuguese king spent days questioning the navigator about his plan. Eager to impress, Columbus told all, and when they finished with him, João II proved to be as duplicitous as he was daring: he commissioned a clandestine expedition based on the information extracted from the Genoese mariner.

The deception continued. João II strung along Columbus while dispatching a supply caravel supposedly bound for Cape Verde and other islands, all the while delaying his official reply to Columbus. When the caravel limped home to Lisbon in appalling condition—with ripped sails and broken masts—the residents questioned the exhausted crew members. The survivors complained of the tempests they had endured at sea and declared it was impossible to reach land over a sea route. Once the voyage's true purpose was exposed, King João's subterfuge was apparent to all.

At this critical juncture, Columbus's young wife, Felipa, died from unknown causes, or disappeared from view forever. A more skeptical tradition hinted that Columbus abandoned Felipa in Portugal, where her family connections had been useful, to try his luck in Spain, where they were not. Although the circumstances of her death, and even the year, remain unclear, his abrupt departure does not necessarily mean he deserted his wife; it is possible that he planned to send for her if he succeeded elsewhere. But it is even more likely that she did not survive, if only because she was never spoken of again.

He had devoted eight years to the great enterprise, with nothing to show for it but rejection and embarrassment. His youth had fled; he was turning forty—advanced middle age for a sea captain—with little to show for his years of wandering beyond unfulfilled ambition. He was a widower in a foreign land with deteriorating prospects and a young son in his care. His long, flowing hair turned white. There seemed to be little for which he could be grateful. But, given the dangers of the Portuguese court, and of the sea, he was fortunate to be alive.

Reluctantly he directed his ambition toward the other patrons of exploration, Ferdinand and Isabella of Spain, even as part of him wished he could one day return to Portugal in triumph. For now, he would seek his fortune in Castile.

Demoralized, he assigned responsibility for the expedition to his brother Bartholomew, and displaying a bit of guile himself, dispatched him to England, to plead with King Henry VII (the father of Henry VIII) for the backing denied by the enigmatic and recalcitrant Portuguese monarch.

To those who knew the Columbus brothers, the sudden transfer of power had a certain logic. Bartholomew's reputation was that of a "very shrewd and courageous man, well versed in the ways of the world and most astute, more full of guile," Las Casas judged, "than Christopher Columbus himself." Bartholomew knew Latin, and "had much more experience in the ways of men." He was reputed to be almost as skillful a navigator as Christopher, and more adept at fashioning charts and nautical instruments.

Overshadowed by his more celebrated son and successor, Henry VIII, Henry Tudor had won his throne by defeating Richard III on the field of battle, and founded the durable Tudor dynasty. He was, for a monarch of the epoch, prudent and responsible. Bartholomew Columbus flattered and cajoled his way into an audience with the king, and to win the sovereign's favor he presented him with a *mappa mundi*, a Latin term indicating a sheet, or map, of the world, and on it were the lands that his brother Christopher planned to claim. The map contained a brief identification of its bearer in Latin: "He whose birthplace is Genoa and whose name is Bartolome Colon of Terrarubia, completed this work in London on the thirteenth day of the month of February in the year of our Lord one thousand four hundred and eighty-eight. Praise abounding be unto the Lord."

Columbus, meanwhile, obtained a copy of a letter composed by the Florentine mapmaker and mathematician Toscanelli, dated June 24, 1474. Toscanelli spoke of a "shorter way of going by sea to the lands of spices, than that which you"—the Portuguese—"are making to Guinea." A ship sailing due west from Lisbon, he claimed, would, after covering five thousand nautical miles, reach Quinsay, the opulent capital of China described by Marco Polo. There was more. Another sea route would take a ship to "the noble island of Çipango," Marco Polo's Japan, which, as readers of the Venetian's enthusiastic account knew, was "most fertile in gold, pearls and precious stones, and they cover the temples and royal residences with solid gold." If true, and that was an immense *if*, Portugal could forge an alliance with a country of unimaginable wealth. Even better, Toscanelli claimed, "By the unknown ways there are no great spaces of the sea to be passed." This simple observation derived from a profound misunderstanding of the globe (and everyone knew it was a globe; there was little dispute about that point). Like Ptolemy before him, Toscanelli omitted the American continent and the Pacific Ocean—features that made such a voyage to Asia impossible.

Even more than Ptolemy, Toscanelli led Columbus to believe that the Caribbean was the doorstep to China. Sooner or later some country, and some monarch, was bound to succumb to the Columbus brothers' siren song of empire.

As Bartholomew was appealing to King Henry, Christopher, revived by his studies, made his way to Spain to interest Ferdinand and Isabella in the same enterprise. But his initial reception in Spain proved so disappointing that late in 1487 he wrote to King João, who had spurned and humiliated him, to ask permission to return to Portugal.

Against all expectations, the Portuguese monarch replied on March 20, 1488, in conciliatory tones, thanking Columbus for his "good will and affection," and, astonishingly, saying, "we will have great need of your ability and fine talent," words certain to inflame Columbus's ambition. The offer came with an assurance that "you will not be arrested, detained, accused, summoned, or prosecuted, for any reason whatsoever, under the civil and criminal code. Therefore, we beg you and urge you to come soon and not to be reluctant to do so for any reason whatsoever."

Columbus arrived in Lisbon in 1488, at the same time Bartolomeu Dias, King João's favored navigator of the moment, returned from his exploration of the coast of Africa. So Columbus endured the humiliation of watching his competitor surpass him in accomplishment and in the affections of King João. Had Columbus been set up? More likely the king summoned him as a substitute in case Dias never returned from his voyage, and Columbus, led by his ambition, his naiveté, and his vanity, had walked into the trap. He left Portugal again in 1488, bound for Spain, where he would make a determined effort to win backing for his enterprise. Humiliated and disappointed, he hoped never to see Portugal again.

Later, Columbus confessed to the sovereign who did back him, King Ferdinand of Spain, "I went to the king of Portugal, who was better versed in the matter of discoveries than any other sovereign, and the Lord blinded his eyes and deafened his ears so that for all of fourteen years he did not understand what I was saying." But Ferdinand listened, and Isabella understood what Columbus was saying. To her ears, he was saying he could bring her the means to administer a transoceanic empire that would surpass that of any other European nation.

Ferdinand of Aragon and Isabella of Castile met for the first time only five days before they married, on October 19, 1469, at the Palacio de los Vivero in Valladolid. He was almost a year younger than she, and on their wedding day, they were just eighteen and seventeen years of age, and cousins. She was not beautiful, and he was not handsome. But they were pious Christians. They were both children of kings of the Trastámara dynasty, and well-known figures. At the age of twelve, Ferdinand had led his soldiers to victory against the Catalans, and when his ambitious mother, Juana Enríquez, a Castilian, died of cancer in 1468, he delivered her eulogy and positioned himself as the next dynastic leader. Months later, representatives from Isabella sought him out and escorted him to Castile to marry.

From the start, theirs was an unusual arrangement that gave Isabella powers equal to, or in some cases greater than, those of her young husband. On terms agreed to by their legions of advisers, she alone ruled the kingdom of Castile in north central Spain. On the basis of their intricate official relationship, their union flourished. Ferdinand had his mistresses and Isabella had her religion for consolation. Whatever their private differences, they demonstrated publicly that they loved and respected each other, as was necessary to maintain their joint rule.

The early years of their reign were a time of testing for them both. They relied on more experienced advisers and intermediaries to rebuff challenges to their power and to their finances. Teetering on the brink of insolvency, they implemented novel methods of taxation, often from the sale of agricultural products, to finance their ambitions. One of the most dangerous tests materialized in 1476 when Alfonso, king of Portugal, invaded Castile with the help of Castilian nobles. The Sovereigns would not let the challenge stand. On March 1 of that year, King Ferdinand won a decisive victory over Alfonso in the wine-producing town of Toro, north of Madrid, and began the arduous task of consolidating the fragmented empire. Ferdinand and Isabella became known as Los Reyes Católicos, the Catholic Sovereigns, a sobriquet that would stay with them throughout their long reign.

In 1479, Ferdinand succeeded his father as king of Aragon, and the territories and kingdoms of Ferdinand and Isabella became one. Not since the eighth century had there existed a unified political entity that could be designated España, or Spain. Los Reyes Católicos did not rest on their laurels. They set about reclaiming political power from both the bourgeoisie and the nobility, and they circumscribed the authority of the Cortes, or General Courts, reduced to mere functionaries in the Sovereigns' quest for glory. They won popular support for their efforts, and consolidated their power. Jews and Muslims, essential components of Spain's commerce, intellectual life, and trade, would be the next to fall. It was perhaps significant that Isabella's royal emblem was a sheaf of arrows, their sharp heads a warning to the perceived enemies of the throne, and that Ferdinand's emblem was a double yoke worn by a team of oxen, signifying his acquiescence to Isabella's authority.

As heresy spread across the realm, the Sovereigns' representatives established the Inquisition in 1480 to bring the accused to trial. Some escaped with no more than the loss of their worldly goods; others were condemned to death. Fear of Ferdinand and Isabella increased, and under their prodding Spain seemed to recover some of its previous swagger and piety. As a potent symbol, the holy city of Jerusalem remained the ultimate spoil of war. Soon there was talk of reclaiming it to complete the unfinished business of the Crusades.

In 1480, Christian forces drove Muslims from the Iberian Peninsula. More than fifty conquered Muslim cities entered the Christian fold within ten years. As mosques became churches, the conquests persisted, relying on artillery and battering rams to lay siege to one town after another. To fund this giant military operation, the Catholic Sovereigns turned to the pope, who permitted the crown to tithe in order to stay solvent. Taxes and obligatory loans also helped to replenish the royal coffers, but the most common method was the confiscation of the wealth of Jews and Muslims. Wealthy Seville was especially hard hit by the exigencies of the Inquisition.

Columbus appeared in the midst of this protracted struggle early in 1485, seeking the backing of Ferdinand and Isabella for an entirely new project, the discovery of a route over the ocean to the Indies. The thirty-four-year-old Genoese mariner's prolonged dalliance with King João of Portugal had proved pointless, and his attempts to interest France and England in his imperial strategy also led nowhere. He had even returned to Genoa to try to generate interest in an expedition, but he met with little enthusiasm in his birthplace.

Discouraged, he had returned to Spain, where his grandiose plan struck a spark when he exhibited a map of the world showing India and other lands of the Grand Khan. According to his confidant Andrés Bernáldez, the demonstration "awakened in them a desire to know those lands." Ferdinand obtained Ptolemy's text, *Geography*, to see for himself just what Columbus was talking about.

Reconquista ground on slowly and relentlessly. Some provinces quietly submitted to Castilian rule and taxation; others stubbornly resisted. In 1487, one of the last remaining strongholds of resistance, Málaga, a port city on the southern coast of Spain, collapsed after a four-month siege, whereupon the Catholic Sovereigns enslaved and sold most of the residents, serving notice on others who would defy the will of Ferdinand and Isabella.

The greatest prize of all, Granada, gradually changed allegiance from Muslim to Christian. In November 1491, the sultan of Granada, his alternatives exhausted, arranged a surrender treaty in secret with Ferdinand and Isabella. On January 2, 1492, Spanish forces occupied the Alhambra, the fourteenth-century "Red Fortress" that had served as the residence for the last Muslim emirs, or sheikhs, of southern Spain; four days later, Ferdinand and Isabella made a dramatic entry into Granada. Columbus claimed he was there to see history in the making that day. "I saw the Royal Standards of Your Highnesses placed by force of arms on the towers of the Alhambra," he later wrote, "and I saw the Moorish King come out to the gates of the city

and kiss the Royal Hands of Your Highnesses and of the Prince my lord."
Perhaps he had merely heard about the surrender. Either way, he wanted his
Sovereigns to know how profoundly he identified with their imperial aims.

Unlike the Jews, who were treated harshly, Muslims could own property,
worship as they chose, and live according to their laws. The accommodation
proved short-lived. Ten years later, a rebellion erupted, and the Sovereigns
ordered the remaining Muslims to convert to Christianity or leave Spain.
A century later, they, too, would be expelled.

The conquest of Granada solidified the increasingly bloody reign of Los
Reyes Católicos, who gained the confidence and the means to undertake a
series of initiatives designed to fortify their Christian empire and pursue
their ultimate goal of retaking Jerusalem. They marched into Africa both
to spread Christianity as far and wide as possible, and to seize gold. On
March 31, 1492, Ferdinand and Isabella signed an order designed to expel
the Jews from Spain. They could either convert to Christianity to preserve
their way of life, their families, and their fortunes or leave the country by
July 31. Years before, in 1477, a more innocent and idealistic Isabella had seen
herself as the Jews' guardian, signing a decree offering them a measure of
protection. "The Jews are mine, and they are under my protection and power,"
she had stated at the time. She later turned her back on them, and by 1489,
Jews in Spain were condemned to be burned at the stake for their supposed
treachery. By now public opinion had turned strongly against them, so
strongly, in fact, that the expulsion was seen as long overdue. Ferdinand and
Isabella found themselves trying to keep pace with the whirlwind of hatred
and civil war that they had sown.

In 1492, Isabella invited Columbus to return to Spain, where the Sovereigns constantly circulated among various friendly castles, palaces, and
monasteries. Their peripatetic existence kept them in contact with their
realm and their subordinates, but it also created a bureaucratic void in which
documents and orders often went astray. Although Columbus's transactions
with the Sovereigns and his voyages are well documented, there are significant lacunae, caused in part by this situation.

When Christopher Columbus again appeared in their midst to ask for
backing for his voyage, his plans, as far-fetched as ever, came as a welcome
distraction from the travails of the Inquisition, and a partial fulfillment of
their goal to forge a Christian empire. He talked at length with Isabella, who
gradually became convinced that his proposed mission could be useful to
them. Consisting of only three ships, it would not cost the hard-pressed
crown much, and the expenses would be paid for by levies and the sale of

indulgences. To demonstrate her sincere faith, she offered her jewels as collateral: a touching gesture, but it was not expected that anyone would claim them. Three weeks after expelling the Jews from Spain, Los Reyes Católicos signed the following decree:

> We send Cristóbal Colón with three caravels through the Ocean Sea to the Indies on some business that concerns the service of God and the expansion of the Catholic faith and our benefit and utility.

CHAPTER 3

Shipwreck

"That night the wind blew hard from the east northeast," Columbus noted on or about December 17, 1492, grateful that Tortuga sheltered their small craft. In the morning, he ordered his crew to put their nets out to fish, and while they did, the inhabitants—now invariably termed "Indians"—frolicked with them and, more interestingly, offered arrows said to have been fashioned by the unseen but ever-present cannibals. These weapons were long, slender "spikes of canes, fire-hardened and sharp." The Indians pointed to a couple of men whose bodies had been mauled and "gave them to understand that the cannibals had eaten them by mouthfuls." If the Indians were seeking to form an alliance with their visitors against this dreaded enemy, Columbus the skeptical Genoese mariner remained unconvinced, and he resumed bartering for gold as he praised the intelligence of the Indians who cooperated.

In the evening, he recorded, a large canoe bearing forty men approached from Tortuga. When the canoe-borne warriors landed on the beach, the local chieftain angrily commanded them to return whence they came, hurling seawater and stones after them. After they shoved off in their canoes, the same chieftain took one pebble and, rather than throwing it at the Spaniards, calmly placed it in the hand of the Spaniards' marshal as a gesture of peace.

When the canoe, and the threat it posed, vanished from sight, the chieftain described—through interpreters—their life in Tortuga. Was there gold? More in Tortuga than in Hispaniola, but no gold mines to speak of. Nevertheless, the "country was so rich that there is no need to work much to sustain life or be clothed, since they go naked." Heedless of these details, which signified the Indians' sinful indolence, Columbus stubbornly persisted in his search for gold, learning that a source could be found within a journey of four days overland, or "one day of fair weather."

With that, the wind died, and Columbus and his men retreated to their ships to prepare for the observance of a feast day, which he called the Commemoration of the Annunciation (now known as Our Lady's Expectation), December 18. As Columbus dined below the sterncastle (a structure above the main deck), two hundred men appeared, bearing the young king on a litter. Everyone, he noted yet again, was naked, or nearly so. Dismounting the litter, "at a quick walk he came to sit down beside me, nor would he let me rise to meet him or get up from the table, but beseeched me to eat." While the Indian's guard arrayed themselves on deck "with the greatest respect and readiness in the world," Columbus invited the young king to partake of the feast, and was gratified to note that he ate all the "viands," and as for the drink, "he simply raised [it] to his lips and then gave to the others, and all with a wonderful dignity and very few words."

After the meal, an Indian courtier offered a gift that pleased Columbus. It was a belt "like those of Castile in shape but different workmanship." The Admiral appraised this item carefully, as if deciding what it would fetch in Spain, and in return gave the chieftain "amber beads which I wore at my neck, and some red shoes, and a bottle of orange water," which elicited exclamations of approval for their recipient.

Hindered by the lack of a common language or reliable interpreters, Columbus took the king's signs and utterances to mean that the "whole island was mine to command." And out of this communication gap was born the conviction, at least in Columbus's mind, that he was acquiring an empire of his own. "After it was late and he wished to leave, the Admiral sent him away in the boat very honorably, and gave him numerous lombard shots; and, once ashore, he got into his litter and went off with more than two hundred men, and soon was borne behind him on the shoulders of an Indian, a very honorable man." It had been a gratifying day's work, rich in hopes and illusions, and in deception.

Weighing anchor, Columbus sailed eastward under a full moon to what was most likely Lombardo Cove, Acul Bay, in today's Haiti: a protected, idyllic spot, even by the standards of the Caribbean. "This harbor is most beautiful," he exulted.

The next day found the Admiral euphoric over his discovery, boasting in his diary, and very likely to his shipmates, that nothing in his twenty-three years at sea equaled it, and it was "superior to all and would hold all the ships of the world" within its four-mile length.

About ten o'clock that night, a canoe laden with Indians made its way from shore to the flagship "to see the Admiral and the Christians and to wonder at them." A session of brisk bartering ensued, and Columbus dispatched a scouting party, who returned with reports of a "big village." To Columbus's chronicler Bartolomé de Las Casas, who spent years living in the Indies, these settlements were a familiar sight in this part of the world. "The inhabitants," he wrote, "make their houses of wood and straw, in the form of a bell. They were very high and spacious, such that ten or more persons lived in each one. They drove in the big poles, as big as a leg or even a thigh, in a circle, half the height of a person, into the earth and close together; they were all joined together at the top, where they were tied with a certain cord of roots that formerly were called *bejucos*." He proceeded to take his readers on an admiring guided tour of an Indian settlement. "With these roots and the bark of trees of a black color, and other bark stripped off that remained white, they made lattice work with designs and foliage like paintings on the inside of a building. . . . Others were adorned with stripped reeds that appeared very white. There were very thin and delicate canes."

At first timid, the inhabitants gradually "lost their fear" and "countless men, women, and children" rushed forward with bread, "which is very white and good," Columbus wrote with surprise, "and they brought us water in calabashes and in earthenware pitchers of the shape of those of Castile," or so they appeared to him. The gifts he received included gold—precious gold!—moreover, the Indians performed their role with conviction. "It is easy to recognize when something is given with a real heart to give," he concluded.

His acquisitive instincts satisfied for the moment, the Admiral praised his generous hosts, who possessed "neither spears nor darts nor arms of any sort." Having decided there was nothing to fear, Columbus sent a party of six to the village, where they tried to explain once more that they had not come from the sky, as the Indians believed, but across the sea in the service of Ferdinand and Isabella, the Catholic Sovereigns of Castile. Amid a sense of heightened expectation, Columbus finally decided to disembark and pay a visit. As soon as he made his intentions known, "there came down to the beach so many people that it was marvelous, men, women and children, shouting that he should not leave but stay with them." Columbus remained safely in his longboat, receiving offerings of food, a portable feast in the making. Receiving parrots and other tributes, and giving "glass beads and brass rings and hawk's bells—not that they demanded anything but that it seemed to him right." And because, with another characteristic leap, "he already considered them Christians."

Wherever he went, he responded with a similar sense of wonder and egotism, as if these spectacular sights had been created for his benefit, and as he later reminded himself, that of his royal patrons. Conditioned by medieval assumptions, his intellect and imagination labored to interpret these astonishing sights according to categories that he understood. The world on which he gazed, and depended for survival, was both natural and supernatural; he needed only to divine the Creator's intentions to exploit them to the hilt. He believed the Indians to be exactly what his views insisted—advanced and attractive and potentially useful creatures—rather than what they actually were, or might be. And if they happened to be in doubt, he would gladly enlighten them. He was bemused rather than displeased to hear that the Indians considered his fleet to have descended from the heavens, especially since the misunderstanding gave him occasion to establish his credentials. Their crowds formed to see him; they displayed their women for his benefit. He in turn admired them as one would admire a prize steed or working dog, still in the wild but capable, even eager, for domestication, noting that "nothing was lacking but to know the language and to give them orders, because every order that was given to them they would obey without opposition." If only Columbus, with his embattled status, could command the same respect in Spain, or anywhere else in Europe.

In the "protected and deep" embrace of Acul Bay, surrounded by "people very good and gentle and without arms," he savored his explorer's paradise. Even the inlet's mouth was wide enough to let ships pass one another without incident. Furthermore, "any ship can lie in it without fear that other ships might come by night to attack them." He decided to name the bay Puerto de la Mar de Sancto Tomás, "for today was his feast."

Come Saturday, December 22, Columbus succumbed to the urge to find gold, and at dawn, the fleet quietly slipped its moorings amid heaving seas. In his mind's eye, he imagined a place with more gold than earth, or so the Indians had led him to believe. Ominously, "the weather did not permit it," and he quickly returned to his anchorage in Hispaniola, where he was courted by the local lord, Guacanagarí, who plied the Admiral with lavish gifts, most memorably a belt bearing a "mask that had two large ears of hammered gold as well as the tongue and the nose." On closer inspection, he found that the "belt was of very fine jewelry work, like baroque pearls, made of white fishbones and some red ones interspersed like embroidery, so sewed with cotton thread and by such nice skill that on the side of the thread and on the reverse of the belt, it seemed very pretty embroidery, although all white, as if it were a web in a frame." He tested it and judged it "so strong that I believe that an arquebus"—a portable muzzle-loaded firearm with limited accuracy but quite deadly at close range—"could not penetrate it, or with difficulty."

On Sunday, Columbus set sail again, after expressing conventional reservations about going to sea on the Lord's Day, "merely from his piety and not from any superstition." No matter, gold was at stake.

Before he came to the gold, the gold came to him, borne by the local ruler. Prepared for hard bargaining, the Admiral reacted with astonishment, "for the Indians were so free, and the Spaniards so covetous and overreaching." He and his men had only to give "a little piece of glass and crockery or other things of no value" to receive pieces of gold, and as these transactions proceeded, the Spaniards found they need give nothing to receive the precious gold, a practice forbidden by their Admiral, who, after observing that the Indians freely gave gold in exchange for just six glass beads, "therefore ordered that they"—Spaniards—"take nothing from them unless they gave them something in payment." Bartered objects included glass beads, cotton, geese, or whatever came to hand. The ranks of the Indians swelled to include 120 canoes, "all charged with people, and all brought something, especially their bread and fish and water in earthen jars, and seeds of many sorts that are good spices, and ended up carrying one another piggyback across rivers and swampy places," as much for the fun of it as for any other purpose, contented to pay their respects and rejoice with the men and their ships.

The festivities became more boisterous. Columbus estimated that more than a thousand Indians approached his tiny ship, each bearing a tribute, "and before they came within half a crossbow shot of the ship, they stood up in their canoes with what they brought in their hands, saying, 'Take! Take!'" And so the Spaniards did, as five hundred more Indians swam out to *Santa María*, standing about a league offshore, to pay their respects.

At night, a convoy of Indian barges entered the harbor to visit the

Spaniards, declaring they had come from afar. By now Columbus and his men, accustomed to receiving tributes of gold without having to seek it out, contemplated spending Christmas in this wonderful harbor, which, he surmised, belonged to an island "bigger than England," his way of conveying the sense that it was very big indeed, as befit its presumed proximity to Asia.

An official visit from an Indian leader prompted Columbus, attentive to matters of status, to ponder the unfamiliar term *cacique*. "The Admiral had been unable to understand whether they used this for 'king' or 'governor.'" As for the designation, Columbus "didn't know whether they say this for 'hidalgo' or 'governor' or 'judge.'" In practice, a cacique could be considered an important chieftain just below the rank of king.

This cacique demonstrated his importance by bringing with him a retinue of two thousand men, who "showed much honor to the ships' people, and the populace, every one," by bringing food, drink, cotton cloth, and especially for the Admiral, colorful parrots. And, of course, more gold. Finally, the Indians took their leave, "carrying on their backs what the cacique and others had given them down to the boats that remained at the entrance to the river."

It was now Monday, Christmas Eve, and as soon as a promising offshore breeze stirred the rigging, he gave the order to weigh anchor, taking with him an Indian "who seemed better disposed and devoted or who spoke with more pleasure," charged with locating the elusive gold mines sought by the Admiral on the basis of his mentioning the word "Çybao." Columbus thought he heard the guide pronounce a near homonym, Çipango, Marco Polo's name for Japan. The actual Cibao denotes the central region of the island of Hispaniola, and on that slender basis, Columbus leaped to the conclusion that his little fleet had made it to Marco Polo's Asia, where the houses had roofs of gold.

Noticing the Admiral's excitement, the cacique compounded the miscommunication by speaking of a "great quantity of gold there." He indicated the "banners of beaten gold" he bore. Columbus yearned to claim this glittering wealth in the name of Ferdinand and Isabella.

By eleven o'clock on Christmas Eve, with his ships running confidently before a light breeze, the Admiral "decided to stretch out and sleep." He was exhausted from the rigors of the voyage, along with the rest of the crew, and had been drinking in celebration of the holiday. And that was when the trouble started. "As it was calm, the seaman who steered the ship decided to go to sleep, and hand over the tiller to the ship's boy, which the Admiral had always strictly forbidden during the entire voyage, come wind come calm; namely that they should let the ship's boy steer." Nevertheless, a lad of about fourteen or fifteen now guided *Santa María*.

"It pleased Our Lord that at Midnight, after they had seen the Admiral lie down and rest, and seeing there was dead calm and the sea like [water] in a porringer"—a shallow bowl usually equipped with a handle—"all lay down to sleep, and the tiller remained in the hand of the small boy, and the currents carried the ship upon one of the banks which, even though it was night, made a sound so they could be heard and seen a good league off." It was the grating thud of the keel grinding into sand. The ship came to an abrupt halt, stranded. The most significant voyage of discovery, years in the making, backed by the most powerful rulers in Europe, threatened to end on a calm night and a gentle sea at the hands—just one small hand, to be exact—of an innocent youth who steered the ship.

"The boy who felt the tiller, and heard the sound of the sea, gave tongue, at which the Admiral jumped up and was so prompt that no one had yet felt that they were aground." Unseen below the water's surface, not one but three coral reefs presented a concealed, treacherous barrier.

Columbus roared at *Santa María's* master and owner, Juan de la Cosa, to secure the longboat they towed astern, grab an anchor, and take it into the longboat. Cosa, accompanied by other desperate crew members, jumped into the longboat as the Admiral assumed they were taking steps to rescue *Santa María*. In fact, they fled to *Niña*, "half a league to windward." But those aboard that ship would not permit them to board. Frustrated, they had no choice but to return to the wreck of *Santa María*.

Alarmed, Columbus surveyed the scene: his own men abandoning his ship, the water becoming shallower as the sea drove the hull ever higher onto the fatal reef, and the ship beginning to list precariously, as if preparing her death throes. He "ordered the mainmast to be cut away and the ship to be lightened as much as they could, to see if they could get her off [the reef]," but *Santa María* persisted in driving up the reef until "she lay on her beam ends across the sea (although there was little or no sea running), and the planking opened."

In this desperate situation, Columbus, overwrought, lay to until daylight. When it became possible to see beyond the beach and into the deep forest, he dispatched Diego de Arana, listed as "marshal of the fleet," and Pedro Gutiérrez, "butler of the royal household," to seek help from Guacanagarí, the Indian leader who had regarded the Spaniards as supernatural beings.

The Admiral, meanwhile, said that he "wept," a remarkable confession. Officers normally commanded, or disciplined, or set an example for others. But the Admiral of the Ocean Sea, overwhelmed, terrified, and possibly disgraced, shed tears. He was Christopher Columbus, the Christ-bearer, as he thought of himself. How could this disaster be happening?

The Indians rushed to the Spaniards' rescue, emptying *Santa María* of her precious cargo. "He cleared the decks in a very short time, such was the great haste and care that the king gave." Columbus noted through his tears that the Indians exercised the same care to secure everything on land that they had removed from the ship. Nor did the king's services and sensitivity toward the afflicted mariners end there. "From time to time he sent one of his relatives to the weeping Admiral to console him, telling him that he must not be troubled or annoyed; that he would give him whatever he had."

As the sun rose over the scene of wreck and recovery, Columbus surveyed the possessions and reflected that not even in Spain would they have been safer, or treated better, than they were here. And he continued to weep, perhaps more with gratitude and relief than with sheer terror, recording the histrionics in his journal for posterity. "He and all the people wept," he observed once more, adding a curious footnote, open to various interpretations: "All are people of love and without greed, and suitable for every purpose. I assure Your Highnesses"—the distant but all-seeing Ferdinand and Isabella—"that in all the world there is no better people nor better country. They love their neighbors as themselves, and have the sweetest talk in the world, and gentle, and always with a smile." Even though they went about as naked "as their mothers bore them," he advised, they maintained "very good manners." The king exercised such admirable self-restraint "that it is a pleasure to see all of it." Perhaps it was the suddenness of the shipwreck, or the aftereffects of the drinking (if it occurred), or the emotional connotations of the holiday—whatever the reason, the wreck of *Santa María* and the rescue of her contents and crew had the makings of a Christmas miracle to his way of thinking. By means of this cognitive shift, he devised an ambitious scheme to salvage the voyage, his honor, and that of Spain from disaster.

On the day after Christmas, while still drying his tears and expressing his gratitude to his Indian saviors, and his Sovereigns, he began to formulate his rejoinder to the Indians' altruistic impulses: a Spanish empire across the sea, and loyal slaves to maintain it. It seemed to Columbus that the Indians were prepared to assume this role; indeed, with their show of subservience they were practically auditioning for it. This was, of course, his assumption, not theirs, and it had its roots in his long experience with slavery, especially female slavery, in Genoa, where slaves formed an essential and intimate component of the economy and of households. To his way of thinking, they were analogous to the Arabs, Asians, and eastern Europeans, non-Christians all, who supplied Genoa with its free labor.

For the moment, he kept his plan to himself, and the generous gestures resumed the following day, when Guacanagarí tearfully promised Columbus and his men "two very big houses, and would give more if necessary," along with canoes necessary to handle the ship's cargo, and sufficient manpower, all "without taking any morsel of bread or anything else." In his desire to repay and validate their kindness with something, anything, the Admiral resorted to offering more hawk's bells, and at the sight of these tinkling trinkets, the Indians called out "*chuque, chuque*" and seemed "on the point of going mad for them." Columbus was gratified to receive four pieces of gold "as big as the hand" in exchange, he was pleased to note, "for nothing." The Admiral became merry, "and the king rejoiced much to see the Admiral merry." That evening, the two leaders dined twice, first aboard *Niña*, the Spaniard celebrating his deliverance and gratification of his greed, the Indian celebrating his own generosity, and later ashore, where they devoured "yams, rock lobsters, game, and other viands they had, and their bread," cassava. The Indians exhibited respectable table manners, Columbus was pleased to note, and afterward he cleaned his hands by rubbing them with herbs in the manner of his hosts.

Striding past "groves of trees next to the houses," the Spaniards found themselves escorted to their guest quarters by "a good thousand people, all naked," except for Guacanagarí, who, out of respect for his guests, "now wore a shirt and gloves that the Admiral had given him, and over the gloves he made more rejoicing than anything." They talked of strategic matters, of the Indians' fierce rivals, the Caribs, who carried bows and arrows reminiscent of the Spaniards' exotic weapons, but made without iron, and of the way the Caribs captured the Indians at will. At once, "the Admiral said by signs that the Sovereigns of Castile would order the Caribs to be destroyed, and would order them all brought with their hands bound." To reinforce his show of strength, Columbus ordered a lombard and musket to be fired. The two shots, powered by gunpowder technology unknown to the Indians, shattered the Caribbean calm, and the Indians fell to earth. A little later, they brought Columbus, their protector, a "big mask that had great pieces of gold in the ears and the eyes and in other parts," together with gold ornaments, which they ceremoniously draped over the Admiral's head and neck.

Thereafter, the idea of a fortress, once the stuff of daydreams, became Columbus's mission and obsession. Once he felt a faint puff of destiny urging him on, he submitted to it as if it were a gale. The "great luck" of running into a reef and wrecking the flagship during a Christmas Eve spree became "the predestined will of God," complete with a purpose that Columbus suddenly divined: "that he might leave the people there" to begin a colony, and to become the catalyst for more voyages to China.

Ruminating on the accident, he made critical revisions to his account. No longer was it caused by the inexperienced hand of the ship's boy on the tiller at precisely the wrong moment, as *Santa María* encountered an all-but-invisible reef at night while Columbus slept; now he insisted it was caused by the "treachery of the master and the people . . . in refusing to run out the anchor from the stern to kedge"—that is, haul—"off the ship as the Admiral ordered." There was no more mention of the hapless boy at the tiller, or Columbus's fatigue, or the holiday celebrations; "treachery" had taken their place.

If only his orders had been obeyed, "the ship would have been saved." He laid the blame on the "men of Palos," the Spanish port where the voyage began, where he failed to receive the "vessels suitable for the voyage" to which he believed himself entitled. The town of Palos, under orders from Ferdinand and Isabella, had provided two of the three ships comprising his fleet, tiny *Niña*, as her name indicated, and delicate *Pinta*. This explanation failed to account for the loss of *Santa María*, in which Columbus himself had a stake. The treachery and accident fit a larger divine plan, "preordained" to bring him into contact with this land and people, so he thought. Until this event, Columbus wrote, "he always went with the intention to discover and not tarry in a place more than one day." No more. His self-serving revelation endowed him with a different goal, one that far exceeded his boast that he could sail from Spain to China.

"Now I have given orders to erect a tower and a fortress, all very well done, and a great moat, not that I believe it to be necessary for these people, for I take for granted that with this people I could conquer all this island, which I believe to be bigger than Portugal"—Spain's principal rival for empire— "and double the number of inhabitants." In this revised world order, he viewed the Indians, his gentle, generous, resourceful protectors, in a harsh new light, "naked and without arms and very cowardly, beyond hope of cure."

His tears had dried, and his meaning was clear; he considered them ripe for exploitation. Their weakness became his strength, and he turned to the God-given task of empire building. "It is right that this tower should be built," he insisted, "and it is as it should be, being so far from Your Highnesses, and that they may recognize the skill of Your Highnesses' subjects, and what they can do, so they may serve them"—Columbus chose his words carefully—"with love and fear."

The matériel for the stronghold came from *Santa María*, transmuted into a new purpose, "boards of which to build the whole fortress." They worked diligently, completing a rudimentary structure in only ten days, a microcosm of confinement and order in a sea of freedom and occasional chaos. Indicating the rapid advance of his plans, he gave orders for "provisions of bread and wine for more than a year, and seeds to sow, and the ship's barge, and a caulker, a carpenter, a gunner and a cooper." He envisioned a stream of wealth in the form of gold and spices flowing from this fortress directly to Castile and the cause of a new Crusade. He became so imbued with a sense of divine mission that he declared that "all the gain of this Enterprise should be spent in the conquest of Jerusalem," as he had once mentioned to his Sovereigns, whom he recalled smiling indulgently at the thought. Inconsistent, inspired, and self-serving, Columbus was proving himself a brilliant but mercurial explorer.

Couched in spiritual and political idealism, the sudden, unauthorized construction of a manned fort served Columbus's interests first and foremost. Until he had hit upon this scheme, he had contracted for a single voyage. Now he would have to return in the name of Spain, if only to relieve the crew, who became hostages to his ambition, marooned off the coast of Haiti, unable to return home until he fetched them. Only Columbus and a few of his officers and pilots knew where in the world this fortress was located, and only they would be able to find it again. If Bartolomeu Dias had been able to think up a comparable scheme, he might not have been cast aside by his sovereign, King João of Portugal. Columbus would not allow Ferdinand and Isabella the same option; they would be duty bound to send him on another journey. For all its anticipation and daring, his voyage to the New World, rather than an end in itself, had become a prologue to a much grander adventure into empire, conquest, and conversion, one that would also serve, he hoped, as his avenue into history.

Guacanagarí returned at dawn on Thursday, December 27, hoping to delay Columbus's departure with the promise of more gold. The Admiral continued to court his favor by inviting Guacanagarí, his brother, and another "very intimate relation" to dine with him, when they suddenly switched tactics and expressed the desire to go with Columbus to the wonderful kingdom of Castile. Their sense of urgency only increased when, in the midst of the meal, other Indians arrived bringing news of *Pinta*; she was anchored "in a river at the end of that island."

Columbus seized the opportunity to send the unstable and insubordinate Martín Alonso Pinzón a letter of reconciliation. Columbus needed Pinzón. The Admiral's plan to establish a fortress in the wilds of India would not succeed so long as his men were threatening mutiny. Worse, Pinzón's returning to Spain to disseminate a different version of events, one that showed Columbus as a naive, self-seeking adventurer rather than an idealistic servant of Castile, could trigger a disastrous chain of events. If Pinzón's version prevailed, the Sovereigns might be inclined to forgive rather than punish him for his near mutiny.

As Columbus tarried among the Indians and presided over construction and staffing of the fortress, the Indians appeared to compete for his favor. In Columbus's telling, one leader entreated him to make use of an elaborate "dais of palm bark," while another at first feigned ignorance of his presence and then ran to him and "hung on his neck a great plate of gold that he carried in his hand" in an effort to outdo his rival. This flattery and bribery continued through Sunday, culminating in a ceremonial send-off, which Columbus found irresistible. The cacique personally received the Admiral with great pomp and formality, and led him by the arm to a sort of dais and chair. He asked Columbus to be seated, whereupon he removed a bejeweled headpiece and placed it on the explorer's head. Returning the gesture, Columbus removed a collar encrusted with multihued gems and placed it around the cacique's neck. He also bestowed the handsome scarlet cloak he wore that day on the Indian, and even sent for a pair of fine boots for the Indian to wear. Finally, he placed on his finger a large silver ring. It reminded the Indian of a silver earring worn by a mariner. With this ceremonial exchange of gifts and show of goodwill, Columbus's voyage was nearing its conclusion, and he wanted to see the Sovereigns before his rival Pinzón got there. He was likely already en route, with malice in mind.

On Monday, the last day of the year, Columbus prepared to set sail for Spain at last, "taking on water and wood," and planning to "give prompt news to the Sovereigns, that they might send ships to discover what remained to be discovered." He could have continued his voyage of exploration, voyaging eastward along the coast "until he had seen all that country," but on sober reflection, he realized that he was left with only one vessel, and "it did not seem reasonable to expose himself to the dangers that could occur in discovering," as well as "all that evil and inconvenience" stemming from the "parting of the caravel *Pinta*." By this, Columbus hinted he was preparing to counter malicious propaganda that he expected to be spread by his rival Martín Alonso Pinzón. The last thing the Admiral wanted the Sovereigns to consider was an unauthorized account of how *Santa María* came to be lost, or the mysterious disappearance of *Pinta*, or the failure to locate the Grand Khan, or other embarrassing incidents. It was preferable to focus on his hastily improvised fortress and plans to colonize the strange land that he had discovered.

The overdue departure finally occurred on January 2, 1493, with Columbus placing Diego de Arana, Pedro Gutiérrez, and Rodrigo Escobedo in charge of the fortress and, in the Admiral's mind, over the Indians. With the threat of the fierce Caribs ever present in the minds of the Indians, the Spaniards demonstrated their lombards, pointing out "how [they] pierced the side of the ship and how the ball went far out to sea." He staged a mock battle between his men and the Indians to demonstrate "they need have no fear of the Caribs, even if they should come." He backed his assurances with tangible resources, designating thirty-nine men, the translator Luis de Torres among them, to remain behind in the fortress, along with sufficient food, and even a physician, all of them good "men of the sea."

Even with these reassurances, the Indians remained fearful, and made their best effort to seduce Columbus, their defender, with an irresistible offering. One of Guacanagarí's men informed Columbus that the king had "ordered to be made a statue of pure gold as large as the Admiral himself." What could be more impressive, or more calculated to appeal to Columbus's vanity than this priceless effigy? They promised it would be ready for delivery in only ten days.

Friday dawned fair, with a light wind, and Columbus made a determined effort to depart, deploying nimble *Niña* to scout a channel and to confirm that it was free of reefs; he noted islets and gulfs as he went, but light wind impeded his progress that morning. He continued to profess, though with less conviction, that the splendid China described by Marco Polo must be close by, but the kingdom remained as elusive as the mythical El Dorado.

On Sunday, while running along the northern coast of the landmass he had named Hispaniola, he feared that reefs and shoals lurked around every point, or were concealed beneath the iridescent water of every harbor like so many sea monsters, their teeth poised to rip his ship's hulls to slivers. Amid these hazards, *Pinta*, presumed lost, appeared on the horizon, racing downwind toward *Niña* and Columbus. The two ships sailed a full ten leagues together to find a safe anchorage, and then Martín Alonso Pinzón came aboard, dispensing with the usual formalities, "to excuse himself, alleging that he had left him [Columbus] against his will."

Exasperated, Columbus dismissed Pinzón's claim as "all false." Pinzón had gone his way out of "much insolence and greed." His behavior was the work of Satan. The Indians believed that Pinzón had abandoned the fleet in the futile pursuit of gold, going all the way to Jamaica—"Yamaye" to the Spaniards—a ten-day journey by canoe. Columbus declared that Pinzón's unauthorized conduct amounted to "insolence and disloyalty."

Water is the enemy of wood, and *Niña* required repairs, pumping, and caulking the following day, January 8, before Columbus considered the craft seaworthy. He awaited news of the life-size gold statue he had been promised, but none was forthcoming. On Tuesday, a high wind from the southeast delayed his exodus yet again. He remained troubled by the actions of the Pinzón brothers, Martín Alonso and Vicente Yáñez, who had abandoned him on November 21. "To get rid of such bad company, with whom he had had to dissemble (for they were undisciplined people), and although he had along many men of good will (but it was no time to deal out punishment), he decided to return and delay no more."

As usual, the slightest mention of gold acted on him like a powerfully addictive drug and sufficed to distract him from his other concerns and goals. Columbus heard from his sailors that they had found gold in the mouth of a river—probably the Yaque—while they were collecting water for *Niña*. He dreamed of the wide and deep river "all full of gold, and of such quality that it is marvelous but very fine." He ordered the sailors "to go up the river a stone's throw," in search of the gold, and when they filled their barrels with water and returned to *Niña*, "they found bits of gold"—gold!—adhering to the barrel hoops. He named the body of water Río de Oro, River of Gold. Columbus's thoughts once again veered toward reality and the necessity of returning to Spain "at full speed to bring the news and to quit the bad company that he had, and that he always said they were a mutinous lot." The ill will was entirely mutual.

After the latest series of delays and maneuvers, he estimated he had traveled only twenty-seven miles from the fortress, which he had taken to calling La Navidad, after the date of the shipwreck and to commemorate the beginning of the Spanish empire in Hispaniola. At midnight, January 9, he set sail once again, soon becoming frustrated by reefs and unseen channels. He took in fine sights, turtles ("very big, like a large wooden shield") and "three mermaids who rose very high from the sea," but, he hastened to add, "they were not as beautiful as they were painted, although to some extent they have a human appearance on the face." In fact, the creatures were sea cows, or manatees, herbivores that generally graze in shallow waters, forbidding-looking beasts weighing over a thousand pounds, nearly ten feet long, with widely spaced eyes and a mournful appearance.

The next day's anchorage brought Columbus, still aboard *Niña*, to the mouth of a broad waterway that he named Río de Gracia. A "good landlocked harbor" beckoned in the distance, but the presence of shipworms, or teredos, warned him away. Once shipworms worked their way into the planks, there would be no getting rid of them, and they would destroy the ship from within. He departed from this uneasy anchorage at midnight on Friday, and confidently reported "great progress because the wind and currents were with him. Dared not anchor for fear of shoals, and so lay-to all night."

Even before dawn *Niña* raised anchor and shaped a generally easterly course. Columbus was tempted to explore "a great and very beautiful opening between two great mountains," which led to an enticing harbor, but he was fearful that once *Niña* entered the harbor, the wind might shift. Instead, he rounded one rocky cape after another, daring to anchor in the midst of a "very great bay" surrounding a "tiny little island." He estimated the depth at twelve fathoms when he dropped anchor, and dispatched a barge in search of water and people, but the inhabitants, he reported, had all fled, and with them the hope of obtaining the life-size statue of gold. He paused to wonder at the immense surroundings, and the configuration of the landmass along whose board he had been coasting. Had he reached a new gulf or island? Or was this endless and varied coastline still "one land with Hispaniola"? If so, "he remained amazed at how big was the island of Hispaniola."

On Sunday, the Admiral had the time and tranquillity to make planetary observations. He patiently awaited "the conjunction of the moon with the sun," which he expected four days later, on January 17, as well as the sun in opposition with Jupiter, which he claimed to be "the cause of great winds."

As Columbus studied the heavens, preoccupied with what the celestial signs portended for his destiny, sailors aboard *Niña*'s barge disembarked onshore in search of food, "and they found some men with bows and arrows, with whom they waited to talk."

One warrior wished to board *Niña* to meet the Admiral himself, and when Columbus came face-to-face with him, the encounter proved unsettling. His face was stained with a substance that Columbus took to be charcoal but more likely was a dye derived from a local fruit. "He wore his hair very long and drawn together and fastened behind, and gathered into a little nest of parrots' feathers, and he was as naked as the others." Columbus believed the Indian was a Carib, but in Las Casas's opinion, the emissary belonged to the Taínos, who had borrowed the Caribs' weapons in self-defense. It mattered little to the Admiral, who talked only of gold. Was there any to be found in this region? A great deal, the Indian replied, gesturing at *Niña's* substantial poop to evoke a massive quantity. *"Tuob,"* he called it, a new designation for the precious substance, and said it could be found on the island of Boriquén, the Land of the Valiant Lord, as the Taínos referred to Puerto Rico.

In exchange for this intelligence, Columbus ordered that the obliging Taínos be given food, "pieces of green and red cloth, and little beads of glass," and sent the man ashore with orders to return with gold. Columbus had seen traces of gold sewn in the Taínos' clothes and assumed it must be readily available. When the barge bearing the Taínos approached the shore, no less than fifty-five men, with "very long hair, as the women wear it in Castile," appeared from behind the trees, each one carrying a bow. The Taíno who had gone aboard *Niña* turned to his own people and persuaded them to lay down their bows, which Columbus's men offered to buy, along with arrows. The mood suddenly turned hostile: "Having sold two bows, they wished to give no more, but prepared rather to attack the Christians and capture them."

They came rushing at them with ropes, prepared to bind their victims as a prelude to imprisonment, torture, and slaughter. "Seeing them running toward them, the Christians, being prepared as always the Admiral advised them to be, fell upon them and gave an Indian a great slash on the buttocks, and wounded another in the breast with an arrow." At that, the rest of the Taínos ran from the scene of battle.

What should have been a peaceful commercial encounter had turned bloody and vicious, but the unexpected turn of events reassured rather than dismayed the Admiral. He confided to his journal that he was sorry about the ill will engendered by the conflict; at the same time, he was not sorry at all: The Indians would have to learn "fear of the Christians." Although he appeared indifferent to the reputation of the Caribs, he came around to the opinion that they had just drawn the blood not of the Taínos but of the Caribs themselves, "bad actors" who "ate men."

Now they had been chastened, or so he hoped. If they encountered the Spanish seamen at the fortress La Navidad, they would "fear to do them any harm." And even if they were not Caribs, "they must have the same customs," and would be deterred in the same way. In either case, the charmed relations and fellow feeling between Indians and Spaniards dissipated. Although Columbus had tried to banish the sinister Caribs from his thoughts, it was apparent from his journal, with its frequent mentions of these fierce warriors, that they were on his mind, and to the peaceful Taínos, they posed an ever-present danger.

By January 15, three weeks after the shipwreck, Columbus had yet to summon the resolve to leave the Indies and their unfulfilled promise of gold for the repercussions awaiting him in Spain. He invited several Indians aboard *Niña* and sent a barge bearing Spaniards to reconnoiter ashore. He confessed that he could not learn much about a country in the space of a few days, "both from the difficulty of language, which the Admiral didn't understand except by guess, and because they knew not what he was trying to say."

To help, Columbus detained four youths aboard *Niña*, communicating with them by sign language. The boys indicated they knew the nearby islands well, and could serve as guides and go-betweens if necessary. So they joined the Spaniards for the journey to Spain, heedless of the elements to which they would be exposed on the open water, and, if they survived, in Europe. From the Indians Columbus also heard a story concerning another island, Matinino, said to contain abundant copper. The island, they added, was "inhabited only by women." Columbus decided to go there directly, see the women, and carry specimens away with him.

The story evoked Marco Polo's account of Male Island and Female Island, located somewhere in "greater India." The legend, beguilingly related by the Venetian, was fact to Columbus and to Europeans. Perhaps the Admiral had managed to locate himself in the Venetian's world after all. "I assure you that in the island the men do not live with their wives or with any other women; but all women live on the other island, which is called Female Island." According to Polo, the men visit for three months of pleasure-taking before taking their leave.

Fumbling for the proper words with which to communicate with the island's inhabitants, Columbus studied their bows and arrows, made from the "shoots of canes." The Indians inserted a fish tooth at the tip, generally coated with poison. He also noted abundant cotton and chili, "which is stronger than pepper," yet "the people won't eat without it, for they find it very wholesome." Traditional European black pepper belongs to the genus *Piper*, while the shiny green and red chili pepper belongs to the genus *Capsicum*, and there was so much in evidence that he estimated he could "load fifty caravels with it in Hispaniola." But was chili pepper worth anything in Spain?

Thick mats of seaweed clogged the harbor, he noticed. He had seen it before, "in the gulf when they came upon the discovery," and in his experience it grew only in shallow waters near land. "If so," he guessed, "these Indies were very near the Canary Islands," his jumping-off point before heading out to the uncharted Atlantic, which he called the Ocean Sea, "and for that reason he believed that they were less than 400 leagues distant." In fact, he would have to traverse more than twice that distance.

The ever-present drifting seaweed was the brown algae, commonly called gulfweed, or sargassum, from which the huge Sargasso Sea takes its name. His fleet had silently and unwittingly entered a sea like no other, stretching two thousand miles east from Bermuda. The water of the Sargasso Sea was intensely blue, so clear that he could gaze two hundred feet into its depths. The sea extends fifteen thousand feet—nearly three miles—to the ocean's floor. This strange, shoreless sea is defined by the confluence of four currents known as the North Atlantic Subtropical Gyre. (In oceanography, a gyre denotes a system of rotating ocean currents generated by large-scale wind movements.) When Columbus sailed through the Sargasso Sea, he experienced a unique combination of wind and water and plant life in the form of sargassum.

Like many sailors, he feared the thick, floating mats would snarl his ships and lead to disaster. In reality, sargassum is too fragile to act as a barrier. It consists of miniature floats containing oxygen, carbon dioxide, and nitrogen for buoyancy, and it derives its name from these little structures, which reminded Portuguese sailors of a grape they called *salgazo*. The designation evolved into the word *sargaço*, or seaweed, and later the floating mats of seaweed were classified as the genus *Sargassum*. (There are six species of *Sargassum*, with two, *Sargassum natans* and *Sargassum fuitans*, predominating.) Columbus called it, simply, "weed," and it was ubiquitous, covering a million square miles, or more, of the Sargasso Sea and Atlantic Ocean. From time to time storms scattered sargassum into the Caribbean Basin, the Gulf of Mexico, and the Gulf Stream, which carried it to the north, along the

Atlantic Coast. In time, the Gulf Stream nudged it ashore, or swept it back into the vortex of the Sargasso Sea. So Columbus encountered its feathery stems wherever he went.

The homeward passage commenced three hours before dawn, on January 16, before a moderate offshore breeze. Relying on his four Indian guides, he headed in the general direction of the Caribs, "the people whom all those islands hold in so great fear, because it is said that with their countless canoes they range over all those seas, and it is said that they eat the men whom they can take."

After traveling sixty-four miles, according to his dead reckoning, the Indian guides indicated that their destination would "lie to the southeast." Instead, he trimmed the sails, proceeded another two leagues, and *Niña* caught what he considered a wind capable of bearing the ship all the way to Spain.

His confidence surged. He had survived the voyage, outlasted a partial mutiny, and discovered a previously unknown part of the world. He had even established and staffed a fort in this remote outpost. Nor did his achievements end there. He had demonstrated the validity of his "grand design" to himself, and soon enough, he would do the same for Ferdinand and Isabella. Nothing could alter those achievements, with the possible exception of Pinzón's malice or divine intervention.

The two surviving ships of the little fleet (*Pinta* was not far behind) headed out to the open sea with all its hazards. What awaited him on the Iberian Peninsula would be far more uncertain and dangerous than anything he had faced in the mild waters and on the powdery white beaches of the Caribbean.

CHAPTER 4

"The People from the Sky"

Symptoms of prolonged isolation from women crept into Columbus's log. He confessed his fixation with the "island of Matinino," said by the Indians to be inhabited by "women without men"—a prospect that answered the prayers of many a sailor and even enticed the more circumspect Admiral. According to the local gossip, newborn baby girls were conveyed to a certain island once a year, while newborn baby boys were sent to an equivalent retreat.

The more he questioned his Indian guides on the exact whereabouts of this island, the vaguer they became about its location, their evasions intensifying his interest in the matter. Columbus was never more zealous than when in pursuit of an illusion. He considered making exploratory gestures, but, he recorded, he "didn't care to tarry," not to mention the way this nautical detour into venery would be portrayed at home by his enemies and rivals. Fair weather and brisk wind encouraged Columbus to put aside thoughts of the Sirens of the Caribbean and to pursue his northing and easting toward Spain. By sunset, he reported, the breeze began to die down.

Columbus's system for marking the days was eccentric, even by maritime standards. Mariners generally began their days at noon rather than at midnight, but Columbus preferred to commence his days at sunrise, at least for the outward-bound voyage. On the inbound voyage, such as this one, he marked his days from sunset to sunset. These variations meant that calculations of his fleet's day-to-day progress were often irregular, and did not always agree.

Similar discrepancies and irregularities marked timekeeping aboard

Columbus's ships. His pilots kept time with a capacious hand-operated hour-glass known as the *ampolleta*. On fair days, he was able to correct time-keeping errors by observing the moment the sun reached the zenith, that is, the highest point overhead. Then, for a few hours, all was regulated, but at sea, nothing stayed the same for very long. On heaven and on earth, everything was in motion.

Never completely breaking free of his medieval frame of mind, Columbus relied on a traditional canonical schedule, even at sea. Prime, or daybreak, occurred at 6:00 a.m., Terce at 9:00 a.m., Sext at noon, Nones at 3:00 p.m., Vespers at 6:00 p.m., and Compline at 9:00 p.m. These hours were occasionally elastic, with Prime, usually indicating dawn, observed whenever it occurred, Vespers in late afternoon or early evening, and Compline before the men went to sleep. At Vespers, when circumstances permitted, Columbus called all hands, who read or looked on while prayers were uttered, and the men of the day watch gave way to the evening guard.

It was then, in the dying light of day, he saw a remarkable sight, a booby, the awkward-looking seabird whose name was based on the Spanish word for "dunce," known to oceangoing sailors everywhere. Soon another booby appeared, and then seaweed: hints and promises of land.

On Friday, January 18, the sea churned with albacore, one of the few species of fish recognizable to Columbus and his crew and an encouraging sign that they were approaching Spain. Repeating sailors' lore, Columbus expressed the belief that they, accompanied by a frigate bird, would lead the ship to a coastal village called Conil, near the city of Cadiz, where they were supposed to congregate. Or as the sailors might have put it, the tuna were towing them toward the city's girls, renowned for beauty and bawdy repartee. The next day brought boobies and other pelagic birds, but no signs of Cadiz or its beauties. And by Sunday, he was yearning for home, imagining the ocean breeze "as soft and sweet as Seville during April and May," as it wafted over a gentle, unruffled sea.

He varied his course between north, north northeast, "and at times did northeast by north," making up so much time that soon *Niña* was bearing down on *Pinta* "in order to speak to her," by which he meant to apprise himself of Pinzón's latest intentions. Suddenly the air turned chill, and he expected more cooling as he proceeded north, "and also the nights were very much longer from the narrowing of the sphere." This observation is but one of many made by Columbus that demonstrate that he fully understood and appreciated that the earth was round, or nearly so, and certainly not flat.

More birds appeared, including petrels, and still more seaweed, "but not so many fishes, because the water was colder." Yet there was no sign of land, and he had scant idea of his whereabouts in the Ocean Sea or in relation to his outgoing voyage. Amid the unease, the wind died down the following day, and with nothing better to do, the ship's Indian passengers went swimming in the briny deep, as their more cautious European keepers looked on from the deck of the *Niña*.

That night, a revived but variable wind teased *Niña* to life, but Columbus and his crew resisted the temptation to proceed. They were waiting for *Pinta* to catch up, yet she appeared crippled. "She sailed badly close-hauled," Columbus noted, "because she had little help from the mizzen owing to the mast not being sound." For that lapse, the Admiral blamed his subversive rival. "If her captain, Martín Alonso Pinzón, had taken as much care to provide a good mast to the Indies," he scolded, "where there were so many and of that sort, as he was greedy in leaving them, thinking to fill the ship with them, he would have done well."

Columbus took comfort in the fact that the ocean remained "always very smooth as in a river," for which he thanked God, who apparently still favored him above all others.

So it went for the remainder of January and into the middle of February 1493. One day, the seamen "killed a porpoise and a tremendous shark." By night, the water, "very smooth," slid silently past the ship's hull, shattering the celestial illumination into glistening fragments.

On the evening of Sunday, February 3, Columbus tried his luck with the astrolabe and the quadrant, instruments on which navigators in many parts of the world had relied for centuries. In its simplest form, an astrolabe consists of a disk marked in degrees, together with a pointer. It is used to make astronomical measurements, especially the altitudes of celestial bodies, and to calculate latitude. Columbus's instrument was rudimentary, and he was by no means expert with it. The quadrant, the other traditional instrument for celestial navigation, consisted of a graduated quarter circle and a sight. This was designed to take angular measurements of altitude in astronomy, and was usually made of wood or brass.

Columbus hoped to take the altitude of the North Star to ascertain his location, but failed. He blamed rough water, or, as he put it, "the rolling wouldn't permit it." Yet his previous sentence notes that the sea was "very smooth." More likely, he was frustrated by his lack of skill in handling the devices, even in calm weather. A sophisticated dead-reckoning navigator who could read currents and clouds and wind with uncanny precision, Columbus lacked mastery of these instruments. In due course he gave up on the quadrant and astrolabe, and relied on his senses, especially his keen eyesight. For all his visionary qualities, Columbus remained the pragmatic Genoese sea captain, impatient with the latest navigational technology.

The trades rapidly bore *Niña* along, and she covered two hundred nautical miles during a twenty-four-hour period beginning on February 6. The pilot, Vicente Yáñez, assisted by a seaman, Bartolomé Roldán, persuaded themselves, and their captain, that they were approaching the Azores, the westernmost projection of European influence into the Atlantic. They convinced themselves that they spied Flores Island, discovered less than twenty years earlier, and then Madeira Island. But on this occasion Columbus's dead reckoning misled him about the position of the two islands and the position of *Niña*. He believed himself seventy-five leagues south of Flores, when he was actually six hundred miles to the east and two hundred miles to the south of his presumed location, yet he remained convinced of his interpretation, and sought confirmation in the appearance of clumps of seaweed that the sailors associated with the Azores.

The longer Columbus remained at sea, the greater the divergence between his actual and presumed locations, which meant the greater the danger. As the voyage unfolded, the ultimate test of his navigational abilities occurred not in the outward-bound journey—which was a demonstration of his vision, not his navigational accuracy, with any landfall in the New World considered a "discovery"—but on the return voyage, when he headed toward a specific destination, not a fanciful idea concocted by Marco Polo or the result of calculations based on inexact measurement. Not knowing where he was as he commenced the return leg of the voyage, and resolute in the belief that he was somewhere off the coast of "India," he found himself at an enormous disadvantage as he attempted to retrace his course, and the problem became worse with every league he traversed. He was lost without realizing it, just as he had been since the day the soft outlines of the Canary Islands faded into the mist.

*   *   *

Amid this relatively calm interval during the inbound journey, Columbus prepared to defend himself against challenges sure to come from Pinzón, the Portuguese, and other rivals, by summarizing his exploits for Luís de Santangel, the Queen's Keeper of the Privy Purse, to pass on to the Sovereigns. (It is conceivable that Columbus wrote two such letters, one intended for each party, but only the letter to Luís de Santangel has survived.) Published only weeks later, in April 1493, it is considered the first instance of printed Americana, and perhaps the most important and valuable.

Columbus's "Letter on the First Voyage" attempted to burnish the events of his first voyage. If his diary reads as a jumbled, frequently contradictory series of impressions made on the fly, his letter reveals his more considered impressions, those he expected to secure his place in the scheme of things. From start to finish, he was determined to accentuate the positive and eliminate the negative aspects of his voyage. "Since I know you will be pleased at the great success with which the Lord has crowned my voyage," he began, "I write to inform you how in thirty-three days I crossed from the Canary Islands to the Indies, with the fleet our most illustrious Sovereigns gave to me. And there I found many islands filled with people without number, and of them all have I taken possession for Their Highnesses, by proclamation and with the royal standard displayed, and nobody objected."

Although he had no idea where he actually had gone, he proceeded to explain his taxonomy of discovery: "To the first island which I found I gave the name Saint Salvador, in recognition of His Heavenly Majesty, who marvelously hath given all this; the Indians call it Guanahani. To the second I gave the name Isla de Santa María de la Concepción; to the third, Fernandina; to the fourth, Isabela, to the fifth, Juana, and so to each one I gave a new name." How splendid it was to conjure and name a new world.

On a more troubling subject, he added, "When I reached Cuba, I followed its north coast westwards, and found it so extensive I thought this must be the mainland, the province of Cathay." Here he rewrote his own history. As his logbook indicated, he initially believed that Cuba was a very large island, and if that were the case, it could not be connected to Cathay, or China, a result that would undercut his promises to the Sovereigns, the purpose of his expedition, and his cosmography. The explorer did not want to confront the consequences of his own discovery, and so he resorted to a convenient fiction, explaining that as he sailed along the Cuban coast, he saw only "small groups of houses whose inhabitants fled as soon as we approached," and stayed on his course, "thinking I should undoubtedly come to some great towns or cities." Worse, the "coast was bearing me northward," and winter was approaching, not that he had any realistic expectation of encountering ice and snow in this subtropical climate, where persistent heat and humidity plagued Columbus and all the men as they went out in their wool and linen clothing, while the Indians went about nearly naked. Pretending that he was fleeing the cold—and how would the Sovereigns ever know the difference, unless they had actually traveled there?—he decided to journey south, but he did not want to carry on in that direction either, preferring to anchor in a "remarkable harbor that I had observed." By the time he finished his little fable about fleeing the harsh Cuban winter, the Sovereigns (and their advisers) would have stopped wondering whether Cuba was an island, after all. More likely, it was some part of "India."

Feigning curiosity when he was, in fact, avoiding a reasonable trajectory for his ships, he sent two men inland to look for "a king of great cities." He dispatched two scouts to find centers of commerce and civilization, and three days of reconnoitering in the wild led only to "small villages and people without number, but nothing of importance." More likely, Columbus deliberately altered parts of his log to conceal his precise whereabouts from his rivals, and it was possible that he was being similarly disingenuous about his half-completed exploration of Cuba.

Rather than pursuing geographical truth, he dashed away to another island, one that he named Hispaniola. Indians had told him about it, or so he said. His story was getting better with the telling, and so he continued to embellish, even when his journal, with its sense of wonder and ambiguity, contradicted his letter's mythmaking.

He portrayed Hispaniola as an extraordinary opportunity for empire building. "It has many large harbors finer than any I know in Christian lands, and many large rivers. All this is marvelous." In fact, everything there was "marvelous"—the plants, the trees, the fruit—and Hispaniola itself "is a wonder" replete with many "incredibly fine harbors" and "great rivers" containing gold (not really), "many spices" (not true), and "large mines of gold and other metals" (a flagrant exaggeration).

As with his fear of the Cuban "winter," only Columbus could verify these statements. He preferred to evoke "lofty" lands, sierras, and mountains. "All are most beautiful, of a thousand shapes, and all accessible, and filled with trees of a thousand kinds and tall, and they seemed to touch the sky." Some flowered; others bore fruit, "and there were singing the nightingale and other little birds of a thousand kinds in the month of November." He wrote on, telling of its rich red soil (true), its powdery beaches strewn with glassine sand (true), its cooperative populace, who seemed wholly of a piece with the soothing environment (hardly), and water of crystal clarity that he had seen nowhere else (for once, the absolute truth). "You could not believe it without seeing it," he exclaimed. Even Marco Polo, also inclined toward hyperbole, had not remarked on such gentle and beguiling natural settings, and for the benefit of the Sovereigns, Columbus wondered if he were approaching the entrance to paradise. In Hispaniola, "the sierras and the mountains and the plains and the meadows and the lands are so beautiful and rich for planting and sowing, and for livestock of every sort, and for building towns and villages." And so Columbus wrote on, soothed by the sound of the sea, encouraged by the prospect of his glorious return to Spain, storms and struggles all behind him as he evoked the magic isles of his voyage.

When he turned his attention to the inhabitants of "this island," he became more candid, and for those who had not seen what he had seen, utterly baffling. They were profoundly human and sensitive, they were savage and dangerous, they flung their arrows at him, they offered to build a life-size gold statue in his image, they considered his fleet the fulfillment of a longstanding prophecy, and they drove him from their land. Their behavior varied from one harbor he visited to the next. Generalizations about them were difficult, if not impossible, to make, but he would try.

To begin, they all "go naked, men and women, as their mothers bore them, except that some women cover one place only with the leaf of a plant or with a net of cotton," he warned, and appraised them as an avaricious Genoese might. "They have no iron or steel or weapons, nor are they capable of using them, although they are well-built people of handsome stature, because they are wondrous timid" and even refused to use the flimsy little sharp sticks they occasionally carried. When Columbus landed, "people without number" were drawn to the sight, only to flee. "Even a father would not stay for his son, and this was not because wrong had been done to anyone." In all, they were "timid beyond cure." And generous beyond reason. "Of anything they have, if you ask them for it, they never say no; rather they invite the person to share it, and show as much love as if they were giving their hearts; and whether the thing be of value or of small price."

He described the efforts he made to prepare for their conversion to Christianity: "I gave them a thousand pretty things that I had brought, in order to gain their love and incline them to become Christians. I hoped to win them to the love and service of Their Highnesses and of the whole Spanish nation and to persuade them to collect and give us of the things which they possessed in abundance and which we needed"—such as their young women, he might have added, if he were to be completely truthful, which he was not. He boasted that he, the Admiral of the Ocean Sea, received a "good reception everywhere, once they had overcome their fear . . . because they have never before seen men clothed or ships like these."

He learned to communicate with them "either by speech or signs," but no matter what passed between them, the Indians "believe very firmly that I, with these ships and people, came from the sky." The conviction remained unshakeable, and ubiquitous. Wherever he journeyed, the startled inhabitants "went running from house to house and to the neighboring towns with loud cries of 'Come! Come! See the people from the sky!'"

Cheered by the adulation, Columbus portrayed his empire building in grandiose terms; he proclaimed that he had discovered the gold mines associated with the Grand Khan, although the claim was based on his having caught glimpses of a few strands of gold. As if trumpet flourishes were sounding all around him, Columbus announced that he had "taken possession of a large town to which I gave the name La Villa de Navidad, and in it I have built a fort and defenses, which already, at this moment, will be all complete."

In fact, this was neither a town nor a citadel, as he implied; it was a modest stronghold cobbled together with timber salvaged from the scuttled *Santa María* and staffed by thirty-nine seamen ill equipped for survival in a strange environment. As the first European settlement in the New World, it served as a powerful symbol. In his Sovereigns' imagination, it would appear as a castle with banners and battlements, a militant monastery in the midst of heathens. It was, in other words, an excellent selling point, secured by the hostages he had deposited there. Columbus insisted that they were not in any danger, and that they enjoyed the protection of the local king, who "took pride in calling me and treating me as a brother." Even if the king underwent a change of heart, "neither he nor his people know the use of arms," Columbus said.

One more thing: he wanted to assure the Sovereigns that "I have not found the human monsters that many people expected. On the contrary, the whole population is very well made." He admitted to hearing reports concerning "a people who are regarded in all the islands as very ferocious and who eat human flesh"—the fierce Caribs, who marauded vulnerable islands and practiced ritual human sacrifice—"they have many canoes with which they range all the islands of India and pillage and take as much as they can," but even these warriors "are no more malformed than the others, except that they have the custom of wearing their hair long like women." Their ferocity derived from the cowardice of their victims. In other words, they were not to be taken seriously as combatants.

He finally bestowed a designation on the people he discovered: they were Indios, a term derived from the misconception that they inhabited India. No matter, they were rich in resources that Spain needed: not only gold, but mastic, "which up to now, has only been found in Greece, on the island of Chios"—as Columbus knew from personal experience during his arduous apprenticeship as a Genoese seaman—together with aloe, rhubarb, cinnamon, and a "thousand other things of value." This appeared to be an impressive tally, but a skeptic predisposed to dislike Columbus would read between the lines and realize that much was lacking, chiefly gold, the most important item on the Sovereigns' agenda. Had Columbus found abundant gold, he would have emphasized it above all. And, of course, he had not found the Grand Khan or his empire, no matter how vigorously he pretended that it lay just over the horizon. And the inhabitants, who today would be called indigenous peoples, were not the highly advanced civilization described by Marco Polo; they lacked the technological, mathematical, artistic, and military abilities catalogued by the Venetian. Columbus tried to turn their lack of technological prowess to his advantage; if they did not have sophisticated weapons, they must be docile. No matter how he couched his description of them, it was apparent they lacked the makings of sophisticated trading partners. He had found little of immediate use to the Sovereigns and their plans for empire. Nevertheless, his voyage triggered an unstoppable impulse for exploration, empire building, and greed.

At the time he wrote this summary, he could not, nor could anyone else, have imagined the immediate consequences or the long-term implications of this voyage. To him, it was the fulfillment of a divine prophecy. To his Sovereigns and their ministers, it was intended as a landgrab and a way to plunder gold. Instead, it became, through forces Columbus inadvertently set in motion and only dimly understood, the most important voyage of its kind ever made.

Columbus signed the document: "Done on board the caravel," as he called sturdy little *Niña*, "off the Canary Islands, on the fifteenth of February, year 1493. At your service. The Admiral." He knew that he was off Santa María island in the Azores that day, rather than in the Canaries, but his habit of obscuring his location remained so ingrained that he could not help but perform this legerdemain even when reporting to his Sovereigns.

By the time the ink dried, his little ship was engulfed in yet another tempest.

On Sunday, February 10, 1493, the Admiral and his crew readied themselves for departure. Even with the help of two pilots, Sancho Ruiz and Peralonso (or Pedro Alonso) Niño, he wrote, "the Admiral found himself much off his course, finding himself much more behind"—that is, farther west—"than they." He supposed they were approaching Castile, and "when, by virtue of the grace of God, they caught sight of land, it will be known who reckoned it more accurately."

Birds glided past, leading him to believe he must be near land. Instead, on Tuesday, he experienced "high seas and tempest, and if the caravel had not been . . . very staunch and well-prepared, he would have been afraid of being lost." The day's sailing involved some of the nastiest weather Columbus encountered on the entire voyage, with lightning bolts shattering the sky. He hauled in his sheets and "proceeded most of the night under bare poles" sustaining only a "scrap of sail" into rougher seas. "The ocean made up something terrible, and the waves crossed each other, which strained the vessels."

By Thursday, they were somewhere west of the Azores, a group of islands that lay a thousand miles west of the Portuguese coast. As the gale lasted into Thursday, February 14, the fortunes of errant *Pinta* became a source of great anxiety, as Columbus related in one of the most emotional entries in his diary: "That night the wind increased and the waves were frightful, running counter to one another, and so crossed and embarrassed the ship that she couldn't make headway or get out from between them, and they broke over her." Even for an experienced sailor, few spectacles are as intimidating, or predictive of drowning, as the sight of towering waves breaking overhead, as if the turbulent sea were engulfing the ship. In response, Columbus ordered the mainsail's yardarm lowered as far as it could go without its sail being shredded or carried away by seawater roaring across the deck. When that strategy failed, and the seas became even more formidable, Columbus "began to scud"—that is, to run before the storm with practically no sail—"since there was nothing else to be done. Then the caravel *Pinta*, in which Martín Alonso [Pinzón] went, also began to scud before it, and disappeared, although all night the Admiral made flares, and the other replied, until it appeared that he could do no more from the force of the tempest, and because he found himself very far from the Admiral's course." That was Columbus's last sight of *Pinta*. Ships disappeared all the time in violent storms such as these, among surging seas and stinging rain, blown sideways between tall waves, and disappearing into a watery trench.

Oblivious to *Pinta*'s destiny, the Admiral's main concern was to survive the night. "At sunrise the wind and sea made up more, sea crossing more terribly," and proceeded with the "main course only, and low, to enable her to rise above the cross-swell, that it might not swamp her." He headed northeast by east for six exhausting hours, traversing seven and a half leagues, or about thirty miles. Columbus vowed that if they survived the ordeal, they would make a grateful pilgrimage to Santa María de Guadalupe, the renowned, inaccessible shrine in Extremadura, Spain, known as the Powerful Lady of Silence, fashioned of wood from Asia. They would "carry a candle of five pounds of wax and . . . all vow that on whomever fell the lot should fulfill the pilgrimage." For them, the ritual was a matter of life and death.

In the midst of the endless storm, Columbus, driven by piety, and possibly driven mad, said that he "ordered as many chickpeas," or garbanzo beans, "to be brought as were people in the ship, and that one [chickpea] should be marked with a knife, making a cross, and placed in a cap, well-shaken." Columbus, ever the child of destiny, went first, placing his hand in the cap, and he "drew the chickpea with the cross, and so the lot fell on him, and henceforth he regarded himself as a pilgrim and bound to go to fulfill the vow." The terrified sailors devised still more schemes to perform acts of religious devotion as a way of improving their chances of survival, their reception in the afterlife, or as distraction from their plight, which became more grave by the hour.

"After that, the Admiral and all the people made a vow that, upon reaching the first land, they would all go in their shirts in procession to make a prayer in a church that was dedicated to Our Lady. Beside the general or common vows, everyone made his special vow, because nobody expected to escape, holding themselves all for lost, owing to the terrible tempest that they were experiencing." Second-guessing himself, Columbus wished, too late, that he had stowed more provisions, more water and wine, if only to have the benefit of their weight on tiny *Niña* at this moment, but he had been distracted by his quest for the Isle of Women, where he had persuaded himself he could take on those precious items. "The remedy that he found for this necessity was, when they were able, to fill with seawater the pipes that were found empty with water and wine; and with this they supplied the need."

Columbus became convinced that "Our Lord wished him to perish." At the same time, he reminded himself of his mission and the news of his exploits that he was bringing to Ferdinand and Isabella. The more important the news became in his mind, the more fearful he became that he would not be able to deliver it, and that all his discoveries and sacrifices would be for naught, "and that every mosquito might interrupt and prevent it." He reflected on his lack of faith, and yet it had been sufficient to bring him to Spain, to win royal patronage, and to enable him to overcome adversity to reach this point, the difficulty of dealing with the sailors, and their mutiny against him. He had managed, with the Lord's help, to prevail. If only he could outlast adversity a little longer.

To leave some record of his accomplishments, he frantically grabbed "a parchment and wrote upon it all that he could of everything that he had found, earnestly requesting whoever might find it to carry it to the Sovereigns. This parchment he enclosed in a waxed cloth, very well secured, and ordered a great wooden barrel to be brought and placed it inside, without anyone knowing what it was, unless they supposed that it was some act of devotion, and so he ordered it to be cast into the sea," his version of a message in a bottle, his testament for posterity, to be washed up on the shores of history. (The barrel was never found.)

As *Niña* helplessly scudded before the wind, heaving and lurching to the northeast, his fervent prayers were not enough to bring him confidence that he would survive the night, let alone succeed in his mission, or, as he put it, his "weakness and anxiety . . . would not allow my spirit to be soothed."

And then, after sunset, "the sky began to show clear in the western quarter." The shift in the wind's direction offered a shred of hope that he might, after all, survive. "Sea somewhat high," he noted, "but somewhat abating." Several hours later, after sunrise, the crew sighted a ghostly apparition that gradually coalesced into a distant landform. Guessing correctly for once, Columbus concluded they had arrived in the vicinity of the Azores, while "the pilots and seamen found themselves already in the country of Castile."

* * *

"All this night went beating to windward to close the land," Columbus wrote on February 16, after the worst of the nightmare seemed to have passed, "which was already recognized to be an island." He tacked to the northeast, and then a bit farther north to north northeast, and at sunrise tacked southward, to reach the mysterious island, now cloaked in a "great cloudmass," and then, to what could only have been his profound relief, he "sighted another island" lying perhaps eight leagues, or fifty miles, away. This was, in all likelihood, São Miguel (St. Michael), with a stiff headwind frustrating his approach. Undeterred, Columbus laboriously tacked upwind all day until, at nightfall, "some saw a light to leeward." Perhaps it emanated from the island they had first seen—Columbus's diary is not clear on this point—and *Niña* spent the night beating to windward. At this moment, Columbus's strength gave out. He had not slept for three or four days, had been living under terrible strain, with little food, "and he was much crippled in the legs from always being exposed to cold and to water."

On Sunday evening, when the seas moderated, Columbus rallied and circumnavigated the sanctuary. *Niña* dropped anchor, and "promptly lost" the equipment while the Admiral attempted to hail someone on land. He had no choice but to raise sail and stand offshore throughout the night. In the morning, he anchored off the northern coast of the island, "and ascertained that it was Santa María, one of the Azores." He was safe, at least for the present.

After mooring securely in the harbor, and explaining how he came to be there, Columbus heard that "the people of the island said that never had they seen such a tempest as there had been these fifteen days past," and they wondered how Columbus had escaped the storm's fury. The apparently innocent question concealed suspicion. Was Columbus telling them the truth?

To impress his audience, the Admiral blurted out his marvelous discovery of the Indies. He proceeded to boast that "this navigation of his had been very exact"—far from the truth—"and that he had laid down his route well," except for exaggerating his speed and, as a result, the distance he had covered. At least his guess that he had arrived in the Azores proved correct.

To save face and avoid the appearance of accidentally washing up on Santa María, he "pretended to have gone further than he had in order to confuse the pilots and seamen who pricked off"—that is, marked with pins—"the chart, in order to remain master of that route to the Indies."

His hosts were not convinced, but they cloaked their skepticism with hospitality. The island's captain, Juan de Castañeda (or perhaps his deputy), sent messengers with refreshments to the ship. In response, "the Admiral ordered much courtesy shown to the messengers, ordering that they be given bunks to sleep in that night, because it was evening and the village was far." In the midst of these diplomatic maneuvers, Columbus recalled the vows he had made on Thursday, "when he was in the anguish of the tempest," and asked the priest of Nossa Senhora dos Anjos, Our Lady of the Angels, to say Mass. The fulfillment of this religious obligation led to a diplomatic contretemps. As the men prayed, the whole town "fell upon them and took them all prisoners."

Unaware of the outrage, Columbus impatiently awaited the return of his men. By 11:00 a.m., they still had not arrived, and he suspected they had been detained. He ordered *Niña* to weigh anchor, and sailed toward the chapel, where a company of armed horsemen dismounted and prepared to arrest him. At the same time, the island's captain "stood up in the barge and asked for safe conduct from the Admiral [Columbus]," who agreed to allow him aboard *Niña*, "and do all that he wished."

Displaying unusual patience and presence of mind after his ordeal at sea, Columbus "tried with fair words to hold him, so as to recover his people, not believing that it would break his word in giving him safe conduct, because he [the captain], having offered peace and security, had broken his word."

As the standoff turned acrimonious, Columbus demanded to know why his men had been seized, and in the midst of a pilgrimage, no less. He claimed that the captain's rude behavior would "offend the king of Portugal," whereas in Spain, the Portuguese were "received with much courtesy and entered and were safe as in Lisbon." He offered to show the official letters he carried from Ferdinand and Isabella naming him "their Admiral of the Ocean Sea and Viceroy of the Indies, which now belonged to Their Highnesses." He had the signatures, he had the seals, and to prove his point he flourished them at a safe distance. If the captain chose not to release the sailors, Columbus argued, he would sail on to Seville, where, the captain could be certain, the outrage would be reported and his people would be punished.

Santa María's captain replied that he knew nothing about the Sovereigns of Castile, was not impressed by Columbus's letters, and as far as he was concerned, Columbus should consider himself in Portugal. His manner, according to the diary, was "somewhat threatening," and Columbus speculated whether a rupture between the two nations had occurred during his voyage. The two of them, captain and Admiral, continued to posture, with Columbus at one point threatening to carry "a hundred Portuguese to Castile and depopulate that whole island." Columbus returned to his flagship without the hostages to ride out yet another storm.

The latest tempest proved powerful enough to part the ship's cables. After making repairs and filling pipes with seawater as ballast, Columbus decided to weigh anchor at the first opportunity. Soon *Niña* was headed away from Santa María and all its troubles toward St. Michael. If he could not find better anchorage—and a better reception—at the neighboring island, "he had no recourse but to flee seaward."

It seemed that he could discover a New World with ease, but he negotiated the Azores only with difficulty. He wanted only to declare his feat, but he could not find anyone who would listen. To the Portuguese inhabitants of the Azores, Columbus was more of a trespasser than an explorer. Only Ferdinand and Isabella, his sponsors, would properly appreciate and validate his accomplishments, once he freed himself from the flytrap hospitality of the Portuguese.

Thursday, February 21, found Columbus again battling rough seas and high winds as he tried without success to locate St. Michael, "owing to the mighty cloud-wrack and thick weather that the wind and sea raised." *Niña* came close to foundering. The force of the storm "amazed" him; in all his experience sailing around the Azores and the Canary Islands he had never seen anything like it, and in the Indies, he had sailed "all that winter without anchoring," or so it seemed in retrospect. (In reality, Caribbean storms had on occasion prompted him to ride at anchor until they abated.)

Sunrise failed to disclose any suggestion of his goal, St. Michael, and he decided to return to Santa María "to see if he could recover his people and the barge and the anchors and cables that he had left there."

The small humiliations resumed as soon as he anchored. A functionary balancing on the rocks overlooking the harbor warned him not to leave. Then a barge bearing "five seamen and two priests and a scribe" boarded the ship. The seamen were armed. Columbus permitted them to spend the night on board, having no other choice. In the morning, they demanded to see signs of the authority conferred on Columbus by the "Sovereigns of Castile," and a scuffle ensued. Columbus related that he broke the deadlock by persuading the intruders of his authority, and the Portuguese finally released all the pilgrims whom they had arrested.

Come Sunday, the unstable weather turned fair, and after taking on food, water, and much needed ballast, Columbus headed due east, toward Spain and the acclaim he expected. Yet the closer to home, the greater the danger he faced. Foul weather blew *Niña* off course. "It was very painful to have such a tempest when they were already at the doors of home," he confided to his diary. On the evening of March 2, "a squall blew up which split all the sails and he found himself in great peril."

As before, the beleaguered men drew lots to select a pilgrim to pray at Santa María de la Cinta, near Huelva, and once again the "the lot fell to the Admiral." There was little time for discussion, as the storm's intensity redoubled, and they found themselves blown not to Spain, as they intended, but toward the one place they did not wish to go: Lisbon.

And the storm grew still more violent.

"Last night," Columbus wrote of the events of March 4, "they experienced so terrible a tempest that they thought they were lost from the seas that boarded them from two directions, and the winds, which seemed to raise the caravel into the air; and the water from the sky, and lightning flashes in many directions." He had no time to consider the irony of his situation: he had gone all the way to the Indies and back, only to face his worst perils in European waters. Columbus's many detractors later charged that the Admiral deliberately headed toward Lisbon under pretext of fleeing the storm in pursuit of a covert agenda influenced by Portugal. On the basis of his account, and others, of the severity of the weather, his agenda consisted solely of survival.

He "made some headway, although with great peril, keeping out to sea, and so God preserved them until day," a task that Columbus said meant incurring "infinite toil and terror." Taking on water, barely navigable, guided by her exhausted crew, *Niña* approached a landmark Columbus recognized: the Rock of Sintra, a peninsula north of the Tagus River, which flows into Lisbon. He had a choice: either attempt to veer off into the storm and the near certainty of oblivion, loss of life, and the failure of his Enterprise of the Indies, or enter the river, and so he did "because he could do nothing else." He made for the fishing village of Cascais, near the mouth of the Tagus, and despite the tempest found anchorage.

The curious gathered onshore, wondering how the crew had survived the ferocious storm and offering prayers. Columbus heard from other seamen that "never had there been a winter with so great storms, and that 25 ships had been lost in Flanders," a frequent destination for ships leaving Lisbon, "and that other ships had been lying there for 4 months without being able to get out." Against this background, *Niña's* survival seemed miraculous.

Columbus's first thoughts were of King João, but there was no satisfaction in proving the disdainful Portuguese monarch wrong. Instead, the Admiral invoked Ferdinand and Isabella, explaining that they had "ordered him not to avoid entering the harbors of His Highness to ask for what was necessary, in return for pay." When the weather cleared, he would be eager to sail to Lisbon "because some ruffians, thinking he carried much gold, were planning to commit some rascality." It would require all his tact and diplomacy to persuade the Portuguese that he had not been raiding their protected interests on the Guinea coast—which Spain had promised to avoid—but was actually returning from the Indies. Either explanation would incite the wrath of King João.

All the more surprising, then, was the appearance of the "master of the great ship of the King of Portugal," riding at anchor nearby: Bartolomeu Dias. When last seen by Columbus in 1488, this courageous navigator was making his triumphal return to Lisbon after the discovery of the Cape of Good Hope. At the time, he enjoyed the great favor of the king who had refused to back Columbus's scheme to find a water route to the Indies. But four and a half years had wrought changes. No longer a captain, Dias was now second-in-command, or master, of a modest vessel in the service of the king. And Columbus, the Admiral of the Ocean Sea, had successfully completed his visionary if misunderstood mission, an accomplishment that further jeopardized his relationship with this deeply suspicious king.

Dias impudently drew alongside *Niña* "and told the Admiral to enter the gig to come and give an account to the king's factors and the captain."

No, Columbus replied, he would do no such thing, "unless by compulsion of being unable to resist armed force." Dias proposed a compromise: Columbus could elect to send his second-in-command, but stubborn Genoese that he was, he insisted he would only go if forced, and "that it was the custom of the Admirals of the sovereigns of Castile to die before they yielded themselves or their people."

Faced with this bravado, Dias relented slightly, requesting to see the letters of authorization from Ferdinand and Isabella, which Columbus had initially offered to show. This he did, and having examined them, Dias returned in the gig to his ship to explain the situation to his own captain, who, "with a great noise of drums, trumpets, and pipes, came aboard the caravel [*Niña*], spoke with the Admiral, and offered to do all he commanded."

By the next day, March 6, Columbus's exploits were the talk of Lisbon, and people regarded his triumph with awe. Of course, both they and the Admiral of the Ocean Sea were misinformed and confused about what he had accomplished. He had not reached Asia, as he would have everyone believe. Yet his actual deeds were even more impressive, and, it would later emerge, more traumatic and transformative, than his fanciful claims. Instead of establishing a new trade route, he had discovered a new world.

Nevertheless, he clinched his argument that he had journeyed to China by displaying the Indian passengers he had brought with him, persuading both himself and his public of the veracity of his claims. He reported, "So many people came from the city of Lisbon today to see him and the Indians, that it was astonishing, and they were all full of wonder, giving thanks to Our Lord."

At long last a letter came from King João II, inviting Columbus to a royal audience at a monastery. The beleaguered discoverer preferred to remain with his ship for the sake of form and for personal security, but he had no choice but to comply with the request, "to disarm suspicion." As an inducement, "The King gave orders to his factors that everything the Admiral and his people and the caravel [*Niña*] stood in need of he would supply without pay."

Columbus set out for the Monastery of the Vertudes, with rain delaying his arrival until evening. The lavish reception he received was calculated to allay his suspicions, and he proudly noted that the king "received him with much honor and showed him much favor." After the honeyed words came the hard bargaining. It was a very impressive discovery that Columbus had made, as everyone acknowledged, but in the process, he had violated the Treaty of Alcáçovas—was he not aware of that? In this agreement, made in 1479 with just this possibility in mind, Portugal exercised rights along Africa's west coast and the Cape Verde Islands, while Spain exercised hegemony over the Canary Islands. And so Columbus's discoveries belonged to King João II, not Ferdinand and Isabella, and certainly not to the Admiral, who suddenly found himself ensnared in negotiations as perilous as the tempests he had recently survived.

Columbus replied that he had never seen the treaty and knew nothing of its provisions. He deferred to the Sovereigns, whose orders to avoid Guinea he had scrupulously followed. Realizing perhaps the impossibility of verifying where Columbus had or had not gone on his voyage, and pleased that the Admiral's answer acknowledged Portugal's right, King João appeared to relent, and replied that he was sure there would be no need for arbitrators in this matter. The king tried his best to draw out Columbus about his voyage. What countries had he visited, and who were the inhabitants? Had he found gold, pearls, and other precious gems? According to Las Casas, the king inquired "always with a pleasant face, dissembling the grief that he had in his heart." Columbus boasted wildly about his accomplishments, without realizing the effect his claims had on the jealous king.

Rui da Pina, a Portuguese court historian who might have witnessed the interview, remarked that the "king blamed himself for negligence in dismissing him for want of credit and authority in regard to this discovery for which he first came to make request of him." So ran the official version. Behind the mask of humility, King João meditated on a chilling solution to the problem of the turncoat explorer. He could execute Columbus; or rather, he could let it seem that others wished him to be killed. And the deed could be carried out discreetly, with blame attributed to some lapse committed by the explorer. In the end, the king instead treated Columbus honorably before booting him out of the country.

On March 15, 1493, *Niña* entered the harbor from which she had departed on August 3, 1492, with *Pinta* following close behind, borne "by a light wind."

Columbus had completed his mission, as he understood it, and expected to be treated with the greatest respect. At last the journey was done, and a glorious future lay before him and Spain. After the years of waiting, the discovery had been accomplished quickly, in a little over seven months, with virtually no bloodshed and with no loss of life, incredibly enough—nothing except a sunken ship from which all hands had been rescued, and bruised feelings on the part of the renegade Martín Alonso Pinzón. Even the threat he posed to Columbus sputtered out when Pinzón turned up in his hometown of Palos de la Frontera, seriously ill, and died within days of his return from the sea. The cause was believed to have been syphilis, and in that case, he might have caught the disease long before he sailed with Columbus, and it had lain dormant in his nervous system for years, until it emerged on the voyage as tertiary syphilis, which would account for his defiant, irrational behavior. He was, in short, going mad, more of a danger to himself than to anyone else.

For now, Columbus savored his achievement. The new lands that he had discovered were closer to Spain and, to hear Columbus tell it, more benign than Marco Polo's version. The soil was fertile, the people nothing like the monsters he had expected to find. Only the fate of the men stationed at the fortress in Hispaniola remained unknown.

He planned to proceed to Barcelona "by sea, in which city he had news that Their Highnesses were, and thus to give them the story of his entire voyage that Our Lord had permitted him to perform." He reminisced briefly about the opposition he had faced when planning his voyage, and the "opinion of so many high personages . . . who were all against me, alleging this undertaking to be folly." Perhaps his critics, like the king of Portugal and his advisers, would see how mistaken they had been.

He had been shrewd, he had been tough, and he had been wily, but most of all, he had been spectacularly lucky. He had been wrong at least as often as he had been right, most blatantly about his destination, but he had also been nimble, capable of reversing himself when it served his purpose. His words, as recorded in his diary, were emphatic, but his strategy was flexible and opportunistic.

"Since I know that you will be pleased at the great success with which the Lord has crowned my voyage," said Columbus in the famous letter to his Sovereigns at the conclusion of his first voyage, "I write to inform you how in thirty-three days I crossed from the Canary Islands to the Indies"—in reality, an island in the Caribbean—"with the fleet which our most illustrious Sovereigns gave to me. I found very many islands with large populations and took possession of them all for Your Highnesses; this I did by proclamation and unfurled the royal standard."

His initial contacts with the inhabitants of the New World were tentative and respectful, even heartening, he claimed. "I hoped to win them to the love and service of Your Highnesses and of the whole Spanish nation," he wrote. "They have no religion, and are not idolaters; but all believe that power and goodness dwell in the sky and they are firmly convinced that I have come from the sky with these ships and people. . . . This is not because they are stupid—far from it, they are men of great intelligence, for they give a marvelously good account of everything—but because they have never before seen men clothed or ships like these."

Still convinced he had reached India, Columbus tailored his understanding of another major discovery, the island of Cuba, to suit his purposes. At first, he accurately labeled it as an island in his journal; later, when he realized he was bound to demonstrate to Ferdinand and Isabella that he had reached the East, he recast it as "the mainland," that is, China, and its inhabitants as subjects of the Grand Khan. Ferdinand and Isabella appointed Columbus as viceroy of these lands without realizing they were creating a monarch potentially more powerful than any in Europe.

PART TWO

Conquest

CHAPTER 5

River of Blood

To Columbus, one question took precedence on his return: the fate of the thirty-nine men left behind at La Navidad. He had placed their lives, and Spain's honor, at risk. And he would have to return to "India" to rescue them, or to discover what befell these hostages to his ambition.

His first voyage had been a qualified success. That he returned with his fleet and its men alive, reasonably healthy, and intact was itself miraculous. He contended that his accomplishment was divinely inspired. Exactly what he had discovered or explored was subject to human interpretation and so less certain. He claimed the dozens of islands he had visited comprised a western extension of India, or China; that the figure of the Grand Khan and the trading possibilities that he offered lurked somewhere to the north and west of the turquoise waters over which his tiny fleet had sailed. He offered his journal as evidence, bolstered by the testimony of the others who had accompanied him, in the hope of claiming the riches and titles and glory to which he believed he was entitled, even divinely ordained, to have. Carefully embellished and edited to meet Ferdinand and Isabella's expectations and his contractual obligations to them, that journal purported to demonstrate that he had accomplished and even exceeded his mission to the point of establishing a Spanish outpost in the islands he had discovered on his way to India. But the lives of thirty-nine Spaniards stationed there hung in the balance. He had created a situation in which he would play the champion, or, if matters went awry, the scapegoat.

The little fort served as the kernel of a vision of empire on which Columbus had been meditating ever since his first voyage, and by now the plan had become firmly established in his mind. He envisioned two thousand colonists settling Hispaniola. They would build "three or four towns"; collect gold, which would be closely guarded; and establish churches with "abbots or friars to administer the sacraments, perform divine worship, and to convert the Indians." He explained his plans to regulate shipping, handle cargo, and protect valuable exports, especially gold, in grinding detail to satisfy Spanish bureaucrats who administered the kingdom's day-to-day operations. He displayed an impressive familiarity with the minutiae of his administrative agenda, which belied the difficulty of carrying it out. Concerning navigation, of which he possessed a singular mastery, he had almost nothing to say.

Between the lines of his communiqué, Columbus urged Ferdinand and Isabella to act quickly, before the Portuguese or another rival outfoxed Spain. Rather than standing as an unprecedented feat of navigation, the voyage would become the first of many to assemble the greatest, the wealthiest, and the largest commercial empire in the world. Or so Columbus hoped. To make his case, the document simplified the complex reality of the "Indies." He omitted references to the menace posed by the Caribs, the difficulty of replicating his feat of navigation, the vagaries of weather, and, of course, the stupendous misunderstanding of the location of his discoveries. He was selective to the point of being deceptive, but there was no mistaking his meaning. Spain would acquire a new empire and he would administer it, becoming wealthy in the process by founding a dynasty. The scheme had the virtue of familiarity; it echoed the Spanish—and for that matter, the Portuguese—approach to exploring and colonizing the African coast and the exotic islands to the south and west of the Iberian Peninsula, Madeira and Gomera and Cape Verde—not quite substantial enough for an empire, but a sphere of influence that might grow into one. Implementing Columbus's plan meant pushing the boundaries of empire thousands of miles to the west.

Pope Alexander VI closely followed Columbus's discoveries, recognizing that they could mightily increase the reach of the Church of Rome and his personal power. But it was crucial that he divide the spoils among the competing states that would administer and exploit their resources. Acting as a mediator, Alexander issued four bulls—formal proclamations—dividing the newly discovered lands and their riches between the leading contenders, Spain and Portugal, who were allies in matters of faith but rivals in matters of politics and trade. (Italy, which supplied much of the manpower for exploration, ranked a distant third behind them.) The bulls were based on the assumption that Christian nations could, by divine right, claim title to newly discovered non-Christian lands and their peoples.

In each bull, he gave to Spain the newly discovered "Indies" (the pope, like all of Europe, was mistaken about the location of Columbus's tantalizing finds), and it was assumed that his Spanish origins influenced his decision. But his effort at clarification led to confusion in April 1493 when he established a line of demarcation that extended from the North Pole to the South "one hundred leagues toward the west and south from any of the islands commonly known as the Azores and Cape Verdes." Anything west of the line—that is, everything that mattered—was Spain's, and if Columbus was able to complete another voyage, partly his as well.

Columbus's son Ferdinand later explained, "As the Catholic Sovereigns knew that the Admiral had been the prime cause of the favors and grants made to them by the pope, and that the Admiral's voyage and discovery had given them title and possession of all the lands, they resolved to reward him well."

On May 20, 1493, they appointed him captain general of a second voyage of discovery, and eight days after that, in an elaborate, finely honed document issued in Barcelona, they conferred rights and privileges on him, and gave him the title "Viceroy and Admiral of the Ocean Sea and the Indies," or "Admiral of the Ocean Sea," as he became known. By then, Columbus was inundated with formal orders for his second voyage with an urgency that seems all the more remarkable given the years of delay and evasion that preceded his first voyage.

Although the document conferred extraordinary powers on Columbus, it reflected the regal self-aggrandizement of Ferdinand and Isabella, determined to shape the stubborn mariner into an instrument of their empire and their will. They treated him as both their Admiral and their vassal, revealing themselves as traditional medieval sovereigns despite the changes swirling about them. The document was studded with entitlements for the newly created Admiral of the Ocean Sea, who was formally empowered to call himself "Don Christopher Columbus," as would his sons and successors, and he was now admiral, viceroy, and governor of the island and mainlands "which you may discover and acquire," as would his sons and

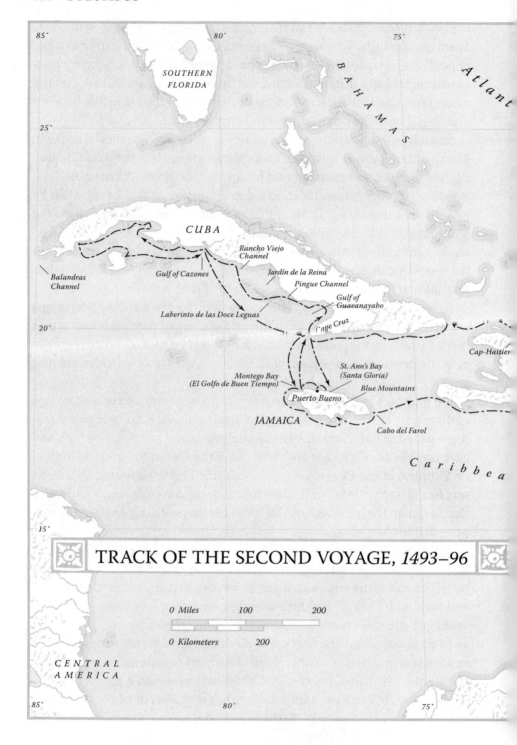

TRACK OF THE SECOND VOYAGE, *1493–96*

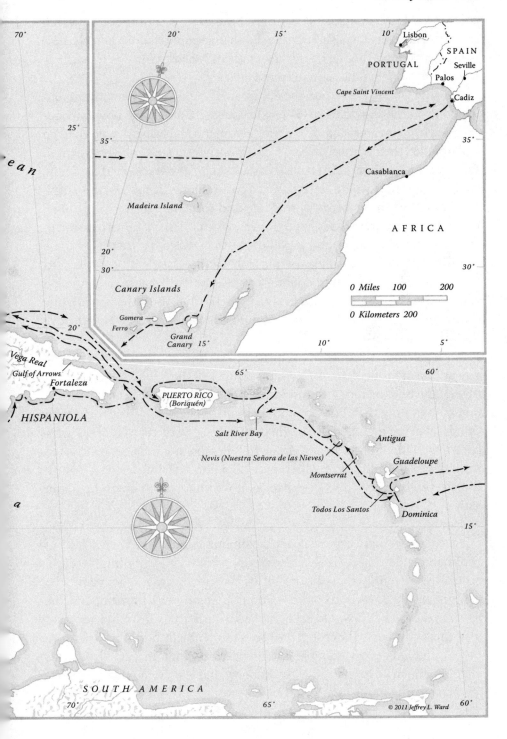

© 2011 Jeffrey L. Ward

successors. That hereditary status meant he could "hear and determine all the suits and causes, civil and criminal," that he could "punish and chastise delinquents," and that he could "levy fees and salaries." It was a long way from being a merchant seaman from Genoa.

On May 29, 1493, the Catholic Sovereigns heaped more honors and obligations on the shoulders of "Don Christopher Columbus," now fully authorized to claim and acquire lands for Ferdinand and Isabella, who charged and directed their admiral, viceroy, and governor to "strive and endeavor to win over the inhabitants" of the islands and mainland he claimed for Spain, which meant they would "be converted to our Holy Catholic Faith." To assist Columbus in his primary mission, and to make certain it was done properly, the Sovereigns assigned a priest, Fray Buil (sometimes referred to as Father Boyle), and several assistants to the voyage "to see that they be carefully taught the principles of our Holy Faith." The identity of this controversial cleric has been in doubt ever since, partly because of confusion surrounding his name. He was likely a Catalan who joined the Benedictine order. Although Columbus was profoundly religious, there was little love lost between the two.

For the record, the Sovereigns insisted that "the Admiral shall, after the safe arrival of his fleet there, force and compel all those who sail therein . . . to treat the Indians very well and lovingly and abstain from doing them any injury." Not only that, but Columbus "shall graciously present them with things from the merchandise of Their Highnesses which he is carrying for barter, and honor them much." In fact, if members of the fleet mistreated the Indians "in any manner whatsoever," Columbus was ordered to "punish them severely." The order, unequivocal in writing, proved anything but in action.

To accomplish these exalted goals, Columbus assembled a fleet worthy of Ferdinand and Isabella. This time, nothing was too good for him, by royal order. This carefully thought-out set of instructions marked a giant step forward in the Sovereigns' appreciation of Columbus's mission, and the rewards they hoped it would bring for everyone in this world, and, for good measure, in the next. The cost of the fleet was nominally borne by the crown. In fact, the Duke of Medina Sidonia lent five million maravedís for this purpose, much of it secured with property and jewelry confiscated from Jews during the Inquisition.

The Admiral's partners in the operational side of the voyage were well known to the crown: Juan de Soria, representing the royal auditors, and Don Juan Rodríguez de Fonseca, representing the ultimate authority, the church, first as the archdeacon of Seville and subsequently as bishop of Burgos. At various times he antagonized and supervised Columbus's efforts to equip the fleet; nevertheless, the Admiral willed himself to consider Fonseca an ally in the cause of conquest.

A new realism informed these instructions. There was no more talk of trading with the Grand Khan, although the possibility that he existed hovered over the voyage. Columbus still tried to reconcile the lands and people he had encountered with those described in Marco Polo's flamboyant travelogue. In reality, the Venetian had died in 1324, and the Mongol empire had rapidly disintegrated.

Columbus's orders also directed him to construct a "customs house for the storage of all the merchandise of Their Highnesses." This plan borrowed heavily from the Portuguese model and made the venture's commercial aspect explicit. Almost as an afterthought, Ferdinand and Isabella permitted Columbus to explore as he saw fit: "If the Admiral, after reaching the Islands, believes it would be well to send some vessels and people to certain parts to discover what has not hitherto been discovered, or for the sake of barter . . . all the captains and mariners whom he may so command are required to carry out and fulfill his orders." Even here, trade was the impetus, and as an incentive the Sovereigns awarded Columbus a healthy share of the proceeds: "The Admiral should have one eighth part of whatever may be acquired from whatever gold and other things there may be on the Islands and Mainland."

Never was there a more exalted moment in his career than this. He had vast resources and royal prestige at his disposal, beginning with the seventeen ships at his command. Three were classed simply as *naos*, or ships. Columbus named the flagship *Santa María*, after the durable vessel he had commanded during his comparatively modest first voyage, and called her by the affectionate nickname *Maríagalante*. She was owned by Antonio de Torres, the brother of the governess of Prince Don Juan. The connection to the Catholic Sovereigns was impressive and implied their approval. *Colina* and *Gallega* were similarly substantial craft. Of the remaining fourteen ships, twelve were light, maneuverable caravels. Sharp-eyed observers recognized *Santa Clara* as *Niña* of the first voyage, under a new name. Several of the caravels were square-rigged, that is, they carried conventional square rigging on the mainmast and the foremast, and lateen rigging on the miz-zen, aft of the mainmast. Learning from the mistakes of the first voyage, Columbus insisted that at least some of his new fleet have a shallow draft to explore rivers and shoals without running aground.

The ships, according to his son Ferdinand, came "well-stocked with pro-visions and carrying all the things and persons needed to settle those lands, including artisans of all kinds, laborers, and peasants to work the land." When he was preparing for his first voyage, Columbus had to scrape for every crew member he could find, and sailed shorthanded, but this time "so many offered themselves that it was necessary to restrict the number of those who might go," even though the fleet was nearly six times larger than his earlier convoy. The ships carried horses—unknown in the Caribbean—and other beasts of burden that could be useful in settling Hispaniola. His company of over a thousand gentlemen, commoners, and criminals comprised a microcosm of Spain waiting and, for once, eager to be trans-ported to a New World and its riches under the leadership of Christopher Columbus.

Many reprised their roles on the first voyage, a circumstance that spoke well of Columbus's reputation as a navigator and the promise of easy riches. There were the Genoese; a few Basques, born to the sea; and still others from the Spanish towns of Palos, Huelva, and Moguer, where the sailors resided between voyages. The influential Pinzón family was conspicuously absent from the roster. Many in Spain believed their claim that they were respon-sible for whatever success Columbus had enjoyed on his first voyage. The Admiral would be on his own this time, with storms and tides mercilessly exposing his shortcomings, and no Pinzóns to come to his rescue.

His captains included bureaucrats and political leaders. Alonso Sánchez de Carvajal, for example, was the mayor of Baeza rather than an experienced mariner. Another participant, Pedro de Las Casas, was the father of Bar-tolomé de Las Casas, who had observed Columbus's return to Seville after the first voyage. (It is believed that Bartolomé's grandfather, Diego Calderón, was Jewish and had been burned at the stake in Seville in 1491.) Three of Bartolomé de Las Casas's uncles were also on board, ensuring strong famil-ial ties to Columbus.

Although the fleet's physician, Diego Alvarez Chanca, had treated Queen Isabella, physicians in Spain were rarely revered, but he enjoyed Colum-bus's trust and was considered one of the better-qualified medical practitioners in the land. Of all those on board the ships with Columbus, Chanca was among the best educated. If not quite brilliant, he showed himself to be reasonably thoughtful and resourceful in the journal of the voyage that he maintained.

Two other members of the fleet's roster went on to win renown. The chart maker, Juan de la Cosa, aboard *Maríagalante,* had sailed on the first voyage as the owner and master of *Santa María,* Columbus's flagship, and he would sail with Columbus on the third voyage; after that, he went to sea with Columbus's sometime rival Amerigo Vespucci. Juan de la Cosa fashioned the celebrated Mappa Mundi of 1500, considered the first European cartographic representation of the New World, and the sole surviving map of Columbus' voyages made by a participant. (His map is on display at the Museo Naval in Madrid.)

Then there was the charming and ambitious soldier of fortune, Juan Ponce de León, who later rose to become the first governor of Puerto Rico, by order of the Spanish government. Only eleven years after participating as a gentleman passenger on the second voyage, he financed his own expedition, a feat that not even Columbus at the height of his influence managed to accomplish. On April 2, 1513, Ponce de León would encounter a landmass he took to be an island. He called it La Florida because of its luxuriant foliage, and because it was Eastertide, observed in Spain as Pascua Florida, Festival of Flowers. He had landed somewhere in North America, and that alone was a significant accomplishment. Columbus, in all his voyaging, never touched, and never even knew, that a North American landmass existed.

While Columbus prospered, King João II of Portugal feverishly tried to reverse the papal decree, which threatened to diminish or even extinguish the Lusitanian empire. A unified Spain could abide without the resources of an overseas empire, but tiny, underpopulated Portugal required its colonies' assets for survival. After enduring threats of naval action and pleas for Iberian cooperation for a year, João II cajoled Ferdinand and Isabella to send representatives to a summit conference in Tordesillas, Spain, on June 7, 1494, where a treaty between the two sovereign powers shifted the line of demarcation to 370 leagues west of the Cape Verde Islands, although this refinement opened the door to further confusion. Where was the line itself—in the middle of the islands, at the western edge? No one could say with certainty. Moreover, the size of the globe was badly misunderstood, so even if everyone came to an agreement on the line's theoretical location, no one could actually find this geographical unicorn.

What seemed merely a technical victory for Portugal turned out to be critical. The alteration meant that ships flying the flag were permitted to ply trade routes along the west coast of Africa. Still more important and less appreciated, the redrawn line of demarcation gave to Portugal the immense, fertile, and largely unexplored land of Brazil.

But for now, the new order favored Spain's emergent empire. It was said that Columbus had personally influenced the pope's thinking, and he was duty-bound to follow up on it. He was already forty-three, an advanced age for a mariner, and he would do well to take action while he still enjoyed royal favor and was strong enough to endure a transatlantic crossing. As his father's example demonstrated, political disenfranchisement was only a revolution away.

A festive atmosphere reigned on the day of departure, September 25, 1493, in the port of Cadiz. "The parting embraces were exchanged, the ships were decked out with flags, while streamers wound about the rigging and the colors of the sovereigns adorned the stern of every ship," recalled one of the passengers, Guillermo Coma, a "nobleman of Spain." All the while, musicians, "playing the flute and the lyre, dumbfounded the very nereids, sea-nymphs, and sirens with their mellifluous strains. The shores rang with the blare of trumpets and the blast of horns, and the bottom of the sea re-echoed to the roar of cannon."

A fresh breeze sped the seventeen ships toward their destination. "On September 28, being one hundred leagues from Spain, many small land birds, turtledoves, and other kinds of small birds came to the Admiral's ship; they appeared to be flying to winter in Africa." They had their fixed route, to the south, and Columbus had his, to the south and east. Holding on his course, on Wednesday, October 2, he reached Grand Canary, a verdant landmass rising from the sea. He set his anchors, but not for long. By midnight, he was sailing for Gomera, and reached the small, lush island three days later.

Gomera had been settled since Roman times, and the island's isolated inhabitants communicated with one another by means of a peculiar whistled language of rising and falling pitches known as Silbo Gomero. Columbus had no time to admire the curious tongue. His mission consumed his attention, as he obtained necessary supplies, especially animals. The transatlantic menagerie included pigs and sows, sheep and goats, twenty-four stallions, ten mares, and three mules. Unable to survive the long weeks at sea in the ships' fetid holds, the animals occupied privileged space on the bridges. Arrayed against the sky, heads bobbing, they imparted a resemblance to that biblical ship, Noah's Ark.

There was one other distraction on the island of Gomera: Doña Beatriz de Bobadilla. Or, as she was known in the Canaries, "Bobadilla the huntress, a woman of rare distinction."

On the outward-bound leg of his first voyage, Columbus had paused at San Sebastián, Gomera, from September 3 through 6, 1492, long enough for a romantic encounter with the island's ruler, Beatriz de Bobadilla. A thirty-year-old femme fatale, she claimed noble lineage from Castile, and served Queen Isabella as a seventeen-year-old maid of honor; in this role she fell under the spell of King Ferdinand. (Despite his professed loyalty to his wife, Ferdinand carried on a series of clandestine liaisons.)

At about this time, the court was visited by Hernán de Peraza, who had the unpleasant task of accounting for the death of a commander associated with him. He received a pardon from Queen Isabella in exchange for vowing to conquer Grand Canary island in the name of Spain. And there was one other condition, a "less onerous penance," as it is traditionally described: to marry young Beatriz de Bobadilla, and thereby distance her from Ferdinand. At one stroke Isabella won Peraza's loyalty and removed the younger and more attractive rival for her husband's affections. Beatriz de Bobadilla and Hernán de Peraza quickly wed and returned to Gomera, where her husband was killed by the indigenous people there, known as Guanches, to protest his tyrannical rule.

As a widow, Beatriz de Peraza proved to be no less cruel. She lured knights and local figures to her castle. Some survived their encounters with her, and others did not. One of her visitors, it was said, spread indiscreet rumors about the *viuda*'s scandalous behavior. She invited him to the castle, where they chatted a bit, and then summoned her servants, who arrested her visitor. He admitted his misdeeds and apologized, to no avail. She ordered her servants to place a noose around his neck and hang him from a tower beam. She calmly watched him in his death throes, and let the body hang from a palm tree, where it warned others who would gossip about Doña Beatriz.

Despite the local uproar over her behavior, she remarried, and soon found herself embroiled in a territorial dispute with a political rival, Fernán Muñoz, whom she also ordered to be hanged. She eventually ended her life by poison.

Those terrible events lay several years in the future. Now the huntress wanted Columbus, at the beginning of his second voyage, to stay with her on Gomera. Columbus dallied, and did his best to impress her. One of his gossipy friends, Michele de Cuneo of Savona, who had come along on the voyage, rolled his eyes at the number of "festivities, salvoes, and salutes we performed in that place . . . all for the sake of the lady of the place, for whom, in a former time, our Admiral had been smitten with love." One account insists that she wished him to remain there permanently as her husband, and to refrain from sailing and exploring. This he was unwilling to do, for her or for anyone else.

On Monday, October 7, 1494, having settled his affairs and accounts on Gomera, Columbus and his fleet of seventeen ships shaped a course for the Indies.

At departure, Columbus gave sealed orders to the captain of each ship, not to be opened unless weather forced a change of course. He insisted on secrecy because he did not want others, especially the Portuguese, to be privy to his route.

By Thursday, October 24, 1494, he had run more than four hundred leagues west, concerned that he had not encountered seaweed, although by this point in his first voyage he had seen quantities. Then, "to the surprise of all," a swallow appeared that day and for two days thereafter. The next day, "[t]he waves rolled high, darkness prevailed everywhere, and black night covered the sea, except where lightning flashed and the thunder echoed. There is nothing more perilous than a shipwreck under these circumstances," Guillermo Coma recalled. The rain and wind blasted the ships with such force that "the yards snapped, the sails were torn to shreds, and the ropes parted. The planks creaked and the gangways were awash, while some [ships] found themselves hanging on the crest of the waves and others saw the waters spread apart and lay bare the floor of the sea." The vessels threatened to collide like toys in a pond.

Amid the turmoil, St. Elmo's fire appeared in their midst. Named for St. Erasmus of Formiae, or St. Elmo, the patron saint of Mediterranean sailors, St. Elmo's fire displays glowing blue or violet air that has been ionized, or electrified, by a thunderstorm, often accompanied by buzzing or hissing. Superstitious sailors, dependent on omens to guide their lives at sea, regarded St. Elmo's fire as a sign of divine favor.

November 2 found Columbus studying the skies, observing "dark, threatening clouds ahead, which convinced him that land was near." He lowered sail, kept watch, and by daybreak on November 3 was rewarded with the sight of a mountainous island called Charis by its isolated inhabitants since time immemorial. No more. Having arrived on a Sunday, he christened it Dominica, as if converting the island itself.

Word of the landfall spread from one ship to another quickly.

¡Albricias!

¡Que tenemos tierra!

The reward! We have land!

He spotted another island, and another, four in all, now known as the Leeward Islands—the northernmost islands of the Lesser Antilles, located at the confluence of the Atlantic Ocean and the Caribbean Sea. ("Leeward" refers to the prevailing winds in the region; the islands are downwind, or leeward, of the Windward Islands, situated to meet the trade winds. The Leeward Islands include the U.S. and British Virgin Islands, Nevis, Saint Kitts, Saint-Barthélemy, Antigua, and Guadeloupe.) The miraculous appearance of these isles cheered all the men, who appeared on deck to intone prayers and hymns of gratitude and relief. As they did, the animals they carried with them, the chickens, the roosters, and especially the horses, raised an excited cacophony.

Columbus had successfully completed his second outbound transatlantic crossing, this time with seventeen ships, all of them avoiding serious accidents, over a distance of eight hundred leagues—about 2,400 miles—from the island of Gomera, in just twenty days. Relying on his judgment, instincts, and favorable winds, he had hit upon the optimal route between Gomera and the Leeward Islands, and demonstrated he could lead a transatlantic crossing without the Pinzón brothers; in fact, he surpassed them at this game. Of course, he was nowhere near his previous landfalls in the Indies, particularly the men stranded at La Navidad. Nevertheless, his men were safe, and the second voyage was off to an auspicious start.

He attempted to moor at Dominica's eastern shore, but found no anchorage. "The sea was heavy and a storm and mist were approaching," he later explained to Ferdinand and Isabella. Trouble was just starting. "I turned back toward the fleet that was quite scattered and brought them all together. Then I dispatched the best equipped caravel to the point in the north," but he ignored her progress. "I was preoccupied because of the bad weather that was raging." Reefing sail and summoning the other ships, he "made for another island ten leagues distant from Dominica." Columbus swallowed his disappointment without realizing he had just been spared encountering cannibals said to be dwelling there. In the years to come, so the story goes, Europeans who fetched up on this island had a rough time of it—that is, until the day the cannibals became so ill after devouring a friar that they avoided anyone dressed as a cleric. For that reason, when Spanish ships from across the Atlantic had no choice but to forage on Dominica for food or water, they assigned a friar, or a sailor who dressed as one, to the task.

Unable to secure anchorage, Columbus ordered his fleet to a nearby island; the predatory Caribs called it Aichi, and the Taínos, their prey, knew it as Touloukaera. Heedless of the island's contentious history, he christened this inviting speck of land Marie Galante, after his flagship. He dropped anchor, ventured ashore, and, in the words of his son, "with suitable solemnities renewed possession that in the name of the Catholic Sovereigns he had taken of all the islands and mainland of the Indies on his first voyage." More powerful than ever, the Admiral of the Ocean Sea had returned to his demesne.

The expedition's physician, Diego Alvarez Chanca, wrote of the landfall with wonder: "On this island there were woods so dense that it was amazing to look at them and especially stupefying were the many species of trees unknown to everyone—some with fruits, others with flowers, and all was green," while the trees in Spain showed only bare gray branches at this time of year. Here, the very air seemed to tremble with magic. "We found a tree whose leaves had the most pleasant clove scent I ever before smelled," he marveled. Tempted, several crew members tasted the unfamiliar fruit. Instantly, "their faces swelled up and they developed such a strong burning and pain to appear seized with rabies, which could not be cured by any means of cold things." Two hours later, the visitors from Spain, tongues afire, departed in their ships.

Just nine leagues to the north, the fleet arrived at a spectacularly lofty island. "This island," Columbus wrote, "is shaped like the point of a diamond, so high that it is a marvel, and from its summit gushes out a tremendous spring that scatters water on every side of the mountain; from where I stood other streams were flowing in on the other side, one of them so big its sharp, high drop made it resemble water gushing out of a barrel, all white, and we could not believe it was water and not a vein of white rock." The sailors wagered: rock or water? When they dropped anchor, they had their answer: it was water, on an island filled with abundant streams. "Upon reaching the island I named it Santa María de Guadalupe," he wrote, referring to a monastery in Santa María de Guadalupe de Extremadura, Spain. It was November 14.

The wind suddenly shifted, bringing bouts of dense mist and torrential rain. Columbus spent a strenuous day battling high winds and heavy seas. When the weather lifted slightly, he produced his spyglass and observed people barely visible through a clearing in the trees. He gave the order to drop anchor, but the panicky island dwellers fled well before the Spaniards could make contact with them. "I reached the north side," Columbus wrote, "where most of the population lives, and I went in very close to land and anchored the whole fleet."

Columbus sent a captain ashore, where he "found a good deal of unspun cotton, yarn, and edible provisions," in Chanca's words. But where were the people?

"Our men," Ferdinand wrote, "found only some children, in whose hands they put hawk's bells in order to reassure the parents when they returned." The Spaniards inspected the structures, and noted "geese resembling our own" and unearthly parrots as large as roosters bristling with feathers of brilliant vermilion, azure, and white. Emboldened, they sampled a fruit similar to melon but sweeter in taste and smell. They noted bows and arrows, hammocks, and took care to restrain themselves from removing anything from the abandoned hamlet so that "the Indians might have more trust in the Christians."

On closer inspection, the peaceful domestic scene turned into a nightmare. "In their houses," Columbus wrote, "I found hanging baskets and great arches of human bones as well as heads hanging up in every house." He was startled to come across "a large piece from the stern of a Spanish ship; I believe it was from the one I left at La Navidad last year." An unnerving silence enveloped the explorers. They assumed they were being watched, but by whom?

"As for the people," Columbus wrote to his Sovereigns, "few were taken and few seen; all of them fled into the countryside, and because the trees were thick could not be captured except for some women, which I am sending to Your Highnesses." They were refugees, victims of brutality and cannibalism. "In my opinion, they were taken as slaves or concubines." By means of gestures they indicated that "their husbands had been eaten and that other women had had their sons and brothers eaten, and that they themselves had been forced to eat them." There was more, sadly. "I also found some boys who had been brought there, and each of them had had his penis cut off." At first, Columbus thought they had been castrated "out of jealousy for their women," but, he learned, "they follow that practice to fatten them up, like capons in Castile, so they can be eaten for feasts; women they never kill."

Had the men at La Navidad met with the same end as the horrifying human remains in the Indians' dwellings indicated? Had Columbus allowed them to be sacrificed in this manner? Stricken with guilt and panic, he intended to go from one island to the next, destroying every canoe he encountered as retribution, "but the desire to aid those whom I had left behind here did not allow time for searches, nor did I have peace of mind."

His exploration of Guadeloupe revealed a string of abandoned villages, but in one hamlet his men came across an "abandoned one-year-old baby who remained alone for six days in this hut." Each day his men passed by the hut, "and they always found the little one next to a bundle of arrows, and he used to go to a nearby river to drink and then return to his hut, and he was always cheerful and content." Consumed by the idea of this small child alone in the wilderness, Columbus intervened, pledging the boy "to God and fortune," adding, "so I had him entrusted to a woman who had come here from Castile." References to this woman and others like her are too skimpy to convey an idea of what role, if any, they played. In this instance, the abandoned Indian child flourished under the care of his nursemaid. "Now he is so well behaved," Columbus boasted to Ferdinand and Isabella, "and he speaks and understands our tongue very well, and that is beautiful." He would send him to Spain forthwith, "but I am afraid he might die, being so young."

Columbus, like other explorers of his day, considered his routes and discoveries trade secrets for which he daily risked his life, and he jealously guarded them from opportunists and rivals. Meanwhile, his trusted chart maker, Juan de la Cosa, amassed data for an official guide to the newly discovered archipelago, but it has not survived, and his famous map dating from the year 1500 contains little detail concerning this region. At some point during the second voyage, he gathered together "drawings of all the islands discovered so far along with those from last year, all of them on a map I made with no small labor," but even if these charts had survived, they might have been of limited value.

Some names chosen by Columbus at this point in his voyage have endured, in abbreviated form, to offer clues to his whereabouts. Santa María de Montserrate, named for a monastery near Barcelona, became Montserrat; Santa María de la Antigua, named for the celebrated Virgin in the Seville Cathedral, before which Columbus is believed to have prayed, became Antigua. But Columbus's San Martín surrendered its name to an island lying to the northwest; afterward, it was known as Nuestra Señora de las Nieves, Our Lady of the Snows. The evocative designation referred to a miracle attributed to the Virgin Mary rather than to actual snow on the island, of which there was none.

As he named these islands, Columbus led his fleet through a world that seemed newly formed each day, mountains emerging from the darkness at dawn, reaching toward stands of cumulus at midday, and receding into the dusk before disappearing into the star-pricked night. Sailing east in search of India, gliding over the quicksilver surface of the sea flashing from gray to cobalt to indigo, the ships seemed to be playing hide-and-seek, not just with islands and currents but with reality itself.

In the morning the Admiral dispatched two small boats to capture an Indian to point the way to Hispaniola and its fort, imperiled La Navidad. The boats returned with two boys, who explained they came from Boriquén, or Puerto Rico, and had been kidnapped by the Caribs. On another sortie, the boats retrieved six women seeking refuge from the Caribs aboard the Spanish ships. Columbus refused, gave them hawk's bells and other small gifts, and sent them back to the island, where the Caribs seized the women and boldly pilfered the trinkets in full sight of the Spaniards.

When the boats returned a third time to take on wood and water, the women pleaded with the visitors for asylum. "Being kindly received and generously plied with food, they thought the gods had come to their aid," Guillermo Coma reported. The women locked their legs around the masts and pleaded to remain rather than be returned to the Caribs, "like sheep to the slaughter."

The grateful women divulged all they knew of the islands in the area, and secretly pointed out Caribs to the Spanish. The Caribs would impregnate women and devour their offspring. Male victims fared no better. If captured alive, they were immediately slaughtered and eaten. Chanca wrote that the Caribs "claim human flesh is so exquisite that a similar delicacy does not exist in all the world." A pile of bare human bones testified to their predilection: "All that could be gnawed on, had been gnawed on, and all that was left, was what could not be eaten, because it was inedible." Chanca reeled at the sight and smell of a "human neck . . . boiling in a pot." Worse, "Young boys once captured have their members cut off and are kept as servants till adulthood, at which time, when the Caribs want to celebrate, they kill and eat them." To demonstrate this last point, however extreme, three Indian boys who had escaped the Caribs and sought refuge among the Spanish "had been castrated."

As Columbus prepared to sail for the island of Hispaniola, he learned that a company of nine men—eight soldiers and their captain—had gone ashore and had yet to return. No one aboard the ships knew what had become of them. Thick undergrowth concealed their location. Caught between abandoning part of his crew and the need to reach La Navidad, Columbus dispatched a rescue party armed with arquebuses, whose deafening blast, it was hoped, would lead the lost men to safety. But after a week of waiting, "we had by then considered them eaten by the natives," Chanca confessed.

During the delay, Columbus, seemingly unafraid of the Caribs, ordered his men ashore to wash their clothes and to procure still more wood and water. Later, he sent a company of forty men under the command of a spirited young captain, Alonso de Ojeda, "to search for the strays and learn the secrets of the country." They found no lost crew members, or their bones, but they did note an abundance of maize, aloe, cotton, ginger, and fowl resembling falcons, herons, crows, pigeons, partridges, geese, nightingales, and twenty-six rivers on this bedeviled isle. "Several times we went ashore, exploring all dwellings and villages that lay along the coast," Chanca revealed, "where we found quite a few human bones and skulls hanging inside the houses and used as containers to hold things." Despite these stark displays, "these people seemed to us more civilized than those living on other islands we had seen." Their straw huts were sturdier; they had more yarn and cotton stored, so much "that they have nothing to envy of those from our country."

More testimony about the voyage came from the pen of Peter Martyr d'Anghiera, a chronicler "tied in close friendship," in his words, to Columbus. Peter Martyr, as he is usually known, was an Italian in residence at the Spanish court. He had originally met the explorer in April 1493, at the conclusion of the first voyage. A month later, in a state of excitement, Martyr dashed off a note to a friend. "There returned from the western antipodes"—that is, India—"a certain Christophorus Colonus of Genoa who had with difficulty obtained from my Sovereigns three ships [to visit] this province, for they considered what he said fabulous; he has returned and brought proofs of many precious things, especially of gold, which these regions naturally produce."

Among the first to recognize the importance of Columbus's discoveries, Peter Martyr related the explorer's latest findings to members of the highest echelons of the church. "I chose these accounts from the originals of Admiral Columbus himself," he said, and went on to explain to Cardinal Ascanio Sforza the ingenious construction of Indian homes and their furnishings: "First, they draw the circumference of the house with logs of very tall trees, set in the ground like piles; then shorter beams are placed inside to prevent the taller ones from falling in; finally they place the ends of the taller posts much like a military tent, thus all the houses have pointed roofs. Next, interwoven leaves from palm trees and some other similar trees are used to protect them very ingeniously from the rain. Across from the short planks and the inside posts are strung cotton ropes or certain twisted roots similar to esparto"—a tough fiber prevalent in southern Spain—"on top of which they lay cotton blankets. Since the island spontaneously produces cotton, they make use either of suspended beds made of raw cotton . . . or heaps of leaves. The courtyard surrounded by these ordinary dwellings is used for gathering and play."

The courtyard, or *batey*, as the Indians called it, served as the arena for games. Ten or twenty athletes clustered at opposite ends of the *batey*, where they served and passed a ball from one player to another. Men and women competed separately. Indian rules prevented athletes from guiding the ball with their hands or feet, so they bounced it off their bodies, taking care to keep it within bounds. During these contests, ordinary spectators sat on the ground, the Indian ruling caste on benches or stools. The raucous games went on day after day, with caciques as well as the players themselves betting on the outcome. Often the teams represented chiefdoms, and took on a political slant, coinciding with significant Indian civic events.

The Spanish visitors had never seen anything like these strenuous games. Nor had they seen an elastic ball, rubber, or rubber plants. From these innocent, spontaneous encounters between cultures, the first traces of an American character began to form, although it went unacknowledged at a time when slaves and spices and gold led the agenda, along with not-so-innocent sexual encounters.

Nor had Columbus's men seen anything like the Indians' fantastic religious rites. The same courtyard where ball games were played served as the setting for elaborate Taíno ceremonies to honor local deities; elaborate observances of marriage and death, and battles; and reenactments of the deeds of their forefathers, all with hypnotic musical accompaniment. On the day of an observance, the pulse-quickening rhythms of Taíno drums and flutes reverberated throughout the public courtyard and the forest beyond. The most conspicuous instrument that Columbus and his men probably heard was the *mayohuacán*, or *maguey*, a drum carved from a substantial tree trunk, with an oval slit—or a slit in the shape of an H—on the top. The design produced a deep, powerful resonance that could be heard for miles around as a drummer used one or two sticks to strike the *mayohuacán*, which was suspended between trees. The Taínos made music, too, with a prototype of maracas, a pair of substantial rattles containing a large ball; slits on the side permitted the rhythmic sound to emerge. Often used in religious ceremonies, they were adorned with carved representations and images of *cemís*, tiny but mighty Taíno religious figures. They were joined by *güiras*, raspers fashioned from hollowed-out gourds with ridges notched into their sides. Today, *güira* and maracas remain integral to Latin American music, as do modern versions of flutes and Taíno whistles called *guamós* or *cobos*. And there were the breathy exhalations of a Taíno trumpet, fashioned from a conch shell. Its notes carried throughout the forest to broadcast warnings of danger to distant members of their tribe.

With these instruments, the Taínos performed hymns and rites called *areítos* to celebrate natural events such as solstices, plantings, and harvests. *Areítos* commemorated the marriage of a cacique, the birth of an important *nitaíno* (a Taíno of the ruling caste), or a military victory. "Since time immemorial, particularly in the mansions of their kings, they have ordered their *behiques* or wise men to instruct their sons in knowledge about everything," Peter Martyr wrote. "With this teaching, they accomplish two goals: one general, playing [songs] about their origins and development, and the other particular, lauding the illustrious deeds in peace and in war of their fathers, grandfathers, great grandfathers, and other ancestors." In each case their "melody is perfectly in accord with each theme."

The Taínos prepared carefully for their sacred *areítos*. The dancers fasted for eight days before the ceremony, imbibing only an herbal tea, or *diga*. Before performing, they bathed in rivers and in sacred *charcos*, natural pools, to purify their bodies. Europeans came to believe that the ritual bathing was meant to propitiate Atabeyra, at times the deity of fresh water and at other times the mother of Yúcahu, the Taínos' principal god. After they purified themselves, the males decorated their bodies with vegetable-dye images of their *cemís*. Concluding the purification rite, they plunged elaborately decorated vomiting sticks made from the ribs of a manatee down their throats to empty their stomachs in preparation for receiving divine enlightenment.

At the start of the ceremony, the presiding cacique took his place on a *dujo*, a stool with four legs, decorated with colorful images of *cemís*. He inhaled the powerful hallucinogenic *cohoba* powder through the slender black stems of his pipe, one for each nostril. *Cohoba* was derived from a slender tree known to botanists as *Anadenathera peregrina*, and to the Indians as *yopo*, which flourished throughout the Southern Hemisphere. Its ground seeds produced the potent snuff, and after inhaling it, the cacique fell into a deep trance lasting three or four hours. When he emerged, he announced to his followers the prophecies he had heard from the *cemís*, and those divine utterances set the program that followed. Drummers and other musicians struck their instruments, and the intoxicating reverberation filled the public square, and floated up to the sky, even as the *cohoba* dust filled the nostrils of the Indians and altered their perception of reality. Three hundred dancers, moving as one, shook the snail shells bound to their arms, their calves, their thighs, and even their heels. "Loaded with these shells they struck the ground with their feet, leaping, singing, and dancing, and they saluted the cacique who, seated in the doorway, received those who came, beating on his drum with a stick," wrote Peter Martyr.

The dancers held hands or clasped each other's shoulders as they danced, the men flashing their body designs in gaudy red, black, and white. "The women, on the other hand, came without any special haircuts or paint, the virgins totally nude," said Martyr.

> At a signal from the *behiques*, or wise men, the garlanded women, dancing and singing their hymns, which they call *areítos*, offered cassava in laboriously woven baskets. Upon entering, they began to circle those who were seated there; these, rising with sudden leaps, celebrated with admirable *areítos* of praise, together with them, to the *cemí*, narrating and singing with the illustrious gestures of their ancestors, giving thanks to the deity for their well being, humbly asking him for future felicity; both sexes on their knees at the end, they offered the deity cassava, which the wise men blessed, and then they divided the cassava into pieces as personal presents.

At the conclusion, each participant carried part of the cassava home and kept it all year as an object of sacred remembrance.

*   *   *

The lost party of nine men suddenly appeared before Columbus on November 8, explaining that they had gone astray in the forest. "We rejoiced at their arrival as though they had come back to life," Chanca wrote, sensibly enough. They were accompanied by ten women and boys, all fleeing the Caribs. To find their way back to the waiting ships, several men had shimmied to the treetops "to get oriented with the stars but were absolutely not able to see the sky." Wandering to the water's edge, they stumbled upon the waiting fleet by accident.

The Admiral was more irritated than pleased by their unexpected return. The tale of their ordeal failed to move his unyielding heart. And he "punished them for their rashness, ordering the captain put in chains and placing the others on short rations," Ferdinand reported.

At daybreak on November 10, Columbus and his fleet departed from Guadeloupe, sailing northwest along the coast to the island of Montserrat. The handful of Indians aboard his ship explained that the island had been ravaged by the Caribs, who had eaten "all its inhabitants." Columbus hastened to Santa María la Redonda—so named because it was round—and then Santa María de la Antigua, and held to a northwesterly course, spotting more islands "all very high and densely wooded" and potentially useful, but as his son tells us, Columbus was "so anxious to relieve the men he had left on Hispaniola that he decided to continue" until November 14, when a storm forced the fleet to seek shelter in Salt River Bay, in the lee of the island now known as St. Croix.

A few of the men went ashore "to learn what kind of people lived there," Chanca noted, "and also because we needed information about which way to follow." Here, as on other islands, "most of the women . . . were prisoners of the Caribs," just as they had expected "on the basis of what the women with us had predicted."

Columbus again dispatched scouts to capture an Indian guide, but they returned instead with several women and three children. As the scouts approached their ship, they found themselves in a pitched battle with four men and a woman in an Indian canoe. The lone woman proved herself a capable archer; her arrow pierced a shield. In retaliation, the Spaniards rammed the canoe, dumping the Indians into the salt water. Swimming to safety, they continued to shoot arrows tipped with a deadly poison believed to have derived from manchineel fruit, sometimes called "beach apples," growing in abundance on bushy trees. These apples were so toxic, wrote

Before winning the backing of Spain, Columbus offered his services to King João II of Portugal. Here the explorer displays a chart of his proposed voyage to the eager Sovereign, who rejected the plan, and tried to mount copycat expeditions despite assurances to the contrary.

Ferdinand II of Aragon, ca. 1495. He met Isabella of Castile only five days before they wed, on October 19, 1469. During their reign, Los Reyes Católicos battled challengers to their complex power-sharing arrangement, sponsored the Inquisition, and commissioned Columbus's voyages.

Queen Isabella was celebrated for her piety and dedication to the cause of a unified Spain. It took Columbus several attempts over a period of years to win her support, but once he did, she remained his steadfast if occasionally critical backer until her death on November 26, 1504, just after the explorer returned from his fourth and final voyage.

D. JOÃO II

King João II of Portugal. Duplicitous and prone to violence, he once stabbed a rival to death. During his fourteen-year reign, he consolidated power and revived Portugal's ambitions for empire. Called the "Perfect Prince," it is believed that he exemplified Machiavelli's notion of a ruler. Queen Isabella called him, simply, El Hombre—"The Man."

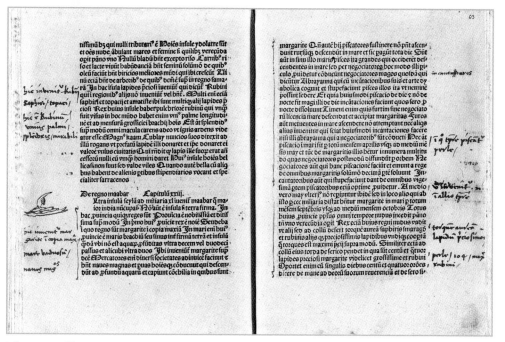

Like many of his era, Columbus studied Marco Polo's *Travels*. The Venetian merchant's account of the Mongol Empire during the reign of Kublai Khan (1260–94) inspired the explorer to find an ocean route to promote trade between the East and Europe. Columbus's numerous "postils," or marginal notes, highlighted items that he wished to exploit for trade.

A view of the harbor of "La Superba" (Genoa the Proud), as it appeared in 1481. Its population at the time, about 75,000, was among the largest in Europe. It was here that Columbus was born in 1451 and where he learned his trade in Genoa's highly competitive commercial culture. According to a fatalistic proverb of the region, *"O mare o lé male"*: The sea is evil.

Adulation of Columbus reached its peak in the nineteenth century, when the example of his visionary courage overshadowed the tragic reality of his voyages. In this romantic representative 1846 portrait, Ferdinand and Isabella receive the worshipful, kneeling explorer on his return from his first voyage.

In this "capitulation," or agreement, of April 17, 1492, Ferdinand and Isabella showered Columbus with rights and privileges that they would later be forced to curtail, lest he administer a larger and potentially wealthier territory than Spain. The capitulation made Columbus viceroy and perpetual governor of all the islands and "mainland" that he would discover in his lifetime.

Christopher Columbus's flagship, *Santa María*, and his two other ships, *Niña* ("Little Girl") and *Pinta* ("Painted One"). About seventy feet long, *Santa María* was a carrack, a capacious sailing vessel with several masts and a high, rounded stern. The other two ships were smaller, lighter, and more maneuverable caravels. With their shallow keels, they became the workhorse of the Age of Discovery.

This woodcut, dating from 1493, was one of the earliest depictions of Columbus's first voyage. In it, the inhabitants of "Guanahani"—their name for the island in the Lucayan Archipelago in the Bahamas on which Columbus first set foot, perhaps San Salvador or Samana Cay, although other candidates have been suggested—flee in panic from the arriving Spaniards.

Before departing on his first voyage, Columbus bids good-bye to his royal sponsors, Ferdinand and Isabella, in this engraving by Theodor de Bry, The background depicts the harbor of Cadiz and the royal Spanish coat of arms.

In this idealized portrayal of Columbus's landfall in the New World, a group of Christians erect a cross while an eager, respectful group of "Indians," as Columbus came to call the inhabitants, offered valuable gifts.

Juan de la Cosa played a crucial role in Columbus's exploration of the New World. He was the owner and master of *Santa María* and a mapmaker, and sailed on three voyages with Columbus. In all, he made seven voyages to the Americas.

In this allegorical 1493 woodcut, King Ferdinand, seated on his throne in Spain, gestures boldly across the sea toward Columbus aboard *Santa María* as she approaches land—the island of "Guanahani"—accompanied by *Pinta* and *Niña* in what is considered the earliest representation of the explorer.

Europe's fascination with Columbus's descriptions of native American customs and political structure remained long after the Indians themselves were gone. In this engraving from about 1725, Indians—presumably the Taínos, whom the Europeans frequently encountered—carry their chieftain, or "cacique," in a grand procession. The dwellings in the background depict sturdy structures reminiscent of Europe rather than the huts, courtyards, and dwellings that the Spaniards actually found.

Martín Alonso Pinzón, mariner, ship-builder, and navigator, was the oldest of the three Pinzón brothers, who all sailed on the first voyage. Unstable and defiant on the return voyage, he became separated from Columbus in a storm and eventually made it back to Palos de la Frontera, Spain, where he died, in 1493.

This woodcut from Girolamo Benzoni's *Historia del Mondo Nuovo*, Venice, 1563, shows Indian fisherman at work. Their canoes and nets for harvesting the sea were admired by Europeans.

A 1493 woodcut accompanying Columbus's "Letter on the First Voyage," illustrating his arrival in the Indies.

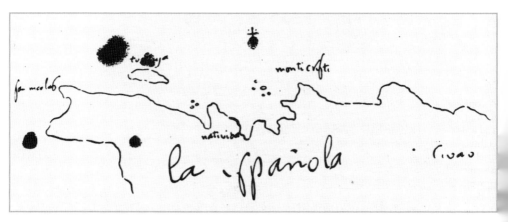

Columbus sketched this map of the Hispaniola coastline and the smaller island of Tortuga, belonging to today's Haiti.

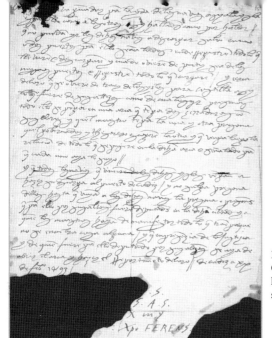

In this manuscript dated November 20, 1493, Christopher Columbus describes the new lands he has discovered on the first voyage. The manuscript concludes with his distinctive signature.

A confident and graceful Arawak (Taíno) woman holding a parrot aloft in one hand and a bow and arrow in the other, in this eighteenth-century rendering by John Gabriel Stedman, a soldier and author of British and Dutch ancestry. Indian women proved themselves skillful archers and leaders as well as alluring companions for the Europeans.

The Columbus home in Genoa, Italy.

Christopher Columbus, his sons Diego and Ferdinand, and an unidentified woman. Ferdinand's mother was Columbus's companion Beatriz de Arana, of Basque origin. Diego's mother was Columbus's wife Felipa Moñiz Perestrello, who died at an early age.

A mariner's astrolabe of the type employed by Columbus; the instrument was used to determine the latitude of a ship at sea. Most mariner's astrolabes were made of brass to withstand heavy weather. This and other navigational instruments often frustrated Columbus, who was more adept at navigating by dead reckoning.

In this illustration from the *Natural History of the West Indies* by Gonzalo Fernández de Oviedo y Valdés, Taínos collect abundant gold. Later, the Spanish strictly regulated supplies of gold as stores of the precious metal depleted. Oviedo arrived in the Indies as a gold mine inspector in 1514.

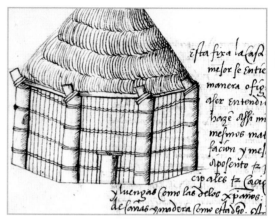

An Indian *bohio*, or dwelling, as it appeared in Fernández de Oviedo's *Natural History of the West Indies*.

Cannibals as depicted in an illustration from the first Latin edition of Columbus's "Letter on the First Voyage." Several of those who sailed with Columbus noted evidence of cannibalism in the Indies.

Theodor de Bry's engraving of Indians dancing with elaborate costumes and musical instruments, 1593. Such images fixed the reputation of Indians in the consciousness of western Europe.

An eye-catching Indian woman displays a parrot and her Taíno attire, as drawn about 1686. At first, the men serving under Columbus maintained a respectful distance from the women of the New World, but eventually Spaniards took one or more as partners.

"The people of this island fight with sharp canes," wrote Columbus's physician, Diego Alvarez Chanca, "which they throw with slings, just like the ones the boys in Castile use." In this 1686 illustration, a well-muscled Indian warrior displays his weapons.

The Columbian Exchange transmitted flora, fauna, culture, technology, and diseases between western Europe and the Americas. Their complex interactions affected the course of evolution and history. This drawing, from about 1700, shows an Indian suffering from smallpox.

Fernández de Oviedo, that "if a man lies down to sleep for only an hour in the shade of one of these manchineel trees, he awakes with his head and eye swollen, and his eyebrows level with his cheeks." The Spaniards called the fruit *manzanilla de la muerte*, little apple of death. The Caribs mixed the poison apples with toxins from vipers and poisonous insects to make an even deadlier concoction. Even the leaves were dangerous, and the Caribs used them to poison their enemies' water supply. The only known antidote was seawater. Out of fifty wounded by poison arrows, "not three survived."

Amid the melee, Peter Martyr reported, there appeared a woman whom the other Indians respected as their queen. Beside her stood her son, "a fierce and robust young man, with a ferocious look and the appearance of a lion." They seemed prepared to finish every last Spaniard, even those in agony from the wounds they suffered from the poison-tipped arrows. Summoning their resources, the Spaniards rowed themselves beside the cannibals' canoe to overturn it. Even with their canoe capsized, the Indian warriors, men and women alike, kept shooting their arrows, one stroke after another. Only when the archers sought refuge on a reef were the Spaniards able to capture them as they fought on to the end. Several Indians perished in this skirmish, and the Spaniards were pleased to note they had "wounded the queen's son twice."

The exhausted survivors were taken prisoner, and "even after being taken on board the Admiral's ship the natives did not lose their fierceness and ferocious looks, not unlike African lions once they feel trapped," in the words of Peter Martyr. Like many in Spain, the classically trained Martyr was of two minds about the Indians. From a safe distance, he compared them favorably to the "tyrants" of the time of "the mythical Aeneas," the hero of Troy, and even portrayed their lives with a touch of envy. "But I feel that our natives of Hispaniola," as he called the Indians, "are happier than they—more so were they converted to the true religion—because naked, without burdens, limits, or death-inducing currency, living in a golden age, free, without fraudulent judges, books, and content in their natural state, they live with no worries about the future." Yet Columbus and his men realized that the Indian tribes they encountered often lived desperate, fear-ridden lives as they preyed on one another in an unending struggle for dominance and survival that mirrored the struggles of European nations. Even the wistful Peter Martyr was aware that the fierce Caribs ranged a thousand miles to find victims, and he admitted that the Indians, despite their apparent freedom and simplicity, were "troubled by the desire to rule and waste each other away with wars."

Unlike the exalted, occasionally desperate sense of mission animating Columbus, his boyhood friend Michele de Cuneo, gentleman of Genoa, did not torment himself with questions about the fleet's location or his role in God's plan. Even the appalling castration practiced by the Caribs intrigued rather than horrified Cuneo. His determination to live in the moment, consequences be damned, prefigured the eventual arrival of buccaneers in the Caribbean.

Cuneo recorded careful observations of the Indians as they appeared to the men of the second voyage. The Indians pressed a heavy plate on the soft brows of infants to produce a profile they considered desirable, as he noted: "They have flat heads and the face tattooed; of short stature; as a rule they have very little beard and very well shaped legs and are thick of skin. The women have their breasts quite round and firm and well shaped." They were carefully groomed, shaving and smoothing their skin with sharpened canes, and "the hair from the nose they uproot with their fingers."

He observed their diet with amazement. "They eat all sorts of wild and poisonous beasts such as reptiles of 15 to 20 pounds each; and when they meet the biggest ones they are devoured by them." He tried a sample, and found it "very good." But the dogs were "not too good" at all; neither were the "snakes, lizards, spiders" that he claimed grew to the size of chickens. The Indians even ate "poisonous insects that breed in the swamps and weigh from a pound to a pound and a half." Those he could not bring himself to stomach.

They acted according to their impulses, or so it seemed to Cuneo. They did not live long ("We have not seen a man who in our judgment would have been past 50 years of age"), they slept "mostly on the ground like beasts," they let the women do most of the work, and they covered their bodies with dye to ward off the "extremely annoying" mosquitoes. (The Europeans, in contrast, failed to find any better remedy than staying in the water.) The Indians ate when hungry, had sex when it suited them, but they were "not too lustful," which he attributed to their inadequate diet. "According to what we have seen in all the islands where we have been, both the Indians"— that is, the Taínos—"and the Caribs are largely sodomites, not knowing (I believe) whether they are acting right or wrong."

Cuneo coolly recorded the brutal treatment the Spaniards accorded the Indians in the canoe as they battled against overwhelming odds. "One Carib was wounded by a spear in such a way that we thought he was dead," he said of the confrontation, "but instantly we saw him swim." The Spaniards quickly caught him and grappled him back to the ship, "where we cut off his head with an axe." They took other Caribs as prisoners, and planned to send them all to Spain, as Cuneo casually recalled, with one striking exception. "While I was in the boat," Cuneo bragged, "I captured a very beautiful woman, whom the Lord Admiral gave to me. When I had taken her to my cabin she was naked—as was their custom. I was filled with a desire to take my pleasure with her and attempted to satisfy my desire. She was unwilling, and so treated me with her nails that I wished I had never begun. I then took a piece of rope and whipped her soundly, and she let forth such incredible screams that you would not have believed your ears. Eventually we came to such terms, I assure you, that you would have thought she had been brought up in a school for whores."

So began the European rape of the New World.

Had Ferdinand and Isabella learned of such escapades, the perpetrators would have paid dire consequences. And if Columbus knew of his comrade's scandalous behavior, he kept the knowledge to himself, and Cuneo had the sense to confide his written accounts of daily life during Columbus's second voyage only to a circumspect friend.

Gonzalo Fernández de Oviedo, the naturalist and scholar, preferred to emphasize the loyalty and sensuality of Taíno women. "They are very fond of the Spaniards and consider themselves highly honored when they are loved by them. Many of these women, after they have known Christians carnally, will remain faithful to them unless they go too far away and remain too long, for they have no desire to be widows or nuns who protect their chastity." For many, chastity was not uppermost in their minds, and pregnancies inevitably followed, for which they had a remedy. "Many of the Indian women eat of an herb that moves and expels the pregnancy," he wrote. "They say the old women are the ones who should bear children. The young women do not want to give up their pleasures, or to become pregnant, because childbearing causes their breasts to become flabby. They have very beautiful breasts and are quite proud of them." If an Indian woman eventually gave birth to a child, Fernández de Oviedo noted, "she goes to the river and bathes, and immediately the flow of blood and purgation ceases, and for a few days she does no work. The sexual organs of Indian women then contract so that the men who have had sexual intercourse with them say that they are so tight that it is with pain that a man may gratify his passion.

Those who have not borne children seem to be almost virgins." This behavior, so resilient and flexible, was very different from that of conventional Spanish and Christian mores, which placed a premium on virginity, abhorred abortion, and often suppressed inherent female sensuality in the name of chastity.

The Indian men emphasized audacious sexual display. The caciques "wear a tube of gold, and the other men large snail's shells, in which they place the male organ. The rest of the body is naked, because the Indians do not feel that the human body is anything to inspire shame"—Fernández de Oviedo wrote in appreciation—"and in many provinces neither men nor women cover their sexual organs nor do they wear anything on any part of the body." Stirring accounts such as this made as much of an impression on European awareness of the Indians visited by Columbus as alarming reports of cannibalism and poison arrows.

In Chanca's account, the battle between the Spaniards and the Indians arose not from provocation, as Cuneo implied, but from happenstance: the unexpected appearance of a canoe with two men and a boy who were so astonished by the sight of the enormous Spanish fleet that "they stayed for a good hour without moving." They were slowly surrounded by Spaniards approaching in boats. "As they kept on wondering and trying to understand what it was all about, they did not notice that they could not flee." When they finally tried to escape, "the men from our boat seized them very promptly."

Chanca sympathized with the small party of captive Indians, far outnumbered by the twenty-five Spaniards who had seized them. Surrounded, the Indians "struck one with two arrows in the chest and the other with one in the ribs, and, had it not been for the fact they wore shields and wooden plates and also that there was a collision with the boat that capsized their canoe, they would have hit the majority of them with arrows." They fought on even after their canoe capsized. Dodging poison-tipped arrows, the Spaniards wounded and captured a single warrior, and brought him back to the fleet, where he died of his injuries.

During the first voyage, the ferocious Caribs had been more rumor than reality. Now Chanca observed them at close quarters, their "very long hair," and a "thousand different decorative images on their faces, crosses and other symbols of varying fashion, as each of them likes best." The few Caribs captured by the Spanish had eerily "painted eyes and eyebrows, which—it seems to me—they do on purpose to appear more frightful." They were, in fact, terrifying. The Spaniards captured their Indian attackers only to find that the men had been castrated: standard practice for the Caribs, who sought to improve the taste of their victims before eating them.

His need to hurry increasing with every league and sign of Carib cruelty, Columbus held to his northwest course, "preferring," said Chanca, "to bring help to our people whom we had left on Hispaniola."

Slicing through cobalt sea, out of sight of land, the fleet was accompanied by the angular black, swooping silhouettes of frigate birds. Chanca accurately portrayed these pelicanlike creatures as "predatory sea birds that do not stop or sleep on the water." Two days later, the men of the fleet spotted land, probably the Virgin Islands; fished for sole, sardines, shad, and even sea horses; passed along the southern coast of Puerto Rico; beheld an Indian watch tower "that could hold ten or twelve persons"; and on Friday, November 22, watched in expectation as the northern coast of Hispaniola finally came into view, solid, fragrant, and mysterious.

This was Chanca's first visit to the Indies, and the scope of Hispaniola overwhelmed him. "A very wide territory," he observed, "to the point that those who have seen its coast claim it could be two hundred leagues long." He was accustomed to the sparse countryside of Spain, the parched soil, and in November, the sunny but chilly Seville.

Here, on Hispaniola, the profusion of strange flora perplexed him. "A very unusual land," he remarked, "with a great many wide rivers, big mountain chains, ample and treeless valleys and high peaks. I suspect the vegetation does not dry up at all during the year. I do not think there is any winter in this territory, since at Christmas there can be seen many nests, some with birds, others with eggs." These birds puzzled him. Their appearance was the result of a separate evolutionary track; as such, they were the product of forces unknown to Chanca or anyone else of that era. Lacking a taxonomy adequate to the formidable task of classifying the fauna all around him, he hesitantly recorded references to "a few multi-colored dogs," and a "furry animal like the rabbit . . . with a long tail and with fore and hind legs like those of mice, and it climbs trees. Many people who have eaten it say it is indeed tasty." At such moments, it seemed as though he were in another world similar to that of Europe, but subtly and enigmatically different, like a foreign language he could only partly decipher. Creatures that he took to be snakes, for instance, baffled him; he claimed that the Indians "like them a lot, much as we like pheasants in our country. They are of different shape but the same size as our lizards," with the exception of one curious beast that he estimated to be the size of a calf "and had the shape of a lance." The creature inspired an outpouring of Spanish abhorrence, yet "many attempts to kill it were thwarted by the dense vegetation where it could hide by the sea and never be caught."

In late November 1493, the fleet paused at the port of Monte Cristi, on the inhospitable northern coast of what is now the Dominican Republic "to study the configuration of the territory," in Chanca's words, "since the Admiral considered unsuitable for a settlement the place where he had left the men." With the benefit of hindsight, Columbus realized that his hasty choice of site on the first voyage had failed to take into account basic considerations such as the availability of water and food, and proximity to the aggressive

Caribs. He concluded he needed to know the territory—and its dangers—better. He soon found them.

A scouting party came across "two dead men near the river, one with a rope around his neck and the other with a rope around his foot." The next day, Chanca wrote, the scouts discovered "two more dead men, one of whom was in a position that revealed he had a long beard." Who were they? With professional sangfroid, the physician observed that "some of our men had more negative than positive feelings, and rightly so, since none of the Indians have beards." Columbus had nothing to say on a subject that could only bring dread to his men. They were about thirty-six miles from the fort.

Columbus departed for La Navidad two days later, on November 28, intending to call on Guacanagarí, the chief who had been entrusted with protecting the life of thirty-nine Spaniards from the first voyage. En route, the Admiral's ship foundered amid the shallows in an eerie reenactment of the mishap the previous Christmas, when *Santa María* had struck a sandbar, but this time Columbus's flagship broke free to arrive after night-fall. "We did not dare to take port near the coast until the next morning when the depth could be surely known and safe passage possible," he recounted. They were still three miles from their goal when a canoe bearing five or six Indians gave pursuit, but Columbus had no intention of waiting for them.

He fired two shots to announce his arrival. As the reports echoed and faded, Columbus waited for the Christians in their garrison to respond in kind. But there was only silence that grew more poignant with every passing minute, "for they suspected that the comrades whom they had left there had been completely wiped out," as Guillermo Coma remembered. Even the detached Chanca admitted to a "lot of concern" among the crew members. "Great sadness was all-encompassing," he sighed. When the Spanish went ashore, they found neither fires nor dwellings.

Four or five hours later, the canoe approached one of the caravels; the Indians signaled that they sought Columbus, and came on board. One Indian identified himself as Guacanagarí's cousin, and, exploiting Columbus's lust for gold, presented the Admiral with gifts of "golden masks." Hours of conversation ensued, and as the sun rose behind them, Columbus emanated "much satisfaction." Perhaps the Christians were safe, after all. Guacanagarí's self-styled cousin assured the Admiral that they were indeed well, with the exception of those who had died from illness, and a few others who had died "because of altercations." And where was Guacanagarí himself? The Indian "cousin" claimed Guacanagarí was busy tending to a wound in his leg, but he would come the next day. There had been trouble, the Indian explained; two other chiefs, Caonabó and Marieni, had launched an attack and set fire to Guacanagarí's village.

The Indians returned to their canoes, promising to come back the next day with Guacanagarí, "leaving us behind, less worried for the night," Chanca recalled. Morning revealed that the village "had been burnt to the ground and all the belongings had been burnt and destroyed but for a few woven pieces of fabric and cloth that the Indians had brought to throw in the houses. All of the Indians who could be seen there seemed very suspicious, did not dare to approach us and indeed fled at first. . . . We nonetheless tried to flatter them by passing out such things as harness bells and seed pearls."

Columbus went ashore to inspect the destruction of the first European fort in the Indies, and from the moment he set foot on blood-soaked foreign soil and imagined the suffering of his men, his sense of mission changed permanently. He "felt much grief at the sight of ruins of the houses and the fort," said his son Ferdinand. "Nothing remained of the houses except some smashed chests and such other wreckage as one sees in a land that has been devastated and put to the sack." He left orders to clean out the fort's well, and to dispose of the gold nearby, but there was no gold to be found, and the well had run dry.

Sailing upriver in search of someone who could explain what had happened, Columbus found the corpses of ten Spaniards, "miserably deformed and corrupted, smeared with dirt and foul blood, and hideously discolored," Coma recalled. "They had lain out in the open neglected and unburied for almost three months." The Admiral and his men offered prayers for their souls, and prepared a Christian burial. "I felt great pain," Columbus reflected, "and though I know it happened through their own fault, there is much to be sad about in such an event, for me it is a punishment greater than any experienced by their relatives, because I wanted them to win great honor at little danger." And so they would have, he believed, "had they governed themselves according to my instructions." Those instructions were clear: "Above all they were to leave alone the women belonging to their fellows as well as those of the Indians." Instead, the Spaniards recklessly "gave themselves over to eating and to the pleasure of women, and so they came to ruin and destroyed themselves."

* * *

Soon after, aboard ship, the Indians informed the Spanish that every single man at La Navidad had died. Who, Columbus wanted to know, had killed them?

Guacanagarí's deputy replied that Chief Caonabó and Chief Marieni had been responsible for burning the fort and wounding the Indians who sided with the Spanish. In fact, he wanted to fly to Guacanagarí's side and return with him to Columbus. The distraught Spaniards let him go: another mistake. "The entire day we waited for them, and when we realized they were not returning," they suspected that the Indians had gotten drunk on the wine served to them aboard ship, climbed into their teetering canoe, capsized it, and drowned.

It seemed impossible that God's will would be thwarted in such a drastic manner. The *fortaleza* had served as the linchpin of Columbus's colonial enterprise and its destruction placed the fleet and all 1,500 men at risk. Columbus had come to believe that divine forces had combined to assist him in his mission. Why had divine favor yielded to divine displeasure?

Columbus ordered a thorough search of the devastated site, not forgetting to look for subterranean caches of gold. They reached a hamlet of seven or eight huts abandoned by their inhabitants the moment they heard the approaching Europeans "after taking with them what they could and leaving the rest hidden in the grass." Within the huts were items once belonging to the men stationed at La Navidad, "in particular a mantle so elegant that one could not explain why it had been brought from Castile." The Spaniards retrieved trousers, a piece of cloth, and even "an anchor from the ship"— *Santa María*—"that the Admiral had lost during the previous expedition." All of these artifacts caused the Spanish concern, especially a small, carefully wrought basket holding a human head. "We inferred it was the head of a father, a mother, or a very dear person, only to learn later that many of these were found similarly preserved."

The elusive Indians' choice of a site struck the Spanish as extremely odd. "These people are so savage that they have no rationality in seeking out a place to live," Chanca wrote in exasperation, "so it appears strange to see how primitively those who live along the sea built their houses, which are all so overtaken by weeds and humidity that I am amazed at how they can possibly survive." But weeds and humidity, along with poisonous insects, snakes, and fevers, would form their environment as long as they remained in these islands.

Columbus's little search party reached an Indian village, received a reassuring tribute of gold, and learned more about the murder of the Christians by Caonabó and Marieni. Chanca reported "indications of quarrels among the Christians, since some of them had taken three women, others four." The story could have been a fabrication to justify the slaughter. The Spanish accepted it at face value. "Therefore, we believed their misfortune was caused by jealousy," Ferdinand said in resignation. He pointed out that his father had heard a comparable tale from Indians who "could say some words in Spanish and knew the names of all the Christians who had been left" at the fort. "They said that soon after the Admiral's departure, they began to quarrel amongst themselves, each taking as many women and as much gold as he could."

As pieced together by Ferdinand, Caonabó's rampage built to a ghastly climax. "Arriving at the town by night, Caonabó set fire to the houses in which the Christians lived with their women, forcing them to flee in fright to the sea, where eight of them drowned; three others, whom the Indians could not identify, were killed ashore." If there was any redeeming element to this grisly tale, it was that Guacanagarí had taken the side of the Christians and was wounded while fighting against Caonabó, just as Guacanagarí had claimed to Columbus.

If that was the case, the Admiral had an ally among the Indians, after all. "I believe this Guacanagarí is not really responsible for the death of our people," he came to believe. "On the contrary, I am most obligated to him." The pendulum in Columbus's mind kept swinging, and he concluded that the Indians were too timid to have murdered the reckless Spaniards: "This also feeds my suspicion that the disaster might have come about from internal quarreling."

The next morning, December 7, Columbus dispatched a caravel to search for a suitable place to build a new city. Another party, including Chanca, set forth with the same goal. Eventually they came to a "very safe port" suitable for settlement, presumed to be present-day Cap Haitien, on Haiti's northern coast. They would have made this attractive harbor their next encampment, but Columbus decided it was too far from the gold mines he expected to find.

The scouting party did locate Guacanagarí, lying "on his pallet in a posture of one who suffers from wounds," in Chanca's careful wording. Deeply suspicious of the chieftain, Columbus's men questioned him about the massacre at La Navidad, and Guacanagarí repeated the story that it had been the work of Caonabó and Marieni, who had also wounded his leg. He displayed the bandages, temporarily convincing the Spanish skeptics, and winning friends by giving each of his visitors a "golden jewel"—finely worked gold that they "hang on their ears and in the nostrils . . . not to show wealth, but to look good."

The following day, Guacanagarí sent his brother to invite the Admiral himself to visit. "The Admiral went ashore along with most of the leaders and so well-dressed that they would have drawn praise even in a great city," in Chanca's words. Columbus took care to bring a few trinkets to reciprocate for the gold he and his men had received. They found Guacanagarí regally suspended in his hammock, accompanied by his wife, twelve ladies-in-waiting—all naked, or nearly so—various companions, and guards reclining watchfully on the ground: the Indian royal court. They had prepared carefully for their visitors.

"He did not get up," Chanca said of the wily Indian leader. "He addressed us with a gesture of courtesy as best he could and showed deep emotion to the point of tears for the Christians' deaths, and began talking about that, saying as best he could that a few died because of illness and others had gone to Caonabó's territory to find the gold mine in the city and were killed there, while the rest had been seized and killed in their own camp." As if to wish away the tragedy, or in recompense for lives lost, Guacanagarí presented Columbus with more gifts—gold, always gold—and belts and headgear adorned with semiprecious stones. The jewels twinkled, they glittered, and the crown was solid and substantial in his hands, conferring the illusion of power and mastery on its grateful, wide-eyed recipient. Guacanagarí then bestowed still more gifts: "eight hundred small figured white, green, and red stone beads together with one hundred figured gold beads, a royal gold crown, and three little gourds filled with gold grains," said Columbus's son Ferdinand.

For the moment, the Admiral was more stunned and flattered than bent on revenge for the deaths of his men, and appeared only too willing to cooperate with his host. The brilliance of gold put the lives of the barely mourned, practically anonymous men who had lost their lives at La Navidad into the shadows of obscurity. A leader who valued gold above the security of his men could be counted on to aspire to great accomplishments at great cost.

Columbus offered Guacanagarí the services of Chanca, the fleet's physician, and the surgeon, both in attendance. Chanca stepped forward and indicated that he needed to inspect the chief's wound in the light of day; it was too dark inside the dwelling. The injured chieftain complied, limping and leaning on Chanca's shoulder. "After he was seated, the surgeon approached him and started taking the bandages off." Guacanagarí explained that the wound had been caused by a weapon made of stone. "When the leg was unbound, we gathered to examine it. It was obvious he felt no more pain in it than in the other leg, although he cleverly tried to show it hurt him very much." Columbus and his men began to suspect that his men had lost their lives not through their own recklessness, or disease, or even starvation (an unlikely occurrence in this fertile land), but had been murdered, every last one of them, by Indians. Nevertheless, he decided the best course was to pretend that he still believed the chieftain's improbable story, to the point of inviting him to dine aboard ship that evening.

Guacanagarí received all the attention he could wish. "When he got to the Admiral's ship," said Guillermo Coma, "he was piped aboard with great pomp, welcomed by the beating of drums, the clashing of cymbals, and the flashing bombardment of the ship's cannon." He took his seat on the deck before a table "sumptuously" set with cakes, confections, and delicacies from the pantries of Castile. As the other members of the Indian party "looked with amazement upon all these things," Guacanagarí "preserved a ceremonious decorum and gravity worthy of his rank," enhanced by his offering gifts of gold to his appreciative hosts. The illusion of dignity dissolved when he noticed the Indian women aboard ship. "Turning to the women who had been saved from the cannibals, he was seen gazing and leering at one of them, named Catalina by our men," Peter Martyr recorded. Guacanagarí would have persisted in his advances, but he was amazed by the strange beasts—horses brought by the Spanish. "They had engraved bits, bright-hued caparisons, and handsomely polished belly-bands," according to Coma. "Their formidable appearance did not fail to terrify the Indians, for they suspected that the horses fed on human flesh."

Employing Indian interpreters who had miraculously survived a spell in Spain after the first voyage and then returned to their homeland, Columbus explained his plans to build another settlement, this time on Guacanagarí's territory. The chief claimed to welcome the arrangement, "although the place was unhealthy, being very humid." Columbus then engaged the startled chieftain in earnest conversation about Christianity. In the past, the Indian leader had been skeptical, but now he "consented to wear about his neck a silver image of the Virgin, something he had refused to do before."

With Guacanagarí aboard ship, wrote Peter Martyr, "there were those who advised the Admiral to keep Guacanagarí so that he could be punished if they learned that our men had been punished by his order. But, realizing this was not the time to irritate his feelings, the Admiral let him go." It was a decision that Columbus would come to regret.

The chieftain's brother returned the next day bearing gold, always gold, and accompanied by women from Boriquén, or Puerto Rico. If the Spaniards assumed the women were intended for them, they were proved wrong as the Indian proceeded to violate them "both in his own name and his brother's the king," said Peter Martyr. After this episode, the Spaniards and, very likely, the exhausted Indian fell asleep aboard ship, at which point the women jumped into the water and fled to land. The Spaniards were slow to awaken to the situation, and by the time they did, the women "had covered such a long distance that our boats were not able to recapture more than four of them . . . when they were getting out of the water." Peter Martyr cast their dash for freedom in sympathetic terms. "Catalina, with seven other women, relying on the strength of her arms, swam about three miles in a not very calm sea: indeed, that was the distance of the fleet from the shore." The Spanish crew gave chase in small boats, capturing only three, but not their leader Catalina, who, they believed, had successfully escaped to Guacanagarí.

By the light of day, Columbus indignantly demanded their return, and sent a search party, which discovered that Guacanagarí himself had escaped in the company of the women with all his possessions. Columbus assigned a subordinate to lead a company of several hundred Spaniards in search of the fugitive Indian, only to wander into "some tortuous gorges, with steep hills on both sides." They spied a substantial hut in the distance, and thinking that it might conceal Guacanagarí, they approached it. They confronted an Indian with a "wrinkled forehead and thick eyebrows, accompanied by a hundred men . . . armed with bows, arrows, painted lances and poles." They ran toward the Spaniards "with a threatening look, shouting they were Taíno, that is, 'noble people,' not cannibals." Though not above violence, the "noble people" were less belligerent, and the company of sailors, breathing a collective sigh of relief, gave a "peace signal," whereupon the Indians "abandoned their arms and their fierceness." The Spanish fostered the friendship by offering hawk's bells that the Indians prized for the brass. Despite the reconciliation in the wild, the Indians had no idea of Guacanagarí's whereabouts, and the Spaniards returned to their ships to ponder the enigmatic ways of the Indians.

The Admiral took the fleet eastward and anchored near Monte Cristi, on the northwest coast of the Dominican Republic. Sand from tall bluffs thickly matted with vegetation gently crumbled under the combined force of wind and rain to form aprons extending into the turquoise water, revealing every fish, crustacean, and reef beneath the crystalline surface. From this vantage point, this seemed to be the most open and inviting of lands, but Columbus, concerned with the island's impenetrable vegetation—Ferdinand wrote of "flowers and bird's nests, some containing eggs and others fledglings, and all the other things that are proper to the summertime," even though the calendar showed it was December—considered the location too daunting for a fort or even a temporary landfall.

The fleet had been making very little progress against a steady trade wind. "The weather was so contrary that it was more trouble for us to sail thirty leagues up-wind than to come all the way from Castile," Chanca complained. It took a full twenty-five days to put the distance behind them.

At last Columbus glimpsed an Indian settlement through trees near the shore. "A suitable site for a fortress," in Ferdinand's words, it featured a plain, a ravine, and palisades sloping to the water's edge. "The plain has marvelous lands surpassing anything in Castile," Columbus boasted in a letter to his Sovereigns. "It is fully covered with tall, green grass, better than a field of barley in Spain in the best season." He estimated that the plain, known as the Vega Real, "has space enough for 20,000 inhabitants to plant grain and vegetables and construct buildings." There he disembarked with the entire crew, food, and equipment necessary for a settlement intended to supplant the bleak memory of the tiny outpost constructed on his first voyage. Columbus and his men "believed it to be an excellent site for a town because it had a large harbor, though open to the northwest, and a lovely river a crossbow shot in width." It was located on a promontory of alluvial soil or silt, nestled between the lapping ocean and a gently rising mountain range, divided by a large river emptying into the bay, and marked off by lagoons.

More relief disguised as exhilaration ensued. "The evenness of the climate seems incredible," he exulted, "it is so sweet and mild; trees, mountains, and herbs are all in bloom and as fresh as Andalusia in April or May." Even the wildlife cooperated with his vision: "The sparrows and other birds are so cheerful, with the nightingales always singing." Nests were everywhere, "and hosts of ducklings are all over, and in the river one finds geese, more than anywhere else, and all the birds are very large: pigeons, herons, and ten thousand other species"—partridges, doves, and others whose names he did not know. "The parrots are countless," and, one presumes, their screeching endless.

The maritime prospects elated him. "Two great leagues west of the city"—which existed only in Columbus's mind at this point—"this land forms an excellent beach, at the end of which is one of the best ports in the world, large enough to hold all existing ships." It commanded a sweeping view of the ocean, so that any approaching ship could be seen and identified at a safe distance. The soil was rich and red; the air pregnant with pollen. Vivid flame trees cast their scarlet sprays, while underfoot, emerald vegetation seemed to glow from within. To an untrained eye, the site looked ideal for the first real Spanish settlement in the Indies, but the beauty of the place proved deceptive. The Indies proved relatively easy to discover, but much harder to settle—impossible, in fact.

Farther inland, a lush, inviting, and tranquil plain charmed Columbus. According to the Indians, the site lay near gold mines. He noted with satisfaction a limestone quarry that with habitual overstatement he claimed was even better "than that of which the church of Santa María in Seville is built," and a "powerful river, better than the Guadalquivir." Columbus probably had the Ozama River in mind; the name is of Taíno origin. In reality, the waterway, less than a hundred miles long, is no match for the broad and mighty Guadalquivir, the second-longest river in all of Spain, but like the Guadalquivir, it was deep and wide enough to accommodate Spanish ships, and it emptied into the Atlantic.

He named the town La Isabela, after the queen who conferred legitimacy on his efforts. Guillermo Coma predicted that "in surpassing all others by virtue of its strategic position and benign climate [it] will within a few years be very populated, and filled and frequented by colonists." And with even less justification, he added, "It will compete with any of the cities of Spain when its buildings are finished and its walls are magnificently raised. They have done the houses, and are constructing the protective walls, which adorn the city and give secure refuge to its inhabitants." He described how a "wide street" would divide the city, crisscrossed by many other streets, with a fortress rising above the beach.

He spun out his extravagant ambitions for the tiny settlement. "The Admiral's residence is called the royal palace, for at some future time, if God, the creator and giver of countless blessings, wills it, the Sovereigns may set out from Cadiz to visit this well-favored land and behold the islands won from them so far from home." They would sail up the Ozama to stake their claim to the new lands Columbus had discovered. Once there, they would find, among other things, "a noble church . . . bursting with the furnishings sent from Spain by Queen Isabella for the worship of God." Although the vision of the Catholic Sovereigns worshipping in these new lands seemed far-fetched, Columbus reported that Christianity was taking hold. The Indians, he said, regarded it with devotion and respect as they knelt in contemplation. It was a beautiful fantasy, eminently suitable for export.

In this spirit, Coma believed that La Isabela was not just another makeshift trading post or embattled fortress, but the early manifestation of a new civilization transplanted from Spain. He advanced the intoxicating but unrealistic conviction that La Isabela, and other new cities like it, would soon rival the capitals of Spain. If Coma expressed a shared sense among Columbus's men, his words indicated a crucial shift in the voyage's rationale: Columbus was no longer looking for ancient India. He had found the raw materials, the workers, and the setting for an entirely new and unexpected realm, something implicitly bigger and better than Spain in the sense that it was purer, and little more than three weeks' journey (weather permitting) from the Canary Islands. Even Las Casas, so quick to condemn Columbus, acknowledged the importance of the new settlement. "When I was appointed prior of the Dominican house in La Plata harbor, I took a large stone from it [La Isabela]. And I laid it as the cornerstone of the monastery I began to build there. For the record," he noted, "this stone stands in the east corner of the ground floor and was the first stone to be laid, right next to the main entrance and the church." In this way, he preserved Columbus's legacy in Hispaniola.

The ambitious task of building a new fort consumed Columbus, who was determined to learn the lessons of La Navidad and construct a safer refuge for his men.

Ferdinand remarked that his father became so overwhelmed that he had no time to keep a journal from December 11, 1493, until March 12 of the following year, when he fell seriously ill. "Suddenly during my sleep I was tormented on my whole right side, from the sole of my foot to my head, as if stricken by paralysis, which caused me not a little suffering," he later reported. "Now I am better, and I have not ceased at that which I ought to concentrate on the best as I can and with contentment. Since then, both night and day, I wear no less clothing than I would in Seville." All the while, he endured cool, dreary weather, which he likened to a "typical winter in Castile." He appeared to have recovered his health, but his medical problems would reappear, each time with more severity.

Raw, incomplete, and unsanitary, La Isabela was formally founded on January 6, 1494, among the most important days in the Christian calendar, the Feast of the Epiphany, that is, the revelation of God in human form, in the person of Jesus Christ. A dozen priests dedicated the settlement in a makeshift church on land. This was the first Mass held in the New World, but under the pressure of events, there was no time to reflect on this milestone.

Two aides, Alonso de Ojeda and Ginés de Gorbalán, immediately set out from La Isabela for the mining region of the Cibao with about two dozen Spanish scouts and a handful of Indian guides. Columbus lingered at La Isabela, tending to his health.

Storms, mudslides, and floods assailed Ojeda's party; the men sought refuge in an Indian village, where Ojeda heard reports of quantities of gold in the hills obscured in the fog and mist. To prove their claims, the Indians displayed three ample nuggets. Ojeda became so excited by the find that he decided to report to Columbus at the first opportunity, and by January 20 he was back at La Isabela, with gold, gifts, and additional Indian servants in tow. His subordinate, Gorbalán, spent an extra day ferreting out additional stores of gold, and arrived at the fort twenty-four hours later. Columbus, his health restored, rejoiced in the find, and readied a mining expedition to the Cibao to bring back a much larger haul, much to the frustration of his men, who yearned for the comfort and safety of Spain.

Without warning, sickness felled the men. Dr. Chanca, so diligent that he insisted on sampling each new kind of fish lest the men poison themselves, found himself treating three or four hundred fallen explorers, and he teetered on the verge of exhaustion himself. At first, Columbus faulted the climate for the outbreak, but on further consideration, he wrote, "I place greater blame on heavy womanizing, which here is very widespread, so if they are immodest and unrestrained it is not strange that they should suffer the consequences," that is, syphilis. The disease presents in many ways, and is often self-healing, simply disappearing after a flare-up. Columbus observed of the afflicted, "Thanks be to God, they get well: four or five days and the illness runs its course." That was not always the case; syphilis sometimes lurks in the nervous system for years until it explodes like a biological time bomb.

Syphilis was the scourge of both continents, and scientific consensus about the pattern of transmission has fluctuated. Reflecting the conventional view of his time, Fernández de Oviedo, the self-taught naturalist, wrote, "Syphilis first appeared in Spain after Admiral Christopher Columbus discovered the Indies and returned home. Some Christians who accompanied Columbus on the voyage of discovery," as he called the first voyage, "and some who were on the second voyage brought this plague to Spain, and from them other people were contaminated." Spanish soldiers brought it with them to Italy during a military campaign, and "from there it spread all over Christendom and was carried by men and women who had the disease." It was so easy to transmit syphilis, Fernández de Oviedo believed, that merely sharing plates or cups or bedsheets would accomplish the deed. "Very few Christians who associate and lie with the Indian women have escaped the malady," he warned. "This horrible disease came from the Indies," where it was "quite common among the natives," but, "not so dangerous there as it is here in Europe." The reason for the disparity, according to Fernández de Oviedo, was that Indians cured themselves of syphilis, so he believed, by gulping drafts of water in which splinters of bark or wood that had been thoroughly boiled—not from just any tree, but the fruit-bearing *guayacán* of Hispaniola, or more precisely, the nearby island of Beata. "Undoubtedly many are cured of syphilis by this treatment."

To meet the myriad difficulties facing the settlements, Columbus resolved to rotate his men; some would sail back to Spain, to be replaced with a fresh contingent of soldier-sailors ready to undertake the difficult work ahead. Those returning could boast of the giant gold nuggets waiting to be mined in the Cibao. The decision would alter the character of the voyage, splintering it yet again, and further weaken his uncertain command.

On the second day of February, 1494, Antonio de Torres, whom Ferdinand characterized as "a man of worth and good judgment, much trusted by Catholic Sovereigns and by the Admiral," departed from La Isabela with a large fleet—twelve ships in all—bound for Cadiz, Spain. Torres planned to provide a full report of the voyage to the authorities, and to ask for more supplies to maintain the Spanish presence in the islands discovered by Columbus. He would also have to convey the grim news about the massacre at La Navidad and the uncertain prospects for the new settlements.

In the grand scheme of things, the promise of gold outweighed the loss of life.

CHAPTER 6

Rebellion

It was an amazing sight: a fortune in gold nuggets direct from the Indies—thirty thousand ducats' worth. Ferdinand and Isabella gazed upon an assortment of misshapen lumps endowed with magical power. To hold them, and to own them, was to feel the weight and might of riches. This glittering plunder was the most powerful of all incentives for the Sovereigns to remain supportive of Columbus and his mission. No matter where he had fallen short, he had kept this pledge.

To bring these nuggets from the Indies, Antonio de Torres had retraced Columbus's route, arriving in Cadiz within twenty-five days, on March 7, 1494. In addition to the gold, he brought a sampling of spices and twenty-six Indians, including three believed to be cannibals. They were considered mere curiosities. The greatest excitement was caused by the fortune in gold nuggets.

Torres carried a lengthy, emotional letter from Columbus to the Sovereigns in which the explorer tried to make the best of the troubled situation in Hispaniola. He explained that he would have sent more gold with Torres's fleet, "had not the majority of the people here suddenly fallen ill." He had thought of employing the few men who remained healthy, but he dreaded the "many difficulties and dangers" they would have faced. He would have had to hike through rugged country to the mining region "23 or 24 leagues away," all the while "fording inlets and rivers on a long journey."

Nor was it wise to leave the sick men alone and unprotected from the Indians. Even if he had led the healthy men to the gold mines, they would have faced "a cacique named Caonabó, a man who, in everyone's opinion, is very evil and even more audacious," and likely to endanger them all. And if they reached the gold, how would they transport it to the ships? "Either we would have had to carry just a little bit every day, bringing it with us and risking sickness, or we would have had to send it with some of the men, still running the risk of losing it."

Nearly as urgent as the pervasive illness was the "great scarcity of all things that are particularly efficacious in fighting sickness—such as raisins, sugar, almonds, honey, and rice—which should have arrived in large quantities but we got very little of." And that had been consumed, "including the medicines." Their situation worsened with every passing day.

Columbus sent several lists to Spain with Torres. One requested basic supplies "for the people":

Wheat
Barley
Biscuit
Wine (about 16,000 gallons)
Vinegar in casks
Oil in jars
Beans
Chickpeas
Lentils
Bacon
Beef
Raisins
Figs
Almonds, hazelnuts, walnuts
Salted fish (300 barrels)
Onions
Garlic (5,000 strings)
Sugar
Mustard
Honey (36 gallons)
Molasses (10 jars)
Seeds
Sheep and goats
Calves (20)
Chickens (400)

Wine flasks
Water casks
Strainers, sieves, sifters

Another list presented requirements expressly "for the Admiral and his household," who, on the basis of their stated needs, craved sweets and other delicacies to soften the hardships of the Indies:

Candied citron (20)
Sweets (50 pounds)
Various preserves (12 jars)
Dates
Quince preserve (12 boxes)
Rose-colored sugar (12 jars)
White sugar
Water scented with orange blossoms (4 gallons)
Saffron (1 pound)
Rice (100 pounds)
Raisins from Almuñécar (on Spain's southern coast)
Almonds
Good honey (16 gallons)
Fine oil
Fresh pig's lard (12 gallons)
Ham (100 pounds)
Chickens (100)
Roosters (6)

The Admiral catalogued other indulgences to ease his stay in the islands: five-yard-long tablecloths, seventy-two small cloths, six towels, six pairs of tablecloths for his men, pewter cutlery, two silver cups, two jugs, a salt-shaker, twelve spoons, two pairs of brass candlesticks, six copper pitchers, four pots, two cauldrons, four frying pans, two stewing pans, two copper pots with lids, a brass mortar, two iron spoons, graters, two forks, a colander, a large basin, candles and tapers, and a "grill to roast fish." He did not explain how these items would help convert Indians, locate the Grand Khan, or find gold, but he did offer a suggestion concerning the islands' cannibals. He urged the Sovereigns to consider "sending some of them to Castile . . . because they will finally abandon their cruel custom of eating flesh. And in Castile, by understanding the language, they can soon receive baptism and save their souls." The Taínos, on whom Columbus had come to rely, would give "great credit when they see that we have taken prisoner those who torment them and of whom they are so fearful as to tremble at the very mention of their name." He proposed regular transports of cannibals between the islands and Spain. "The more that are taken over there, the better."

But the Sovereigns, noting the fatalities among the Indians who sailed for Spain, responded in the letter's margin: "You must tell him what happened here with the cannibals who came." The prospect of caravels filled with dying cannibals crowding the docks of Seville did not sit well with Ferdinand and Isabella; they much preferred that Columbus "should get busy there and, if at all possible, see to it that they submit to our holy Catholic faith, and likewise try to see to that with all the inhabitants right on their own islands." In other words, it was better for Columbus to convert the Indians where they lived.

As if attending to navigation, exploration, the maintenance of his ships, the search for gold, and conversion were not enough to occupy him, the Admiral of the Ocean Sea also interested himself in the sensitive matter of finances. It was his conviction that the major participants of the second voyage, Ojeda, Chanca, and others, deserved recognition in the form of higher pay as well as good honey and fine oil and rose-colored sugar.

He expressed resentment of "these caballeros" who had substituted inferior horses at the last moment ("such nags that the best is not worth even 200 maravedís"). The Admiral declared, "These substitutions were carried out with great maliciousness," and he described the dishonest scheme perpetrated by some of the men on the ships. "These caballeros, in addition to their pay, have had their expenses on the voyage paid so far, including that of their horses, and are still being paid now even though they are the kind of people who, when they do not *feel* well or do not *feel* like doing anything, claim that their horses are not to be used without them; and besides, they expect to do no work except on horseback." The Sovereigns decreed that the caballeros must stay, but required them to make their horses available whenever "the Admiral so commands."

And as for the unruly volunteers, who had a habit of going their own way, Columbus recommended that they, all two hundred of them, receive pay as a means of directing their conduct. (The Sovereigns agreed on this point.) And while he was at it, he asked for essentials such as clothing, shoes, mules, arquebuses, and crossbows to replenish the fleet's dwindling stock of supplies.

* * *

In the midst of these tribulations, Columbus dispatched the restless Alonso de Ojeda with fifteen men to look for the mines of Cibao.

After days in the wild, Ojeda and his men returned, explaining that after ascending a troublesome mountain pass, they had been welcomed by the chieftain of a nearby village, and reached the Cibao in only six days. Once there, he observed Indians panning for loose nuggets of gold in a stream. Hearing from the Indians that many streams contained gold nuggets, Ojeda concluded that the region must be "very rich in gold," an overstatement worthy of Columbus. Recovering from his illness, and "overjoyed," said his son, Columbus decided to see the gold for himself.

Before setting out, Columbus assigned his brother Don Diego to secure La Isabela and supervise its construction. The Admiral ordered all the arms stored in the flagship during his absence "that none might use them to mutiny, as some had attempted to do while he was ill," his son wrote. There was ample motivation. The hidalgos and other amateur explorers on the voyage believed that "as soon as they landed they could load themselves with gold and return home rich," according to Ferdinand, without realizing that his father was as susceptible to the magic spell cast by gold as anyone in his crew, and encouraged the illusion. Sadly, "they did not know that gold may never be had without the sacrifice of time, toil and privations." Once they were confronted with the reality that gold was scarce and difficult to mine, and that transporting it to Spain would be time-consuming and dangerous, disillusionment and resentment quickly set in. And so the stage was set for mutiny.

Columbus intimidated potential antagonists—both Spanish and Indian— with a show of force. Leading his men forth in military columns, as banners bearing royal insignia flapped haphazardly in the moist heat and thick vegetation muffled the sound of their trumpets, he departed from La Isabela on Wednesday, March 12, accompanied by every able-bodied man the expedition could spare, excepting those "required to guard the two ships and three caravels that remained of the fleet," in Ferdinand's words. Peter Martyr, claiming Columbus himself as his source, estimates the force included "all his cavalrymen and four hundred foot-soldiers," bound for the Cibao and its gold.

Led by the amphibious Admiral, the land force embarked on a journey across a landscape "of such perfection, grace, and beauty," wrote Las Casas, "so fresh, so green, so open, of such color and altogether so full of beauty, that as soon as they saw it they felt they had arrived in some part of Paradise."

On the scene, Columbus reported to Ferdinand and Isabella that "*Cibao* is the Indian name, which in our language means 'quarry.' It is a huge region, the land very rough, all the mountains and peaks quite high, and all or most of them not very steep. It has no trees, but it is not without vegetation because of its exceptional fertility; the grass here grows like a weed, thicker and higher than a field of barley at the best time of year, and in forty days it grows as high as a horse's saddle, and it is always thick and green if it is not burnt. The ground below all those mountains and peaks is full of stones as large and round as those on a riverbank or a beach, and all or most of them are bluish." The Cibao's pure water delighted him; it was "clear, delicious, cold and not harsh like those waters that harm people and make them sick; it dissolves kidney stones, and many were cured." Even better, "All the creeks and streams, large and small, have gold nuggets, in the water or nearby where the water has washed them out. I believe, or rather, I am certain, that this gold comes from the mines on the peaks and mountains, and during the rainy season the water carries it into the streams."

The gold, and the men who would mine it, required protection. Columbus decided it was time to establish another fort in the heart of the Cibao. On a hilltop, they erected a small settlement with the intimidating name Fortaleza, or Fortress. But that was not their final destination. "After advancing almost seventy-two miles from the city into the gold region," said Peter Martyr, "Columbus decided to build a fortress on the bank of a large river on a high hill, so that there they could gradually and safely explore the region's hidden places. This fort he named Santo Tomás," after Thomas the apostle, the original "Doubting Thomas" who refused to believe in the Resurrection until he felt Jesus' wounds. This name was, perhaps, Columbus's way of defying all the skeptics who refused to believe this valley produced gold.

Attracted by the industrious Spaniards, Indians gathered in the Cibao, seeking bells and other trinkets as eagerly as the white men sought gold. The Admiral obliged, so long as the Indians brought gold. Some nuggets were so large that Columbus assumed the Indians had melted smaller pieces of gold to form large lumps. Columbus held the nuggets in his hand, as an old Indian man told him there were others as "big as walnuts," or even bigger. "When I received the two nuggets from this old man," Columbus wrote, "I was most happy and indicated that they were very nice and gave him a bell. He received it with a sigh of satisfaction expressing greater contentment than someone being given a fine city." These two nuggets, he said, were as nothing "compared with the others in his land." The old man stooped and picked up several stones, claiming that he had nuggets of gold that were even larger. "They ranged in size from that of a walnut to a big orange," Columbus exclaimed in wonder. But matters were not quite that simple.

Believing that he was close to finding greater amounts of gold, the Admiral "sent a young nobleman with a few armed soldiers to explore the [Cibao] region," wrote Ferdinand. He returned telling fantastic stories of "gold nuggets the size of a man's head . . . found on a riverbank." Curiously, Columbus never followed up, preferring to whet the appetite of his Sovereigns for more voyages. He had his excuses prepared—the distance from the Cibao to the ships was too great, he lacked proper gold-mining equipment, the gold would be there when he got back—but, given the overwhelming importance of gold to Columbus and to Spain, his account is deeply suspect. He had indeed found gold, but not the incredible amounts of which he boasted.

Returning to La Isabela on April 1, just before Easter, Columbus discovered that a group of discontented Spaniards had coalesced around the unlikely figure of Bernal Díaz de Pisa, the fleet's comptroller. In Spain, he had been a constable in the royal court. Now he was a rebel, and he was immediately arrested.

While Díaz de Pisa was confined aboard ship, it emerged that he had fabricated a catalogue of outrageous accusations against the Admiral and concealed it in a buoy marking an anchor. Even Columbus's harsh critic, Bartolomé de Las Casas, expressed dismay at Díaz's treachery: "I cannot imagine just how the Admiral could have committed all the crimes and injuries listed in the short space of two months that he had been out there." Despite Columbus's intercession, rumors of his cruelty toward his own men spread throughout Castile. "I have read the letters he sent to the king and queen in which he explains that he was obliged by law to hand out the punishments he did," Las Casas noted, "which is an indication that he did punish some of them," but the cleric sided with Columbus, for once. "Criminals are always demanding to go unpunished," he wrote, "and always claim their actions are justified and that it is they who are being victimized."

By this time, the formerly unified expedition had split into three parts. First, a small delegation of Spaniards painstakingly constructed the fortress known as La Isabela on the northern coast of what is now the Dominican Republic. Second, Columbus and his loyalists searched through the gold mines of Cibao. Along the way, they confronted Indians who were not allied with Guacanagarí and potential mutineers among the crew. Meanwhile, the third and largest contingent returned to Cadiz, under the command of Antonio de Torres.

Giambattista Strozzi, writing from Cadiz, catalogued the fleet's flora and fauna snatched from the Indies, including gold, spices, parrots, and other fowl. Strozzi also wrote excitedly of "many brown men with wide faces like Tartars, with hair extending to the middle of their shoulders, large and very quick and fierce, and they eat human flesh and children and castrated men whom they keep and fatten like capons, and then they eat them. They are called cannibals."

Guillermo Coma, the nobleman traveling with Columbus, remarked that they were accomplished mariners, traveling from island to island in canoes, "even as far as a thousand miles in search of plunder." And they were ferocious. "They hand over the female captives as slaves to their womenfolk, or make use of them to satisfy their lust. Children borne by the captives are eaten like the captives." It might have been for this reason that the Indian women were quick to resort to self-inflicted abortions.

Despite these repugnant practices, Guillermo Coma considered the Caribs "intelligent, sharp-witted, and shrewd," qualities that gave him hope that "they could easily be led to adopt our laws and manner of life, when they realize that our manners are more mild and our manners more civilized than theirs. It is hoped, therefore, that they will in a short time abandon their savage character as a result both of instruction from us and an occasional threat that, unless they abstain from human flesh, they will be reduced to bondage and carried in chains to Spain"—a "civilized" society with terrors of its own, and which would all but exterminate the Caribs within a few years.

The Admiral marked the three-month anniversary of his fleet's arrival in these islands on a note of nervous rapprochement with the Indians, whom they observed at close range. "All of them," said Chanca, "go naked like they were born, except for the women of this island, who keep their waists covered by means of either a piece of cotton fabric that girds their hips or weeds and leaves. As an embellishment, both men and women paint themselves, some in black, others in white and red, in such an imaginative way that seeing them will make one truly laugh; their heads are shaved in patches with such various lock patterns that it is impossible to describe. In sum, all that in Spain we might wish to do on a madman's head would here . . . be an object of refined attention."

*　*　*

By this time, Columbus's men felt safe enough to make a practice of sleeping on dry land rather than in their leaky, crowded ships. Although they feared another massacre, their encounters with the inhabitants proved peaceful enough, and even enjoyable. "We saw many things worthy of amazement: 'wool-producing' trees"—cotton shrubs—"and of great quality, too, so good that those who know the art affirm they could make good clothes with it," Chanca said with satisfaction. And he found "very good mastic from the mastic tree," the resin with which Columbus was familiar from his apprenticeship in the Aegean.

Concerning the Indians' diet, the doctor approvingly noted a "bread made from a weed root" (cassava), and yams, which he considered a source of "excellent nourishment." Guillermo Coma raved about them: "When eaten raw, as in salads, they taste like parsnips; when roasted, like chestnuts. When cooked with pork, you would think you were eating squash. You will never eat anything more delicious." Michele de Cuneo, on the other hand, favored parrots. "The flesh tastes like that of the starling. There are also wild pigeons, some of them white crested, which are delicious to eat." Not everything that grew on the island attained this high culinary standard. Chanca noted that the Indians routinely consumed "snakes, lizards, spiders, and worms found all over the land," a stomach-turning regimen that made "these people more similar to animals, as far as I am concerned."

By the end of March, La Isabela teetered on the verge of collapse. The physical labor prescribed by Columbus drove the overworked, undisciplined men to the brink of exhaustion. Nearly all the settlement's inhabitants were seriously ill and starving. The little food they had rotted in the heat and humidity. Columbus blamed the ships' captains, who he claimed had neglected to take necessary precautions. He pressed the demoralized survivors—everyone from hidalgos to servants, and even clerics—into service to construct a canal and watermill to grind wheat. Under this regimen, gentlemen had to cook their own meals, if they could find anything edible. The sick received a single egg and a pot of stewed chickpeas, a meager ration considered sufficient to sustain five patients. Death stalked every man at the settlement, including the nobles who had never before had to cope with deprivation.

To enforce his will, Columbus constantly threatened violence. He agonized over how to portray his inglorious efforts before the court of Castile, where jealous bureaucrats waited to discredit him. Success for Columbus meant, above all, identifying with divine will, but for the time being he was in danger of losing the way. Accusations of Columbus's cruelty and "hatred for Spanish," in Las Casas's words, gained credence in the royal court—"accusations that gradually wore him down, ensured he never knew a day's happiness through the rest of his life, and sowed the seeds of his eventual fall."

Columbus and his backers were coming to terms with the fatal calculus of discovery. Despite strenuous efforts to ascribe his motives and deeds to a higher power, the quest remained intensely personal, especially when Columbus confronted sickness, suffering, and the prospect of death. At times like these, he seemed to purchase glory with the suffering of his crew members. The first voyage's unlikely success emboldened Columbus to believe that establishing trade with China could be swift and painless, but that no longer appeared true. It was one thing, he realized, to visit a strange harbor, drop anchor, ask the priests on board to bless their cause, and sail away when the wind and tide permitted, another to establish a permanent, self-sustaining settlement: that was the difference between discovering an empire and maintaining it. Empire building required an innovative and different skill set, as essential as the navigational instincts and abilities he had spent a lifetime acquiring. It meant adding the skills of military commander, merchant, politician, and even spiritual leader—all roles he was barely qualified to play. Grumble though they did, threatening mutiny and retribution for perceived slights, no one else among the hundreds of men on the voyage's roster displayed an aptitude for them or was willing to risk taking them on.

But there was worse to come.

"With the Admiral on the very brink of his tribulations and anguish," a messenger from Fort Santo Tomás appeared with alarming news. The Indians on whom the Spaniards had come to rely were abandoning their settlements. A warrior named Caonabó was vowing to kill every Christian. Roused from his torpor, Columbus immediately assembled seventy of his ablest men to protect the fort. He appointed Alonso de Ojeda to command another group, with orders to proceed to Fort Santo Tomás, which they would use as a staging area to aid the surrounding settlements "in a show of the strength and power of the Christians, which might cow the Indians into learning to obey."

Energetic and responsive, Ojeda ingratiated himself with Columbus and his adjutants, but the decision to put the reckless young man in charge soon proved questionable. Las Casas paid tribute to Ojeda's charisma, and to his fatal flaw. "He was slight of body but very well proportioned and comely, handsome in bearing, his face good-looking and his eyes very large, one of the swiftest of men," the *historiador* sighed. "All the bodily perfections that a man could have seemed to be united in him." For instance, "he was very devoted to Our Lady," and yet, "he was always the first to draw blood whenever there was a war or a quarrel." His fiery temperament would soon pose problems for Columbus.

On April 9, 1494, Ojeda led four hundred men from La Isabela on the pacification mission. They had, at best, only a partial understanding of Indian territories on Hispaniola, and were often unable to tell friend from foe. Occasionally, the Indians were both.

They had divided the island into five kingdoms. The closest at hand was Magua, including La Isabela and the voluptuous Vega Real, ruled by Guarionex. To the northwest, Guacanagarí held sway over Marien. In the east, Guayacoa claimed Higuey, famed for fighters fierce enough to repel Carib invasions. Xaraguá, the island's largest kingdom, lay to the south, and belonged to Behechio, whose sister, Anacaona, was Caonabó's wife. On the strength of this alliance, Caonabó claimed a mountain range in central Hispaniola.

Confronting this network of Indian alliances, Ojeda's small force met with an intimidating show of force. Columbus reported:

> There were over 2,000 Indians, all armed with javelins, which they launch from slings much more quickly than from a bow, and all of them were painted black and other colors, with fancy glass beads, mirrors, masks, and mirrors of copper and gold on their heads, letting out frightening cries, as they are wont to do at certain times. One group had planned to wait on the field for the horses and tip them over by jumping on them. . . . They tried to carry out their plan. But it was the horses that ran over them as they stood in their way, and the horses collided with them and killed them.

Columbus considered this turn of events "a miracle of no small importance, that a few Christians could escape a multitude of people sworn to their death."

Ojeda captured three Indian leaders—a chief and his brother and nephew—and placed them in irons to present to Columbus, waiting impatiently at La Isabela. To add to the spectacle, Ojeda ordered his men to lead another Indian into the midst of his village and "cut off his ears" in retribution for the Indians' failing to be helpful to the Spaniards when fording a stream. When the other prisoners reached La Isabela, Columbus went even further: he ordered them "to be taken to the main square and publicly beheaded."

Columbus's behavior troubled the Spanish no less than his victims. "What wonderful news would now be spread the length and breadth of the land concerning the greatness and goodness of these Christians!" Las Casas exclaimed, thinking of the strategic error caused by Columbus's edict, as well as history's verdict on the explorer, which was sure to be harsh.

To Las Casas, the despicable tactics meant that the Indians "had every right to consider" violence against Ojeda—who had cut off the ears of an Indian for shock value—"and the Christians traveling with him." Columbus should have known better; he should have warned the Indians that he was coming, sent messengers to "notify all the kings and lords of his intended arrival," to let them know that he was coming "for their benefit," and to ask permission. And he should have sent "tokens, as he was formally instructed to in the written orders given him by the king and queen." He should have "extended . . . every courtesy and taken every . . . step, as prescribed in the gentle teachings of the gospel whose minister and messenger he was to assure them that he came in peace and love and to avoid committing any outrage or act that might distress or upset the gentle and innocent."

This gentle diplomatic prescription was all very well, but the massacre at La Navidad remained fresh in the mind of Columbus and all the other members of his party, for whom the time for sending invitations or asking permission had long passed.

Columbus remained at La Isabela to plan more nautical exploration. To administer Hispaniola while he was searching for the illusory mainland, he appointed a council including his brother Don Diego, Fray Buil, Pedro Fernández Coronel, Alonso Sánchez de Carvajal, and Juan de Luxan, a "gentleman of Madrid of the household of the Catholic Sovereigns." With the council in place, Columbus was at last ready to explore the coast of Cuba, still unsure about "whether it was an island or a continent." His instincts told him it was a peninsula extending eastward from the mainland, but his exploration of its coast and accounts provided by the Indians suggested that it was actually a great island. To test his hypothesis, he set out from La Isabela for the coast of Cuba, and when he reached it, he inquired of the Indians whether it was an island or the mainland—not that they understood his meaning. It seemed that they were more interested in eating and their women than in exploring, or even communicating with outsiders. It was even possible they did not grasp the distinction between an island and the mainland. Their world consisted only of islands, and Cuba, they allowed, was an island, but a very substantial one, requiring more than "forty moons" to sail from one end to another—or was that the time required to circumnavigate? It was impossible to decipher the exact meaning.

The imprecision unleashed Columbus's most fanciful geographical notions. From Cuba, he believed it would be only a short distance to the Golden Chersonese, as the Malay Peninsula had been known since the era of Ptolemy. In reality, the distance between Cuba and the Malay Peninsula was more than eleven thousand miles, over land and water. But in Columbus's mind, he was nearing his destination. "I kept following the same course of discovery and reached the island of Jamaica in a few days with a very favorable wind, for which I give infinite thanks to God, and from there turned back toward the mainland and followed its coast west for seventy days." Approaching what he believed was the Golden Chersonese, Columbus turned back, "fearing the winds would shift and the very difficult navigating conditions I was experiencing, for the bottom was shallow and I had large ships. It really is very dangerous to sail through so many channels: many times I came to a standstill with all three ships aground so that none could help the others." He sailed north to Cuba, a distance of several hundred miles, because, he said, "I wanted to assure myself that Juana"—his name for Cuba—"is not an island."

Caught up in his geographical folly, Columbus lost "most of the victuals, which were soaked in seawater when the ships had run aground and at times were about to crack open, but I had with me master carpenters and all the tools to repair and make them like new if necessary." It might have been at this point—Columbus was sketchy on the details—that the fleet entered an inviting harbor on Cuba, complete with food for the taking. "I went ashore and saw more than four quintals"—nearly a thousand pounds—"of fish on spits on the fire, rabbits, and two 'snakes.'" Tied to the trees, they were "the most nauseating sight man had ever seen since all had their mouths sewn shut except some that were toothless; they were all the color of dried wood and the skin on their whole body [was] quite rough, especially around the head coming over their eyes, giving them a poisonous and frightening appearance. Like fish, they were all covered with scales, but hard ones, and down the middle of their bodies, from their heads to the tips of their tails, they had some protuberances, high, ugly, and as sharp as diamond points."

The Taínos called the beasts *iwana*, and the term eventually entered the Spanish language as *iguana*, a type of lizard prevalent throughout Central and South America. To the amazement of the Spaniards, the Indians considered iguanas a delicacy. "Our men did not dare taste them," wrote Peter Martyr, "because their disgusting look seemed to provoke not only nausea but horror." Columbus's brother Bartholomew found his courage, and "decided to put his teeth into an iguana," in imitation of a cacique's sister. To his astonishment, "once that tasty meat began to reach his palate and throat, he seemed to go after it with gluttony." The other Spaniards followed suit, eating bits of iguana at first, and soon "turned gluttons" who "would not speak of anything but of such delicacy, claiming that the banquets prepared with them were more sumptuous than ours based on peacocks, pheasants and partridges."

For him, as for other Europeans, ingesting iguana marked another step on the path toward a new civilization, half wild, half sophisticated. Bartholomew enjoyed the immediate pleasures of Hispaniola that Columbus habitually disdained. He was entertained by naked—or nearly naked—virgins with surprisingly fair skin. He and his party tried sleeping in "hanging beds," or hammocks. He became an enthusiastic audience for Indian dances and songs, including one performance of staged warfare that devolved into hand-to-hand combat claiming the lives of four Indians.

Shortly afterward, Bartholomew himself fought to subdue rebellious Indians and bring their leader Guarionex around to the Christians' side. He was gratified to see that Guarionex became an advocate of the Europeans, praising their mercy and generosity. When the cacique finished his speech, his followers lifted him on their shoulders and jubilantly paraded him about. The rapprochement bought only a few days' peace from the stress of Spanish-Indian conflict.

Meanwhile, the Admiral patrolled the channels between Hispaniola and Cuba in search of the mainland, but found only islands. By this time he had counted roughly seven hundred. The number might have been inflated by his passing the same island several times from different directions.

As disoriented as ever, he expressed the wish to return to Spain—not across the Ocean Sea, but "from the east, by way of the Ganges, Arabian Gulf, and Ethiopia." Columbus was a man of fixed beliefs, and to his way of thinking, east was west, and west was east.

* * *

Alarmingly, Columbus's geographical fantasies found a receptive, uncritical audience in Peter Martyr, who breathlessly wrote to Count Giovanni Borremeo that "daily more and more marvels from the New World"—that controversial term again—"are reported through that Genoese, Columbus the Admiral." This time, "he says that he has run over the globe so far from Hispaniola toward the west that he has reached the Golden Chersonese, which is the furthest extremity of the known globe in the east." So convinced was Martyr of the importance of this spurious finding that he planned to write entire books about it.

The geographical impossibility of dozens of Spanish caravels reaching these landlocked Asian and African kingdoms seemed entirely plausible to another scholar, Andrés Bernáldez, who theorized that Columbus "could arrive by land at Jerusalem and Jaffa and from there board a ship, cross the Mediterranean and finally reach Cádiz." Marco Polo had completed a similar journey; why not Columbus? It might be a dangerous passage, Bernáldez admitted, "for all the populations from Ethiopia to Jerusalem are Moorish," but Columbus was "convinced" that he could sail directly from Cuba "in search of the region and city of Cathay under the rule of the Grand Khan." As precedent, Bernáldez cited John Mandeville, who "went there and saw and lived for a certain length of time with the Grand Khan." In reality, Mandeville had cobbled together an entertaining hoax out of fantastic accounts of the world dating back to antiquity.

Columbus might have acted foolishly, but he was no fool. Some part of his mind grasped the implications of Cuba's being an island rather than part of the Asian mainland. In this case, the geographical premise of his voyages was fatally flawed, and he was nowhere near India but rather had blundered into an unanticipated, unexplored region that we now call the Caribbean. The error—with its conceptual, political, and navigational dimensions—was too large to confess to his all-powerful Sovereigns, to his men, or even to himself. How much more comforting it was to assume that his swift transatlantic navigation, twice accomplished, proved rather than disproved his theory of reaching India. Although he asked the necessary questions, the answers meant that he would have to acknowledge that the world was much larger than he, and nearly all Europeans of his era, believed, that it contained an ocean all but unknown to Europeans, and a continent, also unknown to Europeans. Those realities sounded even more fantastic than his imaginings, and he backed away from them.

Columbus was not the only explorer to have caught a glimpse of a larger, previously unimaginable truth only to retreat to the security of conventional wisdom. A half-dozen years earlier, Bartolomeu Dias had insisted that his men swear oaths when he was exploring the African coast. Columbus had witnessed his return to Lisbon, and might have become aware of the pact, and employed it now to protect the integrity of the voyage as originally conceived. The world was what Columbus said it was.

To enforce his view, he instructed Fernand Pérez de Luna, the official on board concerned with certification of documents, to take depositions from all the men aboard the fleet's vessels. Placing loyalty above the truth, each swore that Cuba was longer than any island with which they were familiar, so it had to be an extension of a continent. Thus, there was no need to explore it any further. Those who dared to violate the oath faced penalties: a fine of ten thousand maravedís and having their tongues slashed. Columbus felt so strongly about the matter that he required the boys among the crew to sign the oath. Any lad who spoke out against it would suffer one hundred lashes, a potentially fatal punishment. Even the expert cartographer Juan de la Cosa signed, although his map of 1500 would show that Cuba was, in fact, an island.

If Columbus hoped the oath would silence debate on this sensitive subject of Cuba, he was disappointed. When the learned abbot of Lucerna arrived in Hispaniola several months later, he declared that, as everyone knew, Cuba "was only a very big island, in which judgment, considering the character of our navigation, most of us others concurred." Columbus had not succeeded in fooling anyone, except, perhaps, himself. Worse, he sowed suspicion that he was manipulating the data to support promises he could not keep.

On Thursday, April 24, Columbus "set sail with three ships," bound for Hispaniola's Monte Cristi. The next day he entered a nearby harbor where he expected to find his Indian ally Guacanagarí.

When the three black caravels appeared, Guacanagarí, as volatile as ever, took flight, "though his people pretended he would soon return." Columbus waited, but by Saturday, he realized that Guacanagarí was unlikely to reappear, and he set a westerly course for the nearby island of Tortuga. The journey meant enduring a sleepless night of choppy seas and a frustrating lack of wind. In the morning, he took his ships in the opposite direction, to the east, dropped anchor near the entrance to the Río Guadalquivir, as he called it, "to await a wind that would enable him to make way against the current."

It blew up eventually, and Thursday, April 29, found the three caravels approaching the southern coast of Cuba, where Columbus located a bay "with a mouth of great depth and one hundred fifty feet wide." He named it Puerto Grande, dropped anchor, and by evening he and his men were devouring freshly caught fish roasted over a fire and sampling plump, eighteen-inch-long rodents known as hutias (*Isolobodon portoricencis*), "which the Indians had in abundance."

By May 1, Columbus was sailing through weed-choked waters, "encountering commodious harbors, lovely rivers, and very high mountains," and waving at locals who believed the black ships had descended from heaven. The well-wishers offered tributes of fish and cassava bread, asking nothing in return. As before, Columbus bestowed hawk's bells and glass beads on his supplicants, "wishing to send them away happy." And with that altruistic gesture, he resumed the crucial task of finding gold. In Ferdinand's worshipful view, the quick departure demonstrated his father's resolve, but Columbus himself took a more pragmatic view. "The wind was fresh and I was using it, because things at sea are never certain, and many times an entire trip is lost because of a single day."

After two days and two nights of "excellent weather" Columbus beheld a view of the island's primeval interior. Through some trick of light and atmosphere the vista seemed close at hand, as though he could reach out and graze a mountaintop with his fingertips. That may have been why Columbus—no aesthete—was moved by the sight. "It is the prettiest that eyes have ever seen," he exulted. "It is not mountainous, yet the land seems to touch the sky, and it is huge, bigger than Sicily, with a perimeter of eight hundred miles. It is most fertile and densely populated, both on the seacoast and inland. . . ."

Once again, he was Jamaica-bound, and in search of gold.

The fleet stood offshore until the next day, when "the Admiral cruised down the coast to explore the island's harbor." All was peaceful until the moment "there issued from the shore so many armed canoes that the boats had to return to the ships, not so much from fear of the Indians as to avoid hostilities with them," Ferdinand said. To avoid a confrontation, Columbus entered another harbor, only to realize he had sailed straight into an ambush. Or was it? On these islands, the Indians' desire to fight, to trade, or just to make noise frequently overlapped, and Columbus resorted to guessing about their real intentions. His own stance was just as ambivalent; within the span of a few days he was capable of regarding the Indians as political allies, trading partners, converts, slaves, or deadly enemies. In the pages of his journal and letters they appeared as wise or primitive, indolent or resourceful, according to his judgment and whims.

Columbus returned to Cuba and resumed his westward course, pondering a familiar question: Was Cuba part of the mainland, a hypothesis consistent with his insistence that he had reached the Indies, or was it an island? If so, he had not yet reached the Indies. In the midst of his reverie, "there arose a terrible storm of thunder and lightning that, added to the numerous shoals and channels, caused him great danger and toil."

In severe weather, Columbus would normally strike sail, but his fleet was in danger of colliding with small islands, their dull trees and beaches just visible through the fog and mist. As the weather brightened, the palm trees and scrub sparkled. Columbus called the islets the Queen's Garden, in honor of his sovereign. "The farther he went, the more islands he discovered, and on one day he caused to be noted 164 islands. God always sent him fair weather for sailing among them, and the vessels ran through those waters as if they were flying," Bernáldez said.

Ashore, they marveled at the profusion of wildlife, "cranes the size and shape of those of Castile, but bright red." Nearby, "they found turtles and many turtle eggs, resembling those of hens but having very hard shells."

Returning to their ships, Columbus's men noticed the strange manner in which Indians fished from their canoes. As they approached, Ferdinand relates, the Indians "made signs not to come nearer until they had done fishing," which meant tying "slender cords to the tails of certain fish that we call *revesos*"—remoras, or suckerfish—"that pursue other fish, to which they attach themselves." Despite Ferdinand's enthusiasm for the technique, the Spanish colonists did not trouble to learn this method of fishing for themselves, preferring to rely on the Indians' largesse.

The Jamaican coast emerged from the fog to take shape before his eyes on May 5. He arrived at what is now called St. Ann's Bay, which he named Santa Gloria, a timeless paradise of powdery beach and gently surging ultramarine sea. In every direction, the Admiral noticed "very big villages very close together, about four leagues apart. They have more canoes than elsewhere in these parts, and the biggest that have yet been seen, all made each of a single tree trunk." The settlements were so prosperous that "every cacique has a great canoe for himself in which he takes pride as a Castilian gentleman"—a station to which Columbus aspired—"is proud of possessing a fine, big ship." The canoes were finely worked, and at least one appeared to be astonishingly long; Columbus measured it to make sure his eyes did not deceive him. It was "96 feet in length [with] an 8-foot beam," he noted with appreciation. The canoes had been fashioned from logs hollowed out by craftsmen who charred and later scraped them with sharp stone axes. The Indians relied on the paddle for propulsion; they had never seen sails until Columbus's ships appeared on the horizon.

While methodically sounding the harbor, he and his men were alarmed by the sight of seventy giant canoes, paddles churning through the sea, Indians shouting, ready to attack. "After I anchored, they came down to the beach in numbers to cover the earth, all painted up with a thousand colors, primarily brown, and all of them naked; they wore various kinds of feathers on their heads, their chests and bellies were covered with palm fronds, and they shouted at the top of their lungs and threw spears, although they did not strike us." Columbus feigned indifference, occupying himself by taking on wood and water, repairing his battered vessels, indirectly letting the Indians know that their bellicose gestures would accomplish nothing. To flee would only encourage the Indians, who, Columbus reminded himself, were so inexperienced that they would grasp a Spanish sword by the blade "without thinking they can be hurt."

According to Ferdinand, Columbus resolved to "scare them right at the start" by sending small craft filled with crossbowmen who wounded at least six or seven Indians by a conservative estimate. The brawl settled matters for the moment.

Columbus's Indian interpreter sailed to shore in a longboat to conduct diplomacy among the inhabitants, and once he had calmed their anxieties, struck a deal, the outlines of which quickly became apparent. "A multitude of canoes came peacefully from the neighboring villages to trade their things and provisions for our trinkets." He obtained all he wished, except for the gold that he believed was just waiting to be discovered.

Having repaired the damage sustained by his flagship in the battle, Columbus was planning to return to Cuba when his departure was delayed by a surprising defection. "A young Indian came aboard saying he wished to go to Castile," and he was followed by canoes bearing his relatives and supporters pleading with him to return, but they failed to persuade him. "To escape the tears and lamentations of his sisters, he hid where they could not see him," Ferdinand noted of the drama. The Indian had his way and remained aboard ship. The defection was complete. "The Admiral marveled at the firm resolution of this Indian and ordered him to be well treated."

That night, the fleet rode at anchor in Santa Gloria's idyllic harbor, and in the morning, May 6, the Admiral raised sail, and traveled fifteen miles west along the Jamaican coast, dropping anchor again in a horseshoe-shaped place of refuge that instantly became Puerto Bueno.

Onshore, Indians donned brightly colored feather headdresses and masks, and hurled their poison spears at Columbus's ships. Undeterred by what he considered a ritual show of force, the Admiral sent a party of men ashore in a longboat to scrounge for water and wood and the opportunity to repair their leaky boats, only to meet with a hail of stones. To tame the warriors, Columbus sent another boat with sailors armed with crossbows, whose arrows injured and killed several. To teach the Indians a lesson, Bernáldez recalled, the Spanish deployed a vicious dog that "bit them and did them great hurt, for a dog is worth ten men against the Indians."

The following day, a half-dozen Indians appeared onshore with offerings of cassava bread, fruit, and fish to appease the Spanish invaders. Columbus and his men helped themselves to the Indians' bounty, all they could want with the exception of gold. On May 9, the newly repaired ships raised anchor and sailed from Puerto Bueno, again in a westerly direction, to a spacious harbor Columbus named El Golfo de Buen Tiempo, the Fair Weather Gulf—now known as Montego Bay. Inevitably, a storm blew up. Without giving a reason, striking out blindly in search of gold and the Grand Khan, Columbus left the Jamaican coast and returned to the mysterious land of Cuba—Juana—reaching Cape Cruz on May 14.

To his surprise, he heard rumors of himself. The Indians had been expecting the man with the large black ships to return.

Within the embrace of Cape Cruz lay an Indian village, where Columbus encountered the cacique, who explained through an interpreter that he had conferred with other Indian leaders, who remembered Columbus from his previous voyage. The Indians had acquired a surprising amount of intelligence about the fleet. They knew that the Indian interpreter was a convert to Christianity, and they were familiar with Columbus's need for provisions, especially water, his noisy but ineffectual firearms, and his obsession with gold.

After reaffirming his good intentions to the Indian sentinels of Cape Cruz, Columbus departed, plying a northeastern route that took the fleet along what is now the Balandras Channel to the Gulf of Guacanayabo. Although the Admiral seemed to have reoriented himself now that he was back in Cuba, he remained befuddled about his global whereabouts, and as reliant as ever on spurious sources, especially Sir John Mandeville.

The fair weather held, revealing a sparkling still life edged with dew. "Next day at sunrise," wrote Bernáldez, "they looked out from the masthead and saw the sea full of islands in all four quarters, and all green and full of trees, the fairest that eyes beheld." Columbus desired to pass to the south of the islands, but he recalled Mandeville, who claimed there were more than five thousand islands in the Indies, and decided instead to sail along the coast of "Juana, and to see whether it was an island or not." Columbus bet that Cuba was part of the mainland.

They sailed on, Columbus anxious to avoid the slightest contact with razor-edged coral reefs and sinister sandbars. From the Gulf of Guacanayabo on May 15, he sailed gingerly to the west, probably past an archipelago off Santa Cruz del Sur, into the Rancho Viejo Channel (as it is now called) and the Pingue Channel, into a gulf guarded by a blockade of islands with the alarming name of Laberinto de las Doce Leguas, Labyrinth of Twelve Leagues. It was but one more maze that Columbus had entered, some geographical, others conceptual, combining to mislead him into exploring dead ends and arriving at false conclusions. He was saved from folly or disaster by his remarkable navigational intuition and his instinct for self-preservation as storms buffeted his ships when they were trapped and vulnerable in the channels. Daily tempests forced him into impossible navigational quandaries in tight spaces—whether to spread sail or take it in, to drop anchor or not to drop anchor—and he often violated his own cardinal rule by scraping the bottom of the channels he explored. The worst transgression occurred when *Santa Clara* ran aground, and for many anxious hours he was unable to dislodge her. Eventually he and his crew freed her, and he regained the freedom of the sea.

As Columbus resumed his exploration of the southern coast of Cuba, he arrived at the massive incursion known as the Bahía de Cochinos (Bay of Pigs). Always persuaded that he was on the verge of reaching India, he suspected that he had located—at last!—a passage from Juana to the mainland. The navigator in him eventually realized that he was in fact exploring a spacious gulf, as he later described to Bernáldez, "on the edge of the sea, close by a great grove of palms that seemed to reach the sky" shielding two gushing springs. "The water was so cold and of such goodness and so sweet that no better could be found in the world." Never had he sounded more charmed by his surroundings. For once Columbus gave himself up to rapt contemplation of the vistas before him.

Departing the bay, Columbus led his fleet past Cayo Piedras and the Gulf of Cazones. All at once, he told Bernáldez, the ships "entered a white sea, as white as milk, and as thick as the water in which tanners treat their skins." Then they found themselves "in two fathoms' depth and the wind drove them strongly on, and being in a channel very dangerous to come about in, they could not anchor the ships." The caravels negotiated the channels for thirty miles until they reached an island in only "two and a half fathoms of water," where they anchored, "in a state of extreme distress." He had inadvertently sailed into the midst of diminutive islands near the Zapata Peninsula, where every swell concealed peril.

He had no choice but to find a way out. For once his gift for dead reckoning failed him. Never before had he seen such an erratic display of water—white, black, milky, and indigo, as if all the formations and currents with which he had become familiar during a lifetime of sailing had lost their meaning. He spent several days cautiously proceeding along Cuba's sweltering southern coast, always near to the shore should disaster strike. He sent an agile caravel into a channel to find water, or signs of human habitation, but the ship soon returned, her crew reporting that the vegetation was "so thick that a cat couldn't get ashore." Columbus tried to pierce the dense mangrove cover, but he, too, complained that the land was "so thickly wooded down to the seashore that they seemed to be walls" that excluded his fleet from the gold, the glory, and the fulfillment of discovery and conquest.

As he coasted along an uninspiring formation he named Punta de Serafín, a wind arose, and the obstructing islands gave way to open water and a prospect of distant mountains. And so, Bernáldez writes, "the Admiral decided to lay a course toward those mountains, where he arrived the following day, and they proceeded to anchor off a very fine and very large palm grove"—almost any grove would have looked appealing after the oppressive wall of mangroves they had endured—"where there were springs of water, sweet and very good, and signs that there were people about." Strange things started happening.

As the Queen's Garden disappeared over the horizon, Columbus slumped in exhaustion. The stress of exploring, the strange diet, the inimical climate, and more than anything else, the lack of sleep had taken their toll. He was, said his son, "worn out," and "had not undressed and slept a full night in bed from the time he left Spain until May 19, the day he made this notation in his journal." Adding to his cares was the difficulty of picking his way through the "innumerable islands among which they sailed," or, to be more specific, the dangers presented—coral reefs capable of slicing a hull to shreds, sandbars that could ensnare a ship as surely as a remora attached itself to its host, unpredictable winds, and even more unpredictable tribes who might attack at any moment.

The very next day, May 20, Columbus negotiated his way past seventy-one islands, "not counting the many they sighted at sunset toward the west-southwest." The vista was anything but reassuring: "The sight of these islands or shoals all about them was frightening enough, but what was worse was that each afternoon a dense mist rose over them in the eastern sky, with such thunder and lightning that it seemed a deluge was about to fall; when the moon came out, it all vanished, dissolving into rain and part into wind." It was such a common atmospheric phenomenon, he said, that "it happened each afternoon."

On May 22, the fleet approached an island that appeared slightly more substantial than the others he had recently passed. Santa Marta, Columbus decided to call it as he went ashore, desperately in need of food and water. The Indians had abandoned their village, and in their huts, the starving sailors found only fish. In the background, large dogs, "like mastiffs," pawed the earth and growled. Unsatisfied and bewildered, the Spanish returned to their ships and sailed onward, "northeasterly among the islands," past stately cranes and gaudy parrots, wandering blindly into a "maze of shoals and islands" that "caused the Admiral much toil, for he had to steer now west, now north, now south, according to the disposition of the channels." Within their confines, the ships could not tack and maneuver. Peter Martyr related that "the water of these channels was milky and thick for forty miles, as if they had sprinkled flour all over the sea." While Columbus and his men frantically sounded the bottom and kept lookout, the keels often scraped bottom. Nevertheless, the fleet made it through and exited into the open sea, where, eighty miles away, lofty mountains hung suspended against the sky. They were approaching Cuba and apparent safety.

The fleet put in, and a lone Spanish scout, armed with a crossbow, went ashore in search of desperately needed water. During his search, he confronted the spectacle of a man dressed in a white tunic. At first, the scout thought he beheld a friar whom the Admiral had brought along. "Suddenly,

from the woods he saw a whole group of about thirty so-clothed men coming," Peter Martyr related. "He then turned around shouting and ran as fast
as he could toward the ships. These men dressed in tunics clapped their
hands at him and attempted to persuade him with all means not to be so
fearful, but he kept running." Stranger still, the men appeared to have complexions as light as those of the Spanish. From what tribe had they come?
Were they lost Europeans? Emissaries of the legendary Prester John? And
if so, had Columbus's fleet finally reached the Indies?

Astonished by the apparition, Columbus sent a delegation "to see if they
could talk with these people, for according to the crossbowman, they came
not to do any harm but to speak with us." They found no one, "which displeased me much because I wanted to speak with them since I had traversed
so many lands without seeing people or villages." Attempting to blaze a trail
inland to the men, the Spanish "got themselves so entangled that they hardly
made a mile," let alone forty. They returned to the ships, exhausted and
empty-handed.

Under way once again, the fleet proceeded ten leagues to the west, past
"marsh and mire," as Ferdinand put it, and within hailing distance of huts
onshore. More canoes approached Columbus's ships, with Indians bearing
water and food, which the sailors were in no position to refuse. They paid
in trinkets, over the protests of their Indian benefactors, who wanted nothing in return.

Columbus snatched one of the Indians, "telling him and the other Indians
through an interpreter that he"—the Indian hostage—"would be released
as soon as he had shown him the way and given him other information about
that region." The information Columbus received was exactly what he did
not want to hear: Cuba, said the Indian, was an island, which meant that
the fleet had not reached the outskirts of the Indies. Ferdinand is silent on
his father's reaction to this news, but the Admiral's sense of bewilderment
can be imagined, and it was compounded by the fleet's having wandered
into a dangerously shallow channel. In the effort to move to a deeper waterway, Columbus "had to kedge it with cables over a sandbank less than a
fathom deep but two ship lengths in size." Kedging meant dragging the ship
from one small anchor to another.

The ship emerged at night into a sea that seemed to be covered from one
end to the other with turtles. (Peter Martyr said the ships "had to slow down"
just to get past them all.) At daybreak, cormorants took wing, "so numerous

that they darkened the sun." And the next day, "so many butterflies flew about the ships that they darkened the air till afternoon, when a heavy rain squall blew them off."

Suffering from exhaustion and malnutrition, Columbus headed back to the safety of La Isabela after nearly three months' absence. The prospect of security turned to peril when the fleet sailed into a channel that quickly narrowed. Before he could react, the ships were trapped in a bottleneck. As his men fought to overcome panic, Columbus, marshaling his inner resources, never appeared more confident than he did at this impasse. "He shrewdly put on a cheerful countenance," Ferdinand noted. In fact, he loudly praised God for making him come by this route; if they had gone another way, "they might have become hopelessly entangled or lost and without ships and provisions with which to return." He sought to calm his men by reminding them that they could turn back at any time, and during the last days of June he was eventually forced to retrace his track through the channel, then coast uneasily over a "green and white sea," which seemed to conceal a massive and hazardous shoal, before he reached "another sea as white as milk," apparently a shoal, but in reality only three fathoms deep.

"All these changes and the appearance of the sea caused great dread among the sailors, since they had never seen or experienced anything of the kind before and accordingly believed themselves to be irretrievably doomed," said Las Casas. They anxiously traversed this sea, only to come to another, black as ink and five fathoms deep, and then, to Columbus's great relief, the fleet made Cuba, where he turned east, negotiating the headwinds and in search of fresh water, safe harbor, and a brief respite from the toil of discovery.

The ships had taken a beating. Their keels had been battered and torn from repeated contact with the bottom. Their ropes and sails had rotted away. The food, sodden with seawater and fouled with vermin, had spoiled. As if these troubles were not enough, while Columbus was writing in his journal on June 30, he felt his ship run aground "with such force that they could not get her off by the stern with the anchors or by any other means; however, with God's aid, they managed to pull her off by the prow, though she suffered considerable damage from the shock of the grounding." Columbus found wind to sail away from the near disaster with as much speed as he could muster "through a sea that was always white and two fathoms deep," and he kept going, enduring every evening at sunset "violent rainstorms which wore the men out," said Las Casas, who continued, "The Admiral was in a state of extreme anxiety."

Even Las Casas pitied Columbus at this point, evoking "the unparalleled suffering of the admiral on these voyages of discovery." Reviewing the misfortunes plaguing the Admiral of the Ocean Sea, the chronicler rose to a histrionic pitch, declaring, "His life was one long martyrdom, something which will lead others . . . to conclude that there is little to be gained and little rest to be enjoyed in this world for those who are not forever conferring with God." Las Casas was unique in considering Columbus impious; from another perspective, the Admiral's misfortunes, and those he caused others, could be traced to his tightly held spiritual convictions, which were both his inspiration and his undoing.

As if they were biblical plagues, Las Casas listed the afflictions: the "sudden squall that placed him in imminent and deadly danger" by "thrusting the neck of his vessel down beneath the waves so that it seemed that it was only by the grace of God that he was able to take in the sails and hold fast by using the heaviest of anchors." That crisis was followed by "the great quantity of water the ship took on board," the exhausted crew, and the lack of food, supplemented only by "the odd fish they managed to catch." Columbus's distress was made all the worse by his oppressive sense of responsibility for the others and for himself. No wonder that he felt moved to cry out to Ferdinand and Isabella: "Not a day goes by that I am not faced with the prospect of the certain death of us all."

The Admiral returned, Ferdinand said, as if under his breath, to the "island of Cuba." Whether island or peninsula, "the air was fragrant with the sweet scent of flowers." Columbus's men devoured fowl they thought resembled pigeons but were larger and tastier and which exhaled an aromatic odor. When their gullets were opened, they revealed partly digested bouquets of flowers.

While resting and overseeing repairs to the ships, Columbus went ashore to attend Mass on the beach; it was now July 7. There he was approached by an "eighty year old man," said Peter Martyr, relying on Columbus, "a leader all respected, though naked, with many followers. During the service, this man remained still, looking surprised, face and eyes still; then, he gave the Admiral a basket full of fruits that he held. Communicating with the Admiral by means of signs, they exchanged religious affirmations." With the help of Diego Colón—an Indian convert to Christianity who had taken the

Admiral's surname—the elderly man "made a speech," and quite a surprising oration it was, covering morality and the afterlife. According to Ferdinand Columbus's version, the chieftain said he had been to Hispaniola himself; in fact, he was acquainted with his counterparts there, and he had also been to Jamaica, and even "traveled extensively in western Cuba." If so, this was a personage who could give Columbus reliable information about these islands, and he even offered an explanation for the apparition the scout had seen weeks before: "the cacique of that region dressed like a priest." A priest: it again seemed possible that Prester John had preceded the Spanish to this partially Christian land, and if he had, so might the Grand Khan, just as Marco Polo had written. If Columbus interpreted the cacique's sign language correctly, they might have arrived in the Indies, after all. The illusion would remain undisturbed, as compelling as ever. He could sail on indefinitely, if uneasily, in search of his elusive Indies, and, of course, gold, passing up countless Edens with their hatching turtles and butterfly storms.

But the cacique had more to say. He talked of human souls following one of two paths, gloomy or pleasant, and he admonished Columbus to decide for himself which direction to take, and what his reward or punishment in the afterlife would be for his actions. Or so the cacique's translated, partly understood words sounded to Columbus, who expressed surprise at the wisdom of the elder. He explained that he was familiar with the concept of punishment and reward in the afterlife, yet he wondered how the cacique, at home in a state of nature, had come to subscribe to the same philosophy.

Columbus explained that the king and queen of Spain had sent him to "bring peace to all the uncharted regions of the world," which, to his way of thinking, meant subduing cannibals and punishing criminals wherever they were found. Men of goodwill had nothing to fear from the Admiral of the Ocean Sea. It seemed to Columbus that his words had pleased the cacique so deeply that the old man would have joined the Spaniards if his wife and children had not objected. Yet the philosophical Indian was puzzled: How was it that the Admiral, who appeared to have supreme power, bowed to the authority of another? Even more incredible to his ancient ears were the descriptions of the "pomp, power, and magnificence of the Sovereigns and their wars, how big their cities and how strong their fortresses," in Peter Martyr's words. Such splendor was overwhelming, and the cacique's wife and children wept at the Admiral's feet.

Keeping his composure, the chieftain "asked many times if the country that gave birth to such men was not indeed heaven," in Peter Martyr's transcription. Among the Indians, Columbus gathered, "earth was a shared as-set, like sun and water, and . . . 'mine and yours' concepts, which are the seeds of all evils, do not apply." The cacique explained that his people were "satis-fied with little, and in that land there are more fields available to cultivate than there is need." It was a golden age for the Indians, Columbus recalled. "They do not surround their properties with ditches, walls, or hedges; they live in open fields, without laws, books, or judges; they behave naturally in a just manner. They consider evil and wicked anyone who delights in harm-ing others."

The old man's ideas challenged the explorer's assumptions about the world beyond Spain. Perhaps the church might not have a monopoly on the afterlife, blasphemous as that notion was. Perhaps Spain did not have a mo-nopoly on empire. Perhaps he was on a voyage of redemption. Or damnation. He would find out.

CHAPTER 7

Among the Taínos

It began with a clap of thunder as the crew raised anchor off Cape Cruz, Cuba, on July 16, "so sudden, violent, and with such a downpour of rain, that the deck was placed underwater," Columbus said. They struck sail and pushed their heaviest anchors overboard to secure a mooring amid the flashes of lightning. By the time they had accomplished that task, so much water had seeped through the "floor timbers that the sailors could not get it out with the pumps, especially because they were all very tired and weak from too little food." To sustain them through their difficult labors, "all they had to eat daily was a pound of rotten biscuits and a pint of wine." Drawing on their last reserves of strength, the men struggled to prevent the vessel from sinking.

Weakened, Columbus cowered before the onslaught of the elements, and confided to his journal: "I am on the same ration as the others. May it please God that this be for His service and that of Your Highnesses. Were it only for myself, I would no longer bear such pains and dangers, for not a day passes that we do not look danger in the face." And yet he persisted; there was no other choice.

The storm eventually blew itself out, and two days later, on July 18, their weather-beaten ship returned to Cape Cruz, due north of Jamaica. A delegation of cheerful Indians brought cassava bread, fish, and abundant fruit to the weak and starving Spaniards. When the men recovered, Columbus desired to sail for Hispaniola, but, with the wind being contrary, he stood for Jamaica.

Four days later, the fleet glided into the translucent waters surrounding Jamaica, where still more Indians plied the sailors with lusty greetings and succulent victuals, "which they liked much better than what they had received on all the other islands."

Early one morning, a canoe approached, bearing an Indian who gave little gifts to every Spaniard in sight, except Columbus. "I was off to one side reciting some prayers I find helpful," he wrote, and "did not immediately see the gifts or the determination of the approach of this man." Eventually he did take notice of the cacique's theatrical entrance. "In the largest canoe he came in person with his wife and two daughters, one of whom was about eighteen years, very beautiful, completely naked as they are accustomed to be, and very modest; the other was younger, and two stout sons and five brothers and other dependents; and all the rest must have been his vassals," Columbus later told his friend Bernáldez. Two or three men had their faces painted with colors in the same pattern, and each wore on his head a large feather helmet, and on his forehead a round disk as large as a plate. Each held in his hand a gadget that he tinkled. As for the cacique, he wore ornaments fashioned of *guanín*, a gold alloy, around his neck. To Columbus, the finery resembled "eight-carat gold." Some were as large as plates, he claimed, and shaped like fleurs-de-lis. Except for a finely worked girdle, the rest of his body was exposed. And his wife was naked, "except in the one spot of her pudendum, which was covered by a little cotton thing no bigger than an orange peel." Her older daughter wore around her middle a single string of small and very black stones, from which hung something made of "green and red stones fastened to woven cloth."

The cacique and his entourage came aboard Columbus's caravel, turned to address the Admiral of the Ocean Sea, and amid torrents of praise for Spain, declared, "I have decided to go to Castile with you and obey the King and Queen of this world."

Columbus considered those words carefully. "He said all this so reasonably I was wonder struck." As a distracting wind shifted one way and then another, he invited the cacique and his entourage to remain aboard ship for the day, "staying out in the open sea until the waves became enormous." The ship heaved and groaned in the heavy weather. "By this time the women were most afraid, crying and asking their husband and father to go back home," Columbus observed. "From that moment, they knew the sea, and what it meant to face the sea." To Columbus, it meant an occasion to master the elements, and by extension, to confront his destiny; to the terrified Indians, it meant the experience of terror before the power inherent in the universe. "And they wanted him [the cacique] to be aware how painful this was for them because they were the ones who most wanted to go to Castile." Reflecting on his wife, his daughter, and his young son, barely six or seven, "whom he always held in his arms," the cacique swallowed his pride and acknowledged the wisest course would be to return to the safety of land. To honor the decision, Columbus and he exchanged gifts, and the Admiral, not to be outdone in magnanimity, said that he also gave gifts to the cacique's brothers and the rest of his retinue.

Shifting his attention to the cacique's children, who were as naked as their parents, Columbus desired "the older daughter dressed, but her mother said no because they were not used to it." In fact, she had been cowering behind her parents, "hugging herself with her arms, covering her chest and face," and uncovering it "only when expressing wonder." She talked throughout the long day at sea, "but always behaved in this honest and chaste manner." When they were safely anchored, Columbus reluctantly dispatched his distinguished Indian guests, who were "very sad at parting, and so was I, because I would have liked very much to bring him to Your Highnesses as he was the very person for knowing all the secrets of the island." They had been spared a grueling transatlantic crossing and an uncertain future in Spain.

Within days, Columbus took it upon himself to explore the southern portion of the island of Jamaica. Perhaps here he would find sufficient quantities of gold to satisfy his avarice.

They appeared behind the mist like a giant turquoise dragon. They were the Blue Mountains of Jamaica, one of the largest continuous mountain ranges in the Caribbean, reaching an altitude of over 7,400 feet at the highest point, swathed in lush vegetation sheltering five hundred species of flowering plants, half of which existed nowhere else on the planet. Fluttering *mariposas* darted among the trees, including the stupendous Homerus swallowtail (*Papilio homerus*), the largest butterfly in the Western Hemisphere, with a six-inch wingspan of flickering black and gold. Hundreds of avian species looked on, in search of their next meal. The richness and diversity of life in the region equaled anything to be found in Marco Polo's extravagant *Travels*.

As Jamaica's Blue Mountains came into view on August 19, Columbus led the fleet past a point that he named Cabo del Farol, or Signal Fire, after spying an Indian bonfire. The ships completed a windward passage to the island of Hispaniola.

In the midst of this natural splendor the fleet spent another three days, until a canoe bearing Indians arrived.

"Almirante!" they shouted in recognition.

Columbus had become a legendary presence in these parts, both feared and welcomed.

They sailed along the suffocating, overgrown coast, enduring dreary afternoon squalls and the menace of distant thunder, until, on August 19, "he lost sight of that island and headed directly for Hispaniola," leaving Jamaica and the promise of easy gratification in his wake. All he had discovered by this point in his voyage was that it would be difficult or impossible to attain his goal without the help of God.

Within a day or two Columbus took refuge on a compact island, Alta Vela, only to realize that he had become separated from the other two ships comprising his fleet. This was not the first time he had lost track of the small fleet. He appeared to be losing his grip on the voyage and on himself. He ordered men to climb to the island's highest point, but even they saw nothing but an endless expanse. Hungry and restless, his men slaughtered seals simply by walking up to the creatures as they slept on the beach and bludgeoning them to death.

After six days, the two missing ships appeared, and the reunited fleet sailed for the island Columbus called Beata, twelve leagues distant. Expecting more of the hospitality to which he had become accustomed, Columbus was startled by Indians "armed with bows and poisoned arrows and carrying cords in their hands issued from that village, making signs that those cords were tying up the Christians they would capture." Undeterred, the three boats landed, and after a brief exchange, the Indians "put aside their arms and offered to bring the Christians bread, water, and all else they had." Even more pleasing, they had heard of Christopher Columbus, and wished to meet him. And so they did, after which the fleet sailed on.

Passing an island, Columbus decided to name it after his companion Michele de Cuneo of Savona, who explained, "out of love for me, the Lord Admiral called it La Bella Saonese. He made a gift of it, and I took possession . . . by virtue of a document signed by a notary public." By such contrivances ancient lands passed into contemporary hands. Cuneo surveyed his new realm, where he "uprooted grass and cut trees and planted the cross and also the gallows." Cuneo was pleased; it was beautiful, he decided, counting thirty-seven villages "with at least 30,000 souls."

* * *

On the night of September 14, Columbus "observed an eclipse of the moon and was able to determine a difference in time of about five hours and twenty-three minutes between that place and Cadiz," said Ferdinand.

This statement has inspired centuries of questions about Columbus's precise whereabouts at this time (uncertain), his facility with celestial navigation (limited), and even his honesty in reporting his findings (open to question). But the deceptions and lapses reveal the limits of his abilities as a navigator and his instinctive desire to obscure his location when it seemed to place him beyond the limits of "India." In "India," he reigned supreme, thanks to the proclamations of Ferdinand and Isabella, and was entitled to great wealth and prestige. If he had inadvertently strayed into some uncharted part of the world, his findings and claims would be open to challenge and probably worthless. Better to hope that all would come right in the end than to try to understand his actual location in a global context. One of the great paradoxes of this explorer's mental habits was his reluctance to contemplate alternative answers to unresolved questions about navigation. He did not wish to "discover" the "unknown." For Columbus, who believed that all had been foretold and guided by the will of God, there was no such thing.

For those who shared Columbus's mysticism, a lunar eclipse was freighted with significance. It occurs when the moon passes behind the earth so that the earth prevents the sun's rays from striking the moon. The sun, the earth, and the moon are aligned, with the earth in the middle. The previous lunar eclipse, May 22, 1453, coincided with the fall of Constantinople, and now it was happening again, imbuing his voyage with cosmic significance.

Columbus was planning to return to La Isabela, when the character of the voyage abruptly changed, and disturbing gaps in the account appear. After five days riding out a gale, the fleet had become separated once more; eventually the two missing caravels reappeared, and on September 24, the restored fleet made for the eastern end of Hispaniola to another island, this one called Amona by the Indians. Instead of returning to what had become his home port in the Indies, Columbus "repaired his ships with the clear purpose of ravaging again the islands of the cannibals and burning all their canoes, so that these rapacious wolves would not injure sheep any longer." But the campaign against the cannibals failed to materialize.

"From that point on the Admiral ceased to record in his journal the day's sailing," his son reported, "nor does he tell how he returned to Isabela." Overwork and nervous strain had broken his health. "He sometimes went eight days with less than three hours' sleep," his son explained. "This would seem impossible did he not himself tell it in his writings." The recent ordeal at La Isabela had taken its toll; as a result of "his great exertions, weakness, and scanty diet" Columbus "fell ill in crossing from Amona to San Juan."

In fact, he was comatose: "He had a high fever and drowsiness, so that he lost his sight, memory, and all his other senses." He was fighting for his life, "more dead than alive," said Peter Martyr. "I attribute my malady to the excessive fatigues and dangers of this voyage: over 27 consecutive years at sea have taken their toll," he later wrote to the Sovereigns. "My own concern was that even the most courageous person could die, and besides, I was preoccupied with bringing the ships and crews back safely." Over the course of the last thirty days, "I slept no more than five hours, in the last eight only an hour and a half, becoming half blind, completely so at certain times of day." He ended his lament with a prayer: "May Our Lord in His mercy restore my health."

The men serving under him realized there was no second-in-command to take his place. Frightened and disoriented, the leaderless crew decided to make for La Isabela, arriving at the beleaguered fort on September 29, 1494. The fleet dropped anchor, and *Santa Clara* welcomed another Columbus, the wandering Bartholomew, who had lived in his brother's shadow. Now he had his chance to step into the light.

For years, Bartholomew Columbus had tried to emulate his brother's exploits at sea. In England, he had unsuccessfully petitioned Henry VII to sponsor a voyage to the Indies, and in France, he approached Charles VIII with the same plan, and met with the same dispiriting result. His skills as a mapmaker stood him in good stead, and he conducted himself as a competent and reliable mariner, but he lacked Columbus's charisma and consuming mysticism. Said Las Casas, "My impression, from talking to him on a number of occasions, was that the commander was a dry and harsh man, with little of the sweetness of character and gentleness of disposition that characterized the Admiral." On the other hand, he had a "pleasing countenance, albeit a little forbidding, with good physical strength and strong character," in the chronicler's estimation, and he was "well-read, prudent, and circumspect" and experienced "in the world of business." During the years of exile in Spain, he had been a "great support to the Admiral, who turned to him for advice whenever he proposed to do something."

In matters of scholarship, Las Casas judged Bartholomew his brother's equal, or better: "He was a notable sailor, and to judge from the books and the navigational charts belonging either to the admiral or to him and covered in marginal notes and annotations in his own hand, he was, in my opinion, so learned in matters of the sea there can have been little his brother could have taught him." In fact, Bartholomew "had a clear hand, better than the Admiral's, for I have many writings by both in my possession."

In limbo, Bartholomew had occasion to study his brother's handwriting. Fresh from the triumphant first voyage, Columbus wrote to Bartholomew, imploring him to come to Spain. If he arrived in Seville in time, the reunited Columbus brothers could have sailed together as brothers in arms, but the fleet had formed so quickly that Christopher led the second voyage from Cadiz long before Bartholomew arrived.

Marooned in Seville, Bartholomew received a communication from Columbus that promised to give him the standing he needed. Bartholomew was to escort Columbus's two children, Diego and Ferdinand, to the court in Valladolid to serve as pages to the sole male child of King Ferdinand and Queen Isabella, the sixteen-year-old infante, Don Juan. At the start of 1494, Bartholomew presented his nephews to the Sovereigns, who in turn elevated him to the status of Don Bartolomé, and gave him a coveted appointment to command a fleet consisting of three ships bound for La Isabela, where supplies were desperately needed. Despite settling in a land of astonishing fertility, the outpost remained dependent on Spain for survival.

By the spring of 1494, Bartholomew, now known as El Adelantado, a Spanish military title meaning "the Advancer," was guiding a fleet bound for La Isabela, where he arrived in late June to join forces with the Admiral of the Ocean Sea. Try as he might, he never inspired the confidence or fear associated with his brother. "Since Genoa was Genoa there has never been a man so courageous and astute in the act of navigation as the lord admiral, for when sailing, by simply observing a cloud or a star at night, he judged what was to come, if there was to be bad weather. He himself commanded and stood at the helm. When the storm had passed, he raised the sails while others slept," marveled his friend Michele de Cuneo, who, unlike Las Casas, doubted the Adelantado's ability to lead a small fleet, let alone a Spanish colony. But nepotism was nepotism, and there was nothing that Cuneo or anyone else on the voyage could do about it.

In an effort to bring a measure of order to their ragtag outpost of empire, Ferdinand and Isabella dispatched another supply fleet, four ships in all, with instructions to Columbus dated August 16, 1494. Although appreciative in tone, the communiqué revealed widening cracks in the royal façade of confidence. They desired their *almirante* to be more forthcoming about his actual discoveries. "We have now read everything you say, and although you go into considerable detail, and reading what you write is a source of great happiness and joy to us, we should like to know still more about, for example, how many islands have been discovered to date and named," they chided, adding that they also desired to know "how far these islands are one from the next, and everything you have discovered on each of them." Furthermore, "You must already have harvested what you sowed, and so we should like to know more about the seasons over there, and what the weather is like in each month of the year, for it seems from what you say they are very different from here." They asked, "If you love us, please write at length."

All reasonable requests, with a common theme: Tell us about our new empire.

Displaying more than perfunctory sensitivity to Columbus's preoccupation with La Isabela, they acknowledged the responsibility was his: "As to the settlement you are building, there is no way anyone can from here advise you or recommend any changes to your plans, and we leave it entirely up to you; even were we on the spot, we should listen to your opinion and take your advice."

To Columbus's dismay, they threatened politely to switch him to a new assignment. Instead of settling the Indies, where the situation was rapidly deteriorating, he could return to Spain to help settle matters with the rival Portuguese concerning trade routes and the Treaty of Tordesillas, whose application was still hotly debated. "If it would be difficult for you to come," Isabella wrote, would he please send his brother "or some other person there who knows" about the issue, "promptly by the first caravels that come home." Given the overriding importance to the shape of the fledgling empire, whose boundaries were being tested every day, she needed to hear all his thoughts "so that we can get back to the question of exactly where the demarcation line is to be drawn within the time laid down in the agreement with the king of Portugal."

Oblivious to these royal requests, Columbus remained at La Isabela, trying to fulfill his grandiose vision of his mission, but his goals were slow to be met. "As each day passed," Las Casas explained, "the Admiral became more and more conscious that the whole of the land was up in arms—albeit the arms involved were a joke—and that the hatred of the Christians was growing." Conversions to Christianity among the Indians proved difficult to accomplish, and often temporary. "As for our holy faith," Columbus wrote of his halting efforts to persuade Indians, "I believe that if the caciques and peoples of this island were called for baptism today all would come running, but I do not believe they would understand or comprehend anything associated with this holy mystery." Often the Indians consented to be baptized—and rebaptized—simply to obtain the gifts they received for complying.

The limited value of the cotton and spices to harvest and ship to Castile hardly justified the expense and danger of maintaining a distant outpost. Most important of all, the gold that had seemed to glisten in every riverbed and hillside in the Cibao had run out. Columbus and his men had picked the mines and waterways clean. He thought there would be an endless supply of gold on Hispaniola, but in fact he had rapidly depleted the island's modest store. To justify his continued presence and his rich entitlements, he turned to the resource of last resort: slaves.

Since February, Columbus had planned to inaugurate a regular slave trade between the Indies and Spain. It would focus on the menacing Caribs, thereby allowing the more peaceful Taínos to remain in place, and it would last until the gold mines functioned. With gold in short supply, the slave trade gradually took on greater urgency. If Columbus had misgivings about his decision, he kept them to himself. Portugal and Genoa had their slave trade; why not Spain? The Sovereigns, no strangers to cruelty, kept their distance from the idea, which was certain to offend the church, political rivals, and even their own sense of morality. "This subject has been postponed for the present until another voyage has come thence, and let the Admiral write what he thinks about it." Ignoring the sentiment expressed in this response, Columbus set about establishing a slave trade including both Caribs *and* Taínos. Despite his intermittent regard for the more peaceful of the two tribes, he would send them all to the busy and profitable slave market in Seville.

According to Michele de Cuneo, Columbus ordered the seizure of fifteen hundred men and women on Hispaniola. Of these, five hundred deemed the most desirable for the slave trade were confined to one of four caravels bound for Spain. He invited his men to select from those left ashore; about six hundred Indians disappeared into captivity this way. The remaining four hundred Indians managed to escape with their lives, among them women who were nursing. Describing the appalling spectacle, Cuneo wrote, "They, in order to better escape us, since they were afraid we would turn to catch them again, left their infants anywhere on the ground and started to flee like desperate people; and some fled so far that they were removed from our settlement of La Isabela seven or eight days beyond mountains and across huge rivers."

In retribution, the Spanish captured Guatiguaná, a cacique believed to have killed Spanish intruders, along with two of his chiefs, and bound them all, but before the Indians could be shot for their misdeeds, the captives chewed through their restraints and fled.

On February 24, 1495, their less fortunate brethren sailed with the fleet, along with Michele de Cuneo, who had finally seen enough of the New World, and Columbus's brother Diego, who had been given the task of defending the Admiral against the charges being prepared in Spain by Columbus-haters led by Father Buil and Pedro Margarit. At that moment, Columbus was ruminating bitterly on the trumped-up charges and outright "false-hoods reported to Your Highnesses by some wretches who came here, and those whom they spoke to." He raged against his accusers, an untrustworthy, ignorant, depraved lot who had no business participating in this noble enterprise: "At dice and other pernicious, infamous vices they lost their inheritances, and since they could no longer find any land that could sustain them they came on this voyage through lies and deception, thinking to get rich quick on the seashore without any work or effort so they could return to their former way of life. This happened no less among the religious [orders] than among the laity; they were so blinded by wicked cupidity that they would not believe me in Castile when I predicted that they would have to work for everything. They were so greedy they thought I was lying."

No matter how low their character and malicious their tales, Columbus's behavior on the voyage was at times even more shameful, but it went unrecognized and unchallenged in Spain.

Antonio de Torres, by now making a specialty of leading these intermediate transatlantic crossings, proved less adept than Columbus at bringing the fleet swiftly home. The Admiral had neglected to advise him of the optimal route, which involved sailing on a northerly course to a latitude approximately that of Bermuda before heading east to the Canaries or Cape St. Vincent on the Portuguese coast. With his tragic burden of captives, Torres drifted around the Lesser Antilles for several weeks before working his way far enough north to catch the trades; after that, he reached the island of Madeira in little more than three weeks.

It was a hellish crossing. "About two hundred of these Indians died, I believe because of the unaccustomed air, colder than theirs," Michele de Cuneo wrote. "We cast them into the sea." Half the surviving Indians were seriously ill by the time they disembarked at Cadiz. "For your information," he informed the authorities, "they are not working people and very much fear cold, nor have they long life."

Desperate to demonstrate the value of the vulnerable human cargo he sent to Spain, Columbus, at a safe distance, put aside his reservations about the Indians to extol their qualities to Ferdinand and Isabella. "I believe they are without equal in the world among blacks or anywhere else," he declared. "They are very ingenious, especially when young," he noted. "Please consider whether it might be worth it to take six or eight boys, set them apart, and teach them to write and study, because I believe they will excel in a short time; in Spain they will learn perfectly." The educational program never came about. Instead, the fleet's overall manager, Juan de Fonseca, sent the survivors to Seville to be auctioned off. Columbus's confidant Bernáldez witnessed the Indians' final degradation at the hands of the Spanish. They were "naked as the day they were born, with no more embarrassment than wild beasts." As if reaching for an even more callous observation, he complained, "They are not very profitable since almost all died, for the country did not agree with them."

As Columbus's plan to establish a slave trade with Spain self-destructed, the Indians of Hispaniola battled Spanish forces, especially in the vicinity of La Isabela. The fugitive Guatiguaná, who had chewed his way out of Spanish bondage, rallied his warriors, and began to kill off the Spanish invaders or force them back onto their ships. The Indians had the advantage of overwhelming numbers and familiarity with their homeland, but Guatiguaná was unable to unite the disparate tribes in this quest. Some leaders wished to remain safely apart, and others, especially Guacanagarí, retained their loyalty to the forces of Spain.

Columbus was still suffering from exhaustion, so weak that his crew carried him from the flagship to the shore. There he spent the winter months recovering, until the end of February 1495. He suffered from the combined effects of several ailments, some more apparent than others. The reliable Las Casas specified arthritis, by which he probably meant the painful and debilitating condition of rheumatoid arthritis, and it appeared that Columbus had begun to deteriorate mentally as well as physically. He was particularly distressed to hear that the Indians had risen in revolt against Pedro Margarit, whom Columbus had appointed to supervise the mines of the Cibao. With his petty authoritarian ways, Margarit had made a mess of things, having "paid no heed to the Admiral's wishes," says Ferdinand, and seemed hell-bent on making himself the new leader of the expedition.

Right after Columbus's departure with his three ships, Margarit had ignored his orders to occupy large swathes of the island, and instead took his men, nearly four hundred strong, to the Vega Real, ten leagues away, where he devoted his energies to "scheming and contriving to have the members of the council established by the Admiral obey his orders, and sending them insolent letters." Frustrated in his plan to usurp Columbus, "to whom he would have had to account for his actions in office," he had caught the first ship bound for Spain, without explanation or placing someone else in charge of the 376 men left behind, who rapidly deteriorated into predators. "Each one went where he willed among the Indians, stealing their property and wives and inflicting so many injuries upon them the Indians resolved to avenge themselves on any they found alone or in small groups." As a result, "the Admiral found the island in a pitiful state, with most of the Christians committing innumerable outrages for which they were mortally hated by the Indians, who refused to obey them." Still inflamed, Guatiguaná slaughtered ten Spanish guards and stealthily set ablaze a shelter containing forty others, all of them ill. Peter Martyr wrote in anguish of the Spanish "injustices" that had occurred in Columbus's absence: "Kidnapping women of the islands under the eyes of their parents, brothers and husbands . . . rape and robberies."

With Margarit gone, Columbus had no choice but to apprehend Guatiguaná. Failing to accomplish that task, he seized some of his followers and sent them as prisoners to Spain aboard the fleet led by Antonio de Torres. The four ships departed on February 24, 1495.

But troubles with the Indians were just beginning.

At La Isabela, Columbus belatedly learned that the Indians served four chiefs, Caonabó, Higuanamá, Behechio, and Guarionex, each of whom commanded "seventy or eighty caciques who rendered no tribute but were obliged to come when summoned to assist them in their wars and in sowing their fields."

One of these many caciques stood out—Guacanagarí—Columbus's occasional ally and overseer of that part of Hispaniola where La Isabela was located. Hearing that Columbus had returned after a long absence, Guacanagarí immediately visited to declare his innocence. He had done nothing to aid or encourage the Indians who had slaughtered the Spanish, and to demonstrate his longstanding goodwill, recalled the goodwill and hospitality he had always shown the Christians. He believed that his generosity toward these visitors from afar had provoked the hatred of the other caciques, especially the notorious Behechio, who had killed one of Guacanagarí's wives, and the thieving Caonabó, who had stolen another. Now he appealed to the Admiral to restore his wives and obtain revenge. As Guacanagarí narrated this tragic tale he "wept each time he recalled the men who had been killed at La Navidad, as if they had been his own sons."

Guacanagarí's tears won over Columbus, restoring the bond between the Admiral and the cacique.

As he considered the situation, Columbus realized that the emotional cacique had provided valuable intelligence about conflicts among the Indians, conflicts that Columbus could exploit to punish enemies of them both. An alliance with Guacanagarí would enable him to settle all scores.

Recovering from his breakdown, Columbus "marched forth from Isabela in warlike array together with his comrade Guacanagarí, who was most eager to rout his enemies," Ferdinand wrote. It was March 24, 1495, almost six months after the Admiral had arrived. The military task ahead presented impossible odds. Columbus and Guacanagarí jointly commanded a regiment of two hundred Spanish guards, bolstered by twenty horses and twenty hounds—beasts who were far more terrifying to the enemy than any European biped. But they faced an immense force, "more than one hundred thousand Indians" defending their own territory against a small band of invaders. Given the Indians' growing anger at the Spanish, it seemed this battle would be the last of Columbus, his mission, his men, and his ships. A massacre in the making, the plan had an air of doom about it, as if Columbus, too skillful a navigator to perish at sea, had deliberately chosen instead to martyr himself—and his men—on land.

Believing that he now understood "the Indian character and habits," Columbus began his campaign by leading his little force on a ten-day march from La Isabela. He divided the men into two groups, one under his command, the other under his brother Bartholomew. Relying on their steeds' ability to strike absolute terror into the enemy, the two brothers would try to trap the massed Indian forces in a pincer movement. Columbus "believed that the Indians, frightened by a din arising simultaneously on various sides, would break and flee in panic."

At first, the "infantry squadrons," as Ferdinand grandly called them, attacked the Indians, beating them back with crossbows and arquebuses. At that point, the "cavalry and hounds" interceded to sow panic amid the enemy, which they did, chasing the Indians into the jungle, and pursuing them wherever they went, "killing many," according to Ferdinand, "and capturing others who were also killed."

The Spanish soldiers chased the Indians into the subtropical thickets, and when they could no longer advance, they unleashed twenty greyhounds. The ravenous beasts, wrote Las Casas, "fell on the Indians at the cry of *tomalo.*" Take it! "Within an hour they had preyed on 100 of them. As the Indians were used to going completely naked, it is easy to imagine the damage caused by these fierce greyhounds, urged to bite naked bodies and skin much more delicate than that of the wild boars they were used to."

The Spanish forces succeeded in capturing Caonabó alive, together with his wives and children. Ferdinand exaggerated the number of Indian warriors participating in the battle, although they greatly outnumbered the Spanish, whose victory, aided by horses and superior weapons, inspired confidence that had been lacking ever since Columbus first arrived in the Indies. "There is not a single one of our weapons which does not prove highly damaging when used against the Indians," Las Casas reported from the front, while the Indians' weapons amounted to "little more than toys."

After the battle, Caonabó "confessed that he had killed twenty of the Spaniards who remained under Arana in La Navidad when the Admiral returned to Spain from his discovery of the Indies." So he had been the prime malefactor all along. And, if his confession was to be believed, there was worse. He had subsequently visited the Spanish at La Isabela "feigning friendship," but with "the true design (which our men suspected) of seeing how he might best attack and destroy it as he had done to the town of La Navidad." Columbus's obdurate aide, Alonso de Ojeda, at first tried to broker a "pact of friendship" between Caonabó and Columbus, Peter Martyr related, and wound up threatening the chieftain "with the massacre and ruin of his people if he would choose war rather than peace with the Christians."

The Italian chronicler skillfully analyzed the chieftain's political dilemmas and pretensions, as they appeared to Columbus. "Understandably, Caonabó was like a reef in the middle of the sea, tossed this way and that by opposite currents, distressed also by the memory of the crimes he had committed, since he had deceitfully murdered twenty of our defenseless men; although he seemed to desire peace, he was nonetheless afraid to go to the Admiral. Finally, after elaborating a plot with the intention of killing the Admiral and the others when the opportunity presented itself and pretending to want to make peace, he set out to meet the Admiral with all his retinue and many others, armed according to their custom." With effort,

Ojeda enticed the exhausted Caonabó to appear before Columbus and make peace. As a reward, Caonabó would receive a coveted bronze bell from the church.

Ojeda brandished steel handcuffs and foot restraints, explaining that no less a personage than King Ferdinand wore these decorative items on horseback. Out of special consideration, Caonabó could try them on and see how it felt to be a king. Ojeda arranged for Caonabó to be mounted on horseback directly behind him, as the Spaniards tightened the restraints so that Caonabó would remain securely astride the horse. At that moment the Spanish soldiers scared off Ojeda's guards, and Ojeda spurred the horse, which galloped across a river with both men. Caonabó had been kidnapped.

Ojeda rode on, pausing only to tighten the restraints of his *prisionero*, until they reached La Isabela, where Caonabó, now a captive, spent his time, in the words of Peter Martyr, "fretting and grating his teeth as if he had been a lion of Libya."

Pressing on with his pacification of the Cibao, Ojeda rounded up other recalcitrant chieftains, although at least one, Caonabó's brother-in-law, Behechio, escaped. When the action was over, Columbus staged a victory march through the subjugated countryside.

That was the Spanish side of the story, recorded for posterity by the chroniclers Ferdinand Columbus, Peter Martyr, and Gonzalo Fernández de Oviedo. But there was another, more troubling perspective, that of the Indians, which emphasized the European rape and kidnapping of the naive Taínos. Even Columbus's sympathies were divided at times between the men he led and those he sought to conquer, but once he had purged himself of compassion, his attention returned to his obsession with gold, glory, and conquest.

Illuminating the moral stakes in the conflict, Las Casas declared, "Such an execrable victory certainly did not redound to the glory of God." To try to make up for these sins in some small way, he would bear witness to their suffering, and serve as their advocate for posterity.

Columbus intended to dispatch Caonabó and his brother to Spain, "for he was unwilling to put to death so great a personage without the knowledge of the Catholic Sovereigns," according to Ferdinand. He judged it sufficient to punish many other Indians. It was a curious decision for such a vindictive man, and stemmed from the fact that Columbus and Caonabó had developed a rapport, from one leader to another, across their vast political and linguistic gulf. They shared an interest in the eternal mysteries of life and death, as Columbus attempted to conquer the Indians' sturdy spiritual realm with the same vigor he had brought to their fragile temporal existence, and with equally baffling results.

"I have taken pains to learn what they believe and know where the dead go, especially from Caonabó," Columbus wrote in a remarkable reappraisal of his former antagonist. "He is a man of mature age, very knowledgeable and sharp-witted," and he gave Columbus his first convincing idea of what the life of an Indian cacique was like: privileged, indulgent, and Edenic. "They eat, have wives, enjoy pleasures and comforts," Columbus marveled. In and around the outbreaks of hostilities, the Spanish had learned more about the lives and resources of their hosts, as Ferdinand noted, their mines of "copper, sapphires, and amber; brazilwood, ebony, incense, cedars, many fine gums, and different kinds of wild spices," including cinnamon ("though bitter to the taste"), ginger, pepper, everything except the gold Columbus ardently sought. There were even "mulberry trees for producing silk that bear leaves all year round, and many other useful plants and trees of which nothing is known in our countries."

What sounds like an idyll, at least in Columbus's words, was anything but. With his two brothers, he established three more fortresses, which he used to enforce a system of tribute that ruined the island's previously resilient economy.

Henceforth, every Indian over the age of fourteen had to give the equivalent of a hawk's bell filled with gold. Caciques were required to give even more to the Spanish occupiers. Indians who lived in regions where gold was scarce could substitute cotton—spun or woven, not raw—if they wished, but everyone had to give his tribute, on pain of death. Those who complied received a stamped copper or brass token to wear around their necks in what became a symbol of intolerable shame. (Of this system, Las Casas charged: "Even the cruelest of the Turks or Moors, or the Huns and Vandals who laid waste our kingdoms and lands and destroyed our lives, would have found such a demand impossibly onerous and would have deemed it unreasonable and abhorrent.")

In time, the Indians depleted the island's limited supply of gold, and what seemed like a modest amount became increasingly difficult to acquire, even with unremitting effort picking through sand and shrubs. The system was in some ways worse than slavery, and it obliterated any chance that the Indians would assist or cooperate with the Spanish in any other endeavor besides the pointless tributes of gold. By imposing this system, Columbus ensured a modest supply of gold would be his, at the cost of everything else he needed or could have wished. For example, Guarionex, the influential cacique, argued that the land used to provide a minimal amount of gold could grow enough wheat to feed all of Spain, not just once, but ten times, but Columbus refused to consider the idea, deciding instead to halve the tribute and perpetuate the offense.

Recounting this policy, Las Casas howled with indignation. "Some complied," he noted, "and for others it was impossible, and so, falling into the most wretched way of living, some took refuge in the mountains whilst others, since the violence and provocation and injuries on the part of the Christians never ceased, killed some Christians for special damages and tortures that they suffered." The Christians responded by murdering and torturing their antagonists, "not respecting the human and divine justice and natural law under whose authority they did it." There is no denying the force of Las Casas's outrage, but Indians were not the innocents of his imagination; they had been slaveholders long before the Europeans arrived. Fernández de Oviedo noted that in war, contesting Indian tribes "take captives whom they brand and keep as slaves. Each master has his own brand and some masters pull out one front tooth of their slaves as a mark of ownership."

Demoralized by the Spanish tribute system, and unnerved by their own prophecies, many Indians took steps to escape in the only way left to them. Columbus became aware of the dimensions of the tragedy decimating the Indians when "it was pointed out to him that the natives had been vexed by a famine so widespread that more than 50,000 men had died, and every day they fell everywhere like sickened flocks," in the words of Peter Martyr.

The reality was even more terrible than famine; it was self-inflicted. The Indians destroyed their stores of bread so that neither they nor the invaders would be able to eat it. They plunged off cliffs, they poisoned themselves with roots, and they starved themselves to death. Oppressed by the impossible requirement to deliver tributes of gold, the Indians were no longer able to tend their fields, or care for their sick, children, and elderly. They had given up and committed mass suicide to avoid being killed or captured by Christians, and to avoid sharing their land with them, their fields, groves, beaches, forests, and women: the future of their people. It was an extraordinary act of despair and self-destruction, so overwhelming that the Spanish could not comprehend it.

All of them, fifty thousand Indians, dead by their own hand.

* * *

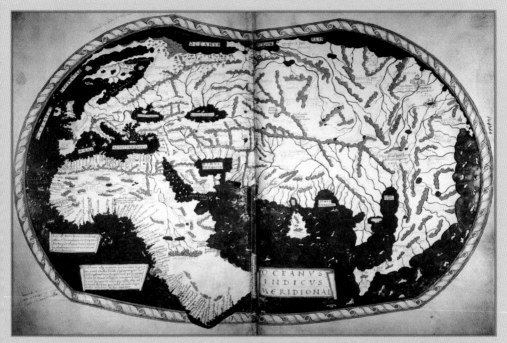

Map of the world, ca. 1489, by Henricus Martellus Germanus (Heinrich Hammer). A similar map is believed to have influenced Columbus's ideas about his voyage. It may have been based on maps devised by his brother Bartholomew several years earlier, in 1485. This truncated view lead Columbus to believe that he was close to Asia when he was in fact in the Caribbean. Relying on maps such as these, as well as classical sources, he maintained that the distance between Europe and Asia was deceptively small.

Virgin of Sailors by Alejo Fernández, 1530. In one of the earliest paintings inspired by Columbus's discoveries, the explorer kneels on her left in a golden robe, and the three Pinzón brothers stand on her right. The painting evokes the spiritual mystique surrounding his journeys, reflecting the exalted manner in which Columbus viewed himself and his voyages.

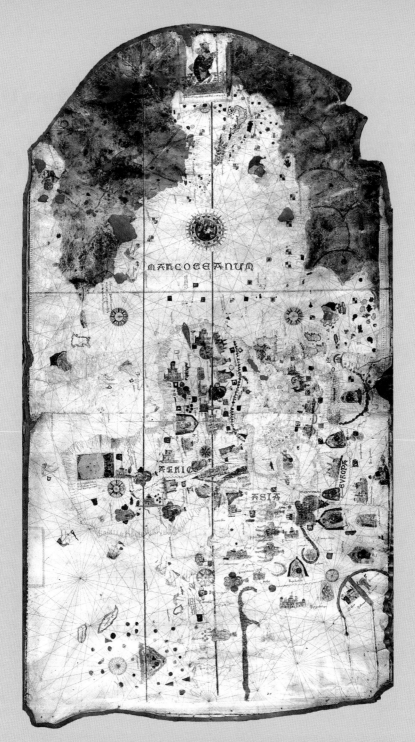

Juan de la Cosa's celebrated Mappa Mundi of 1500, considered to be the first known European cartographic representation of the New World. As Columbus's cartographer, Cosa was obligated to sign an oath that Cuba was not an island, although he suspected that was not the case.

Cartas Previleg̃
Cedvlas
y otras Escrituras
d̃ Dõ Xpoual Colon
Almirante Mayor
dl Mar Oceano Visorey
y Gouernador delas
Islas y Tierra firme

The frontispiece for the resplendent *Book of Privileges* shows the crest of Columbus. This collection of royal documents, assembled between 1492 and 1502, listed the titles, rights, awards, and offices that he believed Ferdinand and Isabella owed him. By the third voyage the Sovereigns were no longer in the mood to grant all his extravagant requests.

Map of São Jorge da Mina. Columbus is believed to have visited this Portuguese fort on the West African coast as a young navigator.

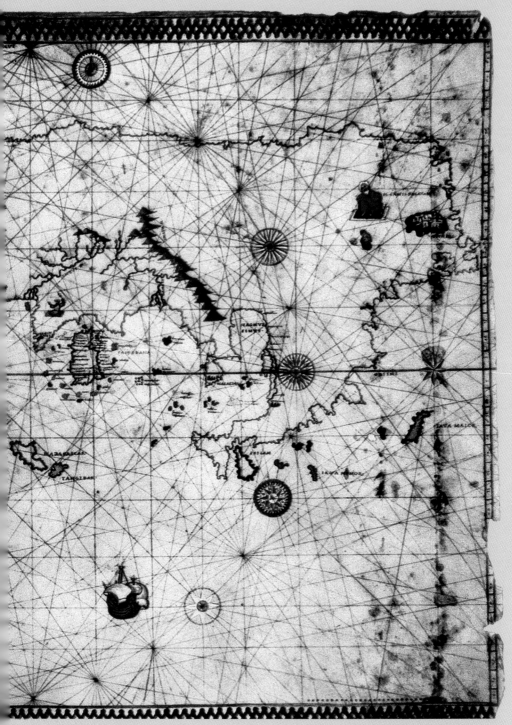

King-Hamy navigational chart, 1502, attributed to Amerigo Vespucci, and named for two of its subsequent collectors.

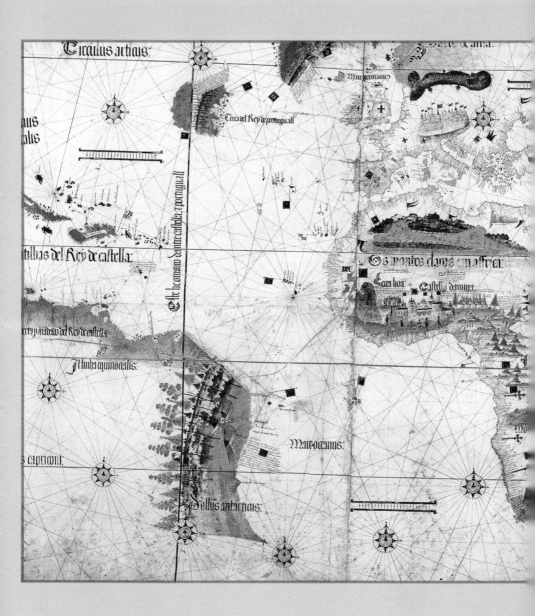

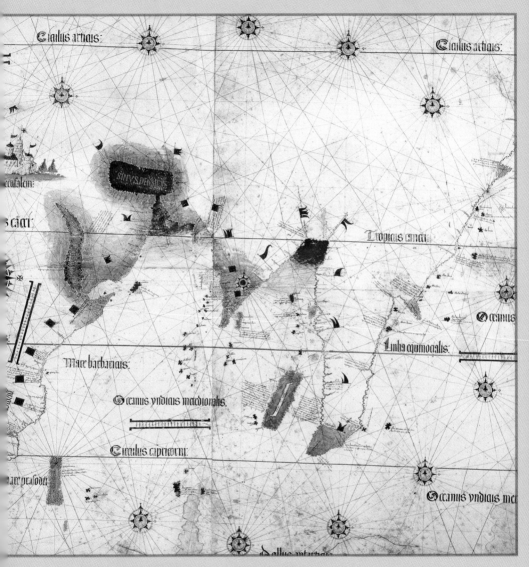

The Cantino World Map of 1502, the earliest surviving map of Portuguese discoveries, features Africa and part of the coast of Brazil. The line on left shows the Papal demarcation of territory (Spain to the west, Portugal to the east) according to the Treaty of Tordesillas.

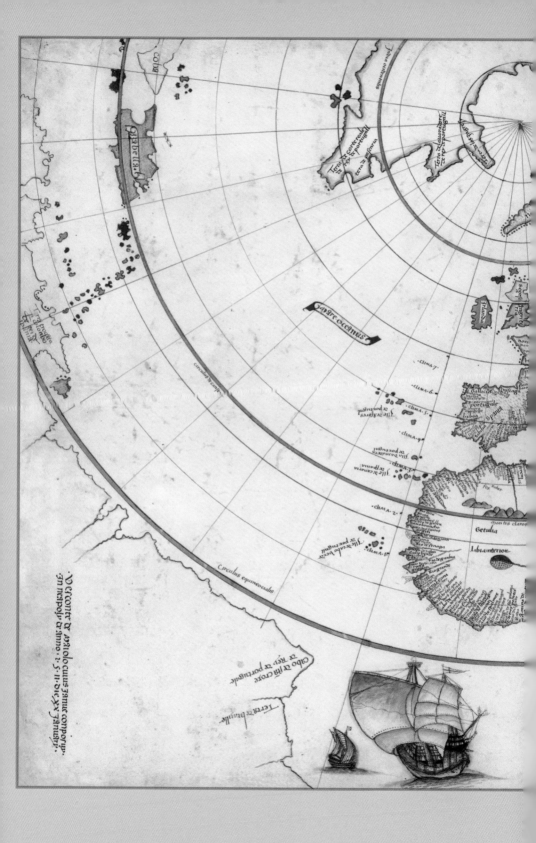

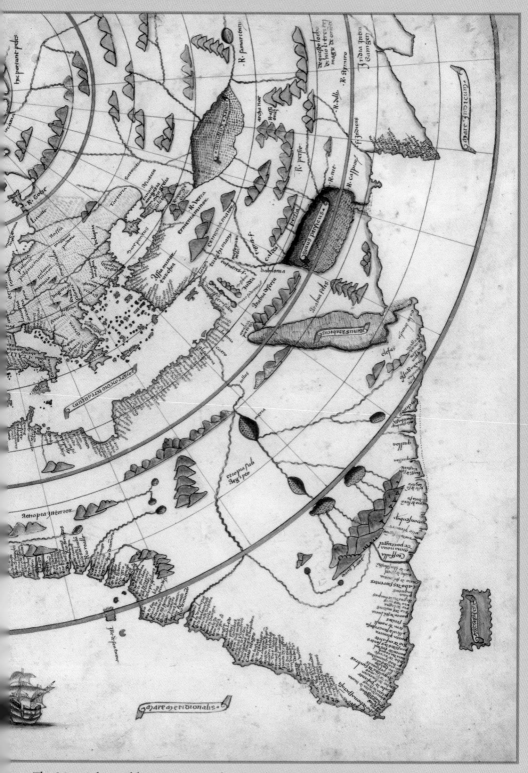

The Maggiolo world map, ca. 1511, showing (extreme left) parts of Brazil and the lands found by Columbus, including Cuba.

Map of the Caribbean by Theodor de Bry, ca. 1594, showing parts of North America, the Yucatán, Panama, and South America with varying degrees of accuracy.

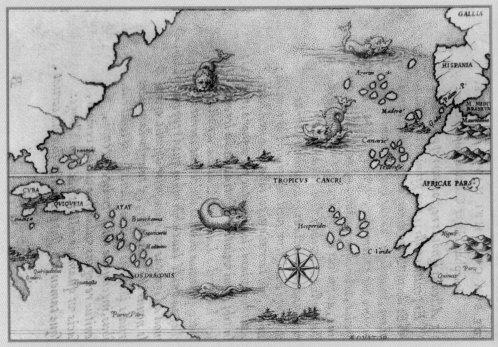

This 1583 map depicts lands visited by Columbus. The Atlantic Ocean is now seen as bounded by Europe, Africa, North America, and South America.

Religious interpretations of Columbus's voyages imparted lasting significance to his journeys. This allegory of Columbus discovering the New World was engraved in 1594 by Theodor de Bry, a Belgian illustrator whose detailed renderings of European exploration became highly popular, although he never visited the New World himself.

The Spanish refused to shoulder the blame. The mass suicide resulted from the Indians' "own stubbornness," said Peter Martyr. "The Indians purposely destroyed all their bread [cassava] fields," Columbus told his Sovereigns in October 1495. "To prevent my searching for gold the Indians put up as many obstacles as they could." At the same time, he acknowledged that "nothing else makes them so sad and upset as the fact that we are coming into their territory." But in reality, the Indians had little interest in gold, especially in comparison to Columbus. In his version, the Indians, after realizing that they would not be able to divert him from his hunt for gold, belatedly "resumed planting and seeding the land because they were starving, but heaven did not help them out with rain this time and they were ruined and died and are dying at an incredible rate." He ascribed their deaths to "starvation."

The dwindling number of survivors found themselves trapped in a survivalist endgame. Some took refuge in the mountains, where Spanish dogs set upon them. Those who avoided the dogs succumbed to starvation and illness. Although estimates of the population are inexact, the trend is plain. Of the approximately 300,000 Indians in Hispaniola at the time of Columbus's first voyage in 1492, 100,000 or so died between 1494 and 1496, half of them during the mass suicide. Las Casas estimated that the Indian population in 1496 was only one-third of what it had been in 1494. ("What a splendid harvest and how quickly they reaped it!" he wrote acidly.) Twelve years later, in 1508, a census counted 60,000 Indians, or one-fifth of the original population, and by 1548 Fernández de Oviedo found only five hundred Indians, the survivors of the hundreds of thousands who had populated the island when Columbus arrived, and who had seen him as the fulfillment of a longstanding prophecy. It was only now that the meaning of that prophecy became clear: his presence meant their extinction.

In time the Taínos made peace with their adversaries. A tribe combining both Caribs and Taíno emerged, and seemed to point the way to coexistence. The arrival of Columbus's fleets, one after the other, disturbed the spontaneous compromise, and added a new level of stress and conflict to this volatile society. The leading figure was Columbus's adversary, Caonabó, the Carib cacique who married a Taíno wife, Behechio's sister, Anacaona. Not long before Columbus's arrival, other Taínos had married Caribs who renounced cannibalism; in this, Caonabó and Anacaona were not alone. A third tribe, the Ciguayo, appeared to be a hybrid of the two former adversaries. Las Casas reported that they had forgotten their native tongue and instead "spoke a strange language, almost barbaric" that might have combined their idiom with the Taínos' speech. Like the Caribs, they grew their hair long, and used liberal applications of red and black war paint, but unlike them, the Ciguayo did not poison their arrows. It was the Ciguayo who fired off arrows at Columbus when he first arrived at the Dominican Republic, and to memorialize the attack, he named the scene of the battle the Gulf of Arrows.

At the time Columbus arrived on the scene, all three tribes—Taíno, Carib, and Ciguayo—were trying to preserve peace and prevent mutual destruction with intertribal marriages, a strategy akin to the many liaisons between the royal families of Spain and Portugal. But the Spanish presence brought the Indian alliances to a halt, and pitched the Indian nations into turmoil.

Columbus's sins—at least, those against the Spanish—eventually returned to haunt him. On August 5, 1495, a fleet of four caravels sailed from Spain under the leadership of Juan de Aguado, a martinet who had been among those who sailed with Columbus at the outset of the second voyage, and who had returned to Spain along with other sick and disaffected would-be conquerors under Torres's command. Thanks to the efforts of Father Buil, sentiment in Spain had turned decisively against the Admiral, and Aguado and his aides returned to Hispaniola with orders to investigate Columbus. At the same time, they carried supplies and—because gold remained paramount—a metallurgist.

On his arrival in October 1495, Aguado made a grand entrance, accompanied by trumpets, and assumed command of the little outpost in the wilderness. Bartholomew, present at La Isabela during the humiliating spectacle, sent a letter of caution to Columbus, who had gone inland to the mines of the Cibao. Returning to the fort, the Admiral surprised everyone by listening respectfully to the new orders Aguado brought from the Sovereigns.

Columbus was to reduce the number of men on the royal payroll to five hundred, and to make sure that everyone received his just share of provisions. Complaints that Columbus had played favorites reverberated from one side of the Atlantic to the other. Worse, everyone else at La Isabela subsisted on short rations, despite the land's incredible fertility. "The soil is very black and good," observed Cuneo. "We brought with us from Spain all sorts of seeds, and tried those that would do well and those that could not." The successes included radishes, squash, onions, lettuce, parsley, melon, and cucumber. Chickpeas and beans shot up in a matter of days, "then all at once they wilt and die." No one knew why. The Spaniards eventually lost interest in growing their own food, "the reason being that nobody wants to live permanently in these countries." Infected with gold lust, they preferred to rely on supplies of foodstuffs from Spain and cassava bread.

Listening to the outpouring of complaints about Columbus, Aguado noticed that the healthiest Europeans engaged in rogue pursuits: petty thievery, searching for gold for themselves, and trapping slaves. He painted a sorry portrait of the Spanish colony's inability to feed itself in the midst of plenty.

> All of the people that have been in this island are incredibly discontented, especially those that were at La Isabela, and all the more for the force, the hunger and the illnesses that they endured, and they did not swear an "as God would take me to Castile"; they had nothing to eat other than the rations given to them from the storehouse of the King, which was one *escudilla* [about a cup] of wheat that they had to grind in a hand mill (and many ate it cooked), and one chunk of rancid bacon or of rotten cheese, and I don't know how many garbanzo beans; of wine, it was as though there was none in the world, and this was the allowance of the Crown. And the Admiral for his part ordered them to work hungry, weak, and some sick (in building the fort, the Admiral's house and other buildings) in such a manner that they were all anguished and afflicted and desperate, for which reasons they complained to Juan Aguado and used the occasion to speak about the Admiral and threaten him to the [Sovereigns].

Absorbing this harsh testimony and surveying the degradation into which La Isabela had fallen, Columbus realized he had little choice but to suspend his exploration of Hispaniola and return to Spain to defend himself. The doors of royal favor and patronage were creaking shut slowly but unmistakably, and he dreaded being cast out. Other mariners stood ready to take his place. All they needed was the Sovereigns' blessing, and Columbus's monopoly on discovery in the name of Spain would end, and with it, the prestige and riches he had been promised.

While he pondered his fate, Columbus, a lifelong autodidact, applied himself to studying the Taínos with the thoroughness he brought to his other endeavors, especially their spirituality, which, he learned, was far more intricate and nuanced than their simple way of life—their small fields, primitive huts, and long canoes—had led him to expect. He noted that their numerous chieftains maintained private shrines in a "house apart from the town in which there is nothing except some carved wooden images." When they saw Europeans coming, Columbus said, they hid them "in the woods for fear that they will be taken from them; what is even more laughable, they have the custom of stealing each other's *cemís*." There was more; the statues were the focus of a private, mysterious, and transformative rite. The images, he added, were accompanied by "a well-made table, round like a wooden dish, in which there is kept a powder that they place on the head of the *cemí* with a certain ceremony. Then, through a cane having two branches that they insert in the nose, they sniff up this powder. The words that they spoke none of our men could understand. This powder makes them lose their senses and rave like drunken men."

The Taínos used the little *cemís* to commune with the spirit world, and as Columbus observed to his dismay and amusement, to manipulate members of their tribe who had not been initiated into the idol's mysteries. He told of a *cemí* that "gave a loud cry and spoke in their language." On closer examination, he discovered that the "statue was artfully constructed," the base connected by a tube or "blowgun" to a "dark side of the house, covered by branches and leaves, where was hidden a person who said whatever the cacique wanted him to say (as well as one can speak through a blowgun)."

To expose the sleight of hand, several Spaniards toppled the talking *cemí*, and the cacique, deeply embarrassed, pleaded with them to say nothing to his tribesmen "because it was by means of that deception that he kept them in obedience to him. . . . Only the cacique knows of and abets this fraud, by means of which he gets all the tribute he wants from his people." (Surely that cynical combination of superstition and deception to control the faithful occurred nowhere in Spain, or anywhere else in Europe.)

Caonabó elucidated other Taíno burial rites for caciques, as Columbus took notes. ("They open the cacique and dry him before a fire that he may keep whole. In the case of others they preserve only the head.") This sojourn through the Taínos' underworld prompted the Admiral, already prone to a morbid turn of mind, to ponder questions of mortality. "I have taken pains to learn what they believe," he wrote, "and know as to where the dead go, especially from Canaobó," who told the explorer that they went "to a valley to join their forefathers."

This was as far as Columbus dared to venture into the twilight of the Taínos' spiritual beliefs and practices. He assigned Ramon Pané, one of the six priests on the expedition, to go further still, "to set down all their rites." This Father Pané did, and compiled a report based on his four years of living in close quarters with the Taínos. His revelations about their religious practices, and the Spanish interference in these rites, contained so many unpleasant truths that Columbus dismissed them as fiction, and considered that "the only sure thing to be learned from it is that the Indians have a certain natural reverence for the after-life and believe in the immortality of their soul." Yet he included the controversial document in his chronicle, which his son reproduced more or less in full, realizing, perhaps, that it offered the best explanation of the deterioration of relations between the Spanish and the Indians.

According to Father Pané, a Catalan who characterized himself as a "poor anchorite"—or scholarly hermit—"of the order of St. Jerome," the trouble went to the heart of their opposing spiritual beliefs. His unsparing reflections are sometimes considered the first anthropological study of the Indians, or, for that matter, of any people. Of all the accounts Columbus's voyages generated, it is certainly the strangest and most penetrating.

"They believe that there is an immortal being in the sky whom none can see and who has a mother but no beginning," he wrote, recording their basic myths in a manner that he hoped would make them comprehensible to Christians like him. Father Pané said that he "wrote in haste and had not enough paper" to record myths passed down the generations: how the sea was created (a giant calabash emptied its contents, water and fish), the origins of the sun and moon (they emerged from a cave populated with two stone *cemís* that appeared to perspire), and the afterlives of the dead (secluded by day, they emerge by night for recreation and to eat a special fruit the size of a peach). Among Father Pané's observations, the Indians had a method for identifying the dead: "They touch the belly of a person with the hand, and if they do not find a navel, they say that person is 'operito,' which means dead." And if an amorous man carelessly lies with a woman without first checking to see that she does, indeed, possess a navel, "she suddenly disappears and his arms are empty."

Suffusing all these beliefs was *cohoba*, the hallucinogenic snuff the Indians snorted through their special pipes with two stems. Father Pané's subjects spent much of their time in an altered state of consciousness, the effect of inhaling powerful *cohoba* dust. "The *cohoba* is their means of praying to the idol and also of asking it for riches," he wrote. The chief initiated the ceremony by playing an instrument. "After he has finished his prayer he remains for some time with bowed head, looks up to the sky, and speaks. All respond to him in a loud voice, and having spoken, they all give thanks; and he relates the vision he had while stupefied with the *cohoba* he stuffed up his nose and that went to his head." During the séance, he spoke of his communing with the *cemís*, of their enemies fleeing, and of the victory to come. Or he might warn of famine, or massacres, "whatever comes into his addled head." Horrified and faintly amused, Father Pané mentions that "they say the house appears to him upside down, and the people to be walking with their feet in the air." He was talking about astral projection, or out-of-body experiences triggered by *cohoba*.

Father Pané believed that conversion to Christianity could break these ancient patterns, and he embraced those Indians who made the leap from their sinful lives to the church. Yet his detailed report demonstrated to Columbus how difficult it would be to conquer and administer this part of the world, trying to bring European ideas of order to people who lived in other spiritual realms and obeyed other voices.

Father Pané heard from Columbus himself about an Indian community with its own language, distinct from the others. It would be his assignment to live with these people and their cacique, Guarionex. Dismayed, the priest questioned Columbus about the wisdom of the order. "Sir, how can Your Lordship ask me to stay with Guarionex, when the only language I know is that of Macorix?" Father Pané beseeched Columbus to provide an Indian companion.

"He granted my wish," Father Pané was pleased to report as he joined forces with a bilingual Indian named Guaicavanú, who later converted to Christianity and took the name of Juan. "Truly, I looked upon him as my own good son and brother." The priest and the sympathetic Indian named Juan took up their new post, where they stayed with Guarionex for nearly two years, "during which time we instructed him in our holy faith and the customs of the Christians." But it was not easy: "At first he appeared well disposed toward us, causing us to believe that he would do all we wished and wanted to become a Christian, for he asked us to teach him the Pater Noster, the Ave Maria, the Credo, and all the other prayers and things that are proper for a Christian to know." Later, "he grew angry with us and backslid from his good purposes on account of the principal men of that country, who scolded him for obeying the Christian law." So they abandoned Guarionex for another cacique, "who seemed well-disposed to us and said he wanted to be a Christian." His name was Maviatué.

"The day after we left the village and dwelling of Guarionex for the land and people of Maviatué, the people of Guarionex built a hut next to the chapel, where we have left some images before which the neophytes could kneel and pray and find comfort." The chapel and its objects immediately became a source of irritation for the lapsed Christians. Two days after Father Pané's departure, "by orders of Guarionex six men came to the chapel and told the seven neophytes . . . in charge to take the sacred images that I had left in their care and destroy them because Fray Ramón [Pané] and his companions had gone away and would not know who had done it." The six followers of Guarionex pushed the guards aside, "forced their way in, took the sacred images, and carried them away."

As if that were not bad enough, the Indian raiders hurled the images to the ground, buried them, and urinated on the mounds, saying, "Now will you yield good and abundant fruit?"

When he heard about the incident, Bartholomew Columbus felt impelled to demonstrate that he could be as decisive in his dealings with the Indians as his illustrious brother had been hesitant. "He brought those wicked men to trial, and their crime having been established, he caused them to be publicly burned at the stake." If Bartholomew believed this punishment would chastise the Indians once and for all, he was quickly forced to realize his error. "Guarionex and his people persisted in their evil design of killing all the Christians on the day assigned for them to pay their tribute of gold." The Spanish discovered the plot just before it was carried out, and imprisoned the Indian conspirators, "yet some persisted in their design, killing four men and Juan Matthew, the chief clerk, and his brother Antonio, who had been baptized."

The rampage grew in intensity, and, it seemed to Christian eyes, yielded a miracle amid the mayhem. "Those rebels ran to the place where they had hidden the images and broken them to pieces. Several days later the owner of the field went to dig up some yams (which are roots that look like turnips or radishes), and in the place where the images had been buried two or three yams had grown together in the shape of a cross." Incredibly, "This cross was found by the mother of Guarionex—the worst woman I ever knew in those parts," yet "she found it a miracle, saying to the governor of the fort of Concepción, 'God caused this wonder to appear in the place where the images were found, for reasons known only to Himself.'" At least it was comforting to imagine that she did.

Father Pané offered sobering advice to Columbus: "This island has great need of men who will punish those Indian lords who will not let their people receive instruction in the Holy Catholic Faith, for those people cannot stand up to their lords." Toughened and wearied by experience, the priest set aside his humility to insist, "I speak with authority, for I have worn myself out in seeking to learn the truth about this matter."

But for the moment, Columbus appeared to have succeeded in his mission against all odds, if his mission consisted only of conquest. Ferdinand claimed that his father "reduced the Indians to such obedience and tranquility that they all promised to pay tribute to the Catholic Sovereigns every three months, as follows: In the Cibao, where the gold mines were, every person fourteen years of age or upward was to pay a large hawk's bell of gold dust; all others were to pay twenty-five pounds of cotton."

Such were the terms of the Pax Columbiana.

Still adhering to their hunger strike, the Indians were starving to death. "If they survive this famine," Columbus euphemistically noted in October 1495, "I hope in Our Lord I can maintain this agreement with them and earn not a little profit." He ordered his men to conduct a census "cacique by cacique," and complained, "no more than a quarter of them could be found because everyone had scattered to the mountains, into unpopulated areas in search of roots to feed the people." Each surviving Indian who delivered a tribute to the Spanish authorities received a "brass or copper token, which he must wear about his neck as proof that he made his payment; any Indian found without such a token was to be punished."

All the while, the Spaniards seethed with resentment. Some had already returned to Spain with Antonio de Torres to spread tales about the callous Admiral of the Ocean Sea. His two brothers, rushing to his side, had only managed to make things worse with their brutal approach to Indian relations. He feared that the longer he was away from the court, the more his rivals would poison the minds of his Sovereigns against him. On his first voyage he had departed in relative obscurity and returned as a hero; on this, his second voyage, he had departed as a hero, but had every reason to believe that he would return in disgrace unless he pleaded his case before the Sovereigns.

Conditions at La Isabela were so chaotic that it took a long time—nearly six months—to ready a ship to bear the Admiral of the Ocean Sea to Castile. She was named, fittingly, *India*, a caravel made of three ships destroyed by a violent Caribbean hurricane, said by Peter Martyr to have occurred in June 1495, and for which the Indians blamed the presence of the Spaniards, who had upset the elements. The only other ship in the little convoy was *Santa Clara*, in which Columbus owned a half share.

The two caravels were designed to carry about twenty-five people each; now they collectively held 235 Europeans and 30 Indians, including the dangerous Caonabó, still a prisoner, along with his brother and nephew. Columbus commended these former enemies to his royal patrons with cheerful optimism: "I am sending Your Highnesses Caonabó and his brother. He is the most important cacique on the island and the most courageous and intelligent. If he starts to talk he will tell everything about this land better than anyone else, because there is no subject he does not know about." The safe arrival of Caonabó in Seville, and his appearance before the Sovereigns, promised to be a major event.

The fleet set out on the morning of March 26, 1496, with Bartholomew aboard, but he disembarked as planned when the ships called at Puerto Plata, not far from La Isabela on the northern coast of Hispaniola. Bartholomew returned to La Isabela overland, and the fleet sailed on without him, under Columbus's sole command.

The going was agonizingly slow. Twelve days later, Columbus put the eastern extremity of Hispaniola astern, sailing "directly east as much as wind permitted." Provisions were low, his men tired and in bad humor. On April 6, the Admiral changed course and headed south. Within three days he dropped anchor off Marie Galante, the island that he had blithely claimed for Spain at the beginning of the voyage. The respite proved brief. The next day, a Sunday, he set sail, contrary to his custom, his ears ringing with the complaints of his men about toiling on the Lord's Day.

Standing off Guadeloupe, he sent a few small boats ashore, taking care to arm the men, and "before they reached the beach a multitude of women armed with bows and arrows and with plumes on their heads rushed out of the woods and assumed a menacing attitude." Those in the boats sent the two Indians among them to bargain with the women warriors, and when they realized the men had come in search of food, not conquest, they directed them to the "northern shore of the island, where their husbands would furnish them with what they needed." The inexperienced Spaniards combed the shore, came away empty-handed, and reeling from hunger and exhaustion, returned to the caravels and set sail on a northerly course. As their ships hugged the shore, Indians assembled at the water's edge, where they "uttered great cries" and fired off volley after volley of poison-tipped arrows at the exposed watercraft.

Undeterred, Columbus sent his men ashore, prepared to meet with a harsh response. The Indians regrouped and tried to stage another ambush, but they dispersed as soon as the Spanish fired their clumsy but noisy guns. In their haste, the Indians abandoned their supplies and their dwellings, "which the Christians entered, looting and destroying all they found," Ferdinand wrote. Most of all they needed food. "Being familiar with the Indian method of making bread, they took their cassava dough and made enough bread to satisfy their needs."

They searched the dwellings with care, noting "large parrots, honey, wax, and iron which the Indians used to make little hatchets, and there were looms, like our tapestry looms, on which they weave cloth." They came across one more item: "a human hand roasting on a spit." The men recoiled in horror.

Soon they were nosing around Guadeloupe, perhaps entering the cove known as Anse à la Barque, marked by serene huts, among other signs of benign inhabitants.

Columbus dispatched a boat with an armed crew, who encountered countless arrows soaring overhead. A few shots scattered the archers, and the landing party raided the huts, looking for food and supplies, but found only huge red parrots staring blankly at them. In frustration, a small group of Spanish marauders gave chase to the Indians and captured three boys and ten women, whom they held hostage as they traded for cassava root.

The ships remained at anchor in Guadeloupe for nine days, as the men busied themselves baking cassava bread on hot griddles, preparing firewood, and gathering water. The leisurely schedule hints that they also enjoyed the "hospitality" of the women they had captured, releasing them shortly before their departure, with the exception of one who appeared to be the wife of a cacique, and her daughter, whom they held captive aboard their crowded ships.

On April 20, 1496, the fleet finally set sail for Spain. In the cramped quarters, illness spread rapidly, and the Indians proved most vulnerable. Caonabó, who had survived so many challenges on his native soil, died at sea. The court of Ferdinand and Isabella, about which he had heard so much, and which had fired his imagination with impossible grandeur, would never greet him, or enslave him.

"With the wind ahead and much calm," Ferdinand wrote, Columbus sailed "as close to the twenty-second degree of latitude as the wind permitted; for at that time men had not learned the trick of running far northward to catch the southwest winds." These conditions made for slow progress, and by May 20, the men "began to feel a great want of provisions, all being reduced to a daily ration of six ounces of bread and a pint and a half of water."

To add to their anxiety, none of the caravels' pilots had the slightest idea of their true location. Columbus believed they were approaching the Azores, confiding his reasoning to his journal. The Flemish and Genoese compasses, or "needles," were not synchronized: "This morning the Flemish needles varied a point to the northwest as usual; and the Genoese needles, which generally agree with them, varied slightly to the northwest; later they oscillated between easterly and westerly variation, which was a sign that our position was somewhat more than one hundred leagues to the west of the Azores." His calculations showed they were getting closer to home with every passing swell, and he expected to see "a few scattered branches of gulfweed in the sea" at any time. Two days later, on May 22, a Sunday, he affirmed that they were one hundred leagues from the Azores.

The compass needles told a different story: the ships were off course and dashing headlong into danger. Columbus "assigned the cause to the difference of the lodestone with which the needles are magnetized." As the men protested, and fear of disaster mounted, the Admiral pursued his course, relying on dead reckoning, that is, arriving at his location by carefully calculating the speed at which his ship traveled, and the distance he had come, since leaving the island of Guadeloupe on April 20.

On the night of June 7, a Tuesday, the pilots estimated they were still "several days' sail from land," but Columbus alarmed them all by taking in sail "for fear of striking land." They were nearing Cape St. Vincent on Portugal's coast, he insisted, as the pilots, eight or ten all told, mocked the misguided Admiral. Some said they would raise the coast of England, and others claimed they were not far from Galicia, in northwestern Spain, and in that case, Columbus should let out all the sheet he could, "for it was better to die by running on to the rocky coast than to perish miserably from hunger at sea." But he did nothing of the kind. Shorn of sail, the ships coasted uncertainly through the dark, gelatinous sea.

Ravenous, the men talked openly about desperate survival measures. The Caribs proposed to eat the other Indians aboard, while the Spaniards conserved their food by heaving the Indians overboard. They were prepared to execute their plan, but at the last minute the Admiral forbade them, reminding them all that the Indians, as Christians and human beings, deserved to be treated as the others.

Columbus held to his course through the night, until, on Wednesday, June 8, 1496, "while all the pilots went about like men who were lost or blind, they came in sight of Odemira, between Lisbon and Cape Saint Vincent." The little town sparkled in the distance, and it lay exactly on the Portuguese coast where Columbus's dead reckoning told him it would. So much for the pilots and their predictions.

"From that time on," Ferdinand noted, "the seamen regarded the Admiral as most expert and admirable in matters of navigation." He had gotten them home alive, and that alone merited their gratitude. He had survived storms, countless Indian attacks with poison-tipped spears, mutiny, the prospect of starvation, and a severe illness.

Now Spain and all its challenges beckoned, and the imperative to extol his accomplishments and justify his actions invigorated him. He had left Hispaniola as the proud Admiral of the Ocean Sea. Preparing to go ashore, he carefully altered his appearance, wearing the simple habit of a friar, out of a mixture of piety, penitence, and cunning. The authorities might jail a captain, but how would they treat the pious man returned from the sea who stood before them?

Columbus had not seen Spain since September 25, 1494, nearly two years before, and great events had occurred during his absence. The Catholic Sovereigns, whom he ardently desired to see, were in Burgos, in northern Spain, preparing the marriage of their only son, the Most Serene Highness Don Juan, Prince of Asturias, to Archduchess Margarita, the daughter of Emperor Maximilian of Austria. Everywhere, the "solemn pomp" of the Spanish nobility was in evidence, said Ferdinand Columbus, privileged to attend as a page to the prince, who was just eighteen years of age and known for his frail constitution.

In Burgos, Columbus displayed mementos of his latest voyage to the Indies: plants, trees, birds, and other animals. He exhibited implements employed by the Indians, their masks, belts accented with gold, and handfuls of gold dust "in its natural state, fine or large as beans and chickpeas and some the size of pigeon eggs." These quantities did not satisfy Columbus's greed, or his promises to return with fistfuls of gleaming nuggets of gold. In a rare moment of ambivalence, he "accepted that up till now the gain had barely met the cost." Despite the Admiral's private reservations, the trophies amazed many who saw them. Columbus and his men seemed latter-day versions of Jason and the Argonauts returning from their quest with rare specimens of the Golden Fleece.

"I send you samples of seeds of every kind," Peter Martyr boasted to Cardinal Sforza on April 29, 1494, "bark, and pitch from those trees they think may be cinnamon." He warned the cardinal to "barely touch them when you draw them near your lips: although not harmful, they produce excessive heat that can irritate and sting the tongue, if you leave them on it a long time." And if the cardinal felt his tongue burn after he tasted them, "the hot sensation is quickly eliminated by drinking water." A "piece of wood," on the other hand, resembled aloe. "If you have it split, you will smell the ensuing delicate perfume."

Setting aside their doubts, the Catholic Sovereigns prepared a stirring announcement that Spain had claimed a new realm, with the pope's blessing. On October 15, 1495, approximately three years after his first landfall in the area, Columbus could inform Ferdinand and Isabella: "The entire island is completely subjugated and its people know and accept the fact that they must pay tribute to Your Highnesses, each one a certain amount every so many moons." So ran the official version of the just-completed second voyage, in which the Admiral of the Ocean Sea consolidated his, and Spain's, control of international trade. Portugal take note: the Treaty of Tordesillas had legitimized the land-and-sea grab.

As if to confirm the Spanish ascendance, João II of Portugal died ten days later. He was only forty years old, and poisoning was strongly suspected. With the Portuguese monarch gone, Ferdinand and Isabella seemed to have a fair portion of the globe to themselves. They had reconquered Iberia, and with the help of Columbus they stood ready to claim still more.

Yet the maintenance of an overseas empire raised more questions than it settled, and troubling, persistent questions they were. First of all, where, precisely, was this newly acquired empire located? Columbus insisted they had reached India's distant precincts yet again, but skeptics and rivals believed that he had only the vaguest idea of where they were located. Next, what to do about the numerous people they had encountered in these islands, the so-called Indians? There were those who were obliging, and offered succor, and those who came racing to the water's edge to hurl spears at their ships. And there were those who committed suicide rather than coexist with the Spanish. There were alarming signs of cannibalism among these "Indians," yet it appeared that no Spaniard had been subjected to this fate. Columbus had tried to form strategic alliances with Indian leaders whom he encountered, yet his supposed ally Guacanagarí had massacred dozens of isolated, vulnerable Spanish scouts. Finally, converting the Indians to Christianity had proved difficult, time-consuming, and frustrating. Even Father Pané admitted that "force and craft" were sometimes necessary to effect conversions, and there was no assurance that Indians who had been baptized would practice the Christian faith after the priests departed. In reality, many fell away from the faith as rapidly as they had embraced it.

So the questions, for now, went unanswered.

As he had at the completion of his first voyage, Columbus guaranteed himself a return trip with the simple expedient of leaving men behind to fend for themselves, and he immediately went about mounting a third expedition to rescue or support them. His friend Peter Martyr wrote that the Admiral, "quite saddened by the murder of our men but of the opinion that he should not delay any longer," immediately began to lobby the Catholic Sovereigns to send a dozen ships to these troubled islands, and it appeared that he would get his wish. Both he and his royal patrons seemed determined to repeat the mistakes rather than learn the painful lessons of the first two voyages. The Admiral of the Ocean Sea remained convinced that the wealth of India and the Grand Khan lay only a short cruise from the islands he had already explored. The age of exploration, or, as it was in danger of becoming, the age of exploitation, continued to be driven by this illusion.

Columbus wished to return immediately to bring his stranded men provisions and weapons. "But insist as he might," Ferdinand commented sharply, "since the affairs of that court are usually attended by delay, ten or twelve months passed before he obtained the dispatch of two relief ships under the command of Captain Pedro Fernández Coronel."

The desperately needed ships finally sailed from Spain for the Indies in February 1497 without Columbus, who "stayed to attend to the outfitting of the rest of the fleet that he required for his return voyage to the Indies." Short of men and supplies, the task would require a year.

During this interval, a noticeable change came over Columbus. "Being a great devotee of Saint Francis, he also dressed from this time on in brown," Las Casas wrote sympathetically, "and I saw him in Seville when he returned from here, dressed almost identically as a Franciscan friar." Wearing the somber garb of a religious order signaled that Columbus had given himself over to his destiny with a renewed vigor.

By the time Columbus departed from Hispaniola, La Isabela had become a ghost town. The highly emotional Las Casas, who later visited the settlement and lamented its failed hopes, noted that "it was advised by many that no one could dare to pass by La Isabela after it was depopulated without great fear and danger" caused by "many frightening voices and horrible ghosts." And he related a fantastic tale:

> One day at some buildings of La Isabela, [some visitors] saw two lines of men, drawn up in formation, all of them apparently nobles and men from court, well dressed, with swords by their sides and all with cloaks of the kind affected by travelers of the time in Spain; those to whom this vision appeared were amazed—how had such elegant strangers come to be there, without anyone's knowing about it? They greeted and questioned them about where they had come from. When the travelers removed their hats, heads disappeared, leaving themselves beheaded, and then they disappeared. Those witnessing this spectacle almost died from fright on the spot and were upset for many days.

In reality, Columbus's final deed before leaving Hispaniola had been to instruct his brother Bartholomew to establish a new city at the mouth of the Ozama River. Santo Domingo was so named because Bartholomew arrived there on a Sunday. The site seemed promising: "a river of wholesome water, quite rich in excellent varieties of fish, flows into the harbor along charming banks," Peter Martyr noted. "Native palms and fruit trees of every kind sometimes drooped over the heads of our sailors, their branches weighed with blooms and fruits." The soil appeared to be even more fertile than that of La Isabela. Work on the fortress of Santo Domingo commenced that year, or the next, 1497, and before long twenty men resided in the future capital of the Spanish empire of the Indies. Santo Domingo is now the oldest continuously inhabited European settlement in the Western Hemisphere.

The rise of Santo Domingo meant the end of La Isabela. The ill-starred settlement became the final resting place of the bones of both Spanish settlers and Indians, finally at peace in death. In their shallow graves, the Indian corpses rested on their sides, according to their custom, and the Spanish on their backs, with their arms crossed over their rib cages and their eyes staring into eternity.

The Columbian Exchange

Millions of years ago, the Old and New Worlds belonged to one giant landmass, Pangaea, meaning "All Land." The geologic paradigm known as continental drift, first proposed by the Flemish cartographer Abraham Ortelius in 1596, slowly drove the continents thousands of miles apart.

As recently (in geologic terms) as 125 million years ago, when dinosaurs still inhabited the earth, large portions of North America were joined to the Eurasian landmass. A giant, amorphous ocean—and its currents—freely circulated the globe. Not until 30 million years ago did the oceans begin to assume their present configuration, but even then, the Atlantic Ocean reached from the poles to the tropics. A new phenomenon, the Gulf Stream, a remnant of the ancient transglobal current, distributed and redistributed life across its length. As Pangaea slowly fragmented, the resulting continents developed divergent evolution—that is, life-forms on each continent evolved separately, sometimes on parallel tracks, and in other cases quite differently.

It seemed that matters would go on this way indefinitely, despite fleeting instances of natural transoceanic contact. But in 1492 the voyages of Columbus and his successors suddenly and permanently altered this age-old pattern, bursting the evolutionary bubbles of previously independent continents. It is challenging to consider that one fleet, led by the vision and determination of a single individual, set in motion the events that brought about this lasting global change, but that is what occurred.

Not that Columbus realized it at the time. Arriving in the Americas, he was dumbfounded by the profusion of unfamiliar flora and fauna he faced. He was at times deeply frustrated by his inability to put a name to plants and animals he saw. The few learned men aboard his ships, such as his physician, Dr. Chanca, were similarly baffled.

The world was a very different place in 1492. When Columbus was journeying across the Atlantic, tomatoes, and tomato sauce, were unknown in Italy, or anywhere in Europe. The same situation applied to chocolate, widespread in the Americas for three thousand years before Columbus, but unfamiliar to European palates. Tobacco presented a similar case: deeply woven into Indian life and ritual, but unknown to Europeans. When Columbus and his men encountered these items, they did not know what to make of them. Yet, as a result of their importing these products to Europe, and transplanting flora and fauna they had brought with them in their ships, some as large as horses, others as small as microorganisms, the Old World and the New became interconnected in ways that no one, least of all Columbus, anticipated.

Nothing would ever be the same. Columbus could not have guessed that the most lasting and irreversible effects of his voyages would transcend his quest for empire and trade; instead, he inadvertently transformed the global environment. More than Christianity, or slavery, or gold, or any of the other forces with which Columbus and Spain grappled, this two-way transmission between the Old World and the New World brought about changes larger than they could have imagined. The transformation was wide-ranging, cataclysmic, and enduring. And it would take years, decades, centuries for the effects of this two-way transmission to unfold.

This slow-moving spectacle is known as the Columbian Exchange, first identified by Alfred Crosby, a professor at the University of Texas in Austin, in 1972. Within a couple of decades, Crosby's insights gave rise to a new way of considering the Columbian legacy. "When Europeans first touched the shores of the Americas," he wrote, "Old World crops such as wheat, barley, rice, and turnips had not traveled west across the Atlantic, and New World crops such as maize, white potatoes, sweet potatoes, and manioc had not traveled east to Europe." These vast differences extended to animal life as well. "In the Americas, there were no horses, cattle, sheep or goats." They were all "animals of Old World origin." In fact, with few exceptions, the New World had no domesticated animals, no chickens, and no cattle until the coming of Columbus. And when they did arrive, their presence changed the hunting, eating, and ultimately the migratory habits and tribal structures of the Indians who made use of them for food, labor, and companionship.

Their effects percolated through the culture in ways that the Spaniards could not have imagined. Take the horses that Columbus brought along with him, for instance. At first, they terrified the Indians, who had never seen beasts such as these. In time, the horses spread north, transforming Indian life. "*The horse gave the Indian the speed and stamina needed to take advantage of the opportunity to harvest the immense quantities of food represented by the buffalo herds of North America and the herds of wild cattle that propagated so rapidly in the grasslands of both Americas,*" Crosby observed. *There were still more unexpected consequences. "The Indians stopped farming; the work was hard, boring, and unrewarding, compared with nomadic life." So the Indians mounted their steeds and roamed the pampas, killing more animals than ever before as they went, more animals than they needed for themselves and their families. The Indian on horseback could increase and multiply. Greater numbers of Indians led to a growing division between rich and poor, to social stratification, and to slavery. As Crosby put it, "the egalitarianism of poverty began to disappear."*

So the animals brought by Europeans were not an unmixed blessing. Along with them—and with the associated black rats and sinister Aedes aegypti *mosquitoes—came deadly disease: smallpox, measles, chicken pox, influenza, yellow fever, and dengue fever. These pathogens infiltrated the New World, leaving destruction and suffering in their wake. The human animal also brought its pathogens, including syphilis.*

Syphilis is the most commonly cited example of disease transmission between the Old World and the New for which Columbus's voyages are held responsible, but there is little consensus about which way the venereal diseases traveled. Did the Indians infect the Spaniards, or was it the other way around? Accounts of syphilis arising spontaneously on both continents further complicated the question of how the disease spread. Clearly some of Columbus's crew suffered from syphilislike symptoms, as Dr. Chanca noted. But did they acquire the disease by mingling with Indian women, or did they bring the disease with them and transmit it to their unsuspecting victims? Or were different strains passed back and forth? This notorious aspect of the Columbian Exchange remains unanswered.

On a more positive side of the ledger, the Columbian Exchange introduced staples such as white potatoes, sweet potatoes, maize, and cassava to Europe, and brought wheat, turnips, barley, apples, and rice from Europe to the Americas. In the two-way transmission of the Columbian Exchange, a fragrant and colorful stream of lilacs and daisies and daffodils, along with lemons, oranges, lettuce, cabbage, pears, peaches, bananas, and coffee traveled from the Old World to the New. Meanwhile, pumpkins, squash, lima beans, and peppers traveled from the New World to the Old, as did peanuts, chocolate, and sweet potatoes. Honeybees arrived in the Americas, turkeys in the Old.

These crops were associated with population growth and economic growth. That was fine as far as it went, and relatively benign. But the Europeans also brought with them alcohol and alcoholism, another scourge that decimated heretofore innocent local populations. The devastating effects of European agriculture and pathogens on American Indians and their land did not mean the New World's ecosystem and its peoples were inferior; it resulted from the novelty of the assault. In time, plants, animals, and people adapted to the invaders, long after the devastation wrought by the initial contact.

Once started, the Columbian Exchange never ceased, and it continues at an ever-accelerating pace. Crosby called the phenomenon a "wild oscillation of nature" that occurs when an isolated region emerges into the larger environment. "Possibly it will never be repeated in as spectacular fashion as in the Americas in the first post-Columbian century, not unless there is, one day, an exchange of life forms between planets."

For better or worse, or rather, for better and worse, this is Columbus's enduring, relentless, inescapable, all-encompassing legacy.

PART THREE

Decadence

CHAPTER 8

"A Great Roaring"

Columbus labored uncertainly on muleback along stony trails and dusty plains toward Valladolid, in north central Spain. Ferdinand and Isabella had wed here twenty-eight years earlier, in 1469, and they occasionally returned to preside over their expanding empire. Columbus's companions included two close relatives of Caonabó, the duplicitous Indian cacique with whom he had formed an alliance. The Admiral of the Ocean Sea had planned to present Caonabó himself to the Sovereigns as a trophy, but he had died of disease at sea. Only his relatives remained.

The Admiral had returned to Spain at the conclusion of his second voyage only weeks before, and he managed this overland journey as if it were an extension of that seagoing enterprise. As the party stumbled on their way, their caged parrots, souvenirs of Hispaniola, screeched in alarm. Caonabó's brother, who had converted to Christianity and taken the name Don Diego, remained nearly as conspicuous, wearing a prominent collar fashioned from gold and his crown, said to be "big and tall, with wings on its sides like a shield and golden eyes as large as silver cups."

Ravaged by illness, Columbus looked a decade older than his forty-six years, drained of the vigor and stamina that had propelled him as a young navigator. His fine mane of hair had gone white, and his vision constantly troubled him, his retinas scorched from long hours of gazing at the sunlit sea. His bones ached with every lurch of the mule on which he rode. Suffering from arthritis and other disorders, he knew his time was limited, and rather than resting on his laurels, and allowing others to win glory and riches by building on the discoveries that he had made in the previous five years, he was determined to cram as much exploration as possible into the time left to him.

At times he brooded on the lack of recognition for his astonishing exploration of the Indies. "I discovered for you," he reminded Ferdinand and Isabella between voyages, "333 leagues of mainland at the very end of the Orient and named 700 islands in addition to what was discovered on the first voyage, and I pacified for you the island of Hispaniola, which is larger than Spain and inhabited by innumerable people." Columbus should have thought twice before making this boast. The Sovereigns had made him, and they could break him, confiscate his discoveries, and strip him of his honors, titles, and wealth if they wished.

Columbus, in contrast, believed that he had been unfairly penalized for his empire building rather than generously rewarded, as he deserved. He decried the "cursing and the scorn for the enterprise" that he had risked his life to set in motion, all because "I had not sent back ships right away laden with gold." No one bothered to take into account the "enormous difficulties" that he faced. "For my sins, or rather, for my salvation, I was held in aversion, and obstacles were raised to whatever I said and asked." He reminded his Sovereigns that he had, in the past, "brought you enough samples of gold and told you about the existence of gold mines and very large nuggets and also copper, and I delivered to you so many kinds of spices that it would be too long to write down," but, he said bitterly, "all of this made no difference to some people"—his critics and rivals at court—"who had very consciously begun speaking ill of the enterprise." He had performed the tasks that explorers through the ages had accomplished on behalf of their rulers and princes: "to serve God while expanding their own dominion." Yet, "the more I argued for [the enterprise], the more the detractors redoubled their jokes on the subject." He had implored Ferdinand and Isabella to hear his plea, but "Your Highnesses responded to me with a smile, saying that I should not be troubled at all by it because you did not view those who spoke ill of this enterprise as deserving authority or credence." Nevertheless, he feared they hovered on the verge of betraying the sacred cause he shared with them.

His many discoveries had whetted his appetite for more. He was driven in part by greed and self-aggrandizement, and in part by a need to exonerate himself, to prove to the Sovereigns that he had kept his sacred promises to them, despite the incomplete and often contradictory evidence of his voyages. Even more troubling, he refused to address his monstrous blunders: the oath he had made his men swear on pain of death that Cuba belonged to the mainland of India, the fifty thousand Indians who had committed suicide in protest of his occupation of their lands, and his failure to locate the Grand Khan.

To proclaim his humility and piety, and perhaps unconsciously atone for the fatal outcome of his administration, Columbus took to wearing the habit of a Franciscan friar, woven of coarse brown cloth. Following the precepts of St. Francis of Assisi, members of this mendicant religious order emphasized penance. Presumably he belonged to the Third Order, the most secular Franciscan subdivision, which did not require its members to live in a Franciscan community but instead to work zealously to improve their lives. He scarcely resembled the imperious Admiral of the Ocean Sea, celebrated discoverer of an empire, and intimate of the Sovereigns. He had carefully concealed signs of worldly ambition and vanity in favor of devotion and humility.

Garbed in plain attire, he had visited at length with Andrés Bernáldez, who appreciated Columbus without challenging him. He entrusted his journals of the second voyage to the curate, who was compiling an ambitious history of the reign of Ferdinand and Isabella, the Catholic Sovereigns who had driven the infidels from Spanish soil. Columbus claimed a small but significant place in this history, one that had more to do with his discovery of gold than of new lands and peoples. A goldsmith named Fermín Zedo claimed that the walnut-size nuggets that Columbus had transported to Spain were alloys. No, Columbus insisted, the gold was pure, and he showed samples to prove his point, justifying himself in Bernáldez's eyes.

Columbus showed Bernáldez the massive gold collar worn by Caonabó's brother. "This I saw and held in my hands," he exclaimed, together with Indian "crowns, masks, girdles, collars, and many articles woven of cotton." On closer inspection, the curate made out the devil "represented in the shape of a monkey or owl's head, or other, worse shapes." Still, he beheld in amazement these souvenirs of another world, "winged crowns with gold eyes on their sides, and especially a crown they said belonged to the cacique Caonabó, which was very big and tall, with wings on its sides like a shield and golden eyes as large as silver cups weighing half a mark, each one placed there in a very strange and ingenious manner." As if that finery were not sufficient, "the devil, too, was represented on that crown." The Indian idolaters, he assumed, "regarded the devil as lord."

Columbus arrived at Valladolid to learn that the Sovereigns had departed for the wedding of Don Juan and the Archduchess Margarita on April 3, 1497, at Burgos. On he went, for at Burgos he could see his sons, Diego and Ferdinand, and finally present the king and queen with the gifts and blandishments designed to secure his monopoly on the lands he had claimed in

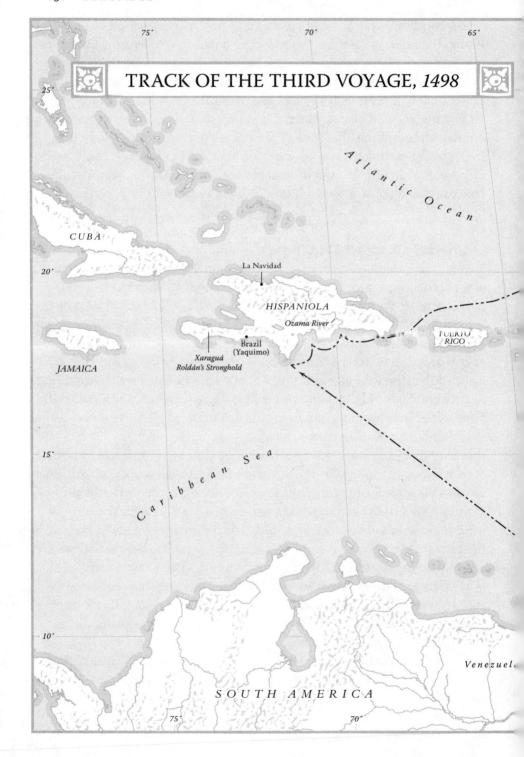

TRACK OF THE THIRD VOYAGE, *1498*

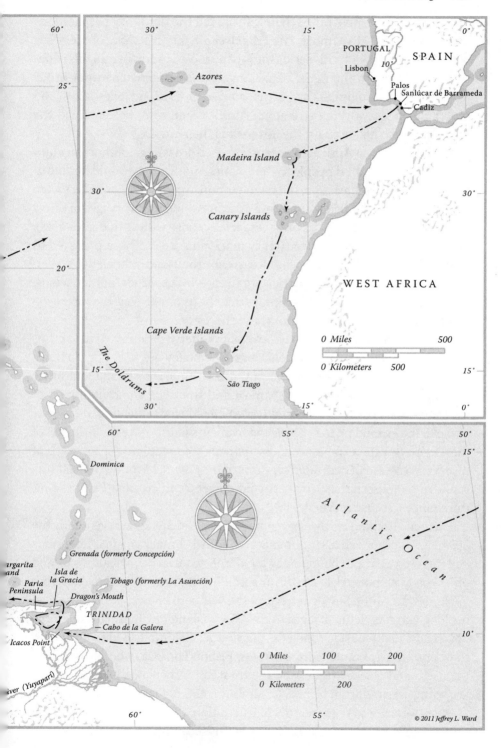

PORTUGAL   SPAIN

Lisbon

Palos
Sanlúcar de Barrameda
Cadiz

Azores

Madeira Island

Canary Islands

WEST AFRICA

Cape Verde Islands

The Doldrums

São Tiago

0 Miles   500

0 Kilometers   500

Dominica

Atlantic Ocean

Grenada (formerly Concepción)

Margarita Island
Isla de la Gracia
Paria Peninsula
Dragon's Mouth
Tobago (formerly La Asunción)

TRINIDAD
Cabo de la Galera

Icacos Point

River (Yuyapari)

0 Miles   100   200

0 Kilometers   200

© 2011 Jeffrey L. Ward

their names. His appearance there galvanized the desultory preparations for his return to Hispaniola. His Franciscan habit, his show of piety, his protestations of loyalty, his seriousness of purpose, and, above all, his experience exploring in the name of the Sovereigns combined to work in his favor. Although Columbus had compromised himself and fallen short, and others had been working strenuously to discredit him, he remained the discoverer who had brought the Sovereigns their empire.

Just days later, on April 20, they approved a third voyage, authorizing him to bring three hundred people to the colony. Another fifty would be able to go at their own expense; spurred by the promise of easy riches, takers were easy to find. Able-bodied seamen and artisans would receive wages of thirty maravedís a day; soldiers, laborers (especially those willing to dig for gold), and cabin boys would receive twenty maravedís a day. Those prepared to stay and cultivate the land would earn six thousand maravedís a year. Women were permitted to participate in the voyage, grudgingly, it seems. Very little is known about this group, but it is assumed that they were expected to work, most likely at domestic chores.

To fill out the ships' rosters, the Sovereigns offered pardons to jailed criminals who agreed to sail with Columbus. The policy did not apply to those convicted of murder, treason, sodomy, arson, or counterfeiting, but other convicts prepared to go to "Hispaniola and the islands and mainland of the Indies" for a year or more would receive a reduced sentence. And in Hispaniola, they would be free. These inducements hardly gave the Admiral of the Ocean Sea the experienced, disciplined force required for a voyage of discovery. Instead of dedicated servants of the crown, he found himself surrounded by mercenaries, amateur gold diggers, and criminals waiting for the chance to cause mayhem.

Financial backing for the voyage was slower to materialize; eventually the Sovereigns authorized 2,824,326 maravedís. By February 17, 1498, Columbus had merely 350,094 in hand to pay for all the necessary provisions, sail, and other costly supplies related to the undertaking. Extra support came not from Spain, but from the Seville bureau of the Genoese bank that had financed his long-ago merchant voyages to the Greek island of Chios. Although the Sovereigns had set aside funds for the voyage, Columbus had to answer to their notoriously cranky administrator, Bishop Fonseca, who disliked him intensely, and blocked or delayed the transfers. When a cargo of wheat for the voyage arrived from Genoa, Columbus could not pay.

After weeks, and then months of frustration, the cantankerous Admiral himself got into a fistfight with one of Fonseca's representatives, Jimeno

Breviesca, who had been ridiculing the Enterprise of the Indies. Hearing criticism once too often, Columbus knocked the bureaucrat to the ground, and kicked him. Breviesca was an officer of the crown, and by losing his temper Columbus had damaged his reputation, especially in the eyes of the Sovereigns.

In fact, his problems extended far beyond this unseemly brawl. He was losing the monopoly he had held for the previous six years over Spain's trans-oceanic empire. Although the boundaries of the Treaty of Tordesillas were still in place, challengers were emerging, some obtaining the backing of Ferdinand and Isabella. Columbus no longer had the Indies to himself.

The exploration squadron under his command consisted of three ships: *Santa María*, the flagship; *El Correo* ("the Courier"), a caravel owned by Columbus and his Sovereigns; and *La Vaqueños*, thought to be leased to the expedition by a widow in Palos, Spain. Columbus planned to sail along a southerly course to the Cape Verde Islands, an archipelago of ten islets off the coast of West Africa. Known, if not well understood, since antiquity, they had been rediscovered by António de Noli of Genoa, who had sailed for Prince Henry the Navigator. King Alfonso V of Portugal later appointed António de Noli as the first governor of Cape Verde.

The Cape Verde Islands proved drab and bereft of the luxurious vegetation of other landmasses. Columbus declared the name "absolutely false . . . because they are so arid that I saw nothing green on them."

Heading into uncharted waters, he planned to go farther south than ever before, in the belief that the closer to the equator he came, the more valuable his discoveries would be. This notion circulated among cosmographers such as Jaime Ferrer, who had advised Columbus that near the equator "great and precious things such as gems and gold and spicery and drugs" could be found. According to Ferrer, Indians, Arabs, and Ethiopians agreed "the majority of precious things come from a very hot region where the inhabitants are black or tan." Therefore, wherever Columbus found such people he would find the precious items he sought.

He set sail at the height of midsummer, June 21, bound for Hierro, on the western edge of the Canary Islands, where during the brief hours of darkness he and his two accompanying vessels bade farewell to the supply fleet bound for Hispaniola. He dropped anchor in a bay near barren Boa Vista—the name roughly equivalent to "land ahoy!" in Portuguese—an island known for its leper colony. The Portuguese notary-in-charge, Rodrigo Alonso, told the Admiral that lepers came to Boa Vista in the belief that eating the meat of turtles and washing in their blood cured the affliction. The islanders caught the turtles by night, first by looking for their tracks with the help of lantern light. When they found one of the sleeping creatures, they flipped it onto its back, rendering it helpless, and then they turned over the next, and the next after that, before butchering the lot.

On Saturday, June 30, 1498, Columbus set sail for nearby São Tiago, the largest of all the islands in Cape Verde. Fog accumulated even in the intense heat, obscuring the sun by day and stars by night. Despite this obstacle, the little fleet departed on a southerly course on July 4, with the Admiral determined to test the boundaries of the recently modified Treaty of Tordesillas. He was, finally, bound for the Indies.

In search of a shortcut, as always, he sailed as far south as he dared, to the latitude of Sierra Leone, 8°30′ north of the equator, before heading west to the island of Hispaniola. On Friday, July 13, Columbus's fleet entered a convergence zone where winds from the Northern and Southern Hemispheres flow together. The wind died, the ocean's surface became ominously flat, and the temperature shot up. They had arrived at the Doldrums, a region that few Europeans, Columbus included, had ever explored, let alone survived.

"I entered a zone of heat so high and intense that I believed that the ships and crews would be burnt up," he confided. "The heat came so unexpectedly and so out of measure that not a single man dared go below deck to salvage barrels of drink and victuals." Becalmed, afflicted by melancholia, Columbus reeled with dread. In the "intense heat," said Las Casas, "he feared that the ships would burn and the men perish." The temperature was already taking its toll on the equipment. Wine and water casks ruptured, breaking the barrels' hoops. Sheaves of wheat withered. Bacon and salted meat rotted almost before their eyes. Only clouds and the occasional rainfall spared them all death by exposure to the pitiless sun.

Suffering from painful gout and disorienting heatstroke, unable to sleep, scarcely able to breathe, Columbus forced himself to conjure a course to more temperate weather. He took heart from the sight of black and white rooks, birds that he believed did not stray far from land. By July 19, the heat was even more intense, and the suffering greater. But then a zephyr filled the ships' sails, a few uncertain puffs at first, followed by more convincing gusts, until the sheets bulged and the air pulsed with vitality once again. "It pleased Our Lord at the end of these eight days to grant me a good wind from the east," Columbus noted, "and I went west . . . always westward on the parallel of Sierra Leone with the intention of not changing course until I reached the location where I thought I would find land and repair the ships and replenish, if possible, our victuals and take on the water I needed." He followed his westward course for seventeen days, believing that he would eventually arrive at a point due south of Hispaniola.

But first he had to find land. His ships were coming apart at the seams, and in urgent need of repair, and their stores were equally in need of replenishment. Sunday, July 22, brought birds flying from the west southwest to the northeast . . . still more birds traversing the skies on Monday . . . and, later that week, a pelican perched proudly on the flagship, suggesting the proximity of land, and drinking water, but where?

Veering north, he made for the big island of Dominica, whose coast he had skirted on the second voyage. Because of its reputation as a cannibal haven, he had chosen to avoid it on that occasion, but now he was so desperate for water and respite from the torments of the sea that he was willing to risk a landfall. Before he did, he sent his servant, Alonso Pérez, up to the mainmast. From his vantage point, "he saw land to the west, fifteen leagues away," Columbus noted. "What appeared were three knolls or mountains." They formed an unexpected deliverance from the anthropophagi. He named the outcroppings Trinidad, after their tripartite nature. As he approached, they appeared to him as "three mountains all at one time, in a single view." Not since encountering land during his first voyage had he felt so relieved. "It is certain that finding this land in this place was a great miracle," he recorded. He had just sighted one of the two islands that comprise today's Trinidad, the southernmost landmass of the Caribbean, only seven miles from the coast of Venezuela and South America. The Spaniards on board rejoiced and chanted the "Salve Regina" as the others nodded in fervent agreement.

He made for a cape that had caught his attention. It seemed to resemble a galley under sail, and so he named it Cabo de la Galera, where, according to his records, he arrived at the hour of Compline, at day's end. In search of a safe harbor, he coasted past miles of shoreline cloaked in forests that "reached to the sea." Finally, Columbus caught sight of a canoe: his first contact with the people of Trinidad. Rather than expressing relief or curiosity, he brushed off the overtures of a small tribe approaching them in canoes. Stressed from the voyage, suffering from aches and pains, and even near blindness, and puzzled that the canoes did not carry Chinese, as expected, he avoided both their friendly gestures and hostile arrows. In reality, he was no closer to India than before, and had happened upon a local community related to the Taíno and Carib tribes.

The next morning, his fleet, rationed to a single cask of water, proceeded along a southerly course until dropping anchor at Point Erin, where the men gratefully refilled their supply of fresh water and cleaned themselves and their garments in heartfelt rites of renewal.

Aboard their ships once again, Columbus's men spied thatched huts ashore, put them astern, and proceeded along Icacos Point, which marked Trinidad's southwesternmost extension. The *icaco*, or cocoa plum, for which the point was named, sends forth glaucous leathery leaves and velvety fruit, often of a purplish hue. Tolerant of salt, cocoa plums provide a natural barrier against the sea's erosion.

The flotilla paused again when Columbus sighted a landmass he took to be an island. But further exploration of the extensive coast—more than twenty leagues—challenged his judgment. On Wednesday, August 1, he arrived at the broad mouth of the Orinoco, among the longest rivers in South America, located at the border of Venezuela and Brazil. The topography persuaded him that he had arrived at the mainland, and the recognition marked the signal discovery of this or any other of his voyages, his first sighting of the continent whose size and location neither he nor anyone else in his ships fully understood or acknowledged. The mystic in him preferred to assume that Providence had led him closer to the entrance to paradise. He shied away from the rigors of geographical adjustment required for nautical reckoning. Nor did he know what to make of the coastal flora beyond noting that it appeared lush and reassuring. "The trees brushed against the sea," in Las Casas's paraphrase, a sign that the sea was calm "because when it is rough there are no trees there at all, but rather sand." Yet a "surging current" appeared to emanate "from above," and a "mounting current" from below.

He led the ships into a shallow, brackish body of water west of Trinidad, now known as the Gulf of Paria. After all he had endured, the sweeping shore seemed a sort of paradise, as befitting one of the best harbors in the continent's eastern coast. "This gulf is a marvelous thing," Las Casas commented, "and dangerous because of the great river that flows into it." He called it Yuyaparí, now the Orinoco River. "This river travels more than 300, I believe 400 leagues." He was describing the Orinoco Delta, a giant, fan-shaped network of waterways. Between the land and sea lurked danger, as

Las Casas explained. "Since that gulf is surrounded by mainland on one side and on the other by the island of Trinidad, and is, as a result, very narrow for the violent force of the opposing waters, they meet in a terrible confrontation and very dangerous battle."

Dropping anchor on Thursday, August 2, Columbus permitted his exhausted men to venture onto a swampy brown beach near Icacos Point "so that they might rest and enjoy themselves" after their anxiety-ridden crossing. Restful it might have been, but the setting had an isolated, melancholy feel, as if time were running out as surely as the tide.

Later that day, a large canoe bearing twenty-four Indians appeared, halting at a safe distance. The Indians shouted over the water, and Columbus's men responded not with words but with a show of objects—"brass pots and other shiny things"—to encourage the canoe to approach for a bit of friendly trading. The Indians came closer, but still kept their distance, even though Columbus improvised a dance of welcome. "I wanted very much to speak with them, and not having anything more that seemed to me suitable to show and lure them to approach, my last resort was to have a tambourine brought up on the quarterdeck to play and have some boys dance, believing that this way they would draw near to see the celebration."

The Indians interpreted the merriment as a war dance and "took up and strung their bows, held up their shields, and began shooting arrows." Their intended targets scurried below deck. Columbus "gave the command to stop the fiesta of drumming and dancing," and ordered his men to bring out their crossbows and fire several warning projectiles at the Indians, who had expended their arrows and positioned themselves at the stern of one of the caravels, as if readying to overrun her. At that moment, the ship's pilot summoned the confidence to dangle from the stern and lower himself into the canoe, armed only with gifts in the form of a "robe" and a "bonnet," quickly accepted by the Indians, who gestured that the Spanish pilot should go ashore to receive their offerings. He agreed, and asked to be taken to the flagship so that he could ask permission from the Admiral. Before he completed the protocol, the Indians had given up and departed.

Columbus thought he had seen the last of them until one of their caciques came to the flagship. The Indian's gold crown caught the eye of every Spaniard, as did his crimson cap and the dignified manner in which he paid his respects to the Admiral. He placed his crown on Columbus's head, sealing their sudden bond. The generous gesture was not quite enough for Columbus, who was hoping for an offering of silk, or brocade, as if to reenact a

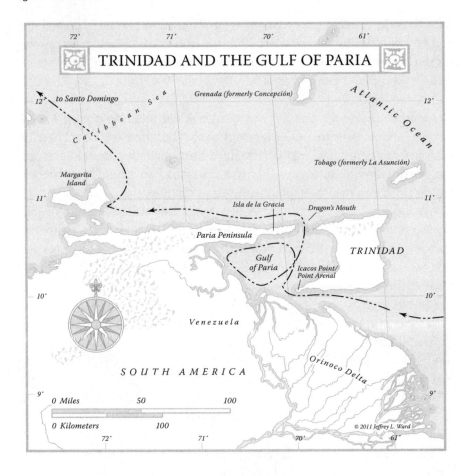

TRINIDAD AND THE GULF OF PARIA

to Santo Domingo

Grenada (formerly Concepción)

Caribbean Sea

Atlantic Ocean

Tobago (formerly La Asunción)

Margarita Island

Isla de la Gracia

Dragon's Mouth

Paria Peninsula

TRINIDAD

Gulf of Paria

Icacos Point/ Point Arenal

Venezuela

Orinoco Delta

SOUTH AMERICA

0 Miles   50   100

0 Kilometers   100

© 2011 Jeffrey L. Ward

scene from Marco Polo's *Travels*. Instead, he met the steady gaze of curious Indians. "They were not so brown as the others," said Las Casas, drawing on the accounts of Columbus and other participants, "rather more white than others that had been seen in the Indies, very good-looking with handsome bodies. Their hair was long and straight, cut in the Castilian style." Their heads were bound with woven cotton, which Columbus, always on the lookout for signs that he had reached the East, took for turbans. Other Europeans eyed the Indians' weapons, especially their bows and feathered arrows tipped with a sharp, barbed bone "like a fishhook."

Negotiating their way past the Indians, Columbus and his men stumbled ever deeper into a boisterous *paraíso* teeming with anacondas, pythons, howler monkeys (the loudest land animals in the New World), capuchin monkeys (whose monkish appearance reminded early European visitors of the habits and hoods of the Order of Friars Minor Capuchin), macaws, toucans, parrots, storks, kingfishers, and woodpeckers. Agile jaguars and pumas wound their way through the impenetrable undergrowth. In search of pearls, Columbus, bewildered, remarked on the "very large oysters" before turning his attention to the plentiful fish and parrots staring at the intruders in their midst. The parrots were "green, of a very bright color tending toward white, while those of the islands are greener and of a darker color. All those of the mainland have yellow necks, like stains, and the points above the wings have colored patches, and there are some yellow feathers on the wings," according to Las Casas.

Surveying from Point Arenal, on Venezuela's northern coast, Columbus studied the islands to the north and the mountains to the south with growing curiosity. They saw tracks of animals—goats, the men assumed, but actually deer—but found the corpse of only one. Like so much else in the "other world," they knew not what to make of the sight.

Columbus resumed searching for an Indian interpreter and for water. His men were at the point of digging wells in the sand when they came upon several boreholes that fishermen had apparently abandoned. He arrived at a channel that he named Boca del Dragón, the "Dragon's Mouth," between the pincerlike land extensions of Trinidad and Isla de Gracia. Refreshed, the Admiral intended to sail to the north toward the familiar sights of Hispaniola, but, he noted with alarm, "there were some great crosscurrents throughout the entrance that made a great roaring . . . like waves breaking and shattering on the rocks." The question was how to get around the churning seawater. He anchored just beyond the opening of the channel, and "discovered that the water came in, night and day, from east to west with a fury like that of the Guadalquivir when it is high, and it flowed so continuously I feared I could not turn back because of the current nor proceed farther because of the shallows." He was trapped.

In the early hours of August 4, the Dragon's Mouth bit.

"Well into the night," Columbus later recalled, "I heard while on deck a terrible roar coming from the south toward the *nao*; I ran to look and saw a tidal wave swelling from west to east like a hill as high as the *nao* coming toward me little by little, and on its crest an advancing line was visible, roaring with a great noise, with the same fury and roar of the other crosscurrents mentioned before and resembling waves breaking against rocks." But he was delivered from destruction as suddenly and inexplicably as he had confronted it. "However, it went by and reached the entrance, where it stopped for a considerable time."

The massive displacement of water snapped the cable securing *La Vaqueños*'s anchor, carrying her to an impossible height. Riding "atop the swell," Columbus marveled that he had never experienced anything approaching this wild and potentially disastrous ride. According to Las Casas, Columbus declared that "if they escaped from here, they could tell stories about how they escaped from the Dragon's Mouth. And because of this, the name stuck, and with good reason." It was one of the few names that did; Las Casas, whose life span overlapped that of Columbus, noted that Columbus generally wrote on water. "Of all the names that he gave to islands and capes of the mainland, which he knew as Isla de Gracia, none remain or are known today except the island of Trinidad, the Dragon's Mouth, the Testigos, and Margarita."

As the wave passed, the ship plummeted toward the ocean floor, coming so close that the men could glimpse the bottom. And then the turmoil ended. He had survived his encounter with the Dragon's Mouth. Months later, the memory of the traumatic event still shook him. "Even today," he later informed Ferdinand and Isabella, "I have fear in my body, for it could have capsized the ship when it came under her."

The monstrous surge was most likely a tidal wave, or tsunami, caused by a significant undersea earthquake: 7.5 magnitude or greater. A tsunami occurs when the earth's crust, or tectonic plate, below the ocean shifts abruptly and vertically dislocates water. The sudden change generates giant, fast-moving waves that propagate in all directions.

Narrowly escaping disaster, Columbus sailed on until he made landfall on Venezuela's Paria Peninsula, August 5, 1498. He sent men to find sweet water, which they soon did. "Since this was a mountainous area," he reasoned, "I thought that farther on, to the west, the land would be flatter for that very reason, possibly more populated." Or so he hoped. He raised anchor and skirted the coastline "to the low edge of this mountain and anchored in a river."

All at once, "many people came and told me they called this land Paria, and farther west there were still more people." There is some doubt about when Columbus himself went ashore. His young page, Andrés de Corral, later testified that the Admiral's inflamed eyes confined him aboard ship. In this version, one of the fleet's captains, Pedro de Terreros, took possession on behalf of the Admiral, and raised a large cross to mark the occasion.

Another captain, Hernán Pérez, claimed that *he* arrived first on the mainland. Others agreed that Columbus did not go ashore at this time.

Later, said Pérez, "the Admiral with about fifty men landed in the country of Paria and took a sword in one hand and a banner in the other, saying that in the name of Their Highnesses, he took possession of the province." Once ashore, he carefully observed the inhabitants who greeted him. "They are the color of all the others in the Indies; some of them wear their hair very long, others like us, but none have cut it as in Spain and the other lands. They are of very fair stature, and all well grown." And, he said, "they wear their genital member tied and covered, and the women all go naked as their mothers bore them."

Taking four Indians as hostage guides, Columbus sailed west for another eight leagues, past a point that he named Punta del Aguja, where the enthralling panoramas ("the prettiest in the world," he enthused) convinced him to drop anchor once more, and go ashore and "see these people." As soon as they saw him approach, they jumped into their canoes, paddled furiously to his ship, and, as he remembered it, "beseeched me, in the name of their king, to go ashore."

Columbus briefly seemed a changed man. In the pages of his letters to the Sovereigns, he expressed an eagerness for the companionship of Indians, rather than sizing up their potential as slaves or converts to Christianity. Blistered by the Doldrums, shaken and humbled by the tidal wave, he sounded simply glad to be alive, and delighted to inhale deep drafts of scented air and to immerse his head in cold, sweet water. For a charmed interval, he saw himself as a fortunate survivor, part of the larger landscape linking divinity and humanity, rather than an overdetermined conqueror and master. Even the sight of gold and pearls adorning the Indians did not make him salivate with greed as it did on the previous voyages: "Many wore pieces of gold about their necks and some pearls on their arms. I was most happy to see those pearls and attempted to inquire where they could be found, and the people replied that they were taken from there, in the north of that land." But Columbus put aside his obsession with riches in favor of the "wheat, wine, and meat" on the verge of spoiling in the holds of his ships, "and since my sole purpose was to see that they did not, I would not tarry for anything in the world"—not even gold. His priorities had altered; for once, he was more concerned with his well-being than with attempting superhuman tasks. The sense of tranquillity soon dispelled. On second thought, "I did try to get some of the pearls and sent the boats ashore."

* * *

The landing party encountered "handsome," "gentle," and "tractable" people who gladly led the way to a "large house with a gabled roof," rather than the expected tent, fully furnished with seats. The newly magnanimous Columbus praised his hosts for their good manners, and for their "fine bodies, tall and elegantly graceful, their hair very long and smooth and held around their heads by embroidered cloth . . . that from a distance seems to be made of silk and gauze." He admired their well-made canoes ("I saw that in the center of each of them is a cabin with a bed occupied by the chief and his wives") and on the setting, which he called Jardínes, or Gardens, "because that name fit it." Absolutely riveted by the Indians' showy gold jewelry, he peppered them with inquiries about where they had found it and how he could reach it, but they warned him away with tales of fierce cannibals or animals, he could not tell which. He considered seeking pearls as a substitute for gold but "did not carry out that search because of the victuals and the problems with my eyes, and because I have too big a *nao*, unsuitable for searching for pearls."

A banquet of bread, fruit, and red and white "wine" awaited them. The alcoholic beverages puzzled Columbus; they were not distilled from grapes, but from some other fruit he did not recognize, and from maize, which he defined as "a grain with an ear shaped like a spindle." *Maize* is the Taíno term for corn. Samples would be sent to Castile at the earliest opportunity.

Men and women remained segregated during the feast, and awkward silences dampened the mood. "Both parties were most sad because they could not understand each other; they wanted to ask us about our homeland, and we wanted to know about theirs," Columbus remarked with laudable equanimity. He was tempted to linger, but "I was most anxious to deliver safely the victuals that would otherwise spoil and to get some remedy for myself since I felt sick from lack of sleep." He calculated that "during this voyage on which I discovered the mainland I went thirty-three days without sleeping," and claimed that he went "without my sight" throughout that period. At the very least, he suffered from impaired vision, and, he complained, "my eyes never hurt as much nor were as bloodshot and painful as they were at this point."

Still unwilling to accept the mounting evidence that he had arrived at a continent, Columbus took refuge in the thought that the coastline delineated an island, and thought about sailing north, in the direction of Hispaniola. Wonder and confusion ensued when he dispatched a "light caravel to see if there was an exit or if a passage was likely." Instead, the caravel reconnoitered a "large gulf," an "awesome river," and "the most abundant and freshest water I ever drank." Yet he became "most disappointed" when he realized he was trapped, unable to sail to the north, south, or west. He had no choice but to turn back, but when he tried to raise familiar landmarks onshore, "the currents had carried me away." Everywhere, "fresh, clear water carried me eastward with great force." And in the distance, the roaring resumed. He decided that the "volumes of water flowing in and through the strait . . . were nothing less than the violent mingling of fresh and salt water: the fresh pushed forward, fighting its way out to the ocean, and the salt resisted it."

At sea once more, he became unusually contemplative. "Sailing from Spain to the Indies I find 100 leagues west of the Azores the greatest change in the sky and the stars and the quality of the air and in the waters of the sea," he reflected, "and I treasure that experience." He noticed phenomena that in his frenzy he had overlooked: the way "the sea here is filled with a certain kind of weed resembling small pine branches bearing fruit like that of the mastic; this weed is so thick that on the first voyage I thought that the sea was shoal and that I would end up running the ships aground." Now, he marveled, "one does not encounter a single twig." His surroundings soothed him, "the sea very calm and peaceful, and even when a strong wind blows, the surface of the sea does not swell or ruffle." The sky itself appeared "very mild" and conducive to stargazing: "I see that the North Star describes a circle with a diameter of five degrees, and the guards are on the right hand; at that very moment, the star is at its lowest point, from which it rises until it reaches the left side."

His eyesight improving, Columbus passed his nights observing celestial objects, but the security such observations afforded him was illusory. The consummate dead-reckoning navigator was not especially adept with the navigational tools and concepts of his day, and on this occasion he came up with an outlandish finding. "I diligently observed it with the quadrant," Columbus said, "and I regularly saw the plumb line fall to the same point," whereas he expected it to shift slightly as his ship slid through the slick sea. Something was awry. "I hold that this is an unknown phenomenon," he declared, and it led him, in this deceptively calm state of reflection, to the most radical hypothesis that he would ever make—more extreme, even, than his misguided belief that he had sailed to India. He believed that he had discovered the entrance to paradise.

* * *

In the grip of this idea, Columbus interpreted the movement of the ship's compass needles as pointing the way to heaven. The farther west they sailed, he believed, the higher their ship would rise. Practically smacking his forehead in dismay at Columbus's folly, Las Casas commented, "From this, he arrived at the idea, against all the common knowledge of astrologers and philosophers, that the world was not round," that is, a perfect sphere. (Most Europeans of Columbus's day realized that the world was round, as mathematicians and geographers of antiquity had predicted.)

Columbus meant something far more elaborate than a slight bulge or distortion in the earth's sphericity. "Each time I sailed from Spain to the Indies, I found that when I reached a point a hundred leagues west of the Azores, the heavens, the stars, the temperature of the air and the waters of the sea abruptly changed," he recorded. "It was as if the seas sloped upward." *Sloped upward?* This observation perplexed him, because he had "always read that the world of land and sea is spherical," yet now "I have found such great irregularities that I have come to the following conclusions concerning the world: that it is not round as they describe it, but the shape of a pear, which is round everywhere except at the stalk, where it juts out a long way . . . like a woman's nipple." This prominent feature led to paradise itself, extending from a watery summit. "I do not believe that anyone can ascend to the top," he cautioned at the end of his fantastic conjecture.

If the gold and slaves and spices he had sent back from his earlier voyages would not silence his critics, perhaps this sighting would. "I do not believe that the earthly paradise is a steep mountain," he explained, "except at its summit, the part I described as the stem of the pear." He believed that "no one could reach the summit," where the water's source lay. He divined this because of the torrents of fresh water he had experienced off the coast of Venezuela, "for I never read nor knew of so much fresh water penetrating so far inland and so near salt water. . . . And if it does not come from there, from paradise, the wonder is even greater, because I do not believe that a river as big and deep is known anywhere else in the world."

In this upwelling from his unconscious ruminations, his search for paradise served as a metaphor for the more elemental surveillance of womankind, of Mother Earth. He took solace in his reveries of inhabiting a world where magic was still possible even as he experienced a troubling sense of confronting the unknown. It was, for him, reassuring to know that the promise of paradise existed, even if he would never reach it himself.

Columbus's visionary propensities remained intact, stronger and more singular than ever. Other explorers felt buoyed by the belief that they were fulfilling the Lord's will, but Columbus's striking conception of the entrance to paradise was unique. It was easy for students of Columbus, beginning with Bartolomé de Las Casas, to separate fact from folly, and science from delusion, but to the Admiral's way of thinking, these seeming opposites remained inextricably intertwined. Even at this late date, eight years after setting out on his first voyage, he still believed that he was on the doorstep of the Indies, as well as the threshold of paradise. Experience fostered his illusions rather than dispelling them. As the voyage proceeded, he gave himself over to reveries. When he considered the globe, he no longer saw the ocean, evidence of currents and tides, sandbanks, reefs, bays, or other geologic features, but a series of shimmering images that might be better described as visions containing coded information about the nature of the cosmos. For him, reconnaissance was the process of deciphering this God-given code as best he could.

"The world is small," he later declared, on the basis of this experience and other mystical flights. "Six parts are dry and only the seventh is covered with water. Experience has already verified that"—even though his voyages demonstrated that, on the contrary, the world was mostly covered by oceans. In his defense, he argued that "I hold that the world is not so large as thought by common men." Columbus based his expert opinion on a conception of the world that included paradise, but excluded the Pacific Ocean and the Americas. His small world had a circumference of about 14,000 miles, when in reality earth's circumference at the equator is about 24,900 miles.

Clinging to his insupportable beliefs, he maintained that as a result of the "navigation and exploration and discovery" promoted by the Sovereigns, he could tell which zones of the earth he had visited by the complexions of the people he encountered. In Cape Verde, he insisted, "the people there are much darker" than elsewhere, "and the farther south one goes the more extreme their color," reaching the blackest at a point "where the North Star at nightfall was five degrees above the horizon."

He explained that after he had passed through the dreadful Doldrums, and reached luxuriant Trinidad, "I found the mildest temperature and lands and trees as green and beautiful as the orchards of Valencia in April, and the people there have beautiful bodies and are whiter than the others I was able to see in the Indies." Not only that, "they have greater ingenuity, show more intelligence, and are not cowardly," qualities that he attributed to the "mild temperature," the result of being in the "highest point in the world," as he had previously explained. And, to clinch his argument, "Over our heads and theirs the sun was in the sign of Virgo." Like others of his day, and Ptol-

emy long before him, Columbus remained a dedicated student of the movement of the planets and their effect on human behavior and destiny. The
positioning of the zodiac was clearly a positive sign, and he confidently went
about correcting the misapprehensions of Aristotle and "other sages" with
his newly acquired—and utterly fantastic—data.

In his search for a paradise, Columbus touched the eastern cape of the Isla
de Gracia, off the Venezuelan coast. Once again, he sent small craft to the
shore, where his scouts encountered cold fires, a deserted dwelling, fish set
out to dry, and other signs of people who had fled the intruders. The Spaniards harvested Jamaican plum, a leathery fruit that Las Casas compared to
"oranges with insides like figs." And they took note of "wild cats." Otherwise,
they had little to report. With every passing harbor, his visions of paradise
faded, and the unresolved tasks of his voyage loomed.

On Monday, August 6, the fleet was approached by a small canoe bearing
four men who belonged to the Guaiqueri Indian nation, and the occasion
probably marked their first contact with Europeans. They wore brilliant
textiles accented by jewelry fashioned from gold and gold alloy, which they
obtained by trade from other Indian groups. This gleaming metal was likely
guanín, an alloy combining gold, silver, and copper in varying proportions.
Columbus had run across *guanín* a couple of times on previous voyages,
thanks to the Taínos, who offered it to him, and he had sent a sample to Spain
to be assayed, with interesting results. The Spaniards, of course, favored gold,
but the Indian alloy contained a high proportion of copper, which lowered
the melting point from over a thousand degrees centigrade for unadulter-
ated gold to two hundred degrees for alloys containing 14 percent to 40
percent copper. For this reason, copper was more valuable to the Indians
than gold.

While they exchanged and examined jewelry, the trading parties imbibed
chicha, brewed from maize. Slightly cloudy and yellowish in appearance,
and tasting like sour apple cider, the potion had a low alcoholic content that
imparted a mild buzz. One of the Spanish pilots indicated to the Indians
that he wished to accompany them to the shore, but as he stepped into the
lightweight craft, he capsized it and the Indians swam away, but not fast
enough to avoid the pilot, who presented them aboard ship to the Admiral.
"When they left here," he reported, "I gave these Indians bells and beads and
sugar, and I sent them to shore, where they had a great battle. And after they
found out about the good treatment, they all wished to come to the ships."
Columbus graciously received the Indians seeking safe haven, and received

tributes of bread, water, and *chicha*. Warmed by the beverage, he cordially engaged them in conversation, with smiles and nods of mutual incomprehension all around.

The next day, the Indians returned to the ships in greater numbers, bearing more gifts, especially their pleasant, murky beverages. In exchange they were happy to accept tiny brass bells. The metal exerted a continuing fascination for the Indians, who gratefully sniffed the gleaming items, attempting to detect properties in European jewelry to which the Europeans themselves were oblivious. The Indians believed they could smell valuable copper, if any, in the jewelry.

The inhabitants offered shrieking, twitching parrots and skillfully woven, brightly colored textiles to the Admiral, who preferred to take the Indians themselves. By day's end, his intended hostages had slipped away. In the morning, when a canoe bearing twelve Indians approached, the Spaniards briskly took them into custody. Columbus selected six to his liking, and dismissed the rest, "without scruple," Las Casas reported, "as he did many other times on the first voyage." Such behavior, according to Las Casas, amounted to a mortal sin, but these concerns did not trouble the Admiral when he was determined to add to his empire.

Several days later, Columbus heard of an Indian bearing a gold nugget the size of an apple. So there was gold, after all. Then men bedecked with gold, as well as ornamental necklaces and beads, arrived in canoes. The women wore strings of colored pearls on their arms. Entranced by the gold, Columbus opened negotiations for more of these precious objects to present to Ferdinand and Isabella. In high spirits, he happened upon an encampment of unusually charming and hospitable Indians, and with his men gladly partook of their red and white fermented beverages. Only the weather troubled him. "I am cold enough to need a cloak every morning, I say, even though I am so close to the equator."

He sailed on in search of pearls, hailing Indians who might be helpful in his quest. As his dependable source, he relied on the *Naturalis historia* of Pliny, the Roman scientist, historian, and compiler, who led Columbus to believe that pearls generated from drops of dew forming within oysters when their shells were open. Observing abundant dew, and sizeable oysters, or creatures that he took to be oysters, Columbus expected to find pearls everywhere, even in the oysters he spotted growing on the branches of mangroves. However, he was mistaken: the mollusks were not oysters, and the pearls elusive. He continued to be undone by his hopes, his dreams, and his avarice.

* * *

Columbus risked leading his squadron to disaster as he entered alarmingly shallow water: only four fathoms deep, equivalent to twenty-four feet. The ships required at least three fathoms' clearance for safe passage. Fortunately, the violent currents—three by his count—running past the Dragon's Mouth carried them past the shoals to deeper waters.

The next day, August 13, he resumed his westward run along Paria's northern coast, giving thanks to God for his deliverance and coming to grips with the new lands he had discovered within days of his arrival.

"Your Highnesses have won these vast lands which are an other world"— *otro mundo,* in his words—"in which Christendom will have so much enjoyment and our faith in time so great an increase." The term "other world" marked a shift in his thinking. He had given up on the idea that he was exploring Marco Polo's ancient India, in search of the Grand Khan, and instead had stumbled across something entirely new and troubling. "I have come to believe that this is a mighty continent that was hitherto unknown." That was a true discovery, something utterly unexpected. That singular fact did not automatically mean that he now realized that Hispaniola and the other islands of the "Indies" lay far distant from India. It meant he was more perplexed than ever before. His voyages of confirmation had become voyages of doubt. He was equipped to confirm cherished myths, not explode them.

After leaving Venezuela's Paria Peninsula, Columbus had seen the islands of La Asunción (now Tobago) and Concepción (now Grenada). On August 14, 1498, he discovered Margarita, located in the Caribbean Sea between latitudes 10°52′ N and 11°11′ N and longitudes 63°48′ W and 64°23′ W. He named the splendid, mountainous island, about fifty miles long and twelve miles across, in honor of Margarita of Austria. The name also punned on the Spanish word for "pearl," in recognition of the nacreous objects scattered about the region.

As his westward cruise lasted into mid-August, he heard reports of the gems from others on his ships, but as his son Ferdinand revealed, "The Admiral . . . could not give as full account of it as he wished because continual watching had made his eyes bloodshot, and therefore he had to write down what he was told by his sailors and pilots."

Later that August, as Columbus gave orders to proceed north and west toward Santo Domingo, the crew spied a small caravel approaching them, the first ship they had seen since their departure from Spain. The approaching craft fired a warning shot, the jolt reverberating across the ocean. Only when she drew alongside the flagship, sails luffing, did Columbus realize that the captain was his brother Bartholomew, also serving the Spanish crown on Santo Domingo. The two Columbus siblings joined forces and sailed into Santo Domingo harbor. Later, a third Columbus brother, Diego, joined them. The Admiral eagerly imagined telling his Sovereigns of his marvelous findings, and the rapid expansion of the Spanish empire that he had brought about.

On the last day of August, the Admiral led his convoy up the Ozama River to Santo Domingo, where he expected a thriving colony to greet him. Instead, "When I arrived from Paria, I found almost half the people in Hispaniola in rebellion, and they have made war on me," he lamented. Their leader was Francisco Roldán, or, as he was now known, the Rebel Roldán, and in Columbus's absence, he had been sowing mayhem.

CHAPTER 9

Roldán's Revolt

It was only a matter of time before Francisco Roldán, or someone like him, appeared on the scene to bedevil Columbus's Enterprise of the Indies. The conditions in Hispaniola were so extreme and uncertain, the temptations so alluring and numerous, the vision of a Spanish empire so vague and unrealistic, and the men who participated in the voyages so casually selected, that discipline was bound to break down during Columbus's prolonged absences, when any kind of mischief was not only possible but also consequence-free.

For a time, his son related, Santo Domingo had remained "fairly peaceful." The settlers expected Columbus's early return from Spain with supplies, weapons, and news from home. "But after the passage of a year, with their provisions running short and suffering and sickness growing, they became disoriented with their present lot and despaired of the future." Appointed by Columbus as the mayor, or chief official, of the colony, Roldán had enjoyed the cooperation of Spaniards and Indians alike, or as Ferdinand put it, "he was obeyed as if he were the Admiral himself." But this eminence led to conflict with Bartholomew Columbus, who, as governor, considered himself the supreme arbiter. As the Admiral's absence stretched on, and it began to seem that he would never return to this little outpost of empire, "Roldán began to dream of making himself master of the island." His scheme was profoundly disloyal: he intended to execute both Bartholomew and Diego. With Columbus's brothers out of the way, Roldán would rule. And he had a plan for bringing Spain to his side.

When Bartholomew traveled to Xaraguá to quell an Indian rebellion and exact tribute, fortune appeared to favor Roldán's plan. Xaraguá, a sprawling, mostly level expanse carpeted with thick shrubs, and bordered by a beach of glistening, powdery sand, occupied a promontory extending to the south of the island. Its serene aspect proved deceptive; Xaraguá became synonymous with the rebel Spanish forces occupying it, with wicked and dissolute behavior, and with indolence. For those seeking shelter, it held strategic advantages, for it was two hundred miles from Santo Domingo, and the sails of approaching ships could be seen for miles. Las Casas paid tribute to the Indians of the district. They were "not to be equaled for fluency of speech and politeness of idiom or dialect by any inhabitants of the other kingdoms" of Hispaniola. They "excelled in stature and habit of body. Their king was Behechio by name and who had a sister called Anacaona"— the "Golden Flower"—who treated the rude, rapacious Spaniards with "civility, and by delivering them from the evident and apparent danger of death, did signal services to the Castilian Sovereigns." A Taíno cacique, Anacaona was also the wife of Caonabó, who had both challenged and joined forces with Columbus.

Bartholomew Columbus placed his brother Diego in charge, with Roldán serving beneath him, secretly seething and fomenting a mutiny. Bartholomew's attention alighted on a caravel lying on the beach at La Isabela; he planned to use the vessel as an escape from the island, if necessary.

Roldán and his supporters insisted that they wanted to launch the caravel as soon as possible, and when they reached Spain they would announce "the news of their distress." Diego Columbus was having none of it; the caravel lacked tackle and supplies. Defying his superior, Roldán ordered the ship to make ready to sail, telling his followers that the Columbus brothers wanted to block their mission, keep them all under their control, and prevent Spain from learning of the evil and corrupt Columbus regime in Hispaniola. Roldán stirred resentment by recalling how callously the three Columbus brothers had treated the settlers, who had toiled in the suffocating heat, erected forts against their will, and exposed themselves to unnecessary dangers. Columbus and his brothers were foreigners, Roldán reminded like-minded Spaniards, and worse, foreigners who had never paid them even though they had made them all work like donkeys. Now it seemed that the Admiral was unlikely ever to return with the supplies and reinforcements.

To remedy their predicament, Roldán proposed that they divide "all the wealth of the island" among themselves, and, just as important, "they should be allowed to use the Indians as they pleased, free from interference," in Ferdinand's words. Many Spaniards had already taken one or more Indian women for pleasure or companionship, despite restrictions. Now anything was possible, even if the men had to suffer the symptoms of syphilis for their excesses.

Bartholomew attempted to restrain this licentiousness, insisting that his men "observe the three monastic vows," as Ferdinand phrased it: obedience, stability (observing the vows indefinitely), and fidelity to the monastic way of life, including the renunciation of private property and strict celibacy. Roldán, in contrast, held out the promise of a commune teeming with easy riches and plentiful women. The riches remained elusive, but, Las Casas reported, "each one had the woman that he wanted, taken from their husbands, or daughters from their fathers, by force or willingly, to use as chambermaids, washerwomen, and cooks, and as many Indian men as they thought necessary to serve them." He reminded the men of the severe rations imposed by Columbus and his brothers, the barbaric floggings, the heartless and humiliating punishments and confinement for the slightest infraction, real or perceived. In contrast to this reign of tyranny under which they had all suffered, Roldán promised that if they followed his leadership, he would protect them from harm. His pandering, combined with his resolute manner, proved effective, and he attracted many, and eventually most, of the disaffected Spaniards to his camp.

By the time Bartholomew Columbus, "the Advancer," returned from his pacification mission in Xaraguá, Roldán's followers had concocted a scheme to stab him and string him up with a rope. Acting on hints of a conspiracy, Bartholomew hastily jailed one of the rebels, Barahona, and condemned him to death, but later changed his mind. "If God had not inspired the Adelantado not to carry out Barahona's death sentence," Ferdinand maintained, "they doubtless would have killed him then and there." Instead, Bartholomew uncovered the full extent of Roldán's plot, in which the rebels would convert a fort named Concepción into a bastion from which they could launch attacks at will across Hispaniola.

Roldán was already familiar with this fort, having once been assigned there by Diego Columbus to pacify surrounding Indians, and while in attendance, he pretended to follow orders. However, the fort's commander, Miguel Ballester, was not taken in by the deception and warned the Adelantado of the mutiny-in-the-making. Bartholomew then sequestered himself in the fortress, thinking his presence would repel Roldán. But the unpredictable rebel went straight to the fort and, as if he had every right to do so, insisted on readying the caravel to carry him and his men away to the relative safety of a voyage to Spain. Although Roldán was better off in his kingdom in exile, he pursued his conflicting strategies at the same time, much to the confusion of his superiors.

Impossible, Bartholomew said on hearing the demand. Roldán was not capable of sailing the caravel to Spain, nor were his followers. They might be able to launch her, but they did not know the sea, and they would perish. Bartholomew spoke as an experienced navigator, "but they were landlubbers who knew nothing," said Ferdinand.

Bartholomew ordered Roldán to resign his office as the mayor; predictably, Roldán refused to comply until King Ferdinand himself so commanded. He declared that he could "expect no justice from the Adelantado," that is, Bartholomew, who would only find some way to kill or harm him. Enraged, Roldán insisted he was a "reasonable man," and to prove it, he would postpone sailing off in the beached caravel and instead coexist peacefully on the island at a place of Bartholomew's choosing, but Roldán expected concessions in exchange for the offer. When he learned the Adelantado wanted to install an Indian who had converted to Christianity and was loyal to Columbus, Roldán rejected the idea, claiming the settlement lacked sufficient supplies. Instead, they would live somewhere else, of Roldán's choosing.

The contest of wills between the two adversaries ended only when the rebel leader stomped off.

Despite his angry demands for a safe haven on Hispaniola, Roldán still yearned for the caravel and the promise of escape to Spain. He returned to La Isabela to take possession of the vessel, but even with sixty-five men at the ready—more than enough to operate the ship—Roldán could not launch it. Instead, they looted the crown's arsenal, equipping themselves with weapons, and the storehouse, commandeering food, clothing, and anything else they desired. While they raided the storehouse, Bartholomew looked on, powerless to stop them. Fearing for his life, he went into seclusion within the fortress, taking a few servants as bodyguards, but not before Roldán tried to lure him to his side to take a stand against the Admiral himself. That, of course, Bartholomew would not do.

Learning that Bartholomew had dispatched armed men to protect Diego from further abuse, Roldán summoned his rebel force, and left La Isabela, and for the time being, the plan to return to Spain. They moved steadily through the thick tropical undergrowth, slaughtering cattle for food as they went, and taking other beasts as needed for the long trek to Xaraguá, the province that Bartholomew had recently pacified. They had their reasons for selecting this remote location as their destination. "It was the pleasantest and most fertile part of the island," Ferdinand explained, "with the most civilized natives and especially the best-looking and best-natured women in the country: This last was their strongest motive for going there." With these seductive promises Roldán, the Lucifer of the Enterprise of the Indies, offered the men everything Columbus withheld: wealth, women, a life of ease, and a sense of control over their own destiny. Roldán's way offered no promise of redemption, no official recognition, and no titles, only a pleasurable limbo.

On their way to Xaraguá, Roldán's men planned one last, murderous scheme. They would overrun the little hamlet of Concepción, and, if they found Bartholomew, the Adelantado, they would kill him. If he was absent, they would lay waste to the town. When word of the plot reached Bartholomew, he countered with a strategy of his own, promising his men "two slaves apiece," said Ferdinand, in exchange for their support. It was a desperate maneuver, but he realized that even those who nominally supported him were tempted by Roldán's offer. Bartholomew summoned his willpower and kept his followers' loyalty If he could not maintain his rule by the power of logic, he was prepared to fight.

He assembled his men, and set off with determined swagger to face the forces of Francisco Roldán, who, intimidated by this convincing show of force, retreated to Xaraguá, dispensing anti-Columbus propaganda as he went. With some justification, Roldán claimed that Bartholomew was cruel and greedy in his treatment of both Indians and Christians; he demanded impossible tributes and broke the spirit and drained the resources of everyone with whom he came into contact. Even if the Indians complied with the onerous tributes, the vicious Adelantado would only demand more, despite the Sovereigns' objections—an unlikely scenario. Roldán, in contrast, proclaimed himself the Indians' champion; if they were unable or unwilling to stand up for their rights, he and his supporters would take up their cause. His unjustified promises persuaded the Indians to defy the tribute system. In reality, Bartholomew received nothing from distant villages, and he was afraid to demand it from those nearby and so push the Indians even deeper into Roldán's camp.

Roldán found a potent ally in the chieftain Guarionex, who formed clandestine alliances with the other caciques and pledged to kill the Spanish invaders. The Indians felt confident that they could exterminate the outsiders who had come from the ships in a series of coordinated surprise uprisings. "Their only way of reckoning time or anything else being their fingers," Ferdinand explained, "the Indians agreed to launch the attack on the first day of the next full moon."

All was ready, until one of the chieftains decided to attack prematurely, either to portray himself as a hero to his people, or, less likely, because he was "too poor an astronomer to know for sure the first day of the full moon." The attack failed miserably. Seeking safety, the disgraced chieftain skulked back to Guarionex, who had him executed for carelessness.

The reversal of fortune reached all the way to Roldán, whose men had expected the Indians to do the slaughtering. Scuttling the pact with Guarionex, they retreated once again to Xaraguá, where they maintained the pretense that they, the Spanish rebels, protected the Indians from the predatory colonial policies of Columbus. "Actually, they were naught but plain thieves," observed Ferdinand, although much the same thing could be said of many of the men who served under Christopher Columbus, men who had exploited and underestimated the Indians for nearly eight years, and counting.

Roldán's misstep occurred when he renewed his promise to protect the Indians from Bartholomew's demands for a tribute, and then seized an even greater tribute for himself. He insisted that the chieftain Manicaotex offer "a calabash filled with gold dust worth three marks every three months," in Ferdinand's words. To ensure that Manicaotex obeyed, even though the supply of gold dust was nearly depleted by this time, Roldán took the chieftain's son and nephew hostage. With characteristic duplicity, he maintained that his gesture demonstrated friendship.

Faced with an impossible situation, Bartholomew and his allies stood by helplessly as their support from their Indian and Spanish allies wilted in the tropical heat. It appeared increasingly likely that either the Spanish rebels or disenchanted Indians, or perhaps an unholy alliance between the two, would wipe out Bartholomew and the loyalists, and claim the island of Hispaniola, bringing a violent end to the Columbian experiment.

Amid the gathering despair, the men at Santo Domingo spotted two Spanish ships on the horizon. They constituted the supply fleet from Spain, carrying food, men, weapons, and provisions needed for survival in the Indies. Roldán and his men intended to plunder the new arrivals as soon as they reached Santo Domingo, but Bartholomew had the advantage of superior intelligence, and he happened to be closer to the port. He placed sentries along the paths leading to the little town to deter Roldán's men so that he, not the rebels, would welcome the supply ships to the troubled realm. And so he did.

Even then, Bartholomew tried to improvise a fragile, temporary peace with the rebels to present a unified front to the newcomers. He dispatched one of the captains, Pedro Fernández Coronel, reputed to be "a man of worth and honor," according to Ferdinand. From the moment he confirmed that Christopher Columbus had safely arrived in Spain, where he received an enthusiastic reception from the Sovereigns, he had won Bartholomew's trust. The Adelantado sent Coronel to convey the situation to Roldán's rebels, but the newly arrived *capitán* found himself staring at the tips of crossbows and arrows. His prepared speech went undelivered. Instead, he spoke privately with a few of the insurrectionists, who made no promises and hastened back to their stronghold at Xaraguá to await the Admiral's return to Hispaniola.

Bartholomew's men learned that Roldán and others planned to tarnish Columbus's name in Spain by means of poison-pen letters. Peter Martyr, from his vantage point in Italy, later wrote that "the rebels, complaining seri ously about both [Columbus] brothers, called them unjust, impious, enemies of the Spanish blood"—code for their Genoese origins—"and squanderers, because they took delight in torturing over trifles, hanging, slaughtering, and killing in all kinds of ways." The rebels, he continued, "depicted them as ambitious, arrogant, envious, unbearable tyrants: so they deserted them, being just wild animals thirsty for blood and enemies of the Sovereigns." Roldán's men claimed that they had seen Columbus and his two brothers plotting obsessively to take over the islands, and they claimed that the Columbus brothers "would allow no one but their own men to reach the gold mines or gather it." From the Sovereigns' perspective, that was precisely what Columbus should have been doing.

The rebels protested that the Admiral resorted to calling them horrible names, "wicked and quarrelsome, pimps, thieves, rapists, kidnappers, outlaws, men deprived of any value or good sense, brainless perjurers, liars either with previous criminal records or escapees fearing being sentenced by judges for crimes." (The accusations stung because they contained considerable truth.) They had heard that Columbus had characterized them as men "originally brought to dig and provide services," yet "did not even walk out of the house." Instead, "they have the poor natives carry them throughout the whole island, like high-ranking magistrates." Columbus related how the rebels, "so as not to lose their blood-shedding habit and test their strength draw swords and compete with each other in cutting off the heads of those innocent people"—the Indians—"with one blow; the man who more swiftly decapitated an unfortunate native in a single blow was declared the strongest and more worthy of honor among them." Even the rebels realized that such appalling behavior would destroy their reputation, if not in Hispaniola, then in Spain.

As the controversy swept Hispaniola, several ships belonging to Columbus's fleet appeared off the coast of Xaraguá, but they were not the ones that Roldán had been expecting.

The three supply ships had made a speedy passage since leaving the Canary Islands in June, too speedy, in fact. When the squadron arrived in the Caribbean, the pilots, said Ferdinand, "were carried so far westward that they arrived on the coast of Xaraguá, where the rebels were." If they had reached their intended destination, Santo Domingo, they would have enjoyed Bartholomew's protection. Instead, the ships were overrun with Roldán's rebels, who falsely claimed that the Adelantado had ordered them to "secure provisions and pacify the countryside." One captain, Alonso Sánchez de Carvajal, saw through the ruse and attempted to persuade Roldán to end his revolt and declare his loyalty to Bartholomew, but sentiment among the crew, already influenced by Roldán's men, and their alluring promises, favored the rebels over the loyalists.

Frustrated, Sánchez de Carvajal joined forces with the two other captains to send a small party of salaried workers to the mines near Santo Domingo. The unfavorable weather and currents that had brought the ships to Xaraguá still held sway; it might take months for the ships to reach Santo Domingo, so the workers, forty in all, planned to set out on foot, under the command of Juan Antonio Colombo. Pedro de Arana would take charge of the three ships, and Sánchez de Carvajal resumed negotiating with Roldán's representatives.

The situation darkened when most of the workers deserted to join Roldán, and Colombo was left with only six or seven men. Furious, Colombo confronted Roldán, insisting that the laborers had come to the Indies to work, not to spend their days drinking Indian wine and their nights with the Indian women. If Roldán refused to cooperate, it would be obvious to all that he had affronted the Admiral and the Sovereigns. Skillful as ever at devising excuses, Roldán pleaded helplessness and ignorance. He could not tell the unruly men how to behave. "His monastery," he explained, "was governed by rules that denied the habit to no man."

Juan Antonio Colombo realized he had been defeated, so he and his handful of loyalists returned to the ships to sail back to Santo Domingo. Battling adverse wind and weather, his food supply rotting in the heat, Sánchez de Carvajal ran onto a shoal, which tore away the rudder and ruptured the keel, admitting so much seawater that the afflicted ship barely reached her mooring. After completing the difficult passage from the rebel outpost of Xaraguá, the three captains were gratified to see the Admiral himself, having completed his northerly passage from Trinidad.

More mariner than warrior, Columbus studied the list of grievances against the rebels, as compiled by his brother, and realized that eventually he would have to punish the malefactors, but first he assembled a new catalogue of accusations. Ferdinand recalled that his father initially "resolved to be as moderate as he could in this affair, that the rebels might more easily be reduced to obedience." To rid the enterprise of troublemakers, he promised, on September 22, free passage to Spain, and food, to anyone who wanted it.

A long voyage westward across an uncharted sea no longer held the terrors that it once did, thanks to Columbus's mastery of winds, currents, reefs, and harbors. The risk of disaster, while never absent, diminished with every crossing until transatlantic travel from Spain to Santo Domingo had become almost routine.

This accomplishment gave rise to a more baffling challenge: how to manage a far-flung empire and its many constituencies: Spanish, Indian, and the brothers Columbus, to name only the major segments. Then there were the hidalgos, or gentlemen; the hired workers; and the fierce Caribs. The Sovereigns' monolithic approach—convert or exploit, or, on occasion, convert *and* exploit—proved tragically ill suited to the varied people of both the "Indies" and Spain, and inadequate to the task of maintaining an empire.

Two days later, on September 24, Miguel Ballester reported that Roldán and another rebel, Adrián de Mújica (or Moxica), were to meet, presenting an opportunity for the Admiral's men to seize the leaders, if Columbus chose to act. As before, he remained idle.

Roldán and his forces, in the meantime, marched to Santo Domingo. Columbus placed the commander, Ballester, in charge of nearby Concepción. Ballester was to deliver a carefully worded message of reconciliation from the Admiral, saying that he "deplored" all that Roldán had suffered, and wished to "bury the past in oblivion, granting a general pardon to all," in Ferdinand's depiction. Roldán should feel that he could meet with Columbus "without fear of reprisal" so that they could jointly determine how best to carry out the Sovereigns' intentions. Columbus would even provide Roldán with safe conduct "in the form he desired."

Whether Columbus made this offer in good faith is not certain. Ballester reported that he had conveyed the Admiral's conciliatory message to Roldán and Adrián de Mújica, "but found them very stubborn and brazenly defiant," with Roldán loudly insisting that he had no interest in negotiations or finding a path to peace. He had the Admiral "in the hollow of his hand," as he expressed it, and could either "help him or destroy him as he pleased." He would not consider negotiations of any kind until Columbus and his brothers released the Indians taken prisoner in the pacification of Concepción: a deeply cynical demand in light of the abuse that his men routinely inflicted on the Indians.

Roldán complicated matters by insisting that he would hold discussions only with Alonso Sánchez de Carvajal, whom he believed to be sensible. The assertion immediately aroused Columbus's suspicions. According to Ferdinand, the Admiral doubted that Sánchez de Carvajal was an out-and-out traitor; after all, he was a person of standing, a hidalgo, and a thoughtful one at that. More likely he sought to be a diligent conciliator, not a double agent. Columbus polled his aides about the best course of action: Columbus would send Sánchez de Carvajal together with Ballester to negotiate with the slippery Roldán.

Roldán refused to meet with the two, citing Columbus's failure to release the Indians he held. Sánchez de Carvajal took up the cause and eventually convinced Roldán, accompanied by several of his men, to speak directly with Columbus. But the rebel leader's own men interfered with the mission, to the point of surrounding him. They did not want their leader making secret arrangements with Columbus; they preferred to convey their "conditions for peace in writing," said Ferdinand, who characterized the terms as "immoderate and insolent," and no doubt they appeared that way to Columbus. Even the combined forces of Ballester and Sánchez de Carvajal failed to convince the rebels to negotiate. Running out of strategies for compromise, the loyalist delegation abruptly conceded to the rebels. Ballester in particular justified the capitulation on the basis of the dwindling morale among Columbus's men, who teetered on the verge of joining the bold and determined rebels. Although Columbus trusted his servants and aides, even they seemed susceptible to Lucifer's blandishments.

Day by day, the number of rebels increased, and loyalists diminished. Preparing to do battle against the renegades, Columbus had only seventy men at his side, and after eliminating those who feigned illness or injury to avoid service, only forty men, or even less, could be considered entirely loyal.

In this vulnerable condition, he dispatched Sánchez de Carvajal with a surprising message for Roldán: Columbus expressed confidence in his worthy antagonist and promised that he would give a "favorable account" of his actions to Ferdinand and Isabella. None of this was put in writing, Columbus explained, to protect Roldán from "the common people" who might be inspired to harm him. Rather, he should talk directly with Columbus's representative, Ballester, "as if he were the Admiral himself," in the words of Columbus's son.

At about the same time, October 17, 1498, Roldán and his outlaw allies sent an oddly conciliatory letter to the Admiral claiming they had "quit the Adelantado because he had plotted to slay them." They implored Columbus to consider their actions "a service to him" and buttressed this strange logic by reminding him that they had protected him and his possessions when they could have resorted to violence. They wished only to act "honorably" and to enjoy their idea of "freedom of action."

The day after this ambiguous negotiation with Roldán, Columbus dispatched five ships to Spain. Those aboard recalled it as a dangerous crossing, filled with "great trials" endured by the six hundred Indians in the convoy. Accompanying them were two emotional letters from Columbus to Ferdinand and Isabella about Roldán's rebels, "of the damage they had done and were continuing to do on the island, plundering and acting violently, killing whomever they pleased for no reason at all, taking other men's wives and daughters and perpetrating many other evil deeds." Las Casas was convinced that matters on Hispaniola had degenerated into a state of anarchy in which Spaniards "traveled from village to village and from place to place, eating at their discretion, taking the Indian men that they wanted for their service and the Indian women who looked good to them." Rather than walking, they commanded Indian men to carry them in hammocks. "They had hunters who hunted for them, fishermen who fished for them, and as many Indians as they wanted as pack animals to carry their loads for them." All the while, the Indians revered and worshipped the Spaniards who exploited them.

Columbus beseeched the Sovereigns to send "devout religious men," in his words, to replace these sinners. As he denounced the wicked behavior of the Spaniards, the Admiral praised the land and its possibilities, "abundant in all things," he wrote, with a biblical cadence, "especially in bread and meat." No one need go hungry, not with the copious pigs and hens and wild animals resembling rabbits so easy to catch that "an Indian boy with a dog brings in fifteen or twenty daily to his master." All that was needed was wine and clothing, items easily transported from Spain. The only problem was that the land of plenty attracted "the greatest loafers in the world."

The lack of dedication among the Spaniards dismayed Columbus. "When I came here I brought many people for the conquest of these lands," he reminded the idealized Sovereigns of his thoughts. "All of these people importuned me, saying that they would serve very well and better than anybody." But in reality, "it was the reverse, because they only came believing that the gold and spices that were said to be found could be gathered with shovels, and that the spices already came tied in bundles on the seashore, so that there was nothing more to do than throw them in the ships. Thus, they were blinded by greed." (As was Columbus, though he refused to acknowledge his own shortcoming.) "I preached all of this to them in Seville. Because so many wished to come, and I realized why, I had to tell them this and all the trials that those who settle in far lands often suffer." Few believed his warnings, at first. "When they arrived here and saw that I had spoken the truth to them, and that their avarice would not be satisfied, they wished to return right away without seeing whether it were possible to conquer and dominate this land. And because I did not consent to it, they began to hate me. And they had no reason." They also hated him because he would not allow them to enter the island's beguiling interior "because the Indians had killed many who had traveled spread out like that, and they would have killed more if I had not prevented it."

As if disruptive settlers did not pose enough of a problem, he had to contend with stowaways; Columbus estimated that a quarter of his men consisted of such *polizones*. And there was one other difficulty: the women of Hispaniola "are so beautiful that it is a marvel," he observed, "even though it should not be said." But everyone did remark on the island's women, with their tawny skin and sweet scent, fertile beauties who displayed a taste for sensual abandon surpassing the settlers' fantasies. To many Europeans, these women, more than any other aspect of Hispaniola, represented the allure of the Indies.

Columbus, as always, tried to calculate the cost, and to make the case to the Sovereigns that his discoveries had given them a historic bargain. "What man of wisdom will say that it was a waste of money?" That was one point of view. Las Casas, in contrast, ruefully observed that Columbus "would have done great things and produced inestimable benefit in this land if he had realized that these people did not owe anything to him or to any other person in the world just because they had been discovered." Instead, Columbus had fostered a system under which the Indians did all the work for the Spaniards, corrupting them in the process. Month after month, he had assigned property to settlers, many of them Indian farms, and given them plants and vines to cultivate, as many as ten thousand to a single person, complete with certificates indicating the quantity and recipient of the items. He initiated cooperative agricultural enterprises among the Spanish settlers, with the unfortunate result that the settlers forced the Indians occupying the land to leave and search for gold to give to their new masters.

Once a wellborn Spaniard established himself as the lord of an estancia ("I think in Seville they call this a country home or a farm or a property," Las Casas noted), he treated the local cacique and the Indians as serfs. If they failed to obey him quickly enough to suit his taste, said Las Casas, he whipped them, cut off their ears, or killed them. At the same time, he took the wives and daughters of the caciques as concubines. Indians bold enough to attempt to flee, or, as the Spaniards put it, rise up, were hunted down and killed. Others were sold as slaves, or loaded into ships bound for Spain and further degradation in a distant land.

"What right did the Admiral have to give them lands, farms, or properties of the unfortunate Indians?" Las Casas asked. By divine right and by order of the Sovereigns, Columbus would have replied.

Among the recipients of Columbus's scandalous bounty was Francisco Roldán, who demanded a settlement known as Ababruco, claiming it already belonged to him. As before, Columbus yielded to Roldán, and soon the estate, the ancestral land of Indians, belonged to the Spanish master, who put the Indians to work for him while he lived a life of indolence. The Indian name was discarded, and the settlement given the name Esperanza ("Hope"), although Robo ("Theft") would have been more appropriate. "He also gave him two cows, two young bulls, two mares, and twenty sows, all from the king's stock, so that he could begin raising them, because Roldán asked it of him," said Las Casas of Columbus. "He did not dare deny him anything."

Columbus's lack of decisiveness damaged his credibility and encouraged the Spaniards' basest instincts. "The Spaniards learned—even the laborers and those who came on salary to dig and work the land and extract the gold from the mines—to loaf and walk proudly, eating from the sweat of the Indians and seizing each by force, three, four, and ten to serve them, because of the gentleness of the Indians, who neither could nor knew how to resist," Las Casas noted of the arrangement, known as the *repartimiento* or *enco-*

mienda system. To Las Casas, Columbus, Roldán, and the other rebels degraded innocent Indians, and in doing so, made "a sacrilege and unpardonable mockery of the Christian religion itself." Fuming, Las Casas declared those Spaniards to blame "deserved to be quartered not just once but fourteen times."

Of the five ships sailing that day in October 1498, two conveyed Roldán's supporters back to Spain. Three others were reserved for Bartholomew to return to the Paria Peninsula and its precious pearls. Roldán remained in Hispaniola, meditating on his next move.

Columbus, meanwhile, reached the lowest point of his career as an explorer. Returning to Hispaniola, he had, once again, been undone by the wily and relentless Roldán. It seemed Columbus had discovered his "other world" only to lose it to a charlatan and thief whose chief aim was the humiliation of the Admiral of the Ocean Sea. Las Casas imagined that "the pain he suffered because of the anger that would come upon the king and queen tormented him most!" Because of his reverses, Columbus's adversaries at court would conspire to make him an outcast, not because of his harsh treatment of the Indians, but because the Spanish rebels had outmaneuvered him.

On October 26, Roldán received a safe-conduct pass from Columbus, and the adversaries convened. After repeating his demands, the rebel leader returned to his supporters without an agreement. Still hoping to reconcile, Columbus sent one of his aides, Diego de Salamanca, to accompany Roldán and negotiate an end to the conflict. On November 6, Roldán finally sent his terms for Columbus's signature, claiming they were "the best he could get from his men," Ferdinand recorded. "If His Illustrious Lordship approved of it, he should send his acceptance to Concepción."

Roldán demanded a swift reply from Columbus. In his son's words, "Having seen this letter and the articles, with their insolent demands, the Admiral would on no account sign them lest he bring justice into contempt and dishonor both himself and his brothers." Overcoming his frustration, the Admiral nailed an announcement to the fort's door on November 11, offering amnesty to Roldán's men. The rebels could safely return to Spain and "the service of the Catholic Sovereigns as if nothing had happened." Passage was free, and wages would be paid in full. The offer would be valid for thirty days. If the rebels failed to accept, Columbus vowed to "proceed against them as the law required." Once more, the rebels ridiculed Columbus and boasted that within a short time he would be seeking a reprieve from *them*.

In reality, there was little Columbus could do with only a handful of trustworthy men at his side. He relied on the power of an empire across the ocean, but as Roldán reminded him, the rebels were genuinely Spanish, while the Columbus brothers were Genoese—outsiders.

As an added provocation, Roldán held the loyalist Ballester hostage without food or water. Sánchez de Carvajal rode to the rescue, Ballester was released, and delegates from the two sides—loyalists and rebels—became embroiled in a marathon argument, from which, miraculously, a written understanding emerged: "The agreement made with the mayor Francisco Roldán and his company for their departure and voyage to Castile."

According to the document, dated November 16, 1498, by Roldán, and November 21, by Columbus, the Admiral would give the rebels "two good ships," properly manned, to transport them from Xaraguá "because most of the followers are there because it is the most convenient harbor for securing and getting ready provisions" to Spain. They would receive their wages, as Columbus had offered. And the Admiral would "write to the Catholic Sovereigns attesting to their good service," incredible as that seemed. The other concessions won by the insurrectionists were even more outrageous. They were to receive slaves "as compensation for the sufferings they have endured on this island," although they could, if they wished, take "mates who are pregnant or have borne them children" in place of the slaves. They could even take their island-born children, who would go free the moment they set foot in Spain.

Columbus also promised to provide the rebels with sufficient food for their voyage in the form of wheat or cassava, to equip them with safe-conduct passes, to return their confiscated goods, and to arrange with the Sovereigns to repay the returning rebels the price of several hundred large and small "hogs" left behind on the island they were abandoning. The only concession that Columbus managed to wring from Roldán was minor; he and his confederates agreed not to "admit into their company any other Christian on the island," although Indians could still join their number. Roldán promised to sail for Spain within fifty days.

"The Admiral knew how wicked were these men," his son explained, "but he did not want to give the rebels any excuse for charging that he did not intend to give them the free passage home he had promised." He ordered the ships to be readied for the voyage back to Spain, and sent the tireless Sánchez de Carvajal overland to Xaraguá to make certain the rebels got on board their ships and departed, as planned. Placing Santo Domingo in his brother Diego's hands, Columbus retreated to La Isabela, and respite from the torments inflicted by Roldán's rebels.

Columbus had demonstrated remarkable patience in his public dealings with the mayor, but in private the Admiral boiled with resentment toward "that ungrateful nobody Roldán." Starting with nothing, he had gained "so much in so little time that he now had more than a million [maravedís]." Columbus had made him and his cohorts wealthy and confident. "Those people pain me," the Admiral lamented.

Not until January 1499 did the ships *Niña* and *Santa Cruz*, with their roster of rebels, embark. A storm arose, and *Niña* sought shelter elsewhere— "another port" was all that Ferdinand had to say—for repair. Columbus sent two of his dwindling number of trusted aides, Pedro de Arana and Francisco de Garay, to guide *Santa Cruz* to Xaraguá. In March, *Niña* rejoined her sister ship there.

Meanwhile, Roldán's rebels remained in Xaraguá to enjoy their easy life, slaves, women, and children rather than face the difficulties of reestablishing themselves in Spain. Roldán excused this reversal by claiming that Columbus had violated their agreement by delaying the ships. In reply, the Admiral sent a blunt communiqué to Roldán and Adrián de Mújica, reminding them of their promises. To reinforce the message, Sánchez de Carvajal, still at Xaraguá, went before a notary to state that Columbus had sent two ships as promised, and he urged Roldán to respect the agreement.

It was now April 25, and still the rebels had not sailed from the island. They amused themselves by claiming that the Admiral had intentionally and spitefully delayed the ships (not true), that the caravels were not sufficiently seaworthy to reach Spain (all too true, thanks to shipworms), and that they had run out of provisions amid the island's plenty (true, but easily put right). So they decided to breach the agreement and stay at Xaraguá indefinitely. Paradoxically, Roldán and his men drew strength from the calamities. The more attention they drew to themselves, and the more anxiety they caused Columbus, the more important they became.

The familiar pattern of defiance followed by conciliatory gestures continued. Roldán sent word through the usual go-between, Sánchez de Carvajal, that he would "gladly confer" with Columbus "to reach a satisfactory agreement," Ferdinand related, and not until May 21, 1499, did the Admiral reply, followed by a more complete answer on June 24. By delaying, he might have hoped that disease, boredom, internal dissension, or starvation would break the rebels' spirit, but Roldán maintained his outpost and his resistance. On August 3, he received a delegation of seven loyalists, dispatched by Columbus, offering him safe conduct to a summit with the Admiral. They planned to meet at the port of Azua, partway between Santo Domingo and Xaraguá.

During these negotiations, Roldán's partner, Adrián de Mújica, revolted once too often and finally was arrested. A brief hearing determined he was guilty of treason, and Columbus ordered him to be hanged. Mújica responded to the sentence with vituperation rather than the expected confession and penance. Las Casas claims that Columbus ordered his loyalists to thrust him to his death from the walls of Concepción, the fort to which he was confined, but it is just as likely that his partisans acted on their own. Columbus evaded the issue by stating, "Our Lord would not permit his evil purpose to be carried into effect." Furthermore, "I had resolved in my own mind not to touch a hair of anyone's head, and owing to his ingratitude, I was unable to save him, as I intended to do. I would have not done less to my own brother, if he had desired to kill me." Troubled by the incident—Mújica was well born and well connected, and his death could not be dismissed—Columbus explained that Roldán's rival for an Indian woman, Fernando de Guevara, bore responsibility for the execution, "without my having ordered it."

At month's end, Columbus's two caravels arrived as agreed at the neutral port of Azua, where a large rebel delegation greeted them. The leaders energetically boarded his flagship, listened to his entreaties and promises of riches and honors, and replied with their outlandish demands, purely for the sake of argument. They wanted land grants and other entitlements for the rebels who elected to remain on the island, and a restoration of Roldán to his former role as the "perpetual mayor." Desperate to break the back of the resistance, Columbus agreed to all of these demands, and still one more: he would announce that the misunderstanding was solely the result of "false testimony of a few evil men."

The rebels added still another demand: if the Admiral failed to meet these conditions, they could use "any means," including force, to compel him to comply. Sick of the rebels and their demands, which had drained his resources and credibility for over a year, Columbus signed. He appointed his antagonist Roldán mayor for life, approved the demands, and so conferred partial legitimacy on a dangerous rival.

Days later, Roldán wielded his newfound authority. He appointed a judge,

Pedro de Riquelme, to sentence criminals, except for "capital offenders," whom he would try personally. Meanwhile, Riquelme broke ground on a rebel fort in Bonao, but work came to a halt amid squabbles. Heartened by this minor victory, Columbus turned his attention to other segments of his fissured empire. Wishing to flee to the relative safety of Spain after his demoralizing spell in Hispaniola, he charged a captain and a company of men "to patrol and pacify" the island (in Ferdinand's words), collect tributes from the Indians, and suppress revolts provoked by the rebels—all formidable tasks.

Confronting a storm or a reef, Columbus displayed an intuitive knack for tactics and an ability to learn from experience. But his behavior on land was quite different. No matter how many uprisings he faced on Hispaniola, he failed to adapt and to acquire the skills necessary for leadership, or even survival, in his own empire. He could command the seas, master the winds, and ride the tides, but he could not fathom his fellow man. He had spent his days studying waves, not people, and knew only the crosscurrents and promptings of his own heart. At that dangerous moment, he appeared stagnant, unwilling to recognize that yielding to the rebels' demands emboldened rather than diminished his enemies.

Then, without warning, four ships appeared on the horizon.

On September 5, the flotilla dropped anchor "in the port that the Christians call 'Brazil,' (and the Indians Yaquimo)," Ferdinand explained, with a simple task: to obtain wood for their ships and fires, and to enslave Indians to perform the labor. It was the identity of their leader that alarmed Columbus: Alonso de Ojeda, the reckless aide who had cut off the ears of several Indians while pacifying a settlement in April 1494. And he had been sent by Columbus's own patrons.

Ojeda's sudden appearance signaled the end of Columbus's monopoly on the Enterprise of the Indies. It meant that the Sovereigns and Bishop Fonseca were now commissioning his rivals to perform many of the same tasks Columbus had set out to accomplish. "Alonso de Ojeda was well loved by the bishop," Las Casas explained, "and after the admiral's account arrived with the chart, Alonso de Ojeda was inclined to go and discover more land by the route that the admiral had traveled, for once the thread is found and in the hand, it is an easy thing to reach the ball." From Columbus's chart, crafty Ojeda learned the basics of the first voyage, what islands the fleet had visited, and other information gleaned from the Indians. Vowing to find the mainland that had eluded Columbus, Ojeda located four ships in Seville, "where he was known as a brave and valiant man," and obtained the means to outfit them.

Violating their contract with Columbus, Ferdinand and Isabella had given Ojeda supplies and instructions; they had appointed him captain and charged him to discover and recover gold and pearls, just as the Admiral of the Ocean Sea had been doing, and on similar terms, giving the fifth part to the king and queen. And, like Columbus, he was ordered to treat the people he encountered in a spirit of peace and friendship. Bolstering his effort, Ojeda induced Columbus's prized cartographer, Juan de la Cosa, to join the expedition, as well as a respected pilot from Palos, Bartolomé Roldán. According to Las Casas, the Sovereigns hoped that Ojeda would carry out his duties with less strife than his hardheaded predecessor.

In 1499, Ojeda's fleet sailed to the Guajira Peninsula, the northernmost part of the South American mainland. In Sinamaica Lagoon, located in today's Zulia state, he encountered Indians dwelling in thatched huts on stilts—*palafitos*—above gently lapping water. According to legend, he and his men decided to call the region Little Venice, or "Venezuela," after the sight, and the name began to appear on maps the following year. Proceeding in a generally southerly direction, they entered brackish Lake Maracaibo, fed with seawater, and explored what is now Colombia. On their return to Spain, Ojeda's men, dazzled by the gold ornaments worn by tribes in the area, circulated fantastic stories about the wealth that could be found inland, in a city called El Dorado—stories that lured one Spanish expedition after another to Venezuela and Colombia. El Dorado and its incredible riches remained forever elusive, and the region became colonized under the spell of this illusion.

Even as Ojeda explored Venezuela, others were challenging Columbus and outdoing his exploits. There seemed to be endless new worlds to discover, conquer, and exploit. In May 1499, Peralonso Niño, who had sailed with Columbus on the first voyage, mounted his own expedition in search of the *margaritas*—pearls—of Venezuela. He navigated the Atlantic with reasonable efficiency for both the outbound and inbound voyages, returning to Spain with a king's ransom in pearls. Charged with cheating the Sovereigns of their share of the bounty, he was arrested and his property seized. He died before his trial concluded.

Vicente Yáñez Pinzón, who had sailed with Columbus on the first and second voyages, arrived at the northern boundary of Brazil on January 26, 1500. Pinzón disembarked on the magnificently desolate beach now known as Praia do Paraíso, in the present-day state of Pernambuco. He returned to

The ubiquitous cassava, cultivated by Indians, provided starch in their diet but required careful preparation to remove harmful acids before it was baked into bread. Cassava roots were not consumed raw because they contain a substance similar to cyanide.

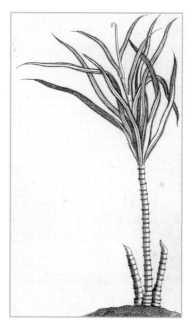

Sugar cane (*Saccharum officinarum*) was among the most significant crops that Columbus brought with him to the New World. Sugar cane plantations in the New World were maintained by slave labor, which ultimately led to slave rebellions throughout the Caribbean and southeastern United States.

The oldest known printed picture of the tobacco plant, 1574. Soon after arrival on the first voyage, Columbus's men encountered Indians smoking an "herb," probably the tobacco plant (*Nicotiana tabacum*) or a much stronger variant in the Nicotiana genus. Tobacco was another of Columbus's highly influential discoveries in the New World.

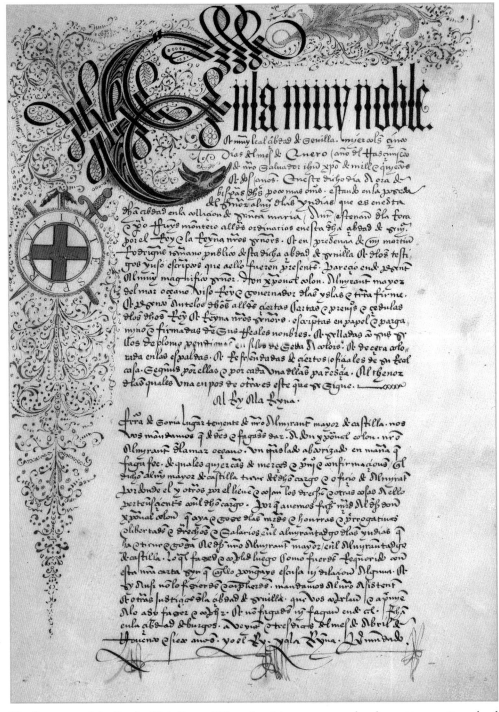

The first page of the *Book of Privileges*. Although raising numerous legal questions as it evolved along with Columbus's voyages, this compilation served as the official basis for Columbus's colonization of the New World.

In this engraving from 1594, Columbus and his brother Bartholomew are taken prisoner on the island of Hispaniola on the orders of Francisco de Bobadilla, the judicial investigator sent by Spain to call the explorer's administration to account.

The specter of cannibalism returned to haunt the soldiers of fortune who shipped out with Columbus on the third voyage. The Taíno were the main victims.

Early reports from the "Indies" blended grotesque fantasy and reality. In this engraving, ca. 1527, cannibals with the heads of dogs butcher men and ready them for eating.

The longer Europeans stayed in Hispaniola and other islands in the Caribbean, the more tangled their alliances and conflicts became. Here western European soldiers do battle with one another as three concerned Indians—two men and a woman—offer escape in canoes.

An estimated fifty thousand Indians committed suicide to protest European occupation of their ancestral homeland, some by hanging, others by jumping off cliffs, as depicted in this 1565 engraving. Still others simply starved themselves to death.

Columbus orders the hanging of mutinous Spaniards, all the while ignoring the pleas of a priest rushing to their aid. This engraving, by Theodor de Bry, was an example of his condemnation of the explorer's cruelty—in this case, toward his own men.

In an even stronger visual statement, de Bry showed Spaniards setting fire to a dwelling filled with Indians, even as another Indian, a female, and probably their leader, hangs from the branch of a nearby tree, ca. 1598. Striking images such as these contributed to the negative image of Columbus in Europe.

On his third voyage, Christopher Columbus discovered pearls and pearl fishers, as shown in this 1594 engraving by de Bry. Relying on the *Naturalis historia* of Pliny, Columbus believed that pearls generated from drops of dew forming within oysters when their shells were open.

Italy versus Spain in the New World: Columbus rallies loyalists against the uprising of Francisco Porras on the island of Jamaica during one of the most desperate moments of the fourth voyage. From a 1594 engraving by Theodor de Bry.

Spaniards brutalizing their victims in the New World.

A land of bounty and promise: After Columbus's death in 1506, his reputation continued to grow, and the debate over his legacy intensified. This allegorical image from 1750 portrays America as an Indian woman seated on an alligator. She holds a cornucopia and a parrot while attended by four figures representing different native American peoples. In the background, Europeans erect a cross as native Americans gambol on a beach.

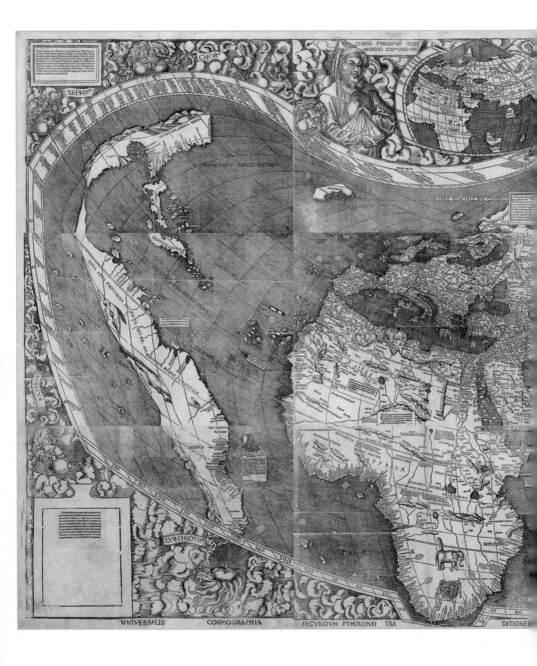

CLAVDII PTHOLOMEI ALEX
ANDRINI COSMOGRAPHI

CHOR

ZEPHIR

OCEANVS OCCIDENTALIS

MARE GLACIALE SIVE CORNELA

AFRICVS

AFFRICA

LYBONOTH

UNIVERSALIS   COSMOGRAPHIA   SECVNDVM PTHOLOMEI TRA   DITIONE

Martin Waldseemüller's spectacular world map, 1507, was the first map on which the name "America" appears, and the first to depict the full Western Hemisphere and the Pacific Ocean. The only copy of "America's Birth Certificate," as it is sometimes known, is displayed at the Library of Congress in Washington, D.C.

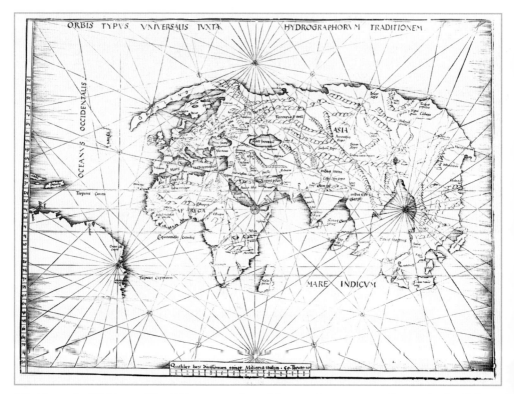

World map by Waldseemüller. This 1513 version of the map incorporates discoveries by Columbus, and is occasionally known as the "Admiral's Map," but the title refers to an admiral other than Columbus.

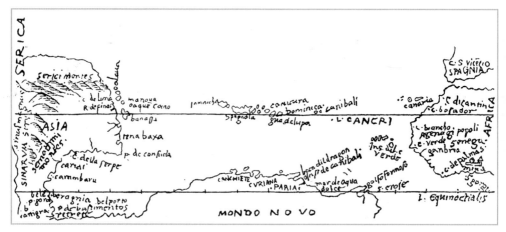

Bartholomew Columbus's tentative map of the New World, included in a letter by Christopher Columbus, dated July 7, 1503. "I cannot recall Hispaniola, Paria, and the other lands without crying," he wrote. This drawing incorporates features he discovered on several voyages; to the end of his days, the explorer struggled to incorporate his findings in his antiquated cosmography.

Ferdinand Columbus in a sixteenth-century Spanish oil portrait. The explorer's younger son accompanied his father on the fourth voyage.

Title page of a biography that Ferdinand Columbus published to defend the reputation of his illustrious father.

A colonialist in the service of Columbus turned monk and historian in later life, Bartolomé de Las Casas was known as the "Apostle of the Indians." His criticism of Columbus was caustic and unrelenting.

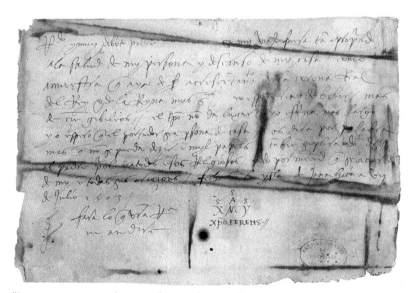

"I came to serve at the age of 28, and now I have not a single hair left that is not white, and my body is infirm and broken; all that belonged to me was taken and sold—and from my brothers, even their clothes. . . . One has to trust that these things were not done by your royal order" —Columbus's letter to his Sovereigns, July 7, 1503, composed in Jamaica.

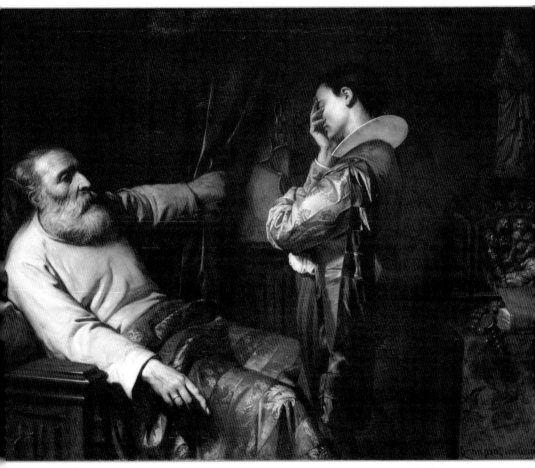

The Last Moments of Christopher Columbus by Claude Jacquand, 1870. In this romanticized depiction, Columbus bids his grieving son to place the chains he wore when arrested in his coffin. Throughout his life, Columbus displayed a penchant for piety and self-dramatization.

QVI RATE VELIVOLA OCCIDVOS PENETRAVIT AP IDOS
PRIMVS ET AMERICAM NOBILITAVIT HVMVM

CHRISTOPHORVS COLVMBVS LIGVR. INDIARV PRIM INVE A 1492

ASTRORVM CONSVLT ET IPSO NOBILIS AVSV
CHRISTOPHOR TALI FRONTE COLVMB ERAT

Christopher Columbus by Jean de Bry.

COLOMBVS LYGVR NOVI ORBIS REPTOR

This portrait of Christopher Columbus emphasizes the explorer's austerity.

Christopher Columbus, by the Florentine painter Ridolfo Ghirlandaio.

Spain on June 23, 1500, having lost many men on the voyage, and taking many slaves to replace them.

Pinzón was followed by the Spanish navigator Diego de Lepe, on a copy-cat mission. He, too, reached Brazil, off-limits to Spain, according to the terms of the Treaty of Tordesillas.

At about the same time, Rodrigo de Bastidas, a wellborn notary from Seville, still in his twenties, sailed with two ships, *San Antón* and *Santa María de Gracía*. He was accompanied by Columbus's mapmaker, Juan de la Cosa, and Vasco Núñez de Balboa, who was later celebrated as the first European to glimpse the Pacific Ocean. After cruising along the coast of South America, and visiting Panama's coast, Bastidas was forced to head north to Hispaniola to repair his shipworn fleet. Shipwrecked off the coast of Xaraguá, he was charged with trading with Indians without permission and sent back to Spain for trial. Acquitted, he later became known as the "Noblest Conquistador" in recognition of the respect he accorded the Indians, who were, in any case, rapidly dying out.

Each of these expeditions both validated and threatened Columbus's voyages of exploration. They demonstrated that it was not so difficult, after all, to sail west from Spain or Portugal across the Atlantic and, thanks to the Gulf Stream and the trade winds, land somewhere in the Americas. Locating a specific island, in this era of primitive navigation, was next to impossible, as even the Admiral of the Ocean Sea learned. With all its promise and challenges, the enterprise he had begun gradually overtook him, like the giant tsunami, irresistible and all-encompassing.

On his voyage, Ojeda brought along a forty-five-year-old Florentine named Amerigo Vespucci, the most enigmatic explorer of his era. By writing or inspiring a letter about a mythical "first voyage" of 1497 preceding his actual debut as an explorer, Vespucci guaranteed himself a controversial reputation. Las Casas, for instance, held him responsible for giving the impression that "Amerigo alone, with no other and before anyone else, had discovered it"—the mainland that came to be known, for no good reason, as America. As a result of Amerigo's "very great fraud," Las Casas acidly observed, "it is apparent then how much injustice was done to the admiral Christopher Columbus." Attempting to right the balance, the chronicler noted, "It was more his due that the mainland be called Columbus, de Colón, or Colombo, after the man who discovered it, or Tierra Santa or Tierra de Gracia, which he himself named it, and not America after Amerigo." But it was not to be. The name "America" stuck to the continent, beginning with the huge, composite *Universalis cosmographia*, a printed wall map of the world by Martin Waldseemüller, published in April 1507, the same year that the cartographer made corresponding globe gores—flat, approximately triangular sections designed to wrap around a ball. This is the first map to include the name "America." For it, Waldseemüller and his assistant, Matthias Ringmann, drew on several sources, including Columbus, for their depiction of the world at the height of the age of exploration, but they decided to award Vespucci preeminence. When it became apparent that Vespucci's role had been vastly overstated, Waldseemüller revised his map and renamed parts of it Terra Incognita; by this time, about a thousand copies of the original had been distributed, too late to correct the misimpression.

Although he gave his name to the continent that Columbus visited before him, Amerigo Vespucci's exploits did not obliterate his predecessor's contribution. Columbus had made such a large impression on the events of his time, and was so well known, if not admired, that the name "America" does not summon the legacy of Vespucci, but the exploits of Columbus.

Amerigo Vespucci began his career not at sea but in finance, working for both Lorenzo de' Medici and his son Giovanni. In the year Columbus made his first voyage, Vespucci had been detailed to the Medici bank in Seville. Cultivating Portuguese as well as Spanish connections, he received an invitation from King Manuel of Portugal to observe a number of voyages bound for South America between 1499 and 1500. One of them, led by Pedro Alvares Cabral, bound for the Cape of Good Hope and India, visited what is now Brazil in 1500. According to the terms of a modified Treaty of Tordesillas, Portugal was entitled to this land. Then, in a situation parallel to the one in which Columbus found himself with respect to the islands making up the Indies, the Portuguese king wished to learn if this newly discovered land, Brazil, was an island or part of the same continent that Columbus had already visited. Another voyage would be required to obtain the answer.

For now, Vespucci, despite his advanced age, benefited from his prestigious connections and arranged to sail with Ojeda's fleet, "but I do not know whether as a pilot or as a man trained in navigation and learned in cosmography," Las Casas confessed. "And even though Amerigo stresses that the king of Castile"—that is, Ferdinand—"put the fleet together, and that they went to discover at his command, it is not so." Instead, a small group of investors "pestered the king and queen for a license to go discover and trade." With the tremendous advantage of Columbus's hard-won chart, his pilots, and sailors, Ojeda stood ready to capitalize on their hunger for empire. He knew about the "Indies," and he even knew about Columbus's much more recent discoveries of Paria, Trinidad, and the Dragon's Mouth. Ojeda took care not to challenge Columbus's claim to have visited the region first; he wanted to be among the subsequent visitors included in its bounty. Imitation was the shortest route to wealth.

As a competitor supported by the Spanish crown, Ojeda posed a graver threat to Columbus's legitimacy than the scheming Francisco Roldán. Believing that Columbus could be assailed with impunity, Ojeda resorted to causing "all other mischief he could," including spreading a false rumor that Queen Isabella "was at death's door and that on her death the Admiral would be without a protector." At that point, Ojeda "could do what injury he pleased to the Admiral."

Treasonous sentiments like these were calculated to inflame Columbus's old adversary Roldán. To Ojeda's dismay, Roldán, having made peace with the Admiral, gathered a force of twenty-six men to pursue their new common enemy, Ojeda, who had taken up residence in an Indian village in Hispaniola. Energized, Roldán searched for his prey by night, but word of his mission reached Ojeda, who came out to confront his adversary.

Posing as a supplicant, Ojeda feebly explained that he had taken refuge on Hispaniola only because his supplies had run out; he meant injury to none. He distracted the skeptical Roldán with an account of his voyage, claiming he had explored six hundred leagues of coastline extending from Paria; survived a furious battle with Indians, who wounded twenty Christians; and yet despite these tribulations, he had bagged "stags, rabbits, tiger skins and paws," examples of which he displayed to Roldán. Refashioning his agenda, Ojeda claimed he would depart immediately to deliver a full report of his exploits to Columbus in Santo Domingo.

Chaos threatened to overwhelm other parts of the island empire. Columbus and his brother crisscrossed the island throughout much of 1499, avoiding peril until the end. "The day after Christmas Day, 1499," wrote Bartholomew, "all having left me, I was attacked by the Indians and bad Christians, and was placed in such extremity that fleeing death, I took to sea in a small caravel." In his vulnerable state, Bartholomew sought God's protection. "Then Our Lord aided me, saying, 'Man of little faith, do not fear, I am with thee.' And he dispersed my enemies, and showed me how I might fulfill my vows."

Ojeda's encounter with Roldán occurred in late September 1499, but not until February 1500 did Ojeda set sail for Xaraguá, Roldán's former haunt.

On arrival, Ojeda did all he could to supplant Roldán, trying to convince his former supporters that Ferdinand and Isabella had actually appointed him as a minder to Columbus, "lest the Admiral do something harmful to the royal interests." To make his claim more appealing, he insisted that the Sovereigns had ordered Columbus to pay those who had served the crown, but Columbus had stubbornly refused to comply, or so Ojeda argued, and he offered his services "to lead them to Santo Domingo to force him to pay up immediately; afterward they could throw the Admiral out of the island dead or alive."

Ojeda's scheme won the support of many former rebels. Under cover of night, he formed a group of the most insistent, or desperate, to attack the others. Ferdinand Columbus related that "there were dead and wounded on both sides." Those who emerged from the fray on Ojeda's side concluded that Roldán had betrayed them. Now loyal only to Ojeda, and his particular brand of mayhem, the misguided insurgents planned to capture Roldán, who learned of the conspiracy and "marched with strong force to punish Ojeda and crush the revolt." Afraid for his life, Ojeda took refuge aboard his ships, where he negotiated with Roldán, who had retreated to *his* ship. They bickered farcically about where to anchor the vessels, "each fearing to place himself in the power of the other."

Ojeda refused to leave his ship. Roldán proposed to parlay there with him, so long as Ojeda sent a boat to take him. After Roldán and his men climbed aboard the vessel, they attacked Ojeda's loyalists. When they had taken control of the boat, they rowed to shore and safety. Humbled, Ojeda realized he had to negotiate with Roldán as best he could.

When the two adversaries finally met, Ojeda apologized for his excesses and vowed to release several of Roldán's men who had been taken hostage. In exchange for these concessions, he pleaded for a "boat and crew." Without it, "he faced certain ruin, having no other boat fit for use," in Ferdinand's account. Conscious of his former status as a rebel, Roldán wanted only to rid himself and the island of Hispaniola of Ojeda, without giving him grievances to carry back to Spain and the Sovereigns, and so he agreed to the request, on condition that Ojeda and his men depart by a certain date. And to make certain that Ojeda complied, he "kept a strong guard ashore."

The leaders and usurpers had changed places. Roldán found himself in the position formerly occupied by Columbus, trying to foil the designs of Ojeda, who played the rebellious role once embraced by Roldán. But none of the men had grown wiser as a result of the conflict, only more cautious and wily. The three-way tussle was symptomatic of the sense of decline afflicting the Enterprise of the Indies; no one even pretended to invoke religious or political ideals anymore.

Roldán and Columbus believed they had rid themselves of Ojeda and other troublemakers. But, Ferdinand observed, "just as a bad weed is not so easily uprooted that it will not grow again, so men of evil habits are with difficulty kept from relapsing into their own old courses after Ojeda had sailed away." The latest threat came from a troublemaker named Fernando de Guevara, who resented Roldán for preventing Guevara's marriage to a young woman who happened to be the daughter of Anacaona, "the principal queen of Xaraguá." With Roldán married to another Indian woman, it became increasingly likely that the affiliations of the women of Hispaniola lay behind this conflict. The longer the Europeans remained on the island, the more their loyalties aligned with their hearts rather than their homeland.

Now Guevara, plotting to supplant Roldán "as lord of misrule," in Ferdinand's words, formed an alliance with another hardened rebel, Adrián de Mújica. By June 1500 they were planning to capture or kill their target. Learning of the conspiracy against him, Roldán rounded up the outlaws, informed the Admiral, and waited for instructions.

Columbus, for once, responded decisively. The men posed a threat to the island's security; they should be punished "as the law required." So Roldán, in his official capacity as the mayor, tried the group, and ordered the apparent ringleader, Adrián de Mújica, to be hanged. Roldán deported the other conspirators and imprisoned Guevara until June 13, when he was conveyed to the Admiral, then in the island's interior, for safekeeping.

Peace had come to Columbus's realm at last.

CHAPTER 10

"Send Me Back in Chains"

On February 3, 1500, Columbus returned from the interior to Santo Domingo, where he made plans to sail to Spain and present his version of events to the Sovereigns. "Throughout these disorders," Ferdinand noted, "many of the rebels, writing from Hispaniola, and others who returned to Castile continually conveyed false information to the Catholic Sovereigns and their royal council against the Admiral and his brothers, claiming they were most cruel and unfit to govern." Why? "Because they were foreigners and had no experience in dealing with people of rank." Columbus was a stranger, speaking in a foreign accent, surrounded by one brother or another, rarely mingling, an aloof, determined, enigmatic mystic. But his accomplishments loomed over all. Everyone on the island toiled in the shadow of Columbus. Even in near disgrace he remained the most powerful European in the Indies. If the Sovereigns did not rescue Hispaniola from his influence, the critics warned, "the total ruin of the Indies would come about." They predicted Columbus would "form an alliance with some foreign prince, claiming the Indies as his possession." And they resorted to more obvious libels—Columbus had hidden the actual wealth of the Indies from Spain; he was planning to use his Indian forces against the Sovereigns—calculated to appeal to his enemies in Castile.

Ferdinand Columbus recalled that when he visited Granada, "more than fifty of these shameless people brought a load of wine and, sitting in the court of the Alhambra"—the Moorish fortress later occupied by the Sovereigns—"loudly proclaimed that Their Highnesses and the Admiral reduced them to the pitiful state by withholding their pay, besides thousands of other lies that they concocted." So great was their resentment, however illusory its basis, that whenever King Ferdinand rode by on his royal steed, they would surround him, blocking his way and bellowing, "Pay! Pay!"

Columbus's son Ferdinand cringed at the memory of his own youthful encounters with the rabble. "Any time my brother and I, being pages to the Queen, would run into them, they would shout and persecute us, chanting, 'Here come the sons of the Admiral of the Mosquitoes, of him who discovered lands of vanity and deceit, the grave and ruin of Castilian gentlemen.'"

To minimize humiliating confrontations with Spaniards angry with Columbus, Ferdinand confided, he and his half brother "carefully avoided their presence." So it was that the offspring of Spain's most influential, transformative explorer went about the countryside incognito, out of fear for their lives.

Mindful of his descent into royal disfavor, Columbus recalled that he prayed "many times" to the Sovereigns to send "someone who might have charge of the administration of justice," and he asked others to make the request on his behalf "since my reputation is such that although I were to build churches and hospitals, they would always be called liars or robbers."

Ferdinand and Isabella listened to the many complaints about Columbus reaching Spain, and they acted as political leaders do: they appointed a special prosecutor. The date was May 21, 1499, and their choice was a man of impeccable credentials: Francisco de Bobadilla, a knight of the Order of Calatrava, the military wing of the Cistercian order, a venerable religious community of monks and nuns. His record reverberated with the pieties of Reconquista, and his new orders expanded on them, making him "Governor of the Islands and Mainland of the Indies." On this basis, he had every right to believe that he, not Columbus, would soon rule the Indies. His mission would be to rid Hispaniola of the corruption wrought by Columbus. On arrival in the Indies, Bobadilla was to investigate Columbus—the presumption in Spain was strong that the Admiral would be found blameworthy—and, Ferdinand related, "should he find the Admiral guilty, he should send him back to Castile and take over the island."

No one, not even Columbus, believed that the administration of Hispaniola had been handled properly. But no one besides Columbus was willing to leave Spain to manage it. Each voyage—and there were now three—demonstrated that Columbus was a brilliant navigator, canny, determined, able to learn from experience and mistakes with breathtaking speed—his Chinese delusion notwithstanding—but that he was ill equipped to serve as a governor of the lands he had conquered. Nearly every landfall showcased his brilliant and fearless navigation even as it exposed his inability to guide men, settle disputes, or instill loyalty.

At the moment Bobadilla's fleet approached Santo Domingo in August 1500, Columbus was at Concepción, putting down the latest Indian revolt. His brother Bartholomew, the Adelantado, was in Xaraguá with Roldán, arresting the allies of Guevara, who had attempted to kill the mutineer. And Diego Columbus remained behind in Santo Domingo, ordering the execution of other rebels. "The Admiral and the Adelantado," explained Las Casas, "anxiously went about arresting those who had again rebelled. They hanged those that they could arrest, and he brought a priest with him to confess them so that he could hang them wherever he might find them." At that point, "he could subject the Indians and constrain them to pay the tribute that he had imposed upon them and that Francisco Roldán had relieved them of during his rebellion." He did all this simply to send money to Ferdinand and Isabella to repay them for their expenses, and to silence his critics. His master plan consisted of baptizing every Indian in the major towns and hamlets of Hispaniola so they could "serve Their Highnesses like the vassals in Castile," in the opinion of Las Casas, who estimated that the scheme would generate sixty million maravedís a year for Spain. If Columbus's plans came to fruition, AD 1500 would mark the turning point in the economics of the Indies, the year the empire began sending revenue to Castile. "But, while preparing his loom, God cut the thread of the cloth that he planned to weave." The instrument was Bobadilla.

At about seven o'clock in the morning of Sunday, August 23, Bobadilla's ships—*La Gorda*, named for her master, Andrea Martín de la Gorda, accompanied by *Antigua*—appeared at the entrance to the harbor, but were forced to tack one way and then another before an offshore wind until late in the morning, when the breeze reversed direction and blew ashore, bearing the caravels before it.

Diego dispatched a canoe bearing three Christians and several Indians to meet the newcomers. One was Cristóbal Rodríguez, a sailor known as the first visitor to master the Indian language. The other two Christians were Juan Arráez and Nicolás de Gaeta. The Indians, whose names have not been recorded, paddled.

As the canoe approached, Bobadilla, "who had traveled in the caravel *Gorda*, then leaned out and said he was sent by the king and queen as judicial investigator of those who were rebelling on this island." Andrea Martín de la Gorda demanded news of Hispaniola, and learned that "seven Spanish men had been hanged that week." Five more were incarcerated, awaiting hanging. The fact that all the victims were Spanish alarmed Bobadilla. What sort of rebellion had occurred? Had Columbus allowed it to get out of hand? The investigator immediately asked for the Admiral and his two brothers, but only Diego was nearby. The Admiral was in Xaraguá, busy preparing still more executions. And to whom did he have the pleasure of speaking? Cristóbal Rodríguez inquired.

Francisco de Bobadilla, the judicial investigator.

The canoe returned to the shore, where expectations ran high that the arrival of the two ships meant better days ahead for the long-suffering colony: supplies, or women, or weapons, or other comforts from home. When they learned that the ships carried a "judicial investigator," said Las Casas, "those who felt guilt reacted with fear and sadness. Those who felt aggrieved by the admiral and his brothers were bursting with joy, along with those who were there involuntarily, mostly those who earned their salary from the king, who had not been and were suffering great need of food, clothing, and necessities from Castile."

When the wind died down, the caravels rode the tide into the harbor. Two scaffolds came into view, "one on this side of the river, which is the western shore where the city has now been built, and the other on the opposite side." Two hanged Christians, imprisoned several days before, dangled from the gallows.

Amid this macabre scene, "people came to and from the ships. They made their courtesies and reverences to the investigator Bobadilla. They asked and they answered, but always with some reserve until they saw what in the world was going to happen."

The next day, August 24, Bobadilla disembarked to hear Mass in the small, ragged settlement that claimed to be the capital of a new global empire. The contrast between the empire of the Indies' aspirations and its shabby reality could hardly have been greater. Bobadilla walked among flimsy, thatched structures housing the Europeans and compact stores of supplies. Most of the business of the settlement was still conducted aboard the ships, in tightly confined spaces, where men felt safer in fetid holds than on land, exposed to mercurial Indians and menacing snakes, flies, and mosquitoes. To an outsider, the settlement would have appeared more of a negligible, makeshift eyesore than an outpost of Christianity and the might of Spain. In contrast, the Indians' villages, huts, hammocks, drums, and fires, graceful canoes and tiny *cemís*, and especially their carefully tended fields of cassava plants, appeared thoroughly in place. Only the Europeans' expansive ships riding at anchor in the harbor or offshore suggested that these white men from afar were capable of better things than violence, rape, and an obsessive quest for gold.

When the observance concluded, the investigator ordered the king's scribe, who had traveled across the ocean with him, to read a letter from Ferdinand and Isabella, in which they summarized the rebellions of Roldán and others, and stated their purpose for sending Bobadilla to Hispaniola: "As we see it, because it was and is a bad example, worthy of punishment and chastisement, and because it pertains to us as king and queen and lords to provide the resolution of it, we command you to go to these islands and mainland of the Indies and gather your information using ways and means you need to find out best and most completely . . . who and which persons were the ones who rose up against the admiral and our justice and for what cause and reason, and what plundering, evil deeds, and damage they have done." When he had completed his investigation, Bobadilla was to "detain those whom you find guilty of it and confiscate their goods." The orders were clear, and, on the face of it, equal to the dire reports from Hispaniola that had reached Ferdinand and Isabella. "Once they have been arrested, proceed against them and against those absent with the greatest civil and criminal penalties you can find by law." Anyone who dared to obstruct Bobadilla's investigation would be fined ten thousand maravedís, a sum larger than any but the wealthiest nobleman could afford.

In the morning, Bobadilla commanded that another royal proclamation be read to remind everyone within hearing that he enjoyed the unreserved backing of the Sovereigns. But skepticism concerning his legitimacy lingered. Having anticipated this reaction, he ordered a clerk to recite still another letter from Ferdinand and Isabella to Columbus himself, with a set of humiliating instructions for the thin-skinned Admiral: "You are required by this letter that without any excuse or delay you give and turn over . . . the fortresses, houses, ships, arms, munitions, provisions, horses, livestock, and whatever other of our things that we possess in these islands" to "the Commander," that is, Bobadilla. If Columbus complied, he could keep whatever personal wealth he had acquired, but if he refused, he would incur the "pain of our displeasure," buttressed with ominous threats about the fate of "those who defied the Sovereigns." Finally, Bobadilla displayed a royal certificate instructing him to pay those owed money by the Sovereigns, implying heavily that even though Columbus had failed to comply with these demands, they would honor the obligations to clear the slate. There was no mistaking the import of these words: the Sovereigns had turned on Columbus, and placed Bobadilla in charge.

The Comendador added to his forces by assembling everyone on the Sovereigns' payroll to inform them that henceforth they served *him*, and their first objective was to rescue several convicts who were about to be hanged. When he produced the document ordering their release, the warden, Miguel Díaz, looking down from the battlements, recognized the signatures of Ferdinand and Isabella affixed to it. Bobadilla persisted: the prisoners were to be released. The warden stalled, asking to examine the fine print. The Comendador shot back that there was no time to produce a copy for him. A delay might lead to the hanging of the convicts. If the warden did not comply immediately, the Comendador would do whatever was necessary to free them, and if injury and death resulted, the warden would bear the burden of responsibility. Cornered, Miguel Díaz insisted that he had to consult with the Admiral himself.

Realizing that the officious warden would not do his bidding, Bobadilla, with his newly assembled forces, advanced on the fortress and ordered him to open the gates and admit them. The warden stood his ground. Sword drawn, standing atop the battlements, he shouted that he had already given his reply. "Since the fortress had more sauce than meat," said Las Casas, "because it had been built to withstand unfortunate people who were naked and without weapons, the Comendador and the people came up and with the great blow they gave to the main entrance, they broke the lock and plate." Just as Bobadilla's men raised ladders and prepared to swarm into the fortress through the windows, the main door swung open. Bobadilla and his forces charged past soldiers offering no resistance to his onslaught and found their way to the chamber holding the prisoners, their feet in painful shackles. Bobadilla delivered them, still bound, to the constable.

All the while, Columbus remained in the interior, preoccupied with ending the uprising. Bobadilla took the Admiral's absence to mean that he had abdicated his role as governor of Hispaniola. And so, Ferdinand said, he "promptly took up residence in the Admiral's palace and took over all that he found there as if it were his by lawful succession and inheritance."

Of this insult, Columbus snarled, "All that he found there, he appropriated for himself; all well and good, perhaps he had need of it; a pirate never treated a merchant so." His personal papers had been confiscated, and those that would have helped him defend himself in Spain, "he has most carefully concealed." While this madman pilfered Columbus's personal effects, the Admiral himself was exposing himself to danger in the interior and at Xaraguá, pacifying rebellions. Even if he overstated his heroism, the Admiral had a point: Bobadilla had usurped the Admiral just as he was bringing a semblance of order to Hispaniola.

To win over the handful of Spaniards still loyal to Columbus, Bobadilla announced that "he had come to pay everyone, even those who had not served properly up to that day." The Admiral looked on in amazement as this bureaucrat usurped his authority and reduced him to a nonperson. "He announced he was to send me back in chains, and my brothers also; and that I was never to return," Columbus recalled. "All this happened the very day after he arrived," with Columbus in the interior.

Bristling with officialdom, Bobadilla had brought letters signed by the Sovereigns that enabled him to do whatever he wished in their names. "To me he sent neither letter nor messenger, nor has he done so to this day," Columbus lamented. A situation so awful "I could not recall even in my dreams," he said. After all he had done for the Sovereigns over the course of three voyages, to be treated this way was beyond imagination and reason. Maybe Ojeda was behind it, maybe he had formed a pact with Bobadilla to dishonor Columbus. Meanwhile, the Sovereigns who owed him so much remained mute.

He unburdened himself in a letter to Doña Juana de la Torre, who enjoyed a close friendship with the queen, and served as conduit as well as confidante. "Consider, Your Grace, what one who held my position was to think!" the Admiral exclaimed to her. "Honors and favors for those who sought to usurp Their Majesties' authority and who have done so much harm and damage; humiliation for one who has sustained it through many perils." He admitted to mistakes in the founding of the Enterprise of the Indies, yet "my errors have not been committed with intention to do ill, and I believe Their Highnesses will credit me when I say so." He had, he pleaded, "fallen into error innocently and under compulsion," unlike the evil Bobadilla, who had plotted to defraud Columbus and the Sovereigns. "Maintaining justice and extending the realm of Their Highnesses to this day has brought me to the depths." But then, inadvertently damning his administrations, he reported that Spaniards bought and sold Indian women for outrageously high prices, enough to buy a farm at home, "and this is very common, and there are now many merchants who go seeking for girls; nine or ten are now for sale; for women of all ages, there is a good price to be had." The situation had become so dire that "if Their Highnesses would command a general inquiry to be made there, I declare to you that they would find it a great marvel that the island has not been swallowed up."

As Columbus retreated into paranoia, Bobadilla established his regime. To begin, he suspended the demoralizing tribute system for a period of twenty years and summoned Columbus to appear before him immediately, as ordered by the Sovereigns. Bobadilla established the legitimacy of this command by conveying a stale royal order to Columbus from the Sovereigns.

> *Don Christopher Columbus, our Admiral of the Ocean Sea.*
>
> *We have sent the Knight Francisco de Bobadilla, the bearer of this letter, to inform you of certain things on our behalf. We ask that you give him full faith, trust, and obedience. Given in Madrid on May 26, 1499.*
>
> *I the King. I the Queen.*

Columbus had no choice but to return to Spain immediately to face his impatient Sovereigns and envious rivals. His exploring, his quest for wealth for the glory of Spain, his awe at the discovery of lands and creatures for which he had no words, the whole magnificent panoply of realms no European before him had visited, had come to a sudden end. Columbus's behavior suggests that he realized that retribution for the excesses he had permitted was coming, but he never imagined it would be so swift and severe.

It was now early October 1500, nearly eight years after Columbus first spied the glittering white shores of the Indies and claimed them in the name of Ferdinand and Isabella. He hastened to Santo Domingo with his brother Diego to confront Francisco Bobadilla, who placed the two in chains and kept them under guard aboard ship. To reinforce the seriousness of the proceedings, Bobadilla insisted on secrecy from everyone with knowledge of the arrest.

And then he confiscated Columbus's gold, a deed certain to torment its target. "Of this gold I had put aside certain specimens, grains as large as a goose's egg, and a hen's egg, and pullet's egg, and of many shapes." Now it all belonged to Bobadilla, who melted down much of it. A large gold chain disappeared. As the days passed, the Comendador raided Columbus's house for silver, jewels, and decorations, appropriating everything for himself. Livestock, books and writings, and personal effects all wound up in his grip. In sum, said Columbus, Bobadilla "showed energy always in everything that he thought would injure me." It seemed incredible, laughable that this man had been sent to "inquire into my conduct," knowing that if he sent back a "very damaging report" he would "remain in charge of the government." If only Bobadilla had appeared two years earlier, "I should have been free from scandalous abuse and infamy."

His influence undermined by rebellions, Columbus felt powerless to resist Bobadilla. The standard by which he was judged was unjust, he insisted. He was being treated as an administrator of "a city or two under settled government, without fear of all being lost." But Hispaniola posed entirely different and greater challenges. "I ought to be judged as a captain who went from Spain to the Indies to conquer a people, warlike and numerous, with customs and beliefs very different from ours, a people living in highlands and mountains, having no settled dwellings, and apart from us." Because of his efforts, "I have brought under the dominion of the king and queen, our Sovereigns, another world, whereby Spain, which was called poor, is now most rich." That was his claim, backed by three perilous voyages of exploration.

Heedless of Columbus's elaborate self-justifying arguments, Bobadilla ordered a "farcical inquest," or so it appeared to Ferdinand Columbus, "taking testimony from their open enemies, the rebels, and even showing public favor." Even a blind man, he said, would recognize that the depositions were "dictated by prejudice rather than truth."

Much later, when passions cooled, the Sovereigns came to agree with this assessment, and "ultimately cleared the Admiral of these charges," and even "regretted having charged such a man"—Bobadilla—"with that mission." But for now, Ferdinand Columbus noted, the Comendador preferred "hobnobbing with the richest and most powerful men on the island," and awarded himself a share of the pay earned by the Indians he assigned to work for the Europeans. And he angrily reported that Bobadilla auctioned off the possessions he had seized, "while making sure some of his cronies acquired ownership of the properties for one third of their value."

Columbus was not quite the innocent victim he proclaimed himself to be. He maintained that he silently endured the investigator's challenge to the point of submitting to shackles and even jail, but witnesses testified that the Admiral had actually assembled a militia composed of Spanish settlers and Indians to resist Bobadilla. If true, Columbus enlisted Indians—heathens—to battle Christians: a serious offense against Spain.

Meanwhile, Bobadilla's inquiry got under way. A priest testified that Columbus ordered Roldán not to baptize Indians without express permission. And another priest, who identified himself as Mateo Valenciano, beseeched the Admiral for permission to baptize a "female servant," only to be denied. Instead, Columbus permitted the Spaniards to take the Indians as slaves to be bought and sold rather than baptized. Stories circulated that Columbus sold attractive Indian boys and girls as slaves rather than converting them to Christianity.

Rodrigo Manzorro, another witness, stated that he heard priests complain that they were unable to convert Indians to Christianity unless Columbus specifically permitted them, insisting that all the Indians of the island belonged to him. This accusation was echoed by Columbus's antagonist Ojeda, who was said to have presided over mass conversions, a practice that upset the Admiral, who insisted that he, and only he, would decide who would be converted and who would be sold into slavery. Capturing a cacique with three hundred followers, the story ran, Columbus decided to send the lot to Castile to offer them as slaves to be bought and sold at auction, even though they were under Roldán's protection. The Admiral's conviction that all slaves belonged to him drove him to inform the island's settlers that they must assign every other servant to him. No longer were they souls to be saved, they were human commodities whose value would be decided by Columbus.

Another witness, Francisco de Sezé, testified that in the previous six and a half years, the Admiral had ordered a dozen or more Spaniards to be whipped in public, tied by the neck, and bound together by the feet because they had traded gold for "a bit of pork and for some wine and bread" when starving. Columbus subjected them to this extreme punishment "because they bartered and gave gold without the Admiral's permission."

More examples of his viciousness surfaced. In one instance, he ordered a woman to be stripped and placed on the back of a donkey, "stark naked," to be whipped because she falsely claimed to be pregnant. In another case, he ordered a woman's tongue cut out because she had "spoken ill of the Admiral and his brothers." She had said that his father had been a weaver—which was true—and that his brothers were "journeymen," a vague insult, perhaps, but hardly a crime.

In La Isabela, a Spanish official arrested a woman named Teresa de Vaeça. With another Spaniard, Rodrigo Pérez, the Spanish official tortured her in secret because the governor had had an affair with a married woman allied with Teresa, who, it was claimed, "deserved the punishment for pimping."

Without trial, she received a hundred lashes "naked and on foot" and had her tongue cut out to chastise her for her transgressions, real or imagined, but in reality—from the context of the accusation—for daring to dishonor a Spanish official.

Columbus punished homosexuality with the same severity. He ordered Juan de Luxan's throat cut for being a "traitor" and "sodomite." The accused objected to the former accusation but not the latter.

Other testimony revealed that Columbus ordered Spaniards to be hanged for stealing bread when they were hungry. He even ordered the ears and nose cut off one miscreant, who was also whipped, shackled, and banished from the island. He ordered a cabin boy's hand nailed in public to the spot where he had pulled a trap from a river and caught a fish.

Whippings for minor infractions occurred with alarming frequency. Columbus ordered one wrongdoer to receive a hundred lashes—which could be fatal—for stealing sheep, and another for lying about the incident. An unlucky fellow named Juan Moreno received a hundred lashes for failing to gather enough food for Columbus's pantry. He received his lashings "on foot and naked" at the hands of an Indian, who was told to proclaim that Moreno was a "scoundrel."

There were hangings, as Bobadilla had seen. And many others that he had not seen. Learning that two Spaniards had sold bread from the ships' stores to hungry Christians, Columbus dispensed with an investigation and trial, and ordered them to be hanged. And so they were. Other hangings were carried out swiftly, without trial or time for the accused to confess.

Witnesses testified to Columbus's bungling management of Hispaniola. Despite the remarkable abundance of fruit and other nourishment on the island, the generosity of the Indians in sharing it with the settlers, and the regular supplements provided by supply ships from Spain, fifty men had died at La Isabela from starvation as Columbus refused them provisions from the ships' bountiful stores. Food that began to decompose was thrown into the sea, and anyone who tried to bargain with a food store's guard was beaten for his trouble. The sick and convalescent discovered that their rations were reduced amid the fertile island's plenty. The accounts, coming from so many witnesses, were abysmal, inexcusable, and served to justify the Comendador's relieving Columbus of command.

After the inquiry, Bobadilla feared that Roldán, now realigned with the Admiral, might free Columbus from his fetters, but the raid failed to materialize. In captivity, both Columbus brothers "displayed much self-restraint,"

Ferdinand reported. That way, "on arrival in Castile they could more easily secure Bobadilla's punishment." If they survived their ordeal.

Their situation was deteriorating by the hour. When Columbus was led to the ship, he believed he was about to be executed by having his throat cut.

"Where are you taking me?" he implored the hidalgo Alonso de Vallejo, who had been assigned the task of conveying Columbus from the fortress to *La Gorda*.

"Sir, your lordship goes to board the ship."

Skeptical that he would be spared, he asked, "Vallejo, is it true?"

And the hidalgo replied, "By the life of Our Lady, it is true that you are going aboard."

Columbus experienced overwhelming relief at the realization that he was being led not to his death but to the ship and to life.

The departure of the caravel *La Gorda*, bearing the Columbus brothers, provoked ugly scenes. The inhabitants of the island realm that the Admiral once ruled now insulted Columbus in the public squares and posted vicious notices on street corners. In the harbor, formerly loyal servants of the Spanish throne blew horns in derision.

Bobadilla feared that Columbus might find some way to escape, and ordered the shipmaster, Andrea Martín de la Gorda, to keep the prisoner shackled tightly throughout the voyage to Spain, until the moment they entered the presence of Bishop Fonseca, charged by the Sovereigns with overseeing the Enterprise of the Indies. Even Columbus's enemies were appalled by this treatment. "A most absurd thing," Las Casas charged, and launched into a stirring defense of the explorer whom he vehemently denounced on other occasions. "At once disdainful, detestable, and wretched. He was, after all, viceroy and perpetual governor of this part of the world and, by most deserved renown, Admiral of the Ocean Sea. He had won those titles—chosen by the singular privilege of God—by enduring so many trials, dangers, and labor, and by revealing to the world this world that had been hidden for many centuries." For that reason, Ferdinand and Isabella owed him "perpetual gratitude. It was unworthy of good reason and more than monstrous that a man in such a lofty position had been treated so inhumanely and shamefully." With his adamantine nature and unflagging purpose, Columbus impressed even his critics, and never more than when he was shackled.

No one could be found who was willing to chain the Admiral of the Ocean Sea, said Las Casas, except for the lowly cook, Espinosa, who attached the manacles "as if he were serving him some plates of new and precious foods." His punishment would mean enduring weeks in a dark, stuffy, sweltering, swaying hold, vulnerable to the elements and to the unpredictable behavior of the crew, who would be tempted to vent their frustration on their two prisoners.

The sails of *La Gorda* slipped below the horizon one day in early October. The Admiral of the Ocean Sea was now a prisoner on his own vessel, waiting to be judged by his Sovereigns.

At sea, the shipmaster offered to strike the chains binding Columbus's wrists and ankles, but Ferdinand reported that his father "would not permit it, saying only that they had been put on him by royal authority and only the Sovereigns could order them struck off." He drew strength from this humiliation, becoming stronger in defeat than in victory. The explorer in chains represented the ideal tableau to express his sense of martyrdom, and he would sustain it as long as possible. Columbus knew the dynamics of redemption, and played his part, even as he resented it. Said his son, "He was resolved to keep those chains as a keepsake of how well he had been rewarded for his many services." Columbus never forgot the ordeal. "I always saw those irons in his bedroom," Ferdinand revealed, "which he demanded be buried with his bones."

On landing in Cadiz, Columbus chose to exhibit himself in chains to elicit sympathy from the curious crowds that had gathered there to watch him and who were duly impressed by the sight of the great explorer humbled. Later, when the chains were finally removed, he would substitute the habit of a Franciscan friar, keeping the sleeves short enough to reveal the marks made by manacles on his wrists as signs of mortification. The spectacle he made of himself was not as bizarre as it sounded, not in a country in which pilgrims on bare, bloody knees paraded through the streets of Seville as part of their Easter observance. Columbus knew what notes to strike with his public acts of penance, and to appear both pious and loyal.

Still manacled, Columbus arrived at the monastery of Santa María de las Cuevas, a fortress of faith on the island of La Cartuja, near Seville. According to legend, an image of the Virgin had appeared in a *cueva*, or cave, beneath the monastery in the thirteenth century.

On December 12, Ferdinand and Isabella ordered Columbus freed from his shackles, provided him with funds, and invited him to court, located, for the moment, at Granada.

Five days later, Christopher, Bartholomew, and Diego Columbus received a cordial reception by the Sovereigns. They let it be known they had not ordered the Admiral to be imprisoned; responsibility belonged to Bobadilla, who had exceeded his authority. Throughout the poignant tableau, "the most serene queen was the one who excelled in consoling him about this and assuring him of her pain for, in truth, she was always the one who favored and defended him more than the king." It was no wonder that "the Admiral placed all of his hope in her."

Columbus's emotions, held in check for months, suddenly burst forth. He knelt before the queen, sobbing. At length, the Sovereigns commanded him to rise, and in a halting voice he conveyed his "deep love and desire to serve them with all the faithfulness that he had always had." He avowed that he had never done anything to give them offense, echoing a letter he had written to them in which he declared, "I swear . . . that I have been more diligent in serving Your Highnesses than in gaining paradise."

In this act of mutual absolution, Columbus acknowledged that he had permitted the misdeeds exposed by Bobadilla's investigation, revealed the pain of being shackled and publicly humiliated, professed his undying love for and loyalty to the Sovereigns, excusing his lapses and abuses on the basis of excessive zeal rather than malice, and begged forgiveness, thereby setting the stage for the possibility of a fourth voyage, as unlikely as that seemed after the lapses of the previous three. His honor was at stake, as were his titles, riches, and role in the Enterprise of the Indies, and he wished to redeem them all before it was too late.

Ferdinand and Isabella undid the work of Bobadilla and restored the Admiral's rights and privileges, at least on paper, by forcing the investigator to disgorge the items he had confiscated. "We command that there be returned and restored to him all the furniture of his person and household, and provisions of bread and wine which the Comendador Bobadilla took from him, or their just value, without our receiving any part thereof," ran part of the Royal Mandate, dated September 27, 1501. The same principle applied to the gold nuggets of Hispaniola (confiscated by Bobadilla), to livestock, expenses, and wages. Columbus's loyal paymaster, Alonso Sánchez de Carvajal, would remain at his post. His books and records would be returned. Most important of all, the Admiral's share of the island's wealth—an eighth of the total, and in some cases a tenth—would remain in his hands.

Ferdinand and Isabella had rehabilitated Columbus, but not enough to suit his taste and vanity. He compiled his personal *Book of Privileges* in which he listed all the properties, titles, rights, awards, and offices that he believed he was still owed, but his grievance went unrecognized. The Sovereigns were in a difficult position as a consequence of the sprawling realm discovered by Columbus. To neutralize the threat he posed, Ferdinand and Isabella cut him down to size.

On September 3, 1501, they declared that he would not be able to return in triumph to Hispaniola, after all. In his place, they chose a younger man, Nicolás de Ovando, as the next governor and chief justice. The appointment meant Columbus no longer ruled the realm he had discovered. Playing to his vanity, they permitted him to retain hollow titles such as admiral and viceroy, and he was allowed to keep the money confiscated by Bobadilla. On one hand, the Sovereigns had honored Columbus; on the other, they had replaced him.

He entered a dark period. His health was declining, his eyesight failing, his body tormented by rheumatoid arthritis. His moods alternated among grandiose ambition, paranoia, and lucid intervals—all because he had lost control of the brave enterprise he had begun, and earned a reputation as a scoundrel rather than the hero of his imaginings.

Despite everything, the third voyage provided important results. Columbus had once again demonstrated his peerless navigational ability, crossing the Atlantic with such efficiency that the accomplishment, all but unthinkable before his first voyage, was becoming commonplace. He had survived a terrible tsunami. And he had finally located the mainland, touching Venezuela, the Orinoco, and the island of Trinidad, and found a region rich in valuable pearl fisheries.

But Ferdinand and Isabella had, in effect, sent the Admiral of the Ocean Sea into retirement. It seemed that his seafaring days were over, and the next shore he reached would be death.

His work done, Francisco de Bobadilla, Columbus's nemesis, embarked on a passage home to Spain, sailing with a convoy of thirty vessels in June 1502. Aboard his ship were Francisco Roldán, the former rebel, now rotated back to Spain; Guarionex, the fierce cacique who had once challenged Columbus, soon to be presented to the Sovereigns as a trophy of the Indies; and the Admiral's steadfast ally Antonio de Torres, the captain. In her hold, the ship carried 200,000 castellanos of gold, equivalent to 87,000,000 maravedís (more than ten million dollars), and a nugget said to be the biggest in the Indies, valued at 3,600 pesos.

Considered the least seaworthy of all the ships in the fleet was little *Aguja*

("Needle"), carrying Columbus's personal store of gold, disgorged by Bobadilla. It was worth 4,000 pesos.

Conditions were forbidding on the day of departure; a swell, *aceitoso y maloliente*, rolled in from the southeast, where hurricanes often formed. A low-pressure system sapped the air of vitality. Shreds of high-altitude cirrus caught fire at sunset, but sea-level breezes did little to dispel the disquieting mood. Dolphins skimming the surface added to the sense of impending mayhem.

On July 11, the fleet was negotiating the Mona Passage, a strait running between Hispaniola and Puerto Rico. With its extensive sandbanks and riptides, the strait was difficult to navigate even in fair weather. On this occasion, wind from the northeast gathered strength until it attained hurricane force, scattering the fleet throughout the passage. There was nothing that anyone aboard these luckless ships could do except to give themselves up to the elements and pray. The flimsy wood and thatch buildings of little Santo Domingo blew apart. The hurricane drove ships ashore, where they broke up. A few shattered craft eventually limped to Santo Domingo, where they sank in the harbor. Twenty other ships foundered at sea, taking all hands to the bottom. More than five hundred colonists and caciques, criminals and nobles, Spaniards and Indians, drowned.

Torres the captain, Guarionex the Indian, Roldán the mutineer, and Bobadilla the judicial investigator all went down with their gold-laden ship.

Of the entire fleet, only fragile *Aguja*, carrying Columbus's treasure, survived the hurricane, a sign of divine favor if there ever was one. The foes of Columbus believed that he had conjured the tempest to vanquish his enemies.

PART FOUR

Recovery

CHAPTER 11

El Alto Viaje

In later life, Columbus's son Ferdinand, whose mother, Beatriz de Arana, never married the Admiral, ascended to wealth and prominence in Spain. Over time, he exhibited patience and a steady temperament—two characteristics for which his histrionic father was not known—and won recognition as a scholar and collector of books. With a significant portion of the fortune he inherited from his father, blood money to be sure, he acquired a library consisting of fifteen thousand volumes, an extravagant amount by the standards of his day. There had always been a bookish side to Columbus, who spent years absorbing arcane learning; his brother Bartholomew shared this passion, dealing in books and maps before his brother appointed him the Adelantado. For the last thirty years of his life, 1509 to 1539, Ferdinand Columbus's renowned library attracted scholars from across Spain and the Continent, including Desiderius Erasmus, the Dutch humanist and Catholic priest.

Ferdinand doted on his book collection. Each carefully chosen volume contained personal notations and the price paid for it. Perhaps the most radical decision he made as a collector was his preference for the newly available technology of printed books rather than gorgeously illustrated manuscripts. He acquired over a thousand priceless examples of incunabula ("swaddling clothes" from the Latin): books dating from the earliest years of the printing press, prior to 1501. His library also included books and papers that had belonged to the Admiral himself, complete with marginal notes, a comprehensive archive of Columbus's intellectual universe. Before his death, Ferdinand inscribed in each volume a statement to the effect that Don Fernando Columbus, son of Don Cristóbal Columbus, the Admiral who discovered India, left this book for the use and benefit of all. Today, a fair portion of the library's inventory, seven thousand volumes, survives intact as the Biblioteca Colombina, lodged in the Seville Cathedral.

Years before, as a boy of thirteen, the studious Ferdinand took the voyage of his life, sailing with his father, the Admiral, and an amalgam of thieves, gentlemen, ambitious enthusiasts, murderers, mutineers, and able-bodied seamen, priests, and pilots. They explored the Caribbean, Central America, and the island of Jamaica, where they passed an entire year in Robinson Crusoe–like desolation on a deserted beach.

It was a journey that no one expected Columbus to make—except for the Admiral himself, that is—and one that evolved into the wildest, most reckless, and grimmest voyage of them all. It was both the culmination and undoing of everything he had tried to accomplish on behalf of Ferdinand and Isabella in the previous twelve years. Responding to the allure of his apparently limitless empire, the Admiral felt impelled to return, as if summoned by the drumbeats of the *mayohuacán* and *maguey*, to distant shores. No other location on the map, real or imagined, would do, not even Marco Polo's dominion. *Otro mundo*—the "other world"—barely hinted at the mingled splendor and terror of what he had found. A perpetual exile and pilgrim, he no longer belonged to Italy, or Portugal, or even Spain. He belonged to Hispaniola, even though he had been banished from the realm by his replacement, Nicolás de Ovando.

But that was a temporary aberration, to Columbus's way of thinking, and he was determined to set matters right.

Now fifty-one, Columbus had become an old man, half-blind, afflicted with rheumatoid arthritis and fits of "paludal poison," or malarial fever. He was more volatile and spiritually intense than ever. He had returned to the Carthusian monastery of Santa María de las Cuevas, where he led an austere, eremitical existence in a solitary cell.

In a Carthusian monastery, the hermit eats in his cell, twice a day or, during days of fasting, only once a day. Meals and other necessities are passed through a small turntable to the occupant, so he does not meet or even see the person who has delivered the items. Anything else he needs— bread, for instance—he may request by means of written communication. Speech is not permitted, even on feast days.

With the cooperation of a Carthusian monk by the name of Gaspar Gorricio, Columbus assembled a work known as *Libro de las profecías*, or *Book of Prophecies*, an idiosyncratic amalgam of biblical texts, commentary, and observations gleaned from ancient authorities, in both Latin and Spanish. It is difficult to know how much of it was composed by Columbus himself— it was written primarily in the monk's hand, with additional entries by his son Ferdinand—but the result was intended to reflect Columbus's spiritual vision of his life's work and destiny. In the explorer's words, it gathered together the "sources, statements, opinions, and prophecies on the subject of the recovery of God's Holy City and Mount Zion and on the discovery and evangelization of the islands of the Indies and of all other peoples and nations," all with Columbus playing a leading, and divinely ordained, role. In it, he appears not as the explorer preoccupied with gold, pearls, and other tokens of greed, nor with titles and his share of the fruits of the Indians' arduous labor, but as a devout servant of the Lord. "The Lord opened my mind to the fact it would be possible to sail from here to the Indies," he reflected, "and He opened my will to desire to accomplish the project."

Columbus portrayed himself as a man who earned scorn and ridicule for his vision from rival mariners, bureaucrats, scientists, and scholars. Only the Sovereigns, to their undying glory, heeded his call. Buttressing his message with biblical citations, he entertained the notion that the time had come to launch a new Crusade to recapture the Holy Sepulchre and spark conversions to Christianity around the world. "I believe that there is evidence that our Lord is hastening things," he declared. According to his calculations, there were only 150 years before the end of the world.

The *Book of Prophecies* reflected Columbus's circumstances of the moment, serving as an *apologia pro vita sua*, and announcing to his critics at court and to posterity that everything he did, all the violence, all the lives lost, was done according to a larger plan. Even in his most ascetic frame of mind, he courted grandeur. Having prepared himself, he yearned for an endeavor he might never live to complete: a fourth voyage.

Inspired by Marco Polo's voyage across Asia with his father and uncle, Columbus decided to bring his son Ferdinand on the fourth voyage to the New World. Polo was about seventeen years old at the time he embarked on his journey, and Ferdinand Columbus only a few years younger, thirteen years old. By voyaging with their families, both Ferdinand and Polo amassed a lifetime of experience and secured their dynastic legacies.

In maturity, Ferdinand recognized that as a young man he had been lucky enough to participate in one of the great events of his era, the exploration of a new world. But he was not merely a propagandist. As a scholar and amateur historian, he portrayed his father as a man determined to make and

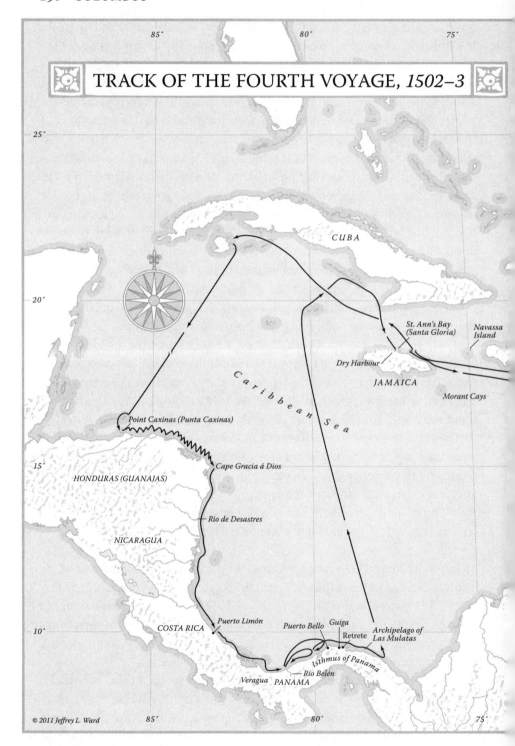

TRACK OF THE FOURTH VOYAGE, *1502–3*

85°   80°   75°

25°

CUBA

20°

St. Ann's Bay
(Santa Gloria)   Navassa
Island

Dry Harbour

C a r i b b e a n   S e a

JAMAICA

Morant Cays

Point Caxinas (Punta Caxinas)

15°   Cape Gracia á Dios

HONDURAS (GUANAJAS)

Rio de Desastres

NICARAGUA

10°   COSTA RICA   Puerto Limón

Puerto Bello   Guiga

Retrete

Archipelago of
Las Mulatas

Isthmus of Panama

Río Belén

Veragua   PANAMA

© 2011 Jeffrey L. Ward   85°   80°   75°

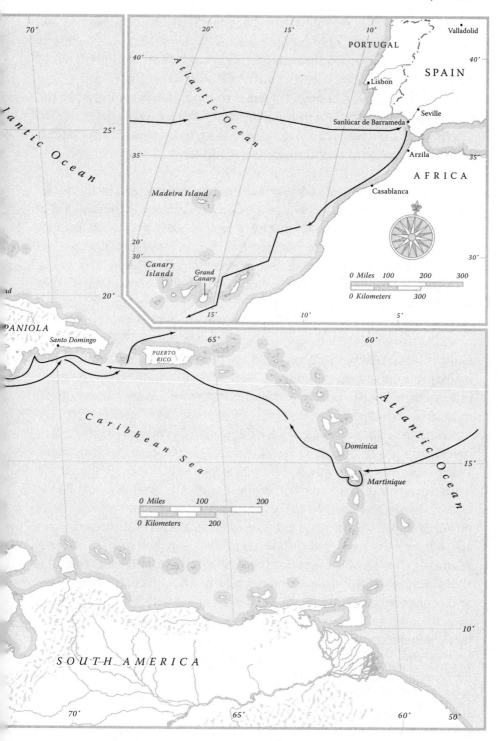

remake history. He generally avoided passing judgment on his father, and subtly censored some of his worst excesses. When matters went awry, as they did time and again throughout this voyage, Ferdinand preferred to blame disreputable Spaniards on board the ship rather than acknowledge his father's failings. Although intended to vindicate the Admiral of the Ocean Sea, the *Historie Concerning the Life and Deeds of the Admiral Don Christopher Columbus* can also be read as an indictment of the Spanish colonial enterprise in all its cruelty and absurdity.

Columbus's fleet consisted of just four ordinary ships leased by the Sovereigns. The flagship was known as *La Capitana*, under the command of Diego Tristán, a Columbus loyalist who received 4,000 maravedís a month for his labors. Ambrosio Sánchez served as master, his brother Juan as chief pilot, each receiving exactly half the captain's salary. They supervised a crew of thirty-four, including fourteen sailors, who received 1,000 maravedís per month, and twenty ship's boys. Specialists included a cooper (to protect barrels holding water and wine), a caulker, a carpenter, a pair of trumpeters to sound alarms and perform music appropriate to maritime events, and two gunners. Afflicted with gout and the poor vision that tormented him on his previous voyage, Columbus assumed a less definite role in the enterprise, in case he again became incapacitated, but he was unquestionably its most important personage.

Santiago de Palos, nicknamed *Bermuda* after her owner, Francisco Bermúdez, was a more compact vessel. Bartholomew Columbus functioned as her captain, without pay, while the nominal captain, Francisco Porras, earned a salary of 3,666 maravedís per month. His brother Diego Porras earned slightly less, serving as the crown's comptroller and representative on board ship. Columbus had not wanted either Porras brother on the voyage, but he was compelled to take them along by the crown's treasurer, Alonso de Castile, who maintained the Porrases' sister as his mistress. This ship's crew consisted of eleven sailors, a boatswain (in charge of the crew and equipment), a dozen or so cabin boys, along with a cooper, caulker, carpenter, and gunner, and six *escuderos* (gentlemen)—volunteers motivated by a combination of greed, lust, and thirst for adventure.

A more reliable crew operated *Gallega* ("the Galician"), with Pedro de Terreros as captain, earning the going rate of 4,000 maravedís per month. A diehard Columbus loyalist, he was sailing with the Admiral for the fourth time. The second-in-command, Juan Quintero, earning half that amount, had been boatswain aboard *Pinta* during the first voyage and, as the ship's owner, had at least as much clout as the captain. A complement of sailors, a boatswain, cabin boys, and an *escudero* completed the roster.

The fleet's smallest ship, *Vizcaína* ("the Biscayne"), boasted a captain with a famous name: Bartolomeo Fieschi came from a renowned Genoese family. Columbus was so determined to keep the fleet under his control that he bought the ship from her owner after sailing. *Vizcaína* carried several Genoese, a chaplain, and a page.

Whatever the flotilla lacked in size and status, it made up for in ambition.

"On May 9, 1502," Ferdinand wrote, "we set sail from the harbor of Cádiz and made for Santa Catalina," a fortress at the port's opening, "whence we sailed again on Wednesday, the 11th of the month, for Arzila," a city sometimes known by its older name, Asylum, situated on the Atlantic coast of northern Morocco, distinguished by stark white walls rising above the sea. In 1471, the Portuguese had wrested the city from Arab control.

Encouraged by King Ferdinand, Columbus attempted to repair his frayed relationship with Portuguese interests by offering to support the city in its struggle to ward off the foe, but by the time he arrived, "the Moors had already raised the siege," wrote his son, for whom the spectacle of greeting one civilization after another assumed dreamlike clarity. "The Admiral sent ashore his brother the Adelantado Don Bartholomew Columbus and myself, together with the ships' captains, to call on the captain of Arzila, who had been wounded by the Moors in the assault. He gave profuse thanks to the Admiral for this courtesy and for the offer of help, sending aboard certain of his gentlemen; some of these proved to be cousins of Doña Felipa Moñiz, who had been the Admiral's wife in Portugal" and the mother of Ferdinand's half brother, Diego.

Having paid their respects, the fleet called at Grand Canary on May 20, and began taking on "water and wood for the voyage" for the next four days, according to Columbus's custom. "The next night we set course for the Indies," said Ferdinand. Although ailing, Columbus performed a navigational marvel on this crossing by catching the trade winds, or easterlies. By the morning of June 15, "with a rather rough sea and wind," they had arrived at Martinique, in the Caribbean Sea north of Trinidad, having crossed the Atlantic in only twenty days, a time frame that even a modern-day sailor would be hard-pressed to equal. If proof was needed that Columbus had not lost his navigational skill and weather eye, this feat surely provided it.

For all his skill, Columbus could not have expected to arrive precisely at this tiny speck, a little over four hundred square miles of sand and scrub at 14°40'0" N, 61°0'0" W. As his previous crossings had demonstrated, sailing west from the Canaries, with a push from the easterlies above and from the Gulf Stream below, he was bound to arrive somewhere in the Americas. But locating a specific port or island was highly unlikely. Except for a storm, little occurred in the open ocean that would affect a ship's course, but coastal navigation was a different story, hit or miss. So it was that he discovered the diminutive island by chance.

On arrival, the men attended to chores, taking on water and wood, and washing their fetid clothing. On Saturday, they sailed the ten leagues to the island of Dominica. "Till I reached there I had as good weather as I could have wished for," the Admiral noted some months and many disasters later, "but on the night of my arrival there was a great storm, and I have been dogged by bad weather ever since." For a novice sailor like Las Casas, the misery of rolling and pitching in the ocean's vastness was even greater, and it was all that he and his shipmates could do to endure the traumatic crossing. "The crew was so worn down, shaken, ill and overcome by such bitterness that they wanted to die rather than to live, seeing how the four elements working against them were cruelly torturing them," he complained, having had a taste of the peril and misery that Columbus and his veteran crew members had endured for years at sea.

Outlasting the storms, Columbus reached Puerto Rico and finally Santo Domingo in Hispaniola. Stripped of his status, he was not supposed to be there at all, having been replaced by Nicolás de Ovando, the new governor and widely known as a Columbus detractor. As Ferdinand carefully explained, Columbus urgently needed to avail himself of Santo Domingo's safe harbor "to trade one of his ships for another because she was a crank and a dull sailor; not only was she slow but could not load sails without bringing the side of the ship almost under water." If not for the need to replace the ship, said Ferdinand, Columbus would have been on his way to "reconnoiter the coast of Paria and cruise down it until he came to the strait" and so on his way to India, at last. (The discovery of the rumored strait, several thousand miles to the south, would have to wait for another eighteen years, until 1520, when Ferdinand Magellan, a Portuguese sailing for Spain, battling mutinies and rivals in a manner that Columbus would have recognized, finally reached it.)

Instead, Ferdinand said, Columbus sailed directly into a confrontation with Nicolás de Ovando, "the Knight Commander of Lares, governor of the island, who had been sent by the Catholic Sovereigns to hold an inquest into

Bobadilla's administration," just as Bobadilla had been sent to investigate Columbus.

Nicolás de Ovando, a decade younger than Columbus, was a son of the Extremadura. Bordering Portugal, this Spanish province served as the cradle of conquistadors—Vasco Núñez de Balboa, Hernán Cortés, Francisco Pizarro, Gonzalo Pizarro, Juan Pizarro, Hernando Pizarro, and Hernando de Soto—those soldiers of fortune, adventurers, conquerors, and narrow-minded visionaries who succeeded Columbus. All carried the region's affinity for the rigors of adventure and exploitation with them.

On the strength of his father's political connections, Ovando joined the Order of Alcántara, devoted to fighting infidels and obeying strict monastic vows. Distinguished by outstanding ability and loyalty, he had won the Sovereigns' appointment to succeed Columbus and reform the administrative shambles left by Francisco de Bobadilla. As governor, Ovando was charged with performing sweeping tasks: transfer powers of government from Columbus to the Spanish crown, establish the church, promote economic development, extend Spanish rule over all laborers and towns, and convert Indians to Christianity, which, in practice, meant teaching them to live as Spaniards in Hispaniola. Although his responsibilities were clear, the way to fulfill them was not. Many colonists, having been brought to Hispaniola by Columbus, remained loyal to the Admiral of the Ocean Sea, while others developed ties to their Indian wives and mistresses. The oppressive climate, the spread of disease, and the strangeness of the setting challenged Ovando. His legacy of making Hispaniola more Spanish than Spain consisted of constructing public buildings of stone, as well as an opulent stone palace for himself. Like Columbus and Bobadilla before him, he fell under the illusion that he ruled the island, and all its inhabitants, the moment he set foot there, so he banned the Admiral of the Ocean Sea.

The Admiral glumly summed up his situation: "I was commanded from Spain not to touch or land there." But land at Santo Domingo he did. It was Wednesday, June 29.

Columbus dispatched one of his captains, Pedro de Terreros, to Ovando, the knight commander, to convey the Admiral's respects and to explain that one of his ships had to be replaced, or lives would be endangered. Adding to the urgency of the situation, he warned of a "great storm" approaching the region, and for this reason if no other, "he wished to take shelter in port."

At the moment, the port was witnessing the final preparations of Bobadilla's convoy of ships bound for Spain. As Columbus knew, one of those ships, the fragile *Aguja*, carried his personal treasure. So he used the storm both as a pretext to return to Santo Domingo and supervise his personal wealth and to deliver a necessary warning. Drawing on his experience in judging weather, he advised Ovando "not to permit the homeward-bound fleet to sail for eight days because of the great danger."

Ovando stubbornly resisted Columbus's prudent, if self-interested, warning. He "would not permit the Admiral to enter the port," said Ferdinand, "much less would he detail the fleet that was homeward bound for Castile" even though the roster included such important personages as Francisco de Bobadilla and Francisco Roldán, "and all the other rebels who had done the Admiral so much hurt." If Ovando and the others had heeded Columbus's warning, matters would have turned out very differently. The fleet would have reached Spain only a few days later than planned. Instead, a calamity occurred.

Defying Columbus, Ovando ordered the fleet to depart, regardless of the storm warning. Ferdinand recorded that when the ships "reached the eastern end of Hispaniola, the storm assailed them with such fury that the flagship carrying Bobadilla and most of the rebels went down."

Columbus recalled the calamity with biblical intensity and resonance: "The storm was terrible, and on that night my fleet was broken up. Everyone lost hope and was quite certain that all the rest were drowned. What mortal man, even Job himself, would not have died of despair? Even for the safety of myself, my son, brother and friends, I was forbidden in such weather to put into land or enter harbors that I had gained for Spain by my own blood and sweat." Meanwhile, "*Gallega* lost her board and all lost a great part of their provisions." Despite these hazards, he noted in wonder, "the ship in which I was traveling, though amazingly storm-tossed, was saved by Our Lord and was completely unharmed." At times like these, Columbus felt singled out by the Lord, yet his salvation was not all that mysterious; he had wisely anchored in the lee of the shore. Even as the fleet's crew found deliverance from the storm, they experienced waves of "grief and chagrin" at being snubbed by the imperious Ovando. And if another disaster appeared on the horizon, "they could expect no aid from ashore." Stateless and unwanted, they were all on the way to becoming outlaws and buccaneers.

"By skill and good judgment he managed to keep the fleet together till the next day," Ferdinand continued, "when, as the storm gained in intensity and night came on with deep darkness, three ships were torn from their anchorages, each going its own way; and though all ran the same danger, each thought the others had gone down. . . . Still greater was the danger of the caravel *Bermuda*, which ran out to sea, where water washed over the deck—from which it is easy to understand why the Admiral wanted to trade her for another." Without Bartholomew, all agreed, the ship would have been lost.

The next day, the surviving ships in Columbus's fleet held a rendezvous in the port of Azua. "As each captain related his misfortune, it appeared that the Adelantado, experienced seaman that he was, had weathered the great storm by going out to sea, while the Admiral had saved his ship by lying close to shore, like a sage astrologer who foresaw whence the danger must come." Believing that he commanded the planets, the weather, and nature itself, the enemies of Columbus "charged that by his magic arts he had raised that storm to take revenge on Bobadilla and other enemies that were with him." In fact, he had relied on his instinct for survival and hard-won nautical experience to warn against the hurricane.

When it was over, the men, utterly drained, went fishing, "one of the pleasures offered by the sea in such time of idleness." The presence of natural splendor roused them from their misery, as did the sudden appearance of a giant manta ray gliding through the water on graceful fins tapered like a bird's: a marvelous fusion of locomotion and beauty. To Columbus's young son, the ray looked "as large as a medium-sized bed."

The crew of *Vizcaína* came upon the creature asleep on the ocean's surface and stabbed it with a harpoon "so it could not escape." They secured it to their launch with a rope, and "it drew the boat through the harbor as swiftly as an arrow." All the while, those aboard *Vizcaína*, "not knowing what went on, were astounded to see the boat running about without oars." The fun ended when the manta ray died and "was hauled aboard with tackling gear used for heavy objects."

Later, the men came upon a manatee, or sea cow. Ferdinand approached it cautiously. "It is not known in Europe," he stated. "It is as big as a calf and resembles one in taste and color, but it is better tasting and fatter." In its strangeness, the bulbous, glistening creature offered further proof that they had entered a world of mystery as well as danger.

By the middle of July 1502, one storm system after another was making up across the Caribbean Sea. It was hurricane season. Having completed repairs to his fleet, taken on supplies, and rested, Columbus and his men strained for the safer waters of Yaquimo, in today's Haiti, to ride out the storm. As soon as they departed on July 14, they "ran into such a flat calm that he could not hold his course, and the currents carried him to some small sandy islands near Jamaica." Ferdinand probably meant Morant Cays, sparsely vegetated islets rising from coral, beautiful to see but hazardous to navigate. Columbus called them the Puddles because "his men soon found enough water for their needs by digging puddles in the sand."

During a leisurely southerly swing off the coast of Honduras, Ferdinand warned, "the map-makers have not traveled in this part of the world." He continued, "They fall into a grievous error," when they depicted Cape Gracias á Dios as a separate landform from Cape Honduras, although in reality they were the same.

As Ferdinand realized, this erroneous depiction was a hoax designed to deprive his father of the fruits of his exploration. Two envious explorers, Juan Díaz de Solís and Vicente Yáñez Pinzón (who had commanded a ship on the Admiral's first voyage), set out in 1508 for Nicaragua, which the Admiral had considered so promising for exploitation. Reaching the islands off the coast of Honduras, which they knew as Guanajas, they ignored the advice given by one of their pilots, Pedro de Ledesma, who recognized the landforms because he had explored them with the Admiral. Instead, they falsely claimed they had arrived at another island for the first time.

Their assertion, backed by phony charts, fooled many, but not Ferdinand, who was determined to expose their conspiracy in his account of his father's life. In Ferdinand's words, the charts clearly "depict that island twice," in different locations. In the short run, there was nothing Columbus or his son could do to correct a deception occurring in such a remote and poorly understood region.

In Guanaja, Columbus sent reliable Bartholomew ashore with two skiffs; there they "encountered people who resembled those of the other islands, but they had narrower foreheads." Treading carefully among pine trees "and pieces of earth called *cálcide*, which the Indians use to cast copper," and which some of the men, mistaking it for gold, pocketed, they came upon a canoe as long as a galley, eight feet across, hollowed out from a single giant tree trunk. Ferdinand wrote that the canoe was "freighted with merchandise from the western regions around New Spain," an observation often taken to mean that Columbus's men had come across an artifact of the Aztec empire, then at its apogee during the reign of the ruler Ahuitzotl.

More likely, the Europeans confronted the highly advanced, complex Maya civilization. In China, Marco Polo had encountered a culture beyond his own; now Columbus faced a similar situation. The Maya were an ancient, hierarchical, deeply spiritual, militaristic society. Their civilization had highly developed mathematics, astronomy, architecture, and letters. They charted the movements of heavenly bodies in books fashioned from the bark of trees. In the years after 1000 BC, when Romans and Celts were struggling to dominate a fragmented and stunted western Europe, Maya civilization flourished in villages and cities. The Maya writing system recorded the deeds of leaders and their political conquests.

By AD 250, Maya civilization entered its Classic era, characterized by the rise of dynasties, whose deeds were recorded in symbolic characters, or glyphs. The Maya population and cities expanded rapidly until about AD 900, when the empire entered a steep, mysterious decline—not all at once, and not everywhere, but the downward trend gained momentum and became irreversible. The Maya collapse was accompanied by civil war, exhaustion of natural resources, prolonged drought, and other calamities. The populace nearly vanished from the face of the earth; during the collapse, the number of inhabitants in one region alone declined 99 percent, or even more. Where there were once millions of Maya, there were now only a few thousand tending to deteriorating edifices, many half-buried by sifting topography, whose origins were lost in the mists of legend. Columbus and his men saw the remnants of a great civilization. Compared with the Maya, he and his European crew hailed from a *New* World, and now they were encountering the *Old* among the Maya in Veragua.

Columbus's journals reveal that he had an inkling that he had stumbled across a powerful and ancient civilization, but ultimately the Maya failed to engage his interest for one overriding reason: they were not Chinese. The only aspects of the Maya that Columbus did appreciate were their seamanship and their long, agile, canoelike craft. Given their prowess on the water, it is worth asking why the advanced Maya did not discover Europe long before Columbus arrived on their shores. The answer has to do with the trade winds, which blow steadily south and west, defeating attempts to sail against them. Columbus benefited greatly from these prevailing winds, which at the same time kept Maya mariners hugging the shore.

The Spaniards paid close attention to the Maya watercraft. "Amidships it had a palm-leaf awning like that which the Venetian gondolas carry; this gave complete protection against the rain and waves. Under this awning were the children and women and all the baggage and merchandise. There were twenty-five paddlers aboard, but they offered no resistance when our boats drew up to them," said Ferdinand. The reception was especially welcome after the unpleasantness of Nicolás de Ovando and near extinction in the hurricane. When the flagship got close enough, Columbus offered "thanks to God for revealing to him in a single moment, without any toil or danger to our people, all the products of that country." Time and again on his voyages he had encountered fleeing Indians, deserted hamlets, and, on occasion, pots and skewers containing human body parts. This time, he had found the opulence he had sought for so long.

Columbus claimed the "costliest and handsomest things in that cargo: cotton mantles and sleeveless shirts embroidered and painted in different designs and colors; breechclouts of the same design and cloth as the shawls worn by women in the canoe, being like the shawls worn by the Moorish women of Granada; long wooden swords with a groove on each side where the edge should be, in which were fastened cord and pitch; flint knives that cut like steel; hatchets resembling the stone hatchets used by the other Indians, but made of good copper." The haul even included crucibles to melt copper.

One other item, mentioned only in passing by Ferdinand, was, if anything, even more valuable than the others: the cacao leaf. When a handful of dried cacao beans used for currency fell to the floor, he noted, "all the Indians squatted down to pick them up as if they had something of great value—their greed driving out their feelings of terror and danger at finding themselves in the hands of such strange and ferocious men as we must have seemed to be."

Columbus and his men were the first Europeans to behold the cacao, traditionally associated with trade and currency in the Americas. A thousand cacao beans could purchase a slave, for example, but beyond monetary value, the cacao itself was prized by the Maya, who called it *ka'kau* and believed it was discovered by the gods. The Spanish word *cacao* also derived from another Maya term, *chocol'ha*, or the verb *chokola'j*, meaning "to drink chocolate together." The Maya used cacao for a variety of medicinal and spiritual purposes; they roasted the beans, mixed them with spices and water, and heated the concoction until it was piping-hot chocolate. Among the Maya, drinking the brew was a privilege reserved for royalty, wealthy princes, shamans, and artists.

Chastened by the Sovereigns' disapproval of slavery, Columbus no longer regarded his dignified hosts as potential serfs and trophies to send to Spain, and his son considered them delegates of a remarkable, highly accomplished civilization. Impressed, Columbus "detained only one, an ancient named Yumbé, who seemed to be the wisest man among them and of greatest authority," who would reveal "the secrets of the land" and persuade his people to talk with the visitors from afar. Satisfied, Ferdinand reported that the elder served them "willingly and loyally." Too willingly, in fact. The more items Columbus displayed, according to Las Casas, "the more the Indians readily agreed that they knew where they were available simply because . . . to say so gave such pleasure, even when they had never before seen or heard of the things they were showing them and he was inquiring about." The Indians went so far as to include fantastic descriptions of "people who lived in the lands of which they spoke [who] had ships and lombards, bows and arrows, swords and cuirasses"—armor—"and anything else they saw the Christians had." Dazzled by the descriptions, Columbus fancied hearing accounts of horses, which were no more part of the landscape than unicorns. As they continued to talk, he misinterpreted their obliging descriptions to mean that he and his men were "only ten days' journey to the river Ganges"—the largest, holiest river in India.

He immediately wrote a report on his findings for the Sovereigns.

The reason for the misunderstanding, besides Columbus's overactive imagination and stubbornly held geographical misconceptions, was simple enough. "The whole conversation was conducted in sign language," in Las Casas's words. "And either the Indians were deliberately playing games with him, or he simply understood nothing of what they were trying to say and only heard what he wanted to hear."

On this basis, the Admiral was elated. Here at last was the "great wealth, civilization, and industry" he had promised his Sovereigns. He had been toying with the idea of returning to Cuba, to his way of thinking still a peninsula, not an island, but the opulence of the region persuaded him that he had found a trade route to India, so "he decided to continue with his search for a strait across the mainland that would open a way to the South Sea and the Lands of Spices." To Columbus, with his rigid yet mystical mind-set, this geographical impossibility seemed logical and in harmony with his interpretation of the Bible, the *Travels* of Marco Polo, and the authors of antiquity. At last everything was falling into place.

So he sailed on, said his son, "like one groping in the darkness."

To judge from his son's words, Columbus no longer assumed he was in Asia, but he believed he could locate a passage—over water, or, surprisingly, over land—leading there. Perhaps echoing the Admiral's rhetoric, Ferdinand grandly described it as the "doorway through which Spain entered upon the dominion of many seas." In search of this chimera, Columbus approached the coast of Honduras and "made for a point of the mainland that he called Caxinas from the name of a tree that grew there; this tree produces fruit resembling wrinkled olives with a spongy core," but on arrival, he found "nothing worthy of mention" with the exception of Indians, dressed, Ferdinand recalled, "like those in the canoe, in dyed shirts and breechclouts"—a loincloth with flaps in the front and back. "They also had thick quilted cotton jerkins like breastplates that were sufficient protection against their darts and even withstood some blows from our swords." The description strongly implied that some sort of conflict, perhaps hand-to-hand combat, had occurred between the Europeans and the Indians. Ferdinand refrained from saying anything critical about these Indians, but wrote about another group with foreboding, characterizing them as "ugly," "black," wearing no clothing, and "very wild in all respects." The fleet's captive Indian guide pointed out that they ate both human flesh and raw fish, and pierced holes in their ears large enough to insert hens' eggs.

By Sunday morning, August 14, 1502, Columbus felt safe enough to go ashore with the captains and a substantial complement of sailors. They celebrated Mass along a placid Honduran beach while Spanish banners fluttered in the humid ocean breeze. Whether or not the participants, the Admiral included, were aware of it, this was the first Mass to be heard on the American mainland, or, as Columbus insisted, in "India."

Three days later, the Admiral dispatched his brother and several launches to hear another Mass ashore and then "take formal possession of the land in the name of the Catholic Sovereigns." In recognition, if not comprehension, of the ceremony, "more than a hundred Indians bearing food came down to the shore; as soon as the boats had beached, they presented these gifts to the Adelantado," who, Ferdinand noted, "ordered them repaid with hawk's bells, beads, and other trifles." These Indians frightened the young Ferdinand as no others had. They communicated in unintelligible languages, and "they tattoo their arms and bodies by burning in Moorish-style designs that give them a strange aspect. Some display painted lions, others deer, others turreted castles." In honor of their pierced ears, Columbus called the region Costa de la Oreja, Coast of the Ear. Their faces, covered with white and red cloth, haunted Ferdinand's dreams. "They really look like devils," he insisted.

Bartholomew attempted to learn more about the region's resources. But his inexperienced interpreter, a native of Hispaniola, failed to comprehend the local language. At least the Indians took pleasure in the gifts from the visitors from afar, and repaid the hospitality the following day, when "more than two hundred others came to the same spot, bringing food of various kinds: chickens that were better-tasting than ours, geese, roast fish, red and white beans resembling kidney beans, and other commodities." The gifts echoed the land's abundance, its pumas, stags, and roe deer patrolling the hills, and its waters teeming with fish.

The Admiral led the fleet from the Honduran coast in an ordeal of beating to windward. Ferdinand reported that "it took them seventy days of sailing to make the sixty leagues from Point Caxinas to that Cape, now tacking toward the sea and again toward land, often gaining with the wind and as often losing, according to whether the wind was strong or weak when they came about."

Columbus recalled the passage as a prolonged test of both his maritime skills and his sanity. "I found myself going against the wind and terrible contrary current. Against them I struggled for sixty days, after which I barely managed to cover a little over seventy leagues. In all this time I did not enter any port, nor could I, nor did the storm from heaven leave me; rain, tremendous thunder and lightning came continuously so that it seemed like the end of the world." More than ever, he believed he was traversing a biblical universe of primordial awe. He took his trial at sea personally; the elements became mortal enemies, determined to claim the lives of everyone on board his ships. His suffering, coupled with piety, validated his discoveries.

> For eighty-eight days the frightening storm did not leave me, to the point that while at sea I saw neither sun nor stars to act as a guide; my ships were devastated, sails torn away, anchor, rigging, and cables lost, as were the boats and much of the provisions; the men were sick to death, all of them contrite, many vowing to devote themselves to religious life, and none neglected to make vows and promise to undertake pilgrimages. Many times they reached the point of making confessions to each other.
>
> Other storms had been experienced, but none ever lasted as long or had been as frightening. Many whom we considered courageous lost all hope time and again.

In the midst of the storm, facing a near-death experience, he was most concerned about the fate of at least one member of the fleet:

> Anxiety for my son, who was with me, wrung at my heart, the more so since I saw him so young, thirteen, struggling so long with such travails. Our Lord gave him such courage that he inspired the others, and he worked as if he had been sailing for fifty years. It was he who consoled me. I had taken ill, and at various times I reached the point of death; from a small cabin that I had ordered built on deck I was directing the course. My brother was in the worst and most dangerous ship. My anxiety was actually greater, because I had brought him with me against his will. Another sorrow lacerated the heart in my breast, and that was for my son Don Diego, whom I had left in Spain, almost an orphan.

On September 12, the fleet arrived at a cape, which Columbus named Gracias á Dios after the gratitude he experienced on deliverance from the storm. "If the coast had not had some good anchorages, it would certainly have taken us much longer to make that distance, but as it was clean and had two fathoms of depth half a league from shore," Ferdinand calmly recalled, "it was very easy to anchor at night or when the wind was slack." The younger Columbus's steady tone stood in contrast to his father's melodramatic recapitulation of events. The Admiral described how it felt to be pummeled in a storm, while the boy about whom he had so much anxiety related circumstances as they arose in a more or less realistic manner. The father was always lunging forward, into the storm, while the son stood back to contemplate it.

On September 16, in Ferdinand's words, "the Admiral sent the ship's boats toward a river that seemed to be deep and easy of entrance. But as they came out, the onshore wind having freshened, and the sea becoming heavy, such a surf built up at the mouth that one boat was swamped, and her crew drowned." Columbus named the unhappy stream in which two men had died Río de Desastres, as its banks were lined with "canes as thick as a man's thigh."

Nine days later, at an island named Quiribirí, the ships anchored tentatively before shaping a course to Cariay (most likely Puerto Limón), off the coast of Costa Rica, whose vistas made an indelible impression on the lad. "Here we found the best country and people that we had yet seen; because the land was high and abounded in rivers and great trees, and the island itself was very verdant, full of groves of lofty trees, palms," and a "great number of Indians, many armed with bows and arrows, others with palm-tree spears black as pitch and hard as bone and tipped with fish bones, and still others with *macanas* or clubs." With his customary composure, he added, "They seemed determined to resist our landing."

Columbus's men signaled that they came in peace rather than war, where-upon the Indians jumped into the water and swam out to the ships to "trade their weapons, cotton cloaks and shirts, and the *guanín* pendants which they hang about their necks." Volatile as ever, the Admiral refused on this occasion, preferring to demonstrate that he and his men "did not covet their possessions." To emphasize his point, he ordered presents from Spain to be distributed. The less interest the Europeans exhibited in trading, the more the Indians showed, and they boldly invited the visitors to go ashore by making signs and "holding up their cloaks like banners." But the Europeans, obeying the Admiral, stayed aboard ship, spoiling the fun. The Indians re-sponded by tying all the trinkets they had received into a neat bundle, which they left on the boat landing for the Spaniards to discover.

On September 25, on Cariay, said Columbus, "I stopped to repair the ships and replenish my victuals and rest the crews, which were very sick, and myself, having, as I said, been many times at the point of death." But he was not too sick to learn about the "gold mines of the region of Çiamba, which I was seeking. Two Indians led me to Carabarú, where the people went naked and wore a gold disk hanging from the neck, which they were unwilling to sell or trade." As mesmerized by gold as ever, Columbus forgot about his suf-fering at sea, and debriefed the Indians about gold and gold mines.

The Indians treated the Europeans with caution. "Thinking that we dis-trusted them, the Indians sent aboard an old Indian of venerable presence bearing a banner tied to a stick; two girls, one eight and the other fourteen years old, accompanied him," Ferdinand wrote. In reply, Columbus dis-patched a skiff to retrieve water from the mainland. Before they returned to the ship, "the Indians urged them by signs to take the girls." By all ac-counts, Columbus treated them well, ordering them to be clothed and fed, and then he sent them ashore, where they rushed into the welcoming arms of the Indian elder and more than fifty others. Later that day, the Indians returned all the gifts given to them by the Europeans, the hawk's bells and other knickknacks.

In the morning, Bartholomew and a scribe went ashore. As soon as he set foot on the boat landing, Indians took him by both arms and sat him down on the tall, whispering grass by the water's edge, in full view of the ships. He asked them a few questions, his amanuensis ready to record their replies, but "the Indians were so terrified by the sight of the pen and paper that most of them ran away. The reason was that they were afraid of being bewitched by words or signs."

And yet, said Ferdinand, "it was they who impressed us as being great sorcerers, but on approaching the Christians they scattered a certain powder in the air; they also burned this powder in censers and with these censers caused the smoke to go toward the Christians," not unlike the incense with which they were familiar. The Indians' reluctance to accept gifts struck Ferdinand as "evidence that they suspected us of being enchanters, confirming the adage that says a rogue sees himself in every other man." There *was* a spark of mutual recognition between the Indians and the Christians, who recognized the sophistication and intelligence—as well as the strangeness— of the other.

It was Sunday, October 2, the ships still anchored in the vicinity of Puerto Limón, when Columbus sent his indefatigable brother ashore once again, this time to "learn of the Indians' dwellings, customs, and mode of life."

Bartholomew and his party came across an amazing crypt, a "wooden palace" covered with cane, containing several tombs. One held a single corpse, "dried and embalmed"; another held two corpses, "with no bad odor, wrapped in cotton cloth: over each tomb was a tablet carved with figures of beasts, and on some the effigy of the dead man, adorned with many beads . . . and other things they most prize." This memento mori illustrated both the brevity of their temporal lives and the longevity of their spiritual horizons.

Columbus being Columbus, he honored the Indians' intelligence by capturing several "so that we might learn the secrets of the country," in Ferdinand's words. Out of seven seized, two were selected to act as guides. "The others he sent home with gifts in order not to throw the country into an uproar." Relying as usual on an interpreter, he explained that he needed their assistance to navigate the coast, promising to set them free at journey's end. The Indians misunderstood, and concluded, not unreasonably, that Columbus was holding them for ransom. The folly persisted into the next day, when a delegation of Indians presented the Europeans with "two native wild boars"—in all likelihood ugly, bristling peccaries, or New World pigs—"small but very savage," in exchange for their kinsmen. Although he refused to yield, he paid them for the "boars" and sent them home politely clutching the same useless gifts they had refused in the past.

The peccaries briefly distracted Columbus, who had become fascinated by the only slightly less bizarre spider monkey, the "size of a small greyhound, but with a longer tail, so strong that if one coils it about something, it holds it as tightly as if it were fastened with a rope," in Ferdinand's deft description. "These animals move about in the trees like squirrels, leaping from tree to tree and grasping the branches not only with their hands but also with their tails, by which they often hang for rest or for sport." Not knowing what to make of the agile, long-limbed spider monkeys, which are indigenous to the New World, Ferdinand called them "cats." Their playfulness led to cruel sport, which Ferdinand never forgot.

> A crossbowman brought one out of the forest that he had knocked down from a tree with a shaft, and because it was still so fierce that he dared not get near it, he cut off one of its legs with a knife. The sight of it scared a valiant dog we had on board but frightened even more one of those boars the Indians had brought, and it backed off in great fear; this surprised us because hitherto it had run at everybody on deck, including the dog. The Admiral then had boar and cat thrown together, whereupon the cat coiled his tail around the pig's snout, seized him by the neck with his remaining foreclaw, and bit him so that he grunted with fear. From this we concluded that these cats hunt other animals, like the wolves and greyhounds of Spain.

The balance of October 1502 passed in an overheated hallucination of voyaging.

October 5 . . . Zorobaró Bay "has three or four channels that are very convenient for getting in and out with every kind of wind. The ships sailed as if in streets between one island and another, the branches of trees brushing the rigging of the ships." Twenty canoes approach, with Indians "as naked as they came from their mothers' wombs," ready to trade gold for hawk's bells. . . .

October 7 . . . Columbus seizes two Indians who refuse to sell their gold mirrors to the Europeans. "The Indians are painted all over their face and body in different colors, white, black, and red." Pedro Ledesma, the pilot, experiences a more elaborate reception, according to Las Casas: eighty canoes, "each with a great deal of gold aboard," approach the Spanish fleet, but "the Admiral refused to take any of it."

Knowing the Admiral's obsession with gold, Las Casas scratched his head. Either the encounter with eighty gold-laden canoes never occurred, or the Admiral concluded their cargo and their message lacked legitimacy.

Within days, the Spaniards are on the move again.

October 17 . . . The Admiral sends boats ashore at the Chiriqui Lagoon, whereupon a hundred Indians rush into water up to their waists "brandishing spears, blowing horns, beating a drum, splashing water toward the Christians, and squirting toward them the juice of some herb that they were chewing." Once the Indians quiet down, Columbus's men trade for sixteen mirrors of pure gold worth 150 ducats. Elation overcomes them.

In the last days of October, Columbus and his men detected "signs of a building," by which Ferdinand meant an edifice made of stone rather than wood, cane, or thatch. For the Europeans, the presence of stone indicated an advanced civilization, in this case, the remnants of the Maya. The Maya's architectural accomplishments were all the more remarkable because, unlike Europeans, they did not use animal or water power to assist in construction; everything was done by hand.

Ferdinand compared the sturdy result to a "great mass of stucco" that "appeared to have been made of stone and lime." And the Admiral was so impressed that he "ordered a piece to be taken as a souvenir of that antiquity." Having found in the Maya a civilization worthy of the name, Columbus appeared on the brink of further study and encounters, but he preferred to search for the Chinese described by Marco Polo, and so he moved on.

On November 2, the fleet arrived at a harbor that Columbus called Puerto Bello, in Panama, "because it is very large, beautiful, thickly populated, and surrounded by cultivated country." Ferdinand extolled the setting, in which vessels could lie close to shore, yet slip away quickly. "The country about the harbor is well tilled and full of houses only a stone's throw or crossbow shot apart, all as pretty as a picture, the fairest thing one ever saw." Seduced by nature, the fleet tarried as rain and foul weather descended.

A week later, the sodden fleet resumed its course eastward, sighting fields of maize from the decks of their ships, and coming to rest in a cove, where the intruders terrified the locals, who frantically swam to safety. When the Europeans tried to catch up with a fleeing Indian and haul him aboard for sport, Ferdinand recalled that "he would dive like a waterfowl and come up a bowshot or two distant. It was really funny to see the boat giving chase and the rowers wearing themselves out in vain, for they finally had to return empty-handed."

In the torpor of heat and rain—temperatures averaged in the high eighties by day, with only a little cooling at night—they were losing track of time.

Suddenly it was November 23, and they were "repairing ships and mending casks"—this was when the coopers played their part—just before they called on Guiga, not far from the Isthmus of Panama, although the men had no idea that they found themselves on a strip of land separating two great oceans.

The sight of hundreds of Indians gathering on the shore, wearing gold pendants in their ears and noses, proved unnerving rather than welcoming. By Saturday, November 26, the fleet was under sail again, squeezing into a cramped harbor that the men called Retrete, that is, "closet," or possibly "toilet," "because it was so small that it would not hold more than five or six ships" negotiating an entrance barely more than seventy feet wide, "with rocks as sharp as the points of a diamond sticking up on either side." The vessels negotiating their way through had so little room that a man could easily jump from the deck to the shore.

"In this harbor we stayed nine days, with miserable weather," Ferdinand mournfully recalled. As before, Indians came to trade, but this time they observed sailors "sneaking ashore from the ships." The moment they saw the intruders, the Indians returned to their dwellings, as this "greedy and dissolute set of men committed innumerable outrages." The Indians lost patience, "and some fights occurred between the two sides" as the Indians circled the fleet trapped in the harbor's confines. Too late, "the Admiral tried to placate them by patience and civility," without success. To teach them a lesson, or, as Ferdinand put it, "to temper their pride and teach them not to scorn Christians," Columbus ordered his artillery to fire at a crowd of Indians on an exposed hilltop. The cannonball fell to earth among them, letting them know "that this thunder concealed a thunderbolt." This time, the show of force worked, and "after that, they hardly dared peep out at us from behind the hills."

In this incident, Las Casas saw the tragedy and folly of the Enterprise of the Indies, for which he blamed one man: Columbus. "Had these people been treated right from the moment they were discovered in a fashion both loving and just, as natural reason dictates they should have been," he explained, "and especially if this had been done in a Christian manner, we should have been able to obtain from these people all the gold and riches that they enjoyed in such profusion in exchange for our worthless baubles, and it is clear that there could have reigned between us such peace and love that their conversion to Christ would, as a consequence, have been both easy and certain." But once again, the Admiral had only made things worse.

Meanwhile, the harbor teemed with "large lizards or crocodiles that came out to sleep ashore and gave out an odor as strong as if all the musk"—popularly known as an aphrodisiac—"in the world were collected together." The sight was understandably unsettling, even terrifying. "They are so ravenous and cruel that if they find a man asleep they will drag him into the water to eat him, but they are cowardly and flee when attacked." The following night, the monsters and their stench returned, as they did each night.

Menaced by man and beast alike, Columbus fled northward on December 5, retracing his route.

"Never was seen more unsettled weather," Ferdinand insisted. "Now the wind was fair for Veragua; now it whipped about and drove us back to Puerto Bello. And just as we were most hopeful of making port, the wind would change again, sometimes with such terrible thunder and lightning that the men dared not open their eyes and it seemed the ships were sinking and the heavens coming down." At times, the booming thunder persisted to the point where "we were sure some ship of the fleet was firing signals for help." Torrential rains soaked the sails and swept the decks. Vicious storms occur regularly in this region, off the coast of Nicaragua, and survival itself was at stake. "All suffered greatly and were in despair, for they could not get even a half hour's rest, being wet through for days on end, sometimes running one way and sometimes another, struggling with all the elements and dreading them all." There was much to fear: "The fire in the lightning flashes, the air for its fury, the water for the waves, and the land for the reefs and rocks of that unknown coast, which sometimes rears up at a man near the port where he hopes to find shelter." But the sailors pressed on, his son trembling before nature's wrath, as Columbus attempted to give orders while struggling to preserve his sanity.

As if these terrors were not sufficient to defeat the fleet, a "waterspout"—Ferdinand's term for a small tornado—appeared on December 13, churning a deadly path between two ships. Catching sight of the funnel from the heaving deck of his ship, Ferdinand noted how "it raises the water up in a column thicker than a water butt, twisting it about like a whirlwind." The only defense was prayer: "Had the sailors not dissolved it by reciting the Gospel according to St. John, it would surely have swamped anything it struck."

As the tempest blew without respite, *Vizcaína* disappeared in the mist, forever, it was feared, until she reappeared "after three very dark and dangerous days, during which time she had lost her boat and once anchored near land, but had to cut her cable." She was safe, for now.

The hurricane had relented, but from within the bowels of her hull, the snakelike shipworms were slowly destroying her.

Even a spell of calm weather, when it finally came "after the fleet had been half destroyed by the battering storm," brought a new menace. A swirl of shadows beneath the rippling surface of the sea coalesced into a school of sharks—probably specimens of the Caribbean reef shark (*Carcharhinus perezi*). *Los tiburones* surrounded the ships and terrorized the superstitious sailors, who considered them the vultures of the sea and portents of death.

"These beasts seize a person's leg or arm with their teeth and cut it off as clean as with a knife because they have two rows of saw-like teeth," Ferdinand noted in revulsion. The sailors killed as many of the streamlined predators as possible, yet "they still followed us by making turns in the water." He was referring to what is now known as a shark threat display, exhibited by sharks sensing danger. When making the display, they exaggerate their usual movements. The gray reef shark, for instance, plunges its rigid fins downward, arches its back, and lashes its tail to the side, swimming in a pattern resembling a figure eight. Sharks behaving in this manner are preparing either to strike or flee.

So ravenous were these sharks, Ferdinand recalled, that they ate carrion, and "one can catch them by simply attaching a piece of red cloth to the hook." Their voracious greed exceeded his nightmares. "Out of one shark's belly I saw a turtle taken that afterward lived on the ship." Another slain shark yielded an entire shark's head previously discarded by the men "because the head, unlike the rest of the body, is not good to eat." Yet the shark had devoured it. Even though the slithering monsters repelled the men, "all did the shark the honor of eating it, for by that time we had been over eight months at sea and had consumed all the meat and fish that we had brought from Spain." The blood, the slime, the foam, the stench, the ships rolling and pitching on the heaving seas: it made a man ravenous and nauseous at the same time. What little food they had caused them to retch in disgust. "What with the heat and the dampness even the biscuit was so full of worms that, God help me, I saw many wait until nightfall to eat the porridge made of it so as not to see the worms; others were so used to eating them that they did not bother to pick them out, for they might have lost their supper by being so fastidious."

Deliverance came on December 17, when the fleet reached Puerto Gordo,

Panama. "In this harbor, resembling a great channel, we rested for three days."

The men staggered ashore, weak from the ordeal, to gaze at a new marvel. "The people here lived in the tops of trees, like birds; their cabins or huts were built over frames of poles placed across branches." The men could not explain the phenomenon, and decided it was a response to "their fear of griffins"—mythical beasts with an eagle's head and wings attached to a lion's body. Or maybe living on raised frames had a simpler explanation, as a precaution against a rival group.

By December 20, the fleet was under sail once again, but "hardly had we put out to sea when the winds and storms returned to vex us, so that we were forced to enter another harbor." Three days later, Columbus judged conditions safe enough for the fleet to try again, "but the weather, like an enemy that lies in wait for a man, suddenly attacked us." The blasts drove the helpless vessels back to the harbor where they had sought refuge on December 12. As Christmas approached, the men occupied themselves with repairs to *La Gallega* and loading maize, wood, and water, when their stomachs craved meat and wine. On January 3, 1503, the fleet put to sea once more, only to encounter "foul weather and contrary winds that actually grew worse each time the Admiral altered his course."

The Admiral took his storms personally; they were contests with cosmic forces, in which he was bound to go mano a mano with the elements. He would not have been surprised to behold a spiteful angel emerge from a massive cumulonimbus, detonating with thunder and lightning, prepared to wrestle him to the bottom of the sea.

"For nine days I was lost with no hope of life," he recalled.

Eyes never saw the sea so rough, so ugly, or so seething with foam. The wind did not allow us to go ahead or give us a chance of running, nor did it allow us to shelter under any headland. There I was held in those seas turned to blood, boiling like a cauldron on a mighty fire. The skies had never looked more threatening. For a day and a night they blazed like a furnace, and the lightning burst in such flashes that every moment I looked to see whether my masts and sails had not been struck. They came with such terrifying fury that we believed the ships would be utterly destroyed. All this time water fell unceasingly from the sky. One cannot say it rained, for it seemed like a repetition of the Deluge. The crews were now so broken that they longed for death to release them from their martyrdom. The ships had already twice lost their boats, anchors, and rigging and were stripped bare of their sails.

On January 6, the battered fleet came to rest in today's Panama off the mouth of a river that Columbus chose to name Río Belén, an abbreviation for Bethlehem. After three days of ambiguous encounters with Indians and fruitless expeditions in search of gold, *La Capitana* (Columbus's flagship) and *Vizcaína* rode the flood tide over the bar and proceeded up the Río Belén. The sight of the strange ships summoned droves of Indians peddling their fish with all the vigor of the dockside merchants of Genoa or Seville. Ferdinand was astonished to learn that the fish swam *upstream* to meet their fate. Cadging a little gold wherever he could find it, Columbus gave over hawk's bells and strings of beads for samples of the precious metal. The next day, the other two ships in the fleet crossed the bar, and, with his forces massed, the Admiral prepared to claim what he believed was gold hidden in the mines of Veragua.

"On the third day after our arrival the Adelantado took the boats down the coast and ascended the river to the village of the Quibián," wrote Ferdinand, "which is the name those Indians give to their king." Learning of visitors from afar, the Quibián immediately came downstream with his canoes to greet them. The result was perhaps the most decorous initial contact of the entire voyage: "They treated each other with much friendship and civility, each giving the other the things he most prized; and after they had conversed for a long while, the Adelantado and the Quibián each went their own way very peacefully." The next day, the sociable cacique returned to greet the Admiral himself aboard the flagship, where they chatted for an hour without rivalry or rancor.

Then, on Tuesday, January 24, a storm broke. Moments before, the Spaniards had been feeling calm and secure, but now, in the deluge, the Río Belén overwhelmed its banks. "Before we could prepare for or run a hawser ashore," Ferdinand wrote breathlessly, "the fury of the water struck the flagship with such force that she broke one of the two cables and drove with such force against *Gallega*, which lay astern, that the blow carried away her bonaventure mizzen"—the short, lateen-rigged fourth mast. "Then, fouling one another, they drifted so as to be in great peril of going down with all hands." If they sank, all would be lost, and both Columbus and his son would go down with them.

Eventually the ships managed to untangle themselves, and they floated down the river to the sea. "So violent a storm raged there that the fleet would have been shattered to pieces at the mouth of the river." There was nothing to do but wait, and pray. The outcome vindicated Columbus's risky decision not to seek refuge at sea, where disaster lurked.

When the skies cleared several days later, he assigned his brother Bartholomew "to settle and conquer the land." Columbus would give up his search for a strait leading to India in mid-voyage to return to Spain and his Sovereigns. The abruptness of the decision suggested that he was far sicker than anyone—even his son—realized, and he desired above all to return to Spain to recover, or die in the attempt.

CHAPTER 12

Castaways in Paradise

By February 6, Bartholomew was leading a complement of sixty-eight men in rowboats along the coast to the mouth of the Río Veragua, west of the Río Belén, up the river to the Quibián's village, where they spent a day resting from their labors and inquiring about the way through the jungle to the gold mines. The Quibián obligingly sent guides to show them the route, and within hours of their arrival, the men were collecting gold, many of them for the first time in their lives. That night they returned to their ships, feeling tired, content, and rich.

The men later learned that the promising mines they had visited were not in Veragua, as they had assumed, but in Urirá, a neighboring province at war with Veragua. "The Quibián had guided the Christians there to annoy his enemies," and, even worse, "in the hope that Christians would go to that country and quit his own," said Ferdinand. The stately, civil Quibián was capable of more guile than the Europeans realized, and began to plot against them.

As Columbus prepared to return to Spain, his brother the Adelantado undertook yet another expedition in search of gold. With the exception of the sleight of hand concerning the gold mines, the Europeans were treated as ambassadors or honored guests wherever they went rather than as dreaded or reviled conquerors. By February 24, they had ventured so far inland that Bartholomew became concerned; he had wandered too far from the ships, and decided to retrace his route.

Along the way, and almost as an afterthought, so casually did Ferdinand mention it, the Adelantado—Bartholomew Columbus—laid the basis for a new European settlement, the first in the region. Divided into eight groups of ten, the men "set about building houses on the banks of the Río Belén about a lombard shot from its mouth, beyond a gully that comes down to the river, at the foot of which there is a little hill," Ferdinand recalled. Step by step, building by building, the Spanish empire extended into Central America (not that Veragua was recognized as such at the time). Before long, "ten or twelve houses" emerged in the jungle. They were no match for the sophisticated edifices of the Maya, but they offered proof that the Europeans who fashioned them were there to stay. "Besides these houses, which were of timber and thatched with the leaves of palm trees that grow on the shore, they built a large house for use as a storehouse and arsenal, in which they placed many pieces of ordnance, powder, and foodstuffs." However, "the necessities of life, such as wine, biscuit, garlic, vinegar, and cheese, being all the Spanish food they had," were stored aboard *La Gallega* for maximum security. Columbus intended to leave the ship for the Adelantado's use.

Catching his breath, Ferdinand recorded his on-the-fly impressions of Veragua's Indians, the curious way they turned their backs when they spoke to each other; their habit of incessantly chewing an herb ("We decided that must be the cause of their rotten teeth"); the way they caught fish with hooks "sawed out of tortoise shell" and then wrapped the fish in leaves to dry.

As his impressions of Indian customs accumulated, the young Ferdinand came to regard his hosts from a very different perspective than that of his father. The Admiral appraised the Indians' abilities, trying to be as utilitarian as he could, assessing their tactical value, fitness for conversion to Christianity, and usefulness. Ferdinand was simply in awe of their gracefulness and mastery of their environment, and quite unlike his father, never forgot that he was in their homeland, rather than the other way around. In his descriptions, they had a way of materializing and disappearing without warning, usually benign, occasionally sly, always cloaked in mystery. To the young man, they were *Indians*, not potential slaves or in need of conversion. They were already complete.

Europeans in Veragua lived by its waterways, and, Ferdinand discovered, died by them. "The river, which had before placed us in grave peril by flooding, now placed us in an even worse plight by a sharp drop in water level," he grimly observed. "The reason was that the January rains having ceased, the mouth of the river became so choked up with sand that instead of four fathoms, which had barely permitted our entrance, there was only half a fathom of water over the bar. We thus found ourselves trapped and without hope of relief." Hauling the ships over the sand to the ocean was out of the question, and "even had we the equipment to do it, never was the sea so quiet but that the least wave could break a ship to pieces against the shore—especially ships like ours that were already like honeycombs, riddled through and through with shipworm." All the men could do was pray for rain, which, in sufficient quantities, would float the ships over the bar to open water.

They preferred risking the hazards of the ocean to those on land, where their onetime ally the Quibián, "greatly offended that we had settled on that river," now "planned to set fire to the houses and kill the Christians." In retaliation, the Spaniards would spirit the Quibián and "all the leading local citizens" away to Castile, and make sure those who remained behind "accepted the overlordship of the Christians."

As unrealistic as his plan to double-cross the cacique sounds, Columbus's men counted on their horses, their dogs, and most of all their firearms to prevail. And so the scene was set for another confrontation between the righteous Christians and the threatened Indians.

On March 30, the Adelantado set out with seventy-four men to a hamlet in Veragua to confront the Quibián. From his hillside hut, the cacique warned the Spaniards away. He did not want his kin seeing him with the outsiders, nor did he want the outsiders violating the sanctity of his home. To discourage the cacique from fleeing, Bartholomew arrived with a detachment of only five men. What could be the harm in that? The other Europeans, meanwhile, lurked in the jungle in widely spaced pairs, ready to spring a trap. "Having come within a musket shot of the house, they were to surround it and allow no one to escape." It was an absurd exercise, trying to place Indians under house arrest in their own village, but Bartholomew proceeded with a stubbornness worthy of his brother. As he approached the hut, "the Quibián sent word that the Adelantado must not enter the house, that although he was suffering from an arrow wound, he himself would come out to speak with him. He did this to keep the Christians from seeing his wives, for the Indians are very jealous. So he came out and sat down in the doorway, saying that the Adelantado might approach, and this the Adelantado did, telling the other Christians to attack as soon as he had grasped the Quibián by the arm."

With scores of his men lurking just out of sight, Bartholomew feigned concern for the cacique's injured arm, reaching for it, and holding it tightly until his complement of four Spaniards ran to the hut to take the Quibián hostage. "Thereupon the fifth man fired off his gun, and all the Christians rushed out of their ambush and surrounded the house." Within, they found fifty Indians, whom they captured without inflicting a single wound. The number included the Quibián's wives and children. The sight of their chieftain taken prisoner paralyzed the other Indians, who, rather than resisting, "offered a rich ransom for their freedom, saying they would give us a great treasure that was hidden in a nearby wood." The Adelantado was having none of it, and brusquely ordered the Quibián, his wives, children, and followers to confinement aboard the ships before other Indians could effect a rescue. ("This was one among several great deeds accomplished that day and in that place by the commander," Las Casas commented sarcastically.) As the Indians departed, Bartholomew and his men stayed behind to pacify the Quibián's allies and family.

The Spaniards' plan began to come apart when the men debated who should accompany the dozens of captive Indians to the ships waiting at the river's mouth. In the end, said Ferdinand, responsibility fell to Juan Sánchez of Cadiz, the fleet's highly regarded chief pilot. He offered to take the cacique "bound hand and foot."

The Adelantado agreed, admonishing the pilot to keep the Quibián secure at all times. If the cacique escaped, Sánchez vowed to "permit the hairs of his beard to be plucked out one by one." With that, he went down the river with the Quibián under close watch. When they neared the mouth of the river, the cacique started to complain that his restraints were painful. Taking pity on him, Sánchez loosened all the ropes binding the captive except for those tying his hands.

Carefully watching his captor, the Quibián chose a moment when the pilot's attention wandered, and jumped overboard. The rope tying the two men together tugged so powerfully at Sánchez that he was forced to let go in order not to be pulled to his death by the fugitive cacique. "By this time it was dark, and the other prisoners made such a racket that the Christians could neither hear nor see the cacique swim ashore, and he vanished like a stone fallen in water." The Quibián had escaped into the night as Sánchez realized to his chagrin that he had violated his oath. If the hairs of his beard were actually plucked out, no mention was made of it.

Determined and fearless, the Adelantado roamed the lush hills in search of escaped Indians. By April 1, he was having doubts. The populace had abandoned the countryside; empty huts lay scattered about the hills like silent sentinels. Even he acknowledged that it might be difficult to return home safely if attacked, but he made it back to the waiting ships without losing anyone. He presented Columbus with "about 300 ducats' worth of booty in gold mirrors and eagles, gold twists that the Indians wear around the arms and legs, and gold cords that they wear about their heads in the manner of coronets." The men set aside the fifth part, owed to the Sovereigns, and "divided the rest among members of the expedition, giving the Adelantado one of the crowns as a token of victory"—a victory that would prove worthless.

For now, fortune favored the Admiral's cause. The rains returned, summoned, the men believed, by their fervent prayers, and swelled the river to the point where the ships could clear the bars and sail into the ocean. Columbus seized the opportunity to begin the inbound voyage with three ships "to be able to send to the settlement as quickly as possible"—a settlement that consisted of only eight or ten dwellings, a handful of men, and countless Indians waiting to overwhelm them. The Admiral gave every indication of resorting to the dubious strategy he had adopted during the first voyage to guarantee himself a second voyage: stranding a small number of men, vulnerable, ill equipped, and of wavering loyalty, in the midst of a hostile wilderness, and so requiring eventual rescue.

Although Columbus had repeatedly shown masterful command of the Atlantic, resulting in swift, safe crossings, the ships seemed to be in constant peril from the start, and the men had to load and then unload the ballast to lighten the ships sufficiently to skim pass the shifting sandbars. Even Ferdinand, who placed all his trust in his father's seamanship, began to have doubts. When "we reached the open coast," he recalled, "a league from the mouth of the river, and were about to depart, God put it into the Admiral's mind to send the flagship's boat ashore to take on a supply of water . . . whereby the boat was lost but many men were saved both on land and sea." What could his father have been thinking?

After this lapse in judgment, things were never the same.

"When the Indians and the Quibián saw that the caravels had sailed," Ferdinand wrote, "and we could not help the men who remained behind, they attacked the Christian town at the very time the ship's boat was approaching the shore. The dense woods allowed the Indians to creep up unobserved to within fifty feet of the huts; they attacked with loud cries, hurling darts at every Christian they saw." Stunned, Columbus's men fought back for their lives, led by Bartholomew, who had increasingly filled the leadership void left by his infirm brother.

Seizing a lance, the Adelantado, having found new sources of courage, charged the Indians, who retreated into the forest bordering their dwellings.

Both sides hurled their darts, or spears, at the other, as if "in a game of jousts," Ferdinand commented. The Spaniards repelled the Indians "by the edge of the sword and by a dog who pursued them furiously." The toll: "one Christian dead and seven wounded, one being the Adelantado, who received a dart wound in the chest." But he would survive.

Ferdinand, close to the action, appeared satisfied with the outcome, but Las Casas sputtered with rage as he considered this latest example of Spanish barbarism: "As ever, it is the poor naked and defenseless Indians who come off the worse while the Spaniards are free to butcher them with their swords, lopping off their legs and arms, ripping open their bellies, and decapitating them, and then setting their dogs on them to hunt them down and tear them to shreds." Las Casas might have been grimly satisfied to note that the Indian darts later claimed many Spanish victims attempting to flee the warriors in their canoes. One of the survivors, a cooper from Seville named Juan de Noya, escaped by swimming underwater to the riverbank, running to safety in the jungle, and eventually reaching the tiny European settlement, where he warned the others about the attack and casualties. "At this news, our men were beside themselves with fear," said Ferdinand. They were vastly outnumbered, many of their comrades were dead, and "the Admiral was at sea without a boat and unable to send them aid."

They had no choice but to flee the settlement before they, too, were killed. "They would have done this, too, in a disorderly, mutinous fashion, if not prevented by the closing of a river through the onset of bad weather." They could not launch the caravel set aside for them, and "they could not even send a boat to inform the Admiral of what happened because the sea broke so heavily over the bar." They were stranded, castaways in paradise. The "India" that Columbus had sought so eagerly, and explored so thoroughly, had ensnared him. With no seaworthy ship, and no prospect of rescue, they were bound to perish in utter obscurity. In desperation, they resorted to mutiny, "crowding into the ship with the intention of making their way out into the open sea, only to find their way blocked by a sandbank." The rough, buffeting seas prevented their sending a vessel to Columbus with a message.

The Admiral was also imperiled, anchored off an extremely rocky coast, without a ship's boat, and with his force decimated by the Indians. Worse, the Spaniards stranded on land experienced the anguish of seeing the corpses of their compatriots float downstream, pierced with gaping wounds. In the stormy skies overhead, crows and vultures, "all of them croaking and wheeling about," swooped down to feast on the corpses "as though possessed."

Meanwhile, Ferdinand wrote, the men quietly moved to a "large cleared space on the eastern bank of the river," where they constructed a makeshift fort from casks and pieces of artillery. The structure did its job, and the Indians, terrified of the cannonballs, kept their distance.

The thunderstorm took its toll on Columbus, who experienced the roaring wind and sickening swells as apocalyptic manifestations, all of it made worse by the fear that the Indians had killed the men he had left behind. All the while he remained confined to the captain's cabin, hardly more than a closet, too weak and ill to mount a struggle against his adversaries and the elements.

Recalling the trauma for the benefit of Ferdinand and Isabella, who could only have considered him mad as they listened to his account, he described how his predicament worsened with every flash of lightning. "My brother and the rest of the crew were on a ship that remained inside [the bar] while I alone was outside, off a wild coast with a high fever, laid so low that all hope of recovery was gone."

Finally, the incredible occurred; aboard the flagship *La Capitana* Columbus heard a voice from heaven, designating him the recipient of new scripture:

In such a state of torment, I got up to the highest part of the ship, calling for help with a frightened voice, crying, and with great intensity invoking to the four winds the succor of Your Highnesses' captains of war, but no one ever responded. Overcome by weariness, I fell asleep moaning. I heard a merciful voice saying,

"O fool, O man to believe in and serve your God, the God of all, what more did He do for Moses or David, His servants. From birth He always took great care of you; when He saw you were of an age that seemed right to Him, He caused your name to resound marvelously throughout the world. The Indies, that part of the world that is so rich, He gave to you; you divided them as you thought best, and He permitted you to do so. To you He gave the keys to open the barrier of the Ocean Sea, which were closed with such strong chains; you were obeyed in so many countries and this acquired such glorious fame among all Christians. . . ."

As if in a swoon I listened to it all but could make no reply to words so certain, and I could do nothing but weep for my errors. He who was speaking to me, whoever He was, ended thus:

"Fear not, have faith."

It is unclear whether Columbus actually reached the "highest part" of his ship. His son, among others, mentioned his inability to leave his cabin. Perhaps he scaled these heights in his imagination. No matter what his location, he believed he had heard the voice of God.

In Columbus's telling, his faith was rewarded nine days later, on April 15, when the weather cleared sufficiently to rally the survivors of the massacre and the storm for one last voyage. Despite everything, he remained determined to return to Spain, offering this justification: "I would have stayed with everyone to garrison the colony if I had had a way to inform Your Highnesses." Having made his apologies to the distant Sovereigns, he left "on Easter night"—April 16. Ravaged by shipworms, his fleet was no longer seaworthy. He abandoned fragile *La Gallega* at Belén, and would soon forsake *Vizcaína* just before she broke up. "That left only two, in the same condition as the others, without boats or provisions, to cross 7,000 miles of sea and water or else to die along the way with a son, brother, and so many men," he lamented. To those who would dare to second-guess Columbus's decisions, he replied: "I would like to have seen them on this voyage!"

While Columbus underwent his catharsis, emerging with his faith intact, the situation aboard *Bermuda* rapidly deteriorated. Cowering in the fetid hold were the wives, children, and other relatives of the Quibián, the cacique who had freed himself from his fetters and escaped his guard, Juan Sánchez. They, too, resolved to escape.

One night, the sailors who slept on deck neglected to secure the hatch cover with chains. Below, the Indians gathered the ship's ballast, loose stones, into a mound. Balancing precariously on it, they pushed their shoulders against the underside of the hatch, sending the sailors asleep on it sprawling, and quickly, before the other Europeans aboard ship could react, several of their leaders climbed out and leaped to freedom. When they awoke and realized what had happened, the sailors closed the hatch, this time with a chain, and realized they had better not fall asleep again while on watch.

The Indians below deck lost all hope of regaining their freedom. They might drown or suffocate, far from their ancestral lands. In despair, they gathered ropes and, one by one, hanged themselves from the deck beams, "bending their knees because they had not enough headroom to hang themselves properly," said Ferdinand. By the time they were discovered, it was too late to rescue them.

Ferdinand callously assumed that "their death was no great loss to us of the fleet, but seriously worsened the plight of the men ashore." He believed that holding the Quibián's children hostage had kept the cacique at bay, but now that their hostages had killed themselves, the Europeans on land and sea were vulnerable to retaliation by the Indians. The Admiral's son lamented not the deaths of the Indians but these "misfortunes and vexations, with our lives hanging by the anchor cables, and ourselves completely in the dark on the state of affairs ashore." Given the way the hardhearted Spaniards treated the innocent captives on their ship, it was hardly surprising that the Indians onshore responded in self-defense.

As the siege continued on land, the Spaniards realized that the men trapped in the makeshift fort had to be rescued, or they would be murdered. A few able-bodied seamen offered to be rowed in the boat—now the sole remaining launch for the entire fleet—that would take them to the bar. Columbus had little choice but to "accept the offer," and *Bermuda*'s boat took them to "within a musket shot of land; closer than that they could not come because of the waves that broke on the beach." Upon reaching this point, Pedro de Ledesma, the pilot from Seville, "boldly leapt overboard and swam across the bar to the settlement." On arrival, he listened to the men stranded there beg for deliverance from their "hopeless situation; they begged the Admiral to take them aboard, for to leave them behind was to condemn them to death." Some threatened mutiny; they were prepared to steal a canoe from the Indians and return to the ships that way, if need be, preferring to "risk their lives in this way rather than wait for death at the hands of those cruel butchers, the Indians."

Considering the pitiful story brought back by Ledesma and the others, together with the threat of mutiny, the Admiral softened a bit, and decided he would grant their pleas, even if it meant "lying off the coast with no possibility of saving them or himself if the weather grew worse." After eight days "at the mercy of the prow cables," by which Ferdinand meant that a single anchor stood between the ship and disaster, the weather lifted, and the stranded Europeans began to "transport themselves and their gear over the bar, using their single boat and two large canoes lashed together so as not to overturn." The transfer took two agonizing days, after which "nothing remained ashore, except the worm-eaten hulk of *Gallega*."

Relieved to the point of euphoria, the survivors set sail on April 16, 1503, on an easterly course along the coast. A navigational dispute arose. The pilots, relying on their crude charts, believed that Hispaniola lay to the north, whereas the Columbus brothers "knew it was necessary to sail a good space along the coast before crossing the sea that lies between the mainland and Hispaniola." Their decision prompted ominous grumbling among the sailors, convinced that "the Admiral intended to sail a direct route to Spain with unfit and ill-provisioned ships."

The tiny fleet held its course until returning to Puerto Bello, where "we had to abandon *Vizcaína* because she was drawing much water and because her planking was completely riddled by shipworms." Retracing the fleet's route, the remaining ships, *La Capitana* and *Bermuda*, bypassed Retrete, and the Archipelago of Las Mulatas—130 miles east of Puerto Bello—to sail toward a mottled promontory that Columbus called Marmóreo, Portuguese for "marbled."

Propelled by the trades, excused from misfortune for the moment, Columbus's diminished fleet reached Cape Tiburón, Colombia, on May 1, and stood northward, "with winds and currents easterly, always endeavoring to sail as close to the wind as possible." Again, the pilots tried to tell the volatile Admiral "that we had passed eastward of the Caribbee Islands, but the Admiral feared he would not be able to fetch Hispaniola." On May 10, a Wednesday, they espied tiny islands swarming with turtles—"as was all the sea thereabout, so that it seemed to be full of little rocks"—and named them Las Tortugas, now the Cayman Islands, which they soon put to stern.

May 13 found Columbus approaching Cuba in a desperate state. Ferdinand catalogued their miseries: "As we lay here at anchor, ten leagues from Cuba, suffering greatly from hunger because we had nothing to eat but biscuit and a little oil and vinegar, and exhausted by working three pumps day and night to keep the vessels afloat (for they were ready to sink from the holes made by the shipworms), there came on at night a great storm in which *Bermuda*, being unable to ride it out, fouled us and broke our stem"—the foremost part of the hull—"nor did she get off whole, but smashed her stern into the helm." In the midst of wind and rain lashing the masts, sail, and rigging, while the ships rode heaving seas, the men managed to separate the two ships before they did more damage.

The storm had strained the cables running to the anchors to the limit. In the morning, the crew found only a single strand intact. If the storm had lasted just an hour longer, the men estimated, that strand would have parted, and the hull would have smashed into the rocks. But the ship held on by this slender thread. "It pleased God to deliver us then," Ferdinand gratefully noted.

*   *   *

Throughout the storm, Columbus appeared to be in command of his faculties, but a letter that he wrote weeks later confirmed his pilots' misgivings. He was half-mad, half-blind, and hearing voices. His biblically inspired geography insisted that he had, in his words, "reached the region of Mango, near Cathay." Somehow he would have to find Hispaniola from that illusory location.

He fought on. If only he could reach a more northerly latitude, he could catch the trades to Spain and safety, but, he admitted, "the rough sea had the upper hand, and I had to turn back without sail. I threw out anchor at an island where I lost three anchors at a single stroke, and at midnight, when it seemed the world was about to disappear, the cables of the other ship gave way and it bore down on me, so that it was a wonder that we were not dashed into splinters; it was the anchor and the way it held that, after God, saved me."

When the weather lifted slightly, the fragile fleet returned to the open sea, but, Columbus wailed, "with all the rigging lost, the ships more riddled with shipworms than a honeycomb, and the crew so frightened and depressed, I got a little farther than I had before." Foul weather forced him to return to another harbor in the island he had just left—it is difficult to specify which island, because Columbus thought he was approaching China—where he languished for eight anxiety-ridden days, at last reaching Jamaica by the end of June, "always with contrary winds and with the ships in worse condition than ever." The vessels took on water so quickly that even with three pumps operating, the crew could not prevent the water from rising; they resorted to bailing water with kettles and tubs, all to no avail. The ships appeared headed for certain disaster.

His misery was so intense, and prospects for surviving from one day to the next so uncertain, that as his ships nosed their way toward Hispaniola, he confessed, "I wished I had never set out." The conditions were the most adverse that he had endured during his years in the Caribbean. "The other ship, half-submerged, hastened to find a harbor. I struggled against the sea in the midst of the storm. As my ship sank Our Lord miraculously brought me to land." He stopped scratching his pen to reflect, "Who could believe what I am writing?"

Paraphrasing Marco Polo's celebrated remark that his *Travels* did not contain even half of all that had occurred to him, Columbus claimed, "In this letter, I have reported but a hundredth of what happened. Those who were with the Admiral can bear witness to it." Even if much of the tumult had occurred in his mind, it was nonetheless overwhelming.

* * *

In these dire conditions, Columbus changed course once again. Now the fleet stood for Jamaica because, Ferdinand explained, "the easterly winds and strong westward-running currents would have never let us make Hispaniola—especially since the ships were so riddled by shipworms." The crew continued to work the three pumps morning, noon, and night, but by Midsummer Day's eve, June 23, "the water in our ship rose so high that it was almost up to the deck." The men clung to a floating wreck, capable of only rudimentary navigation. But the instinct to survive drove them on against overwhelming odds. "With great toil we continued in this state until daybreak when we made a harbor in Jamaica named Puerto Bueno" on the northern coast, later called Dry Harbour.

From the deck of his sinking ship, the broad harbor appeared benign, but no source of fresh water was apparent, nor did they see an Indian village where they could replenish themselves. Risking one more day aboard the flimsy ship, Columbus sailed eastward to a haven that he named Santa Gloria, now St. Ann's Bay, a sequence of shallow bay, alluvial fan, and marsh. Approaching the shore, Columbus and his men beheld aromatic cedar, rosewood, ebony, mahogany, palmetto palm, coconut palm, and blue mahoe, which grows to sixty feet, whose wood contains blue, green, and yellow tints and whose flowers change color from yellow to orange to dark red. Through the trees, the men caught sight of showy parrots, iridescent hummingbirds, and cuckoos. Plump little todies, similar in shape to kingfisher birds, with green wings and crimson gorgets, flitted nervously from branch to branch.

The crew angled the boats toward the beach. "Since we were no longer able to keep the ships afloat, we ran them ashore as far as we could, grounding them both close together board and board, and shoring them up on both sides so they could not budge." When beached, the ships were nearly swamped at high tide, but they were alive and safe—for now.

Having exhausted their usefulness at sea, the ships became makeshift fortresses. On the fore and stern castles, the exhausted men cobbled together cabins, "making our position as strong as possible so the Indians could do us no harm; for at that time the island was not yet inhabited or subdued by Christians." A sense of loneliness and stillness descended, relieved only by the fluttering wind, the muffled crash of distant surf, and faint birdcalls. Stranded in these rotting structures only a "crossbow shot from land," Columbus, Ferdinand, and the other crew members faced another test of survival.

"The Indians of that country, who proved to be a kind and gentle people, presently came in canoes to barter their wares and provisions," Ferdinand remarked. Columbus designated two of his men to monitor the trading for food with the eager hosts. To keep track of his small band of survivors, and prevent mischief, Columbus endeavored to keep his men aboard the beached shipwrecks rather than wander into the woods. As he knew from experience, "Our people by nature being disrespectful, no punishment or order could have stopped them from running about the country and into the Indians' huts to steal what they found and commit outrages on their wives and children, whence would have arisen disputes and quarrels that would have made enemies of them." The Admiral confined the men aboard ship, and required them to sign out if they intended to go ashore. The Indians appeared so grateful for the protocol that they offered everything the sailors needed "in exchange for our things." Colored beads, or lace, a red cap, hawk's bells, scissors, and small mirrors fetched hutias and substantial cassava cakes for the hungry seamen.

With their most pressing needs provided for, Columbus and his men convened repeatedly to discuss their return to Spain. No ship was likely to appear on the horizon to carry them away, and they lacked the means to build a new vessel or to repair the wrecks sheltering them. A raft, or jury-rigged ship, would not suffice, not with the weather and winds and currents they had to face on the return journey. "We had neither the implements nor the artisans needed for the task."

Columbus decided to send messengers back to Hispaniola with an urgent request for a rescue ship with provisions and ammunition. The bearers of that news would have to contend with Columbus's nemesis, Nicolás de Ovando, who would no doubt be pleased to learn that the Admiral of the Ocean Sea was stranded on Jamaica, desperate and powerless, but the castaways had no other choice but to seek help; they could not go on trading with the Indians indefinitely.

For now, the bay enclosed and protected them. The days offered reassuring breezes, calm seas, and radiant vistas. The nights revealed the immensity of the heavens, and their suspension in the sea of infinity. Like all sailors, they gazed on the flickering stars and the moon's spectral countenance, and traced the trajectory of the occasional meteor streaking across the night sky. Beyond the harbor, moonlight glistened across the swell. The celestial spectacle revealed their insignificance in the scheme of things; God ordained their place, and Columbus urged them toward their homeland, more distant than ever. They had food for now, but if the Indians became distracted or hostile, the shipwrecked Spaniards faced the prospect of starvation on the pristine sands of a beach found on no map. Their bleached bones might be discovered a hundred years later, or never; they and their little expedition to the edge of nowhere would be memorialized, celebrated by partisans and condemned by rivals, and soon forgotten. Only by the trick of survival could they fend off the inevitable for a while, and live out the span of years left to them.

"None of my people realize the danger of our situation," Columbus confided to his chief clerk, Diego Méndez de Segura. "We are very few, these savage Indians are very many, and we cannot be certain that their mood will not change. One day, when the mood strikes them, they may come and burn us here in these two ships." With their straw roofs, the structures would instantly catch fire "and roast us alive."

Columbus proposed sending "someone"—Méndez knew whom the Admiral meant—to make the risky crossing to Hispaniola in a canoe, purchase a ship, return to Jamaica in her, and rescue them all. The dutiful Méndez envisioned playing a heroic role in this assignment; he could emerge as the savior of Columbus and the voyage. Méndez aired his doubts, as Columbus listened patiently, and "firmly persuaded me that I was the man to undertake the voyage."

Méndez worried that the other men resented him because "Your Lordship entrusts all the most honorable responsibilities to me." He suggested that Columbus assemble his men to see if anyone else would undertake it—which Méndez doubted—"and if they all hold back, as they will, I shall risk my life once more in your service."

When Columbus explained the mission to the others, no one came forward to offer his services and his life, and several were overheard to say that crossing forty leagues of open ocean in rough weather in a canoe was impossible. Then Méndez rose to his feet. "My Lord," he said, "I have but one life, but I will risk it in Your Lordship's service and for the good of all here present."

Columbus approached him, kissed him on both cheeks, and declared, "I knew very well that nobody here except you would dare to undertake this mission." That was how Méndez chose to remember the event; more likely, Columbus chose that moment to assign twelve or fourteen men to the rescue mission. They would occupy two canoes in all, one under the command of Diego Méndez, and the other under the command of Bartolomeo Fieschi, the Admiral's comrade from Genoa.

Méndez set about readying the fragile craft that would carry them to rescue or disaster. He affixed false keels to the canoe for stability in the open water, covered the hull with pitch and grease, and "nailed some boards to the prow and stern to prevent water from coming in, which it might, owing to the low freeboard"—the narrow portion of the hull above the waterline. Other modifications included the addition of a simple mast and sail, and stores. Each canoe would carry six Spaniards, in addition to several Indian paddlers. They would cover approximately 124 miles.

After bidding farewell to the Admiral and putting to sea, Méndez reached the easternmost end of Jamaica. Lingering at the cape, waiting for a calm sea before commencing the crossing to Hispaniola, Méndez saw that Indians had assembled "with the intention of killing me and taking my canoe and its contents." They even "drew lots for my life" to decide who would carry out the deed. He and his men quietly reclaimed their canoes, beached several miles away, raised sail, and returned to Dry Harbour, where Columbus was stationed.

Relieved that Méndez and his men had escaped slaughter, the Admiral sent them all back to the cape, accompanied by seventy men under the direction of the Adelantado. The squadron waited four days for favorable seas. "When I saw the seas growing calm I very sadly took leave of my escorts and they of me," Méndez recalled.

Ferdinand remembered watching the Indians deftly settling into the canoes with gourds of water and "native food" as the brave Spaniards took their places, carrying "swords, shields, and foods." They launched into the sea, Bartholomew escorting them to the island's eastern end to ward off Indian attacks. None materialized. The Adelantado waited until dark as the canoes became specks on the horizon. When they had vanished, he walked back to his men, "urging the Indians he encountered on the way to be friends and trade with us."

The men in the canoes commenced paddling for five days and four nights. Méndez recalled "never taking my hand off the oar and steering the canoe while all my companions rowed." They were rowing for their lives, and those of the men they left behind with Columbus. For the last two days of this marathon, with their stores of food and drink exhausted, the men aboard the canoes neither ate nor drank.

On arrival in Hispaniola, Méndez was to move on to Santo Domingo, the tiny capital, to beseech Ovando for help, and Fieschi was to return to Jamaica forthwith "to spare us worry that and fear that he might have perished." As Ferdinand knew, "this could easily happen with such flimsy craft if the sea turned at all rough." In fact, they were setting off on a journey of great hardship.

The two canoes proceeded eastward along the coast, the Indians diligently paddling, encountering "only little islands or rocks along the whole course." The final leg from that island to Hispaniola, eight leagues of open water, proved to be the most uncertain. "They had to wait for a perfect calm before starting to cross that great space in such frail craft." As if by divine will, the sea turned to glass for them.

After the rescue mission had departed, those left behind languished in their improvised fortresses in Jamaica. In the enforced idleness, morale deteriorated at an alarming rate; the men, barely loyal to Columbus at the voyage's outset, complained and conspired. They wove elaborate theories about their enigmatic, unstable Admiral, designed to prove that he had no intention of returning to Hispaniola, where he had been forbidden to land. In this scenario, Méndez and Fieschi would return to Spain and secure Columbus's fortune with the Sovereigns. To fit this theory, they persuaded themselves that Columbus was content to remain "in exile right there," on a splendid broad beach with Indians doing his bidding until matters at home were settled to his liking.

The empty days passed. Where was Fieschi? He should have returned by this time. What if he had perished at sea? What if Méndez had perished? What if Fieschi and Méndez had *both* perished? Dependent for the moment on the Indians for survival, the forgotten castaways on Jamaica lost all hope of rescue.

Sequestered on his wrecked ship, an apt symbol of his mind and body, the Admiral afforded the men scant confidence. He could hardly get out of bed, much less endure the hardships of a canoe voyage to Hispaniola. He was broken in body, and damaged in spirit, preparing to make his final voyage, from which there would be no return. He had demonstrated that the world was a more varied and richer place than any in Christendom had suspected, but now he confronted the limits of mortality.

In July, he composed an epistle to the Sovereigns laying bare his regret, self-pity, and recrimination. "I cannot recall Hispaniola, Paria, and the other lands without crying," he wrote of his miscarried adventures. "I used to believe that their example could serve for these others; on the contrary, they are in a depressed state: though they are not dying, their illness is incurable and prolonged. Let them who reduced them to this state come forward with the remedy, if he can or knows how. Everyone is a master at destruction," except himself, of course. "Those who left the Indies, shirking work and speaking of the Indies and me, later returned with appointments; the same will now happen with Veragua." He had seen it all coming, and had tried to govern "in your royal name. You accepted that," he forcefully reminded them at this great distance, "granting it with privileges and by agreement, with seal and oath; you named me Viceroy, Admiral, and Governor General of all, and you assigned me a boundary 100 leagues from the Azores and Cape Verde Islands, with a line running from pole to pole, and over all that I might discover later you gave me full powers."

Now they, or those around them, were stripping him of those powers, despite his accomplishments. "Seven years ago I was at your royal court," he said, at a time when "all who heard of this undertaking agreed it was foolishness." He had given them new lands, new riches, and a new world. But they had rewarded him by ending his monopoly, creating an absurd state of affairs. "Now even tailors want to make discoveries," he groused. "One is led to believe they go to make clothes; they are given permission and make a profit, greatly prejudicing my honor and severely damaging the economy." Columbus believed he deserved to be treated more respectfully, and generously, than a merchant. The lands he discovered "are vaster and richer than any other in Christendom," and he had been the one who placed them "under your royal and eminent rule, and in a position to render tremendous profits." On the beach at Jamaica, he relived the trauma of his confinement for the benefit of the Sovereigns, for whom he had arranged to receive "tremendous profits" from ships that were "victorious and with great news of gold," while he, their Admiral, "full of faith and joy," was suddenly, without warning, "arrested, and thrown in a ship with two of my brothers, brought in irons, naked and mistreated"—here he was stretching a point, for he had insisted in keeping the chains when his captors wished to remove them— "without being summoned or charged by the law."

He gave vent to the roaring in his head:

Who would believe that a poor foreigner could rebel under such circumstances against Your Highnesses without cause or the aid of another prince, alone in the world, surrounded by your vassals and subjects and having my sons at your royal court? I came to serve at the age of 28, and now I have not a single hair left that is not white, and my body is infirm and broken; all that belonged to me was taken and sold—and from my brothers, even their clothes—without my being heard or received, to my great dishonor. One has to trust that these things were not done by your royal order.

They could redeem themselves, Columbus told his Sovereigns, by punishing "those who did this and stole my pearls"—a blatant reference to the turncoat Alonso de Ojeda, who poached on the pearl fisheries that Columbus had discovered off the coast of Venezuela. If the Sovereigns put matters right, "the greatest virtue and exemplary fame would redound" to them. Descending into melodrama, he confided, "I am desperate."

> I used to weep for others; now may heaven show me mercy, and the earth weep for me. As for temporal things, I do not possess even a penny to give to charity; as for spirituality, I have been stranded here in the Indies . . . isolated in this torment, sick, expecting death every day and encircled by a million savages—filled with cruelty, our enemies—so far from the holy sacraments and Holy Church that she would forget this soul if it were separated from the body here. May whoever possesses charity, truth, and justice weep for me. I did not set out on this voyage to earn honors and riches; that is certain because hope of that is already dead. I came to Your Highnesses with an honest intention and good zeal, and I am not lying. Humbly I beseech Your Highnesses, if God be pleased to release me from here, to permit me to go to Rome and other places of pilgrimage. May the most Holy Trinity preserve and increase your life and high state.
>
> —Written in the Indies on the island of Jamaica, July 7, 1503.

CHAPTER 13

February 29, 1504

Columbus fretted and hallucinated about his shattered career in the privacy of his quarters. The other men stranded on Jamaica, no less isolated and desperate, tormented themselves by imagining the favored few who had departed in canoes arriving to a royal welcome in Spain, where they would "enjoy the favor of Bishop Juan de Fonseca and the High Treasurer of Castile," Ferdinand commented.

At this moment of maximum vulnerability, two of the castaways, Francisco Porras and his brother Diego, decided they could no longer endure Columbus's infirmity and tyranny. Lives were at risk, and something had to be done as quickly as possible. They were an influential pair of traitors—one was *Santiago*'s captain, the other comptroller of the fleet—and together they cajoled forty-eight men to affix their signatures to the articles of mutiny. The uprising was scheduled to commence on the morning of January 2, 1504.

Captain Francisco Porras burst into Columbus's makeshift cabin, demanding, "What do you mean by making no effort to get to Castile? Do you wish to keep us here to perish?"

As calmly as possible the Admiral said that no one wished to leave the island more than he did, but they needed a ship. If Porras had another plan, he should propose it to the other captains to consider; Columbus would convene them as often as needed. Talk of meetings merely annoyed Porras. Either Columbus decided to leave the island immediately, or the others would abandon him. He turned his back on the Admiral, a sign of profound disrespect, and shouted, "I'm for Castile. Who's with me?"

The other mutineers cried out, "We're with you!"

At that, they overran the makeshift cabins and roundtops, or masthead platforms, aboard the two shipwrecks, bellowing "Death to them!" and "To Castile! To Castile!"

A few loyalists, their voices drowned by the madmen, inquired, "Captain, what do we do now?"

Crippled by arthritis, Columbus was barely able to stand. Ferdinand reported that he "hobbled to the scene of the mutiny; but three or four honest fellows, his servants, fearing the mutineers might slay him, forced him with great difficulty to return to bed."

With Columbus safe for the moment, the loyalists rushed to his brother the Adelantado, who was fighting off attackers with a lance. The loyalists relieved him of the weapon, and shut him in the cabin with Columbus. Then they pleaded with Porras to leave before he inspired a "murder which was bound to harm them all and for which he would certainly be punished." If Porras complied, "none would seek to hinder him from going."

As negotiations concluded, the mutiny lost some of its vehemence. Columbus had "scoured the islands to procure canoes" to prevent the Indians from using them. Porras and his men commandeered the canoes, and "they set out in them as gaily as if they were embarking from a harbor in Castile." As they began to pull away, many others, "not mutineers but . . . desperate at the thought of being abandoned there by the greatest and healthiest part of the company also piled into the canoes"—much to the distress of the few remaining loyalists and of the sick, who with good reason believed they were "doomed to remain there." The humiliating sight of nearly all of the men abandoning the Admiral who had brought them on this adventure remained with Ferdinand, who sadly noted, "If all had been in good health, I doubt that twenty of those people would have stayed with the Admiral." Their morale lower than ever, those who stayed behind beheld the Admiral emerge unsteadily from his cabin to comfort and reassure his men as best he could. In fact, there was little consolation he could offer while Francisco Porras led the canoes laden with deserters to the same location on Jamaica's easternmost shore from which Méndez and Fieschi had set out on their rescue mission.

Ferdinand painted an ugly picture of the deserters preparing to depart for Hispaniola: "Wherever they called, they inflicted outrages on the Indians, robbing their food and other possessions; they told the Indians to collect their pay from the Admiral and authorized them to kill him if he would not pay." To feed the Indians' disdain, Porras's renegades explained that all the other Christians hated Columbus, that Columbus was the author of "all the misery of the Indians on Hispaniola," and, if they failed to kill Columbus, he would "inflict the same suffering on them."

Setting out from the Jamaican coast, they made uncertain progress toward their goal. After they had traversed four leagues, "the wind turned contrary," and the men feared the rolling seas would swamp their overloaded craft. Before long, water was coming over the gunwales, and they resorted to tossing everything overboard, with the exception of their weapons and food for the return journey to the Jamaican coast from which they had departed. When the wind gained in strength, terrifying the renegades, they decided their only course of action was to kill the Indians and toss them overboard, as if they were excess supplies. Once they started killing Indians, the others jumped overboard, swimming away from the canoes until fatigue overcame them. In desperation, they returned to the canoes, holding on to the gunwales in a death grip, until the mutineers hacked off their hands.

Ferdinand acidly commented on the "Christians'" behavior: "They killed eighteen this way, sparing only a few needed to steer the canoes; this was the Indians' reward for listening to their false promises and their pleas for aid."

The renegades returned to the marshy Jamaican shore, where they fell to arguing about what to do next. Some of the men aimed to flee to Cuba, thinking "the easterly currents and winds" would carry them to their destination; once in Cuba, they assumed it would be an "easy jump" to Hispaniola, without realizing that many miles separated the two islands. (Ferdinand recognized that Cuba was an island, even if his father clung to the belief that it was a promontory extending eastward from the "Indian" mainland.) Other renegades wanted to return to the relative safety of the wrecked ships they had recently abandoned. They could either make peace with the Admiral or attempt to confiscate his weapons. A third group advocated waiting to try for better weather and attempt to reach Hispaniola again, and eventually they prevailed.

The desperate rebels passed more than a month in a Jamaican village Ferdinand called Aomaquique, relied on the Indians for sustenance, and waited for a favorable wind. When they judged conditions were right, they tried again, failed again, and tried yet once more, defeated each time by contrary winds. Broken in spirit, they trudged back to the harbor where their ships and the remnants of the crew remained, living off the land and, when they could, stealing food from the Indians. The glorious voyage had come to this, a band of scavengers and robbers, unable to save their own skins, or souls, or those of anyone else.

In charge of the ruins of two beached ships, Columbus, though enfeebled, tended to the sick among his loyal men. At the same time, he made certain to give the Indians the respect needed to do business. The ailing loyalists, many of them, regained their strength, and the Indians continued to serve, until the system broke down under unequal requirements. "They are an indolent people who will not cultivate on a large scale," Ferdinand wrote in a cruelly revealing passage, "and we consumed more in a day than they in twenty."

Worse, as the Indians acquired goods from the Europeans in barter transactions, they "began to be influenced by the arguments of the mutineers" and brought fewer provisions to the visitors. As January 1504 gave way to February, the situation steadily deteriorated. The loyalists were faced with a dilemma: if they abandoned their makeshift dwellings to attack the Indians for more of the cassava, fruit, and water on which their lives depended, they would be "leaving the Admiral to face great danger in the ships." The Europeans came to realize that the Indians, by starving the intruders by degrees, "believed they had us at their mercy."

In all honesty, Ferdinand confessed, "we did not know what to do."

Throughout his years of exploring, from the Mediterranean to the Atlantic, Columbus had revealed a genius for survival, whether shipwrecked off the coast of Portugal, pleading for support from the Sovereigns, fending off mutineers, or trying to reclaim his legacy from rivals. Now, with no ships at his disposal, Indians slowly starving him, his men reduced to a paltry few, and his health so poor that he could barely stand, he faced his greatest challenge, and to meet it, he devised a supreme ruse in which he virtually became the sorcerer that others had feared he always was. They held that the Admiral of the Ocean Sea could command the tides and even the weather; now, in the name of survival, he plotted to demonstrate that he controlled the heavens themselves.

Columbus's hidden advantage had always been his sophisticated knowledge of navigation. Turning to his store of charts and books, he studied the *Almanach perpetuum*, compiled in 1496 by Rabbi Abraham Zacuto, the Sephardic Jewish astronomer and mathematician who had served João II after the Inquisition drove him from Spain. Portuguese captains often consulted this work, consisting of hundreds of pages of astronomical tables accurately predicting celestial phenomena. Columbus may also have relied on Regiomontanus's *Ephemerides astronomicae* (1474), which conveniently enough included a table of lunar eclipses occurring between 1475 and 1540. In the past, he had relied on these reference works to calculate latitude and longitude, often with mixed results, and now he turned to them to save his life.

According to Regiomontanus, an auspicious event would occur on February 29, 1504: a lunar eclipse. In this eerie celestial spectacle, the moon passes through the earth's umbral—or inner—shadow, turning ever deeper shades of orange, and eventually bloodred, before returning to normal. The sight was enough to spark foreboding in superstitious sailors and, Columbus hoped, in credulous Indians.

Regiomontanus included the dates of the eclipses, and diagrams of how completely the moon would dim, hour by hour. But the times of the occurrence differed across the globe, and Columbus could not reliably determine the local time in Jamaica. (Regiomontanus's calculations applied to Nuremberg, Germany.) And he could not say how accurate Regiomontanus's prediction for February 29, 1504, might be. He had no choice but to take his chances according to his best estimates. If he succeeded, he would demonstrate supernatural power to the Indians that would deeply influence their behavior. If he failed, he and his men would likely succumb to starvation or slaughter at the hands of the Indians.

He summoned the caciques of the region to a feast. Ferdinand recorded, "He told the gathering through an interpreter that we were Christians and believed in God, who . . . rewarded the good and punished the wicked, as he had punished the mutineers by not permitting them to cross over to Hispaniola, as Méndez and Fieschi had done, and by causing them to suffer many trials and dangers, as the Indians well knew." Columbus warned the Indians that "God was very angry with them for neglecting to bring us food for which we had paid them by barter, and had determined to punish them with famine and pestilence."

As the audience absorbed the import of the old Admiral's words, laughter broke out, at first hesitant, then boldly derisive. He told the doubters, "God would send them a clear token from Heaven of the punishment they were about to receive. They should therefore attend that night the rising of the moon: She would arise inflamed with wrath, signifying the chastisement God would visit upon them." He stopped, rested, and observed as "the Indians departed, some frightened and others scoffing at his threats."

The eclipse commenced, as predicted. The earth's shadow expanded and darkened until it covered the entire moon, turning it into a faint red disk suspended in the night sky. Most lunar eclipses are plainly visible to the naked eye, and based on Ferdinand's account, the occurrence of February 29 was especially dramatic.

Under the influence of this magical transformation, Columbus's immense power of suggestion took hold. He appeared to interpret, if not control, the heavens. "The Indians grew so frightened that with great howling and lamentation they came running from all directions to the ships, laden with provisions, and praying the Admiral to intercede with God that He might not vent His wrath upon them, and promising they would diligently supply all their needs in the future."

Extracting as much benefit as possible from the moment, Columbus announced to the throng that he wished to have a word with God, and he disappeared into the depths of his ramshackle cabin, an old necromancer at the height of his powers. In the near darkness, the Indians cried and shrieked at the bloodred, malevolent moon waxing overhead. In seclusion, Columbus consulted an hourglass to calculate the time remaining *para el eclipse lunar.* "When the Admiral perceived that the crescent phase of the moon was finished and that it would soon shine forth clearly, he issued from his cabin, saying that he had appealed to his God and prayed for them and had promised Him in their name that henceforth they would be good and treat the Christians well"—and here was the crucial part—"bringing provisions and all else they needed."

Drawing on his reserves of strength, Columbus informed the awestruck Indians that God had pardoned them, "in token of which they would soon see the moon's anger and inflammation pass away." They needed no more persuading, and unified by terror and relief, they paid tribute to the Admiral and offered prayers to God, who had spared them. "From that time forward," Ferdinand intoned, "they were diligent in providing us with all we needed, and were loud in praise of the Christian God." It was apparent to the young man, as to the other marooned Europeans, that the Indians feared eclipses and, at the same time, "were ignorant of their cause." It did not occur to them that "men living on earth could know what was happening in the sky." It never troubled Columbus, his son, or any of their company that the Admiral had practiced a grand deception in the name of God. They were safe, and that was all that mattered. God would forgive them.

It had been eight months since Fieschi and Méndez set off to Santo Domingo on their rescue mission. By this time they should have returned or sent word of their whereabouts, but there was nothing—no canoe, no Indian, no Spanish survivor of the mission, and no sail on the horizon to indicate their fate. Rumors spread that they had drowned, or been slaughtered by Indians, or, in Ferdinand's words, had "died on the way from sickness and hardships. They knew that from the eastern end of Jamaica to the town of Santo Domingo in Hispaniola stretched over one hundred leagues of very difficult navigation by sea on account of contrary winds and currents and of travel over very rugged mountains by land." Indians whispered about a ghostly shipwreck that had been spotted "drifting down the coast of Jamaica," but its substance remained a mystery.

Yet another mutiny broke out, this time led by an unlikely candidate, the apothecary Vernal. It grew unchecked until late March 1504, when a sail appeared on the horizon. The ship, a little caravel, had been dispatched by Nicolás de Ovando, and it anchored close to the hulks of Columbus's shattered flotilla.

"The captain, Diego de Escobar, came aboard and informed the Admiral that the Knight Commander of Lares, the Governor of Hispaniola, sent his compliments and regretted that he had no ship large enough to take off all the Admiral's men." He hoped to send one soon, and as a token of his goodwill, Captain Escobar gave Columbus a "barrel of wine and slab of salt pork," both welcome luxuries in this isolated outpost, before returning to his vessel, raising anchor, and sailing that night "without even taking letters from anyone."

The caravel's appearance, to say nothing of the gifts of food and wine, so astonished the stranded mariners that the mutineers immediately "covered up the plot they been hatching," although the alacrity with which Captain Escobar departed inspired a new set of conspiracy theories. The men speculated that Nicolás de Ovando had no intention of rescuing his despised rival Columbus, whom he wanted to perish in his obscure Jamaican refuge. As Ferdinand saw matters, Ovando "feared the Admiral's return to Castile," and worried that the Sovereigns would "restore the Admiral to his office and deprive him (Ovando) of his government." For this reason, Ferdinand theorized, Ovando had sent the little caravel not to assist the Admiral but "to spy on him and report how he might be totally destroyed."

Another rumor, mentioned by Las Casas, held that Columbus was plotting a "rebellion against the king and queen with some notion of handing these Indies over to the Genoese or to some other country apart from Castile." Even Las Casas dismissed the allegation as "false and invented and spread by his enemies as a wicked calumny," but the chronicler could not resist discussing it, especially because the claim gained enough currency to reach the Sovereigns. Not knowing whether he would ever be rescued, or whether his words would ever reach Ferdinand and Isabella, Columbus demolished this theory in a passionate self-defense: "Who could entertain the notion that a poor foreigner would, in such a place, dream of rebelling against Your Majesties, for no reason whatever, with no support from any foreign ruler, surrounded by your subjects and countrymen?"

Even if those arguments held the Sovereigns at bay, Columbus still had to assuage his rival Ovando, whom he tried to lobby and flatter in equal measure. "When I left Castile, I did so to the great rejoicing of Their Majesties, who also made me wonderful promises, and in particular that they would see all my assets restored and would heap still more honors on me; these promises they made both by word of mouth and in writing." Having put Ovando on notice, Columbus shifted his argument. "I ask you, my lord, not to entertain any doubts on that score: please believe that I shall obey your orders and instructions in every particular." Not only that, but Columbus had heard from Escobar "how well and how tirelessly you have looked after my affairs, and I acknowledge this, my lord, with a grateful heart." Rising to heights of artful insincerity, Columbus sighed, "Ever since I met you and got to know you, I have always understood, my lord, deep in my heart, that you would do everything you could for me no matter what the circumstances." He knew that Ovando would "hazard anything, even your own life, to rescue me."

And if these words succeeded in calming Ovando sufficiently to spare Columbus death on a distant shore, the Admiral faced the fears of his own men, and had to persuade them all that he had ordered the caravel to depart without them—not as part of a devious plot to put them all at risk, but because it was simply too small to carry them. Either all went, or none.

Ovando's caravel brought one other item of particular interest: a letter from the absent Méndez. The day after departing from Jamaica, Méndez's letter began, he and Fieschi enjoyed a cruise through blissfully calm weather, "urging the Indians to paddle as hard as they could with the sticks they use for paddles." In the heat, the Indians refreshed themselves by jumping into the water, and resuming their place. "By sunset, they had lost sight of land." At night, half of the Indians continued paddling as the Spaniards aboard the canoes kept a vigil, and by dawn, everyone was exhausted. Even the captains took turns paddling, and with the dawn of the second day, the voyage continued without interruption, with "nothing but water and sky" surrounding them. As the day wore on, the Indians, thirsty from physical labor, depleted the canoes' water supply. By noon, the sun tormented everyone. The sole respite from debilitating thirst came drop by drop from the captains' "small water casks." The trickle proved to be "just enough to sustain them till the cool of the evening."

The canoes plowed through heavy seas, their diminutive masts and flickering paddles barely visible above the waterline, as their occupants, drenched and exhausted, hoped to raise the little island of Navassa, about eight leagues distant. Even with the benefit of the most determined paddling, these canoes could make no more than ten leagues against the current in a twenty-four-hour period.

The unending exertion put the paddlers at risk of dehydration, a common affliction in the Caribbean, even on the water. One Indian died on the second night, as others, prostrate with exhaustion, lay on the bottoms of the canoes, and still others tried to paddle but strained to move their arms. With one feeble stroke after another they made their way, dabbing salt water on their parched tongues. By the time night fell for the second time, they still had not reached land.

At moonrise, Ferdinand learned from Méndez's letter, they raised the white cliffs of Navassa, all two square miles of it, shimmering above the frosted wave tops. The whiteness came from the exposed coral and limestone poking out beyond the uninhabited island's grass cover. They were still one hundred miles south of Guantánamo Bay, Cuba. Nevertheless, Méndez "joyfully" pointed out Navassa, and carefully doled out water to the paddlers. By dawn they had reached the island.

What they found was "bare rock, half a league around." No Indians greeted them with water, food, or counsel. After they hurriedly offered thanks to the Lord for their survival, they realized that Navassa was nearly treeless and, worse, appeared to lack the drinking water they needed so desperately. In search of streams, they clambered and crawled from one steep cliff to another, collecting trickles of precious water in gourds. Eventually they found enough to fill their stomachs despite warnings not to drink too much. Nevertheless, some of the Indians drank without restraint, and grew violently sick, or died.

The rest of the day passed in relative tranquillity, the men playing and "eating shellfish that they found on the shore and cooked, for Méndez had brought flint and steel for making fire." But they could not tarry; foul weather could arrive at any time. That evening they pushed off for Cape San Miguel, the nearest point on Hispaniola, traveling throughout the night to arrive by dawn, the fourth day after leaving Jamaica. They arrived exhausted once again, and spent two days recuperating before facing the challenges ahead.

Fieschi wished to return to Columbus, as arranged, to report their safe arrival on Hispaniola, but his traveling companions, both Europeans and Indians, were "exhausted and ill from their labors and from drinking sea water," and refused to accompany him, "for the Christians regarded themselves as having been delivered from the whale's belly, their three days and nights corresponding to those of the prophet Jonah."

But Méndez had a different idea. Despite suffering from "quartan ague," an archaic term for malaria, he led his men inland "over wretched paths and rugged mountains" to the western province of Xaraguá, formerly the refuge of Roldán and his rebels, where Nicolás de Ovando busied himself putting down another Indian rebellion. The cold-blooded governor feigned delight when these emissaries from Columbus appeared from nowhere, and in keeping with his anti-Columbian agenda, delayed giving the exhausted travelers permission to trek the seventy leagues to Santo Domingo.

During the seven months they were detained at Xaraguá, Méndez witnessed the governor's cruelty. "He burned or hanged eighty-four ruling caciques," including Anacaona, "the greatest chieftain of the island, who is obeyed and served by all the others." She was also known as a composer of *areítos*, or narrative poems, and had been considered friendly to the Spaniards. At a feast in her honor organized by eight caciques, to which Ovando was invited, he set fire to the meetinghouse, arrested her and other Indian leaders, and executed all of them. Most were shot; Anacaona died by hanging. She was thirty-nine years old. Her husband, Caonabó, had been captured by Alonso de Ojeda, and died at sea en route to Spain. Even the Spaniards were appalled by Ovando's brutality toward friendly Indians, but there was little they could do about it.

When the governor finally considered the pacification of Xaraguá complete, the indefatigable Méndez got permission to go on foot to the capital, all but forbidden to the Admiral himself. There he drew on Columbus's "funds and resources" to buy and equip a caravel. "None had come for more than a year," Méndez recalled, "but thanks be to God three arrived during my stay, one of which I bought and loaded with provisions: bread, wine, meat, hogs, sheep, fruit," all now available, for a price, in this remote outpost of the Spanish empire.

He supervised provisioning the caravel for the voyage, and dispatched her to Jamaica in late May 1504, so that the Admiral "and all his men might come in it to Santo Domingo and from there return to Castile." Méndez went ahead with two ships "to give the King and Queen an account of all that had happened on that voyage." There would be much to tell.

At about this time, in Spain, Queen Isabella fell seriously ill at Medina del Campo, a city known for its trade fairs, a little more than twenty miles from Valladolid. "The doctors have lost all hope for her health," wrote Peter Martyr in despair. "The illness spread throughout her veins and slowly the dropsy became apparent. A fever never abandoned her, penetrating her to the core. Day and night she had an insatiable thirst, while the sight of food gave her nausea. The mortal tumor grew fast between her skin and flesh."

As her strength ebbed and her thoughts turned to eternity, she cut back drastically on official business coming before her.

As for Columbus and "all his companions," having spent an entire year marooned in a lush, obscure, and troubled paradise on Jamaica, they "were highly delighted with the ship's arrival." When Méndez and Columbus later renewed their friendship in Spain and recalled the rescue, "His Lordship told me that in all his life he had never known so joyful a day, since he never expected to leave Jamaica alive."

For the moment, Columbus still had to neutralize the mutineers led by the Porras brothers, who had little appreciation for Méndez's heroics. To bring them around, he dispatched two representatives—Ferdinand described them only as "respected persons"—considered friendly to both parties; they came bearing a gift in the form of the mouthwatering salt pork that Ovando had sent to Columbus. Captain Porras warily conferred with the two envoys by himself, fearing that they "brought an offer of a general pardon that his men might be persuaded to accept." Nothing, not even Porras, could keep them from learning about the arrival of the caravel and its promise of a safe return to Spain, and, eventually, of Columbus's offer of clemency.

The mutineers made a counteroffer: if given another ship all their own, they would leave. Failing that, they might consider leaving if they were guaranteed half the space on the little caravel Ovando had sent. And they wanted access to Columbus's stores, because they had lost all of theirs. Becoming impatient, Columbus's envoys explained why these demands were "unreasonable and unacceptable," whereupon Porras's men declared that if they were not willingly given what they wanted, they would seize it. With that, they turned their backs on the envoys, and the promise of a peaceful resolution. They went back to their followers, decrying Columbus as a "cruel and vengeful man," and they told the others not to be afraid, they had friends at court who would rally to their side against the Admiral. (Ferdinand Columbus reflected on Roldán's recent rebellion: "And see how well their enterprise turned out; assuredly it would be the same with them"—that is, with Porras's followers.)

Porras devised an argument to defeat the powerful presence of the caravel and Méndez's return. Do not believe your eyes, he told them. The ship was not real. It was merely, as Ferdinand recalled, a "phantasm conjured up by the magic arts of which the Admiral was a master," an image evoking Columbus's striking fear into the Indians by appearing to conjure a menacing lunar eclipse. "Clearly, a real caravel would not have left so soon, with so little dealing between its crew and the Admiral's men." If it had been real, "the Admiral and his brother would have sailed away in it."

Columbus's behavior these past eleven months invited this kind of wild speculation. Confined to his cabin, grumbling orders, leading the Indians to believe that he controlled the heavens, he acquired the aura of a man possessed if not by supernatural skills then by the gifts of prophecy and revelation. Spain had come to regard him as the discoverer of new lands, but he believed himself an instrument of divine revelation. Others had come to accept that Columbus was making history, but he wanted to see his deeds emblazoned in Holy Scripture, glittering with fire, and, if need be, soaked in blood. Other explorers, especially those seeking to usurp him, wrote on water, while his accomplishments would stand as monuments, or so he believed. He created history as he went, as if time and place were two aspects of the same entity that he had chased for twelve years, guided by Marco Polo, inspired by the Bible, and driven by his lust for gold.

If not wholly convincing, Porras's crude deception caused the mutineers to doubt what they could plainly see. So he strengthened the mutineers' resolve, and prepared them to lay siege to all the ships, confiscate their contents, and even take the Admiral prisoner. Emboldened, they occupied an Indian village called Maima, close to the beached ships, to prepare an assault. As he had in similar situations, Columbus dispatched his brother Bartholomew "to bring them to their senses with soft words," reinforced by fifty armed loyalists in waiting to repel an attack, if it materialized. On May 17, the Adelantado positioned himself on a hilltop "a crossbow shot" from the village and charged the two aides who had negotiated unsuccessfully with Porras to try again. The mutineers refused even to speak to the representatives. Six rebels conspired to slaughter Columbus's brother, believing that once he was out of the way, the other loyalists would surrender.

In battle formation, they cried out "Kill! Kill!" as they attacked the Adelantado and his company. Five of the six would-be assassins fell before the loyalists.

The Adelantado responded with a fierce attack of his own, dispatching at least two men: Juan Sánchez, who had never lived down his reputation as the man who allowed the Quibián to escape, and Juan Barbara, who had initiated the scuffle with drawn sword. Others were wounded, and, most important of all, Francisco Porras was captured. The other mutineers, in Ferdinand's words, "turned tail and ran away with all their might," Bartholomew taking off after them, until his aides restrained his lust for vengeance, murmuring that "it was well to punish, but in moderation."

If they slaughtered all their enemies, the many Indians who were observing the conflict might decide the moment had come to take on the loyalists. Bartholomew relented, and escorted Porras and the other prisoners to the beached ships, where Columbus received them gratefully, with prayers and "thanks to God for this great victory." The loyalists, though victorious, did not escape unscathed. One of Columbus's servants died, and the Adelantado was wounded in the hand, but recovered.

In the heat of battle, Pedro de Ledesma, the pilot turned rebel, tumbled unnoticed over a cliff, and hid until dark. Indians who discovered him were curious how he had survived the Europeans' keen swords. They reopened his wounds with "little sticks," examined a "cut on his head so deep one could see his brains," and took note of other wounds that nearly severed his shoulder, cut his thigh to the bone, and sliced the sole of one foot from "heel to toe so it resembled a slipper." Whenever the Indians approached, he shouted, "Beware, I can get up!" And they ran as if from a ghost.

Eventually the Spaniards rescued Ledesma, transporting him to a "palm-thatched hut nearby, where the dampness and mosquitoes alone should have finished him off." The ship's surgeon spent eight days treating Ledesma's wounds ("so terrible that it would defy the human imagination to devise any more horrible or grave," as Las Casas would have it), until, against all expectations, he recovered. "I met him after all this in Seville, as fit and well as though nothing had ever happened," said Las Casas, although, not long after, "I heard that he had been killed with a dagger." In any event, the mutineers' spirit had been broken.

On Monday, May 20, the dispirited band of rebels sent their own emissaries to Columbus to make amends and beg for mercy. They all confessed in writing to their insubordination and inhumanity, begged forgiveness from the Admiral, and expressed repentance. They swore loyalty anew "on a crucifix and missal," and if they ever broke their word, no priest, no Christian of any kind, would hear their confession, and they would be considered to have renounced "the holy sacraments of the Church," which meant that as wicked Christians they would be denied burial on consecrated ground, and instead be disposed of "in no man's land as one does with heretics."

Columbus read their pleas and confessions with satisfaction and relief. The renegades received full pardons, with the exception of Porras, who was held prisoner "that he might not be the cause of new disturbances."

Now the question arose of where to billet the men. With space tight on the two shipwrecks housing the loyalists, and lingering tensions between the rebels and loyalists, Columbus assigned the former mutineers to a camp onshore, to wait for the ships that would carry them to Spain. They could "wander the island as he directed, bartering their trade goods, until the arrival of the ships," according to Las Casas. "And God knows what damage this party inflicted on the Indians and what outrages they committed."

Days later, the anniversary of their arrival came and went. His recent pledge of loyalty to Ovando forgotten, Columbus fumed at the delays he had been forced to endure, "asserting that the delay was deliberate, and occasioned by [Ovando's] hope that the Admiral would die there." But he had not died. He had survived, intent on vindication.

Days later, Diego Méndez's caravel dropped anchor in the bay. After their struggles to survive and their battles with one another, the men who had been stranded, without hope, were more relieved than ebullient to board the vessel that would take them away. "In this ship we embarked, friends and enemies alike," Ferdinand laconically recalled. It was June 28, 1504.

Winds and currents remained contrary throughout the crossing from Jamaica to Santo Domingo, where they did not arrive until August 13. When they reached the island of Beata, off the coast of Hispaniola, they encountered currents that defeated their progress. As he did in times of enforced idleness, Columbus unburdened himself. In a letter to Ovando, he described the actions taken to end the mutiny, singling out the Porras brothers for their evil deeds. Columbus again swore loyalty to the governor, and concluded the letter with his distinctive, and cryptic, signature:

which, in his private language, meant "Columbus, the Christ-bearer." He adopted this signature as his special imprimatur. His heirs, he urged, should also "sign with my signature which I now employ which is an X with an S over it and an M with a Roman A over it, and then an S and then a Greek Y with an S over it, preserving the relations of the lines and points." Despite these highly specific instructions, the full meaning of the signature, the product of Columbus's fertile spiritual imagination, has yet to be fully decoded, but it likely includes biblical as well as maritime references. In its shape, some see a ship's mast, others a cross, and still others cryptic references to invocations and hymns.

On arrival in Santo Domingo, to his great surprise, Columbus received a welcome distinguished by "great honor and hospitality" (said Las Casas) from an unlikely source: Nicolás de Ovando. After a year of living in the shadow of obscurity, Columbus had emerged into the dazzling sunlight of prominence. The governor's unexpected goodwill extended to sheltering Columbus in the newly built governor's residence, "with orders that he was to be accorded every consideration."

The show of hospitality concealed persistent conflicts between the present and former governor of Hispaniola. Columbus was quick to take offense at perceived slights; these unnamed actions he "regarded as insulting and as affronts to his dignity," Las Casas learned. Ferdinand took Ovando's hypocritical behavior as "a scorpion's kiss." The concealed poison within the kiss consisted of Ovando's freeing Francisco Porras, the acknowledged "ringleader of the mutiny," in the presence of Columbus himself, in a gesture designed to humiliate his predecessor. "He even proposed to punish those who had taken up arms to defend the Admiral." Later, Columbus muttered darkly to his son Diego about the Porras brothers, "They did such bad things, with such raw cruelty as was never heard before. If the King and Queen leave them unpunished I do not know who will dare take more people out in their service." Their mutiny forgiven and forgotten, the Porras brothers received their back pay, positions, and titles.

In the same spirit, Ovando excluded the Admiral of the Ocean Sea from official dealings with Ferdinand and Isabella. With that, Columbus realized he was more prisoner than honored guest, disgraced and endangered by Ovando, who refused to recognize the Admiral's credentials as the "captain general" of the fleet. The bona fides, declared Ovando, were none of his business. It is difficult to imagine Columbus, a man of soaring vanity, reduced to the status of a vassal in the capital of the empire he had discovered as Ovando went about humiliating him, but he had no choice. It was left to Ferdinand to express indignation on his behalf.

A month later, on September 12, Columbus, his son Ferdinand, and servants sailed for Spain in a chartered caravel accompanied by one other ship. The rest of Columbus's crew, the men who had endured a harrowing year on the beach in Jamaica, stayed behind on the island of Hispaniola. Of those men, many former mutineers, Las Casas noted in passing, "some of them later crossed over to Puerto Rico to settle the island—or, to put it more accurately, to destroy it."

The weather turned fierce. Two leagues offshore, the mainmast of one of the ships in Columbus's little fleet split "right down to the deck," most likely the result of heavy winds. Columbus ordered the damaged vessel to return to Santo Domingo, and he resumed the journey to Castile in the accompanying vessel. But "after sailing with fair weather for almost a third part of our course," Ferdinand reported, "we had a terrible storm that placed us in great jeopardy." That was October 19. The following day, the ship's mainmast "broke in four pieces," precipitating still another emergency.

Ferdinand ascribed their survival to the "valor of the Adelantado and the ingenuity of the Admiral, who could not rise from bed on account of his gout." Nevertheless, the two brothers "contrived a jury mast"—that is, a replacement—"out of a lateen yard"—a triangular sail's spar—"which we secured firmly about the middle with ropes and planks taken from the stern and forecastles, which we tore down." The ship remained seaworthy, so long as the weather did not trouble them.

Presently another storm descended, cracking the mast.

After more repairs, the ship made the final seven hundred leagues to the port of Sanlúcar de Barrameda, in southern Spain, last seen by Columbus two and a half years earlier. Frail and vulnerable, he had survived, and so long as he lived, the promise of a Columbian empire—sanctioned by the Sovereigns, of course—remained alive. Despite the tranquil splendor of Dry

Harbour, Jamaica, his time there had been extraordinarily dispiriting, time spent tending to his physical and psychic wounds. His year on the beach had been no idyll; there was no coming to terms with himself, or with the "Indies." It was, at best, a refuge.

Many of the 140 men who had set out with Columbus did not live to see the end of the voyage. Several deserted at Hispaniola. Thirty succumbed to disease, or drowned, or died in battles with the Indians or with mutineers. Columbus, confronting disease, mutineers, hostile Indians, and his own delusions, was among those who survived, as were his son and brother.

Despite his extensive reconnoitering of the coast of what is now Panama and Costa Rica, he never grasped where in the world he had been. Yet Columbus realized he had found some great entity that seemed to expand the more he explored it, a place without clearly defined borders, poorly understood or described by the writers of antiquity, to which even the Bible made scant reference, simultaneously concealing and revealing incalculable riches. He later claimed part of its wealth as his own, even while he devoted the whole of his time in Spain not in palaces or brothels but in austere monasteries or tottering on muleback along steep mountain trails, driven by the twin demons of vanity and duty.

To his loyal son, Columbus's accomplishments were anything but foreordained or clear-cut. An aura of chaos hovered over his entire life and adventures, against which he tried to impose his will. In Ferdinand's retelling of events, his father was always vulnerable—to the whims of monarchs, the caprices of Indians, the power of tides and storms, and the moods of the impressionable men serving under him. He emerged as a hostage to fortune in the high-stakes game of European expansion; time and again, his exploits could have gone one way or another, were it not for his singular vision, or so Ferdinand would have his readers believe. The adventure gave impetus to his imagination and intellect for the rest of his days.

For Columbus's brother Bartholomew, the Adelantado, the journey had been the occasion for acts of heroism, at least in the eyes of the Spanish. If not for his vigilance, Columbus and his band of loyalists would not have lasted a year on the beach. Yet the most heroic acts of all had been performed not by his brothers, but by the self-effacing Diego Méndez, who had survived a perilous journey in an open boat and a year in the realm of Nicolás de Ovando to bring the caravel to Jamaica to rescue Columbus and his men.

Despite these hardships and frustrations, Columbus retained a particular affection for El Alto Viaje—the High Voyage—perhaps because it gave him a chance to show off his navigational skills as never before, and to accomplish feats that would make less accomplished explorers gasp in wonder. Or perhaps because the hardships of the voyage, its reversals and privations and narrow escapes, brought him closer to God, to his son Ferdinand, and to his sense of mission.

It was now November 7, 1504. He planned to return to Seville to recover his health, and then journey once again, this time to make amends with the queen who had backed his voyages for a dozen years. As with many of his expectations, it was not to be.

Queen Isabella, still at Medina del Campo, continued her decline. Only weeks before, on October 4, she signed her will, in which she exhorted her husband and daughter to conquer Africa—considered by some to belong to the Spanish empire—and to complete the Crusade. There were other requests: she would be buried in a habit of St. Francis, and she appointed her daughter, Juana, her "universal heir." As for King Ferdinand, she was thankful for his labors, and he would receive half the income flowing to Spain from the empire that Columbus discovered for them both—the Indies.

Beyond that, a codicil to her will maintained that "our main aim was to arrange the introduction there of our holy Catholic faith and to ensure that the people there accepted it, and also to send prelates, monks, priests, and other learned people who fear God to instruct the people in the faith and to teach and indoctrinate them with good customs."

By this time she had given her blessing to a new mission to the Indies, led not by Columbus or one of his brothers, but by Juan de la Cosa, the mapmaker. Later, she assigned Alonso de Ojeda, whom Columbus considered a poacher on his demesne, as the governor of the bay of Urabá, between today's Colombia and Panama. Although the mission, backed by an amalgam of conversos and nobles, was slow to start, its mere existence was enough to alarm the Admiral, who complained that "nobles of the realm now sharpened their teeth as if they had been wild boar, in the expectation of a great mutation of the state."

Although Columbus was already sketching out another voyage in his fevered imagination, it was apparent that his remaining strength would not be equal to the demands of life at sea. He had deteriorated badly, like one of his ships too riddled with shipworms to endure another squall.

On November 26, nineteen days after Columbus had arrived in Sanlúcar de Barrameda, Isabella I, Queen of Castile and Léon, died in Medina del

Campo. She was fifty-three years old. With her went Columbus's hopes of obtaining backing for another voyage. For all her reign's brutality, she had been a powerful leader, bringing the nobility under control and a semblance of order to Castile. Reflecting the conventional opinion of the era, Peter Martyr described her as "the mirror of virtues, refuge of good things, scourge of evil." But she would always be remembered as the sponsor of the Inquisition—and of the voyages of Christopher Columbus.

"Her death caused the Admiral much grief," wrote his son, "for she had always aided and favored him, while the King he always found somewhat reserved and unsympathetic to his projects." Ferdinand was not the only observer who noticed the disparity in the way the two monarchs treated Columbus. "The Catholic king," Las Casas observed, "I know not why nor with what motive, not only failed to show him any material sign of gratitude but also, while very complimentary in what he said, did his level best to ensure that [Columbus's] route to advancement was blocked." The chronicler shook his head in wonder, and suddenly came to the defense of the man he had devoted volumes to condemning. "I never managed to get to the bottom of this dislike," he admitted, "unless it was that the king paid more attention than was warranted to the false witness brought against the Admiral by those at court who were jealous of him." The whispering campaign against Columbus continued unabated.

It is painful to contemplate Columbus entering into his final round of negotiations with King Ferdinand. Like Nicolás de Ovando, the king acknowledged the explorer's accomplishments and service to the crown, without promising anything for the future. Refusing to recognize this reality, Columbus persisted in beseeching his Sovereign for confirmation of his titles, and even for backing of future voyages, although he was barely capable of traveling overland, let alone over the Ocean Sea. He had lived long enough to see his moment pass, all too briefly. Now he bargained with the king as with death itself for more time, money, and glory. Columbus regained enough strength to plan a visit to the movable Spanish court, guessing that it was at Valladolid. He proposed to travel aboard the ornate palanquin once used to transport a cardinal's corpse to be interred at the Seville Cathedral, but put the plan aside in favor of journeying as he did so often overland, on the back of a mule.

After many delays, he finally set out, accompanied by his brother Bartholomew, in May 1505. It was imperative to persuade the Sovereign one last time to clear his name and to restore his privileges, his wealth, and his honor.

He bluntly outlined his intentions in a letter that he wrote to the king the following month: "The government and the position that I had was the height of my honor"—the concept had become an obsession with him—"I was unjustly expelled from there; very humbly I beg Your Highness that you give orders to put my son in possession of the government I once had."

When they met, the king "received him courteously and professed to restore all his rights and privileges, but it was his real design to take them all away," his son observed, "and this he would have done but for his sense of shame, which is a powerful force to noble souls." Now that the Indies, discovered by Columbus, were beginning to fulfill their promise, "the Catholic King begrudged the Admiral the very large share he had in them by virtue of his capitulations with the Crown."

At the time of the original capitulation, Columbus had promised to find a maritime equivalent to Marco Polo's trading route, and to establish trading relations with the Grand Khan, to Spain's benefit. Dominion over the lands he might discover en route, and the wealth thereof, were granted to Columbus almost as an afterthought, a by-product of his voyage of commercial discovery, but the Admiral placed an entirely different emphasis on the Enterprise of the Indies, seeing himself as fulfilling a mission inspired and even directed by God. Under these auspices, Columbus believed himself the recipient of a great and lasting honor, one that extended beyond the laws and memories of mortals.

Once the Sovereigns became aware of his failure to deliver what he had originally promised and the overwhelming extent of all that he had discovered, they changed the terms of the agreement to ensure that Columbus remained in his place, as their servant rather than a rival. From their point of view, they were entitled to treat him as they wished; from his perspective, the Sovereigns had unaccountably breached their contract. Columbus rallied, and tried to persuade Ferdinand to maintain Columbus's status and entitlements. "I shall serve you all the remaining days of my life, few though these may be," and according to Las Casas he vowed that in the future, his service "will prove a hundred times more illustrious than I have done Your Highness to date."

These promises restarted negotiations between Ferdinand and his tarnished Admiral, whose son realized that the king "wished to regain absolute control" over the Indies and "dispose as he pleased of the offices that were only the Admiral's to grant." Acknowledging that Columbus still had some life in him, and some claim to his discoveries in the Indies, the king offered a new capitulation and requested the name of an arbiter to bring this about; Columbus, taking the bait, put forward the name of his friend at court Diego Deza, a former Franciscan friar who was now the archbishop of Seville and the successor to Tomás de Torquemada as the Grand Inquisitor for all Spain, and whom the pope himself later reprimanded for being overzealous. The archbishop affirmed that Columbus was entitled to the governorship but referred the entire business to lawyers to sort out. In exceptionally strong language, Las Casas wrote, "The king proceeded to prevaricate on this issue and so the Admiral again petitioned him, reminding His Majesty of the service he had done him, the unjust imprisonment he had suffered, and the unwarranted way he had been stripped of the dignities, rank, and honors Their Majesties had bestowed on him."

Later, in Seville, Columbus, as persistent as ever, told the king that "he had no desire to go to law or argue his case before judges. He simply wanted His Majesty . . . to give him that which he thought fit." The Admiral explained that he was "weary to the bone and simply wanted to go off somewhere on his own and rest." Fruitless meetings exhausted his patience and strength. Growing weaker, Columbus wrote a formal petition, concluding, "I do believe that it is the pain caused by the delay in dealing with my business that is responsible for my being as crippled as I am."

He filled the idle hours fretting about his lost income from the Indies, explaining that the Indians "were and are the island's real wealth." They grew the food, baked the bread, and excavated the gold on which the "Christians" all depended, yet he was disturbed to hear that "six out of every seven Indians has died as a direct result of the inhuman treatment meted out to them: some hacked to pieces with swords, others clubbed to death, and yet others succumbing from abuse, hunger, and the appalling conditions under which they had been forced to exist." This expression of regret did not lead to a mea culpa, as might be expected. Rather, the dire situation meant that a great deal of income had been lost—Spain's income, and his.

He offered a similarly shallow excuse for his sending ships filled with slaves back to Spain. It was purely a temporary measure, he now explained. He had intended them to convert to the holy faith, and to learn Spanish customs and skills, and then return to Hispaniola, where they could pass all they had learned to their kin.

The debates and petitions continued without respite. Even Columbus came to realize he had run out of options, out of luck, and out of time. His persistence would get him nowhere. From his sickbed, he wrote to the archbishop of Seville that since the king seemed determined not to honor "the promises he had made along with the Queen (God rest her soul) both by word of mouth and in writing, I feel that it would be like banging my head against a brick wall for a simple countryman like myself to continue the battle."

The death of Queen Isabella reverberated throughout Spain and its expanding empire, threatening political instability and even civil war. Juana, the daughter of Ferdinand and Isabella, had married Philip the Fair. Mentally unstable, she became known as "Juana la Loca"—Juana the Mad. Supported by the nobility, her husband, Philip, became king of Castile, replacing his father-in-law. For a time it appeared that Juana was destined to rule, despite her infirmity, with the understanding that Ferdinand would become permanent regent. To make this plan a reality, Ferdinand struck coins with the impression "Ferdinand and Juana, King and Queen of Castile, León, and Aragón," the control of currency being the fastest route to control of government. At the same time, Philip sought to form an alliance with Juana la Loca to fend off Ferdinand. In the fall of 1505, the failure of the harvest, driving the price of wheat to unconscionable levels, added to the sense of chaos afflicting Spain.

The crisis deepened when Ferdinand arranged to marry Germaine de Foix, all of eighteen years of age, compared with Ferdinand's ripe fifty-four, and, even more unsettling, the niece of the king of France, long persona non grata in Spanish diplomatic circles. Given Germaine's age, the prospect of heirs suddenly loomed, and the old order of Ferdinand and Isabella, and the kingdoms of Aragon and Castile, and the stability and grandeur that they had represented, appeared to fade into the chronicles of the past.

On March 22, 1506, Ferdinand married his young bride, setting the stage for civil war. Philip and Juana made every effort to assert their authority. Then, one day in September, Philip overexerted himself while playing a Spanish ball game called pelota, but appeared to recover. A few days later, on September 25, he exercised again, fell ill, and by nightfall he was dead. Poison was suspected as the agent of Philip's demise, and King Ferdinand the culprit, but nothing was ever proved. The death prompted riots and pushed fragile Juana la Loca, now in her late twenties, into a profoundly affectless state in which she refused to speak or eat. Ferdinand and his newly acquired queen Germaine rebounded, having won the support of—or at least not alienating—the necessary church authorities. He remained in place as regent.

Against this tumultuous background, Columbus sought to have his rights, as he saw them, restored and confirmed for all time.

* * *

King Ferdinand left Valladolid to call on Columbus, who, his son explained, was "much afflicted by the gout and by grief at seeing himself fallen from his high estate, as well as by other ills." The old navigator, out of favor if not actually in disgrace, still mattered enough for the king to display concern. They had a long history, beginning with Isabella's sponsoring the first voyage, and continuing with both of Columbus's sons serving as pages in the royal court.

It had taken Columbus years to win standing at court. For all his ambition and desire to impose himself on Spain and its rulers, there was something profoundly otherworldly about him, something that went well beyond conventional piety and mysticism, something that drove and tormented rather than comforted him. His faith brought him no peace. He had driven himself well past the limits of endurance, and had little strength left.

Columbus felt too weak to rise from his bed to greet the king; in his place, he sent his reliable brother Bartholomew, who carried a letter in which Columbus, "in adverse and distressing circumstances," apologized for being unable to greet the king.

Ferdinand intended to rescue his father's reputation from the conspiracies arrayed against him, but his account revealed the ancient mariner in rapid decline, dwelling on his reputation and entitlements rather than the tasks of discovery, all the while needlessly endangering the lives of those who served him. He had created crises in order to demonstrate his ability to escape them, or to show his martyrdom to the world. In the name of discovery, or divine will, or the Sovereigns, he concocted confrontations, or persisted in misunderstanding his pilots or the Indians, cajoling them through the force of his personality into telling him what he wished to hear. Only in the midst of a crisis, stranded on a beach, or in the grip of a deadly storm did Columbus steadily focus on the tasks necessary for survival; otherwise, he indulged his grandiose fantasies and half consciously looked for occasions to place himself in harm's way, to tempt the devil and then loudly praise God for rescuing him from disaster. His fertile psyche devised great problems, as well as the great discoveries for which he became known.

Although Columbus's voyages had resulted in monumental discoveries, he took scant delight in them. He remained convinced that China lay just over the horizon, that paradise was accessible from the ocean, and that he had sailed to the outskirts of "India." His morality remained absolutely fixed. It could be said that over the course of his four voyages, he had discovered everything, but learned nothing. His preconceptions might have been tested and stretched a bit by his experiences, but they remained intact, an edifice of faith and will in a world that he had helped to change.

The world, in fact, was already moving beyond him, taking his discoveries into a new realm in which the "other world" became known as the New World. He was credited with discovering a continent that he had never recognized and that was named for someone else—Amerigo Vespucci. Discoveries happen in that capricious and convoluted way; often as not, credit is arbitrary.

Columbus languished in his humble lodgings in Valladolid, but, contrary to legend, he was neither isolated nor impoverished. His sons Ferdinand and Diego were in attendance, as were several of his companions on recent voyages, notably the heroic Diego Méndez. It was apparent to all that he was dying.

The ills afflicting him at the end of his life have been the subject of much speculation. The symptoms he reported, and which others confirmed, are consistent with crippling and painful arthritis—which Columbus called "gout"—and with malaria, caused by a parasite transmitted by the anopheles mosquito, marked by the high fevers, shaking chills, and anemia afflicting him. Headache, nausea, vomiting, and diarrhea are common symptoms, and if he suffered from malaria, as he likely did, he was often miserable. Reviewing his symptoms, some modern doctors have diagnosed a form of reactive arthritis formerly known as Reiter's syndrome. Caused by infection, this condition can lead to severe inflammation of the eyes (such as conjunctivitis) and painful swelling of the joints, both of which had tormented Columbus for years. If he had contracted reactive arthritis, he might well have suffered from genitourinary and gastrointestinal inflammations. Many of these conditions came and went over time, but there is no doubt that he suffered mightily from their combined effects.

After a winter spent in steady decline, Columbus dictated his will on May 19. In it, he appointed his son Diego executor, and included provisions for his son Ferdinand's mother, Beatriz de Arana, who "weighs heavily on my conscience." But he refused to elaborate: "The reason for this I am not permitted to explain."

On May 20, 1506, Columbus died in Valladolid, "having received with much devotion all the sacraments of the Church and said these last words, in *manus tuas, Domine, commenda spiritum meum,* God, in His great mercy and goodness, assuredly received him into his glory. *Ad quem nos cum eo perducat. Amen.*"

He was fifty-four years old.

Las Casas commented, "And so it was that a man who had, by his own efforts, discovered another world greater than the one we knew before and far more blessed, departed this life in a state of distress and bitterness and poverty without, as he put it himself, so much as a roof he could call his own where he might shelter from the rain and rest from his labors. He died, dispossessed and stripped of the position and honors he had earned by his tireless and heroic efforts and by risking his life over and over again."

Columbus's modest funeral procession wound its way through Valladolid to a Franciscan monastery, where his mortal remains were buried in a crypt. That was not to be his final resting place; rather, it marked the beginning of an endlessly unfolding and often bitterly contested saga of his remains and his legacy.

In 1509, three years after his death, his remains were removed to the Chapel of Santa Ana in the monastery of Santa María de Las Cuevas, near Seville, where he had spent the years in retreat and reflection between his third and fourth voyages. His son Diego, who became the second admiral, died in 1526, and he was also buried at Las Cuevas. A decade later, in 1536, the third admiral, Luís Columbus, transferred the remains of father and son, along with those of his brother Bartholomew and his wife, Felipa Moñiz, to the Cathedral of Santa María la Menor in Santo Domingo on the island of Hispaniola.

Several years after that, Luís Columbus, who had given up his family's administrative responsibilities in exchange for a title—Duke of Veragua—and an annuity, was convicted of bigamy, and sentenced to ten years' military service in North Africa. Even when confined to remote outposts, Luís Columbus, who had a long history of entanglements with women, bribed his guards, found a mistress, and married her, although his three previous wives were all living. He was exiled again, this time to Oran, a large port city in Algeria, where he died at age fifty, in 1572. He was interred in what had become the Columbus family burial place in the cathedral of Santo Domingo.

In 1697, Spain ceded part of Hispaniola, now Haiti, to France, and later the rest of the island. To prevent the remains of the Columbus family from going to the French, they were shipped to Havana, Cuba, in 1795, where they were entombed in another cathedral, apparently for all time. But it was not meant to be. In 1877, a priest in the cathedral at Santo Domingo uncovered a lead casket filled with bones, several legends identifying the "Discoverer of America, First Admiral," and a lead bullet. A year later, further excavations yielded another sign, this one reading "Last of the remains of the first admiral, Sire Christopher Columbus, discoverer." It could not be established who had placed the signs there, or the significance of the bullet.

It was later determined that the remains in Havana were actually those of Diego Columbus, the Admiral's son, and that Columbus himself was still buried in the cathedral of Santo Domingo. In 1879, a report compiled by the Spanish Royal Academy of History listed no less than five burial places for Columbus. After the Spanish-American War in 1898, Spain transported what appeared to be Columbus's remains in a lead casket to Cadiz, and then up the Guadalquivir River. On January 19, 1899, the lead casket was reburied in the Seville Cathedral, the third cathedral to host the Admiral. As he did in life, the Admiral of the Ocean Sea simultaneously unites and divides three countries and two continents.

Today, Spain considers Seville the final resting place for Columbus's remains. The Dominican Republic insists that Columbus and his errant grandson Luís are buried in Santo Domingo, and that Seville has only the remains of his son Diego. DNA tests on the remains proved inconclusive. The controversy is not likely to be resolved anytime soon. And no one knows what to make of the lead bullet found with Columbus's remains. The exhumations and re-interments of his remains evoke the unquiet soul of a voyager with no final resting place, fated to haunt the shores he explored in his lifetime.

Columbus Day

The drastic devaluation of Columbus seems a recent phenomenon, but it originated at the time of his voyages. The Spanish judicial investigator, Francisco de Bobadilla, sent him home in chains. King Ferdinand disdained him. Bishop Fonseca's intense dislike for Columbus was widely known. Amerigo Vespucci fostered the impression that he, rather than Columbus, had discovered a New World, and gave his name to the continent. His former lieutenant, Alonso de Ojeda, laid claim to territories first visited by Columbus. Nicolás de Ovando, who succeeded Columbus as governor of Hispaniola, endangered his life and mocked him. The Porras brothers, Francisco Roldán, and others who sailed with Columbus staged mutinies with little or no retribution.

The most lasting damage to Columbus's reputation came from the pen of Bartolomé de Las Casas. Arriving in Hispaniola with the new governor, Nicolás de Ovando, in 1502, Las Casas began as a slave owner. In 1510, he became the first priest to be ordained in the Americas, often called the "Apostle to the Indians." In his influential jeremiad, *A Short Account of the Destruction of the Indies* (*Brevísima relación de la destrucción de las Indias*), written in 1542, he laid out the torture and genocidal practices of the Spanish colonialists who followed Columbus.

Las Casas championed the nearly extinct victims of this outrage—"the simplest people in the world," he wrote of the Taíno Indians, "long suffering, unassertive, and submissive, . . . without malice or guile, utterly faithful and obedient"—in short, the kind of subjects the Spanish crown would want to have. Yet instead of cultivating these gentle and intelligent people, "we know for sure our fellow-countrymen have, through their cruelty and wickedness, depopulated and laid waste an area which boasted more than ten kingdoms, each of them larger than the Iberian Peninsula." They slaughtered their children, "on occasion running through a mother and her baby with a single thrust of their swords." The Spaniards were even more brutal with the Indians' leaders, whom they lashed to a "griddle consisting of sticks resting on pitchforks driven into the ground and then grill[ed] them over a slow fire, with the result that they howled in agony and despair as they died a lingering death."

All this Las Casas witnessed. He estimated that "the despotic and diabolical behavior of the Christians has, over the last forty years, led to the unjust and totally unwarranted deaths of more than twelve million souls, women and children among them." Indeed, he believed fifteen million to be a more accurate tally of deaths caused by Christians resorting to torture, wholesale slaughter, and "the harshest and most iniquitous and brutal slavery that man has ever devised for his fellow men." Las Casas's figures have long been debated, but even conservative estimates are stark: of 250,000 Indians under Spanish rule, only 40,000 survived after fifteen years. After a few decades, only a few hundred survived. Many died from infectious diseases caused by exposure to germs borne by the Europeans or their livestock, against which the inhabitants of the New World were defenseless.

And the reason for this tragedy? In his words, "Purely and simply greed."

Las Casas's indictment found a receptive audience in Spain's nascent rival, England, where it took root as the Spanish "Black Legend." For centuries thereafter, Spain and the explorers who sailed under the Spanish flag were widely condemned as murderers and thieves. The shadow of the Black Legend hung over Columbus as it did over other explorers from Spain. Explorers who sailed under the Spanish flag were widely condemned as murderers and thieves who habitually resorted to inhuman extremes of cruelty. Without meaning to, Las Casas's account served as a call to arms for Spain's mostly Protestant rivals to save the New World from further horrors. The surviving Indians became pawns in a geopolitical struggle beyond their comprehension. Even religion offered little guidance concerning the explorers' deeds and the acquisition of empire. Both Las Casas and Spain's pious rulers believed God was on their side, as did England.

In 1510, eight years after arriving in Hispaniola, Las Casas became a missionary to the Taínos of Cuba. For a time he exploited Indian labor, then renounced the practice, and by 1514 declared his opposition to the Spanish Enterprise of the Indies, even while encouraging the conversion of the Indians to Christianity. In his later years, he formulated the Doctrine of Self-Determination. It stated, simply, that all power derives from the people, that the people delegate power to rulers to serve the interests of their people, and that significant government deeds require popular approval. "No state, king, or emperor can alienate territories, or change their political system without the express approval of their inhabitants," he affirmed. Las Casas lived on until July 17, 1566, and died at age ninety-two.

Not everyone was hostile to Columbus or indifferent to his suffering and accomplishments. His loyal friend Diego Méndez always considered his desperate rescue mission in a modified canoe across the open sea to Hispaniola as his life's great adventure. In his will, dated June 19, 1536, he directed his executors to erect a tomb made of stone—"the best to be had"—to commemorate the event. In the middle of the stone, he ordered, "let there be a canoe, which is a hollowed log in which the Indians navigate, since in one such I navigated 300 leagues, and above it let them carve merely the letters which read CANOA."

Nowadays, Columbus the explorer is everywhere. Sculptures, monuments, and memorials of Columbus abound in public squares in Genoa, Barcelona, Madrid, Mexico City, Seville, and in cities throughout the Caribbean and the Americas. From street level these statues reveal themselves by turns as heroic, grotesque, and fearsome; they portray a gargoyle of conquest. Rivers, cities, towns, thoroughfares, and the nation of Colombia have been named in his honor.

In the United States especially, his example and his voyages answered an unceasing need for self-definition and identity. Beginning in the eighteenth century, his name was given to the capital of South Carolina, the capital of Ohio, and the mighty Columbia River in the Pacific Northwest. Through an act of Congress in 1871, the site of the nation's capital was named the District of Columbia. New York City has Columbia University, Columbus Circle, and Columbus Avenue.

His marble statue sits atop a seventy-foot granite column rising above Columbus Circle. Designed by Gaetano Russo in 1892, the monument's marble base proclaims:

To

CHRISTOPHER COLUMBUS

The Italians Resident in America,
Scoffed at Before,

During the Voyage, Menaced,
After It, Chained,
As Generous As Oppressed,
To the World He Gave a World.

Columbus held up a mirror to the Old World, revealing and magnifying its inhumanity and greed along with its piety, curiosity, and exuberance. Columbus's voyages revealed many harsh truths about the limits of human understanding, but it is too late to undo the consequences of these voyages. Their crimson thread is now woven deeply into the fabric of European and global history.

For all the scorn Columbus engendered, his four voyages constitute one of the greatest adventure stories in history. Although he was not the first explorer to glimpse or visit the distant shores of the Americas, his was the discovery that permanently planted the reality of the New World in the imagination—and political schemes—of the Old. Columbus forever changed the idea of what a European empire could be. He had the vision—and, at times, the delusion—to imagine, and to persuade himself and others that he had found something immense, important, and lasting.

For all their accomplishments and liabilities, Columbus's voyages were just the beginning, setting in motion consequences—political, cultural, and scientific—that persist to this day. In its complexity and powerful contradictions, his example speaks more urgently than ever to our contentious era.

✼ ACKNOWLEDGMENTS ✼

During the years I worked on Columbus's voyages, the comment I heard most frequently was "You mean he made *four* voyages? What happened on the others? Where did he go? Do the other voyages matter?" I replied that I thought the other voyages mattered greatly, that they were at least as important as the first, which, in context, set the stage for the later ones, each more adventurous and tragic than those preceding it. Many people helped make this idea a reality.

My literary agent, Suzanne Gluck, at William Morris Endeavor, once again demonstrated why she is the best. Her resourcefulness carried me through my Columbian labors. At WME, I also acknowledge the very capable assistance of Sarah Ceglarski, Caroline D'Onofrio, Elizabeth Tingue, and Eric Zohn.

In Wendy Wolf, editorial director of nonfiction at Viking Penguin, I feel fortunate to have found the ideal editor for this book. From the moment we started discussing Columbus's voyages, we seemed to jump into the midst of a conversation that had been going on for some time. I also extend my appreciation to Susan Petersen Kennedy, Paul Slovak, Carolyn Coleburn, Hal Fessenden, Sharon Gonzalez, Carla Bolte, Sonya Cheuse, and Margaret Riggs at Viking Penguin in New York; and to mapmaker Jeff Ward.

In both New York and Genoa, Italy, Anna Basoli performed tireless research and translation assistance. I must also acknowledge Dr. Alfonso Assini, coordinating director of the States Archives in Genoa. Also in Genoa, the resources of the Società Ligure di Storia Patria proved helpful.

Alfred Crosby, professor emeritus at the University of Texas, generously elaborated on his influential "Columbian Exchange." Professor Kathleen Deagan, coauthor of *Columbus's Outpost among the Taínos*, advised on my Caribbean research. Carter Emmart, director of astrovisualization at the Rose Center for Earth and Space of the American Museum of Natural History, brought his scientific and philosophical perspectives to bear on Columbus's exploration. Larry Fox held forth on navigation issues based on his extensive sailing experience; Daniella Gitlin offered translation and useful commentary concerning *Columbus et su secreto* (1976). Ash Green, who edited my book about Marco Polo's travels, intervened at the right moment to encourage me to write about Columbus. Toby Greenberg, my photo researcher, tracked down numerous Columbus-related images. Heather Halstead, executive director of Reach the World, shared her enthusiasm about sailing across the Atlantic in the wake of Columbus. Gail Jacobs literally saved my life, for which I will always be grateful. Payne Johnson offered his insights into Columbus's later voyages. Edmund and Sylvia Morris offered inspiration and camaraderie over the years. Vincent Pica, flotilla commander of the United States Coast Guard Auxiliary, brought his knowledge of seamanship to bear. David Hurst Thomas, curator in the Department of Anthropology at the American Museum of Natural History, called my attention to the Columbian resources of his institution. I also wish to acknowledge the contributions of Chip and Susan Fisher, Cesar Polinia, Nicole Robson, Jeannette Watson Sanger, Matthew Schaeffer, Olga Valdes Skidmore, Joseph Thanhauser III, and, of course, Henry. My thanks also go to Daniel Dolgin and to Loraine Dolgin Gardner for travel expertise. Dan, one of the most helpful people on the planet, also read the manuscript with care, and the book has benefited from his scrutiny.

My daughter Sara brought her impressive editorial skills to bear on the manuscript. And my son Nicholas, a competitive sailor, shed light on some of the navigational issues faced by Columbus.

At the New York Society Library, chief librarian Mark Bartlett was always there to answer queries with his customary resourcefulness. Daniel M. Rossner, my fellow trustee, pointed out V. S. Naipaul's provocative article about Columbus and Robinson Crusoe, and Sara Elliott Holliday brought to light material relating to Bartolomé de Las Casas.

In addition, I consulted the Hispanic Society of America's trove in upper Manhattan, and the LuEsther T. Mertz Library at the New York Botanical Garden, where Jane Dorfman, reference librarian, retrieved items relating to the Columbian Exchange; as well as the collection of Taíno artifacts at El Museo del Barrio New York. At Columbia University, Butler Library's collection of works concerning Columbus became an essential resource. My thanks to the library's reference librarians for pointing me in the right direction. I am also obliged to Columbia's MFA research internship program and to Patricia O'Toole for providing Aaron Cutler to assist with research on this book.

My friend James B. Garvin, chief scientist of NASA's Goddard Spaceflight Center in Greenbelt, Maryland, brought his expertise to bear on retracing Columbus's track across the Atlantic and on the Columbian Exchange.

The Harvard University Archives, Cambridge, Massachusetts, graciously gave me access to the complete Columbus collection of Samuel Eliot Morison, the author of *Admiral of the Ocean Sea* (1942). At the John Carter Brown Library, Brown University, I appreciate the assistance of Edward L. Widmer, director, and Ken Ward in making the most of the resources of this exceptional collection. Richard Ring, formerly of the John Carter Brown Library at Brown University and currently head curator and librarian, Watkinson Library, Trinity College, Hartford, Connecticut, brought his agile thinking to bear on my research.

At the Library of Congress in Washington, D.C., I owe a debt to Thomas Mann, reference librarian, as well as to Everette Larson in the Hispanic Division and to John Hébert, chief of the Geography and Map Division, for their insights into the complex historical record of Columbus's voyages. In May 2009, I attended the Library's symposium, "Exploring Waldseemüller's World," where presenters Owen Gingerich and Nicolás Wey Gómez thoughtfully analyzed this seminal cartographic representation of the New World. Anyone wishing to step back in time to 1507 need only stand in front of this giant map on display at the Library.

It was a delight to conduct research again in the Archivo General de Indias in Seville. These days elements of its collection, including digital facsimiles and images relating to Columbus, are available online at http://pares .mcu.es. I wish to thank Pilar Lazáro and the staff for their cooperation with my inquiries. I also wish to extend appreciation to the Biblioteca Columbina, located in the Cathedral of Seville (www.institucioncolumbina.org). Here thousands of volumes from the libraries of Christopher Columbus and his son Ferdinand can still be inspected. To step into this library is akin to peering into the mind of Columbus.

In Palos de la Frontera, Spain, I visited La Rábida Monastery, where Columbus planned his first voyage. Much of its environment has been preserved or restored to its appearance during the explorer's day. In Madrid, the collection of the Museo Naval proved as helpful as it had been during my previous visits, especially its celebrated oxhide chart by Juan de la Cosa.

In Rio de Janeiro, Brazil, I conducted research at the Real Gabinete Português de Leitura, where a variant scholarly tradition emphasizes Columbus's Portuguese connections. (Baretto Mascarenhas's 1977 work, *"Colombo" Português*, is one example.) I am extremely grateful to Jacqueline Philomeno for the warmth of her friendship and the breadth of her understanding.

My research in the Dominican Republic, once the seat of Columbus's empire, took me to La Isabela (Puerto Plata), the site of Columbus's fort and home. In Santo Domingo, the collections of the Museo de las Casas Reales, the Museo Alcáza de Colón, and the Museo del Hombre Dominicano, with its comprehensive collection of Taíno artifacts, illuminated aspects of Columbus's voyages. Mayra Castillo, Tiffany Singh, and Alejandro Tolentino made me feel welcome and provided guidance with my research, as did the capable personnel of my hotel, the Hostal Nicolas de Ovando, the former residence of Columbus's successor in Santo Domingo. For additional expertise relating to the Dominican Republic, I am indebted to Marcela Manubens, senior vice president of Phillips–Van Heusen Corporation for Global Social Responsibility, and her colleague Juan Carlos Contreras, PVH's regional manager. I wish to extend particular appreciation to Frank Moya Pons, the Dominican historian, for making available several works about Columbus.

🐚 NOTES ON SOURCES 🐚

The ever-expanding literature on Columbus encompasses diverse languages and historical traditions. To give some idea of its size, Simonetta Conti's *Bibliografia colombiana, 1793–1990*, which includes books and articles in a variety of languages, runs to well over seven hundred pages, yet even this massive compendium ends before the outpouring of additional documents and translations inspired by the Columbus Quincentenary in 1992. As my own narrative makes plain, Columbus's legacy and reputation were highly controversial right from the start. Throughout his career, glory and dishonor ran neck and neck, and the race continues to this day.

Fortunately, Columbus, his son, various Spanish ministers, sailors, and historians all left accounts of his actions—often voluminous and impassioned, pleading for the Admiral of the Ocean Sea or against him, and in some cases, both for *and* against him. These firsthand reports, with their often contrasting testimony, make it possible to understand Columbus's voyages in a multidimensional way. The *Repertorium Columbianum*, comprising over five thousand pages of original source material published in thirteen volumes overseen by Geoffrey Symcox of UCLA beginning in the late 1980s, contributed greatly to the subject, as did the multivolume *Nuova Raccolta Colombiana*, published in Italian and English by the Istituto Poligrafico e Zecca dello Stato, Libreria dello Stato, in Rome over a period of years around the quincentenary of his first voyage, in 1992.

Among outstanding American works on the subject, Samuel Eliot Morison's *Admiral of the Ocean Sea* (1942) remains the largest maritime database pertaining to Columbus. Morison is preoccupied with comparisons between Columbus's routes and his own journeys by sea and air, which often loom larger than his subject's. His views of the people and cultures that Columbus and his crew encountered in the New World are reflected in his patrician outlook and that of the World War II era. In trying to retrace some of Columbus's voyages with a modern fleet, he occasionally relied on flawed data, and as a result many of his landfalls occurred scores of miles from Columbus's presumed original course. (To paraphrase the song, Morison was at times looking for the Admiral in all the wrong places.) For more on this, see Hobbs, "The Track of the Columbus Caravels in 1492."

Washington Irving's exhaustive and well-sourced *Life and Voyages of Christopher Columbus* (1828) provides the color and context absent from Morison's more technical study—and even Morison relies heavily on Irving's account. More recently, Felipe Fernández-Armesto's succinct biography, *Columbus* (1991), presents an astringent critique of its subject, and John Noble Wilford's *The Mysterious History of Columbus* (1991) offers provocative commentary about questions concerning the Admiral's voyages. Finally, *The Worlds of Christopher Columbus* (1992), by William D. Phillips Jr. and Carla Rahn Phillips, brings context to bear on Columbus's life and times. Foreign-language biographies of Columbus often take their lead from Morison, for example, Paolo Emilio Taviani's *Cristoforo Columbo* (Istituto Geografico de Agostini, 1974, two volumes). An exception is Henry Harisse's thorough *Christophe Columbe* (1884–5), which portrays Columbus in a benign light that seems remarkable by today's standards. I am indebted to all these historians for their energetic, rigorous approaches to the formidable subject of Christopher Columbus.

In most cases, I have indicated the source of quotations in my own text, whether it is Columbus himself, his son Ferdinand, Bartolomé de Las Casas, or commentators such as Peter Martyr.

Prologue

Of all the unresolved questions surrounding Columbus's voyages, the location of his first landfall is among the most persistent and revealing of his motives. Columbus had a strong incentive to announce that he had found something of significance, and to claim it for Spain (and for his future wealth and titles), so it would seem to be in his interest to be as precise as possible about what he had found, and where. But there were also reasons for him to obscure the exact location. Laboring under his Chinese delusion, he assumed he was approaching Asia. In addition, he did not want to divulge this vital piece of information to his rivals, including those at court in Spain. So he had to steer between the Scylla of revelation and the Charybdis of his geographical handicaps. Anyone capable of making his crew, boys and men alike, swear an oath that Cuba belonged to the mainland rather than admitting it was an island, as Columbus did, was capable of obscuring his route. Add to these considerations the changes wrought by five hundred years of erosion, and the chances of pinpointing his first landfall are slim indeed. Nonetheless, hypotheses abound.

The *National Geographic* of November 1986 offered an account by Joseph Judge of a thorough scientific investigation into the location of Columbus's first landfall, the result of five years of analysis. "No fewer than nine landfall islands have been suggested, defended, and opposed," Judge writes. "Cat, Watling, Conception, Samana Cay, Plana Cays, Mayaguana, East Caicos, Grand Turk, and Egg in the northwestern Bahamas." Each candidate for first landfall had a distinguished proponent. Samana, for example, was the choice in 1862 of Gustavus V. Fox, who was Lincoln's assistant secretary of the navy; the *National Geographic* itself endorsed this choice in 1894, and there the case rested until 1942, when Samuel Eliot Morison came out in favor, unequivocally, of Watling Island, now known as San Salvador—sixty-five miles to the west of Samana Cay. However, in a dissenting opinion in the same November 1986 issue of *National Geographic*, Luis Marden argued, after an exhaustive examination of the evidence and navigational techniques available to Columbus, that Morison and others might well have been mistaken about the most basic unit of measurement, the sea league, which Marden puts at 2.82 nautical miles, which ruled out Samana Cay as the first landfall by some ten miles. He concluded, "We cannot say that we have established with absolute certainty the precise point of Columbus's landfall. Currents may vary, and there are still unknown factors." Nevertheless, the uninhabited island of Samana Cay remains the choice of Dr. James B. Garvin, chief scientist at NASA's Goddard Space Flight Center in Greenbelt, MD, based on his careful analysis of satellite data of Columbus's track.

All of these choices share an assumption: Columbus meant to indicate the actual location of his first landfall. On this basis both Morison and Judge insisted that the answer must closely fit Columbus's description in the log. But that approach might well be flawed. Columbus's description was curiously generic, as if he were not paying close attention, or deliberately trying to be vague. And what about erosion altering the reefs, shoals, harbors, and beaches, as was likely to happen over time? What if Columbus camouflaged the location to protect his claim, as if it were buried treasure that he wanted no one else to find? He was not above manipulating data in the log to suit his purposes, and what more likely occasion than his first landfall to throw others off his track? Or was he sincere, but having one of his delusional episodes? Keep in mind that this is the same Columbus who, on a later voyage, believed the seas sloped upward in the vicinity of paradise. He wrote about that phenomenon with as much conviction as he reported any of his other findings. Who is to say exactly when Columbus was delusional and when he was not? Because of these questions, it seems unlikely the exact landfall will ever be determined with complete assurance.

For another consideration of the erratic history of the first landfall, see John Noble Wilford's *The Mysterious History of Columbus*, pages 129 and following.

Chapter 1: Thirty-three Days

Luis de Torres was not, as has been sometimes claimed, subsequently the owner of an enormous estate in the New World.

Tobacco is mentioned in *Journals and Other Documents on the Life and Voyages of Christopher Columbus*, page 91, note 2. Fernández de Oviedo discusses pineapples on page 99 of *Oviedo on Columbus*.

The subsequent journey, beginning around December 16, was as follows, based on Columbus's log:

Daring to enter "an arm of the sea" reaching inland aboard one of his longboats, he observed villages consisting of attractive dwellings, all the while terrifying their dwellers. One look at the approaching Europeans and their weapons, one whiff of their unfamiliar scent, and "they all fled." The explorer assumed "those people must have been persecuted because they had so much fear." Persecuted by whom? Columbus did not say, but his guess was a good one. As soon as he and his crew drew nigh, "signal fires" illuminated ubiquitous lookout posts, warning of, rather than heralding, his arrival in this strange land. "These people must have been persecuted because they had so much fear." Overwhelmed by the sand, the sea, and the fragrant air, Columbus named the region Paradise Valley, and the river the Guadalquivir after the main waterway to Seville.

At midnight, Sunday, December 16, a "light offshore breeze" picked up, and along with it, the explorer's fortunes. He "sailed close-hauled along the coast of Hispaniola." At three in the morning, "a wind sprang up" and as he approached the "middle of the gulf"—anyone's guess which one, with Columbus obscuring his track to preserve secrecy—his fleet encountered a tiny, isolated craft: one canoe bearing one Indian. Columbus wrote that he wondered how this "Indian could stay afloat with such a strong wind," and moved quickly to seize him and have him "brought aboard ship." Columbus resorted to his standard procedure for dealing with unwilling guests, bestowing glass beads, bells, and brass rings on the Indian, whom he transported sixteen miles to a position "near the sea." Disembarking at another settlement consisting of new houses, the Indian became the explorer's goodwill ambassador, telling the locals that the great chief and his men, the Admiral and the Christians, as they thought of themselves, were "good people," and confirming rumors that had already reached the ears of the inhabitants.

Walking out of the dense, leafy growth came five hundred men, and eventually, their chief. Impressed and gratified, the Admiral described the extraordinary sight: "One by one, and many by many, they came to the ship, bringing nothing with them, although they wore the finest gold in the ears or in the nose, which they gave with good grace." He responded to their generosity, and to the lure of gold, by ordering them to be treated honorably because "they are the best people in the world and above all the gentlest." During these respectful rituals, their twenty-one-year-old king remained safely on the beach, earning Columbus's goodwill by encouraging a flow of intelligence concerning the location of gold. Even they reminded him of his adopted home. "This king and all the others went naked as their mothers bore them, and so too the women, without any shame; and they are the most handsome men and women that he had found hitherto; so white that if they went clothed and protected themselves from the sun and air they would be almost as white as in Spain." The gratifying potential of gold prompted Columbus to lavish praise on their island, and he went so far as to claim that in all Castile "nothing compared with it for beauty and excellence." The very trees were exceptional, to his way of thinking, "so luxuriant that their leaves ceased to be green, and were of blackish verdure." Here, he concluded, could be found "everything that man could want."

That night, the young king ventured aboard the flagship, and cast doubt on the story of King Ferdinand and Queen Isabella, and Columbus's mission. Through interpreters, the navigator and his officers heard that the king believed these three ships had come from the sky, as did the "Sovereigns of Castile," who were "not of this world."

Columbus interpreted these naive words with dismaying opportunism. "You may believe that this island and all the others are as much yours as Castile," he advised. "There is nothing wanting save a settlement, and to command them [the inhabitants] to do as what you will." Having made this assessment, he naturally took the next step: "I, with the people on board, who are not many, could overrun all these islands without opposition; for already I have seen that when only three of the mariners went ashore, where there was a formidable multitude of these Indians, all fled, without seeking to do them ill." Even better, "they bear no arms, and are completely defenseless . . . so that a thousand [of them] would not face three [of Castile]; and so they are fit to be ordered about and made to work, to sow and do all else that may be needed, and you may build towns and teach them to go clothed, and to [live by] our customs." In other words, their nakedness, their innocence, and their gentleness could be employed against them; these "best people in the world" would make ideal slaves of Castile, or so he wanted his Sovereigns to believe. If he could not bring Ferdinand and Isabella gold and a direct route over water to the Indies, he would instead bring them slaves and an empire.

Chapter 2: Son of Genoa

For an insider's appreciation of La Superba, "Genoa the Proud," see Emilio Pandiani, *Vita privata genovese nel Rinascimento* (1915) and *Vita della Repubblica di Genova nell'Età di Cristoforo Columbo* (1952).

The Piccolomini quotation is drawn from Gaetano Ferro, *Liguria and Genoa at the Time of Columbus* (1992), page 197 (vol. 3, *Nuova Raccolta Colombiana*).

Paolo Emilio Taviani discusses the genealogy of Columbus's mother in *Cristoforo Colombo: Genius of the Sea* (1990). Also see Genoa, Commissione Colombiana, *Christopher Columbus: Documents and Proofs of His Genoese Origin* (1932) and Silvio A. Bedini, *The Christopher Columbus Encyclopedia* (1992), vol. 1, page 283.

Details of the plague can be found in Pandiani, *Vita della Repubblica di Genova* (1952).

The descriptions of Genoa harbor, city, and trade are drawn from *Vita della Repubblica di Genova*. Pandiani's *Vita privata genovese nel Rinascimento* describes Genoese trade and sailing. Accounts of slavery in Genoa, which imprinted itself on Columbus's consciousness, come from the same author's *Vita privata genovese nel Rinascimento*, pages 205–13.

Among the earliest to sing Genoa's praises was the fourteenth-century Italian scholar and traveler (sometimes called the "first tourist") Francesco Petrarca, or Petrarch. In his "Itinerarium ad Sepulcrum Domini" ("Journey to the Holy Sepulchre"), a travel guide that he wrote for a friend in about 1350, Petrarca said, "Let's go to Genoa. Here you will see rising from a rocky mountain an imperious city of proud walls and superb men, whose very appearance announces her as the Lady of the Sea."

Works on the Inquisition are numerous. Useful summaries include François Soyer's *The Persecution of the Jews and Muslims of Portugal* (2007), pages 140 and following. Also, Felipe Fernández-Armesto's *1492* (2009) contains a lucid consideration of the subject in a global context, beginning on page 99.

An analysis of the evidence of the Perestrello-Columbus marriage can be found in Rebecca Catz's "Christopher Columbus' Portuguese Family," a paper presented at the XIII Symposium on Portuguese Traditions at UCLA on April 21, 1990, and in her book *Christopher Columbus and the Portuguese* (1993), pp. 15–16. See also Las Casas on Columbus, pages 30–47. For more on the controversy surrounding Felipa's death, see Justin Winsor's antique but reliable *Christopher Columbus* (1892), pages 154–55.

Columbus's assertion that he observed Ferdinand and Isabella occupy the

Alhambra can be found in Wilford's *The Mysterious History of Columbus*, pages 25–26. Finally, Morison's *Journals and Other Documents on the Life and Voyages of Christopher Columbus* discusses the peripatetic Sovereigns on page 299.

Chapter 3: Shipwreck

To navigators, coral reefs pose a lethal menace, but to an oceanographer or naturalist, they rank among the wonders of the deep: fragile, varied ecosystems of hard corals made of skeletons secreting calcium carbonate, the primary component of pearls, eggshells, and especially seashells. There is more to a coral reef than a pile of shells, however. Sponges, worms, and bivalves, among other marine creatures, bore into the calcium carbonate, reducing the coral skeletons into sediment filling the gaps in the reef. Eventually, algae and other microorganisms hold the reef in position. Nearing the end of his voyage aboard the *Beagle*, a naval survey brig, Charles Darwin became fascinated by reefs during his passage through the Indian Ocean in 1836, and after intense study, offered a theory of coral formation the following year in which he identified three main types: the fringing reef, the barrier reef, and the atoll. Fringing reefs commonly border continental and island shorelines, especially in the Caribbean. Farther offshore can be found barrier reefs, which come into being when the ocean floor sinks, and fringing reefs are pulled away from shore.

Barrier reefs are prevalent in the Indo-Pacific, and also in the Caribbean. Australia's Great Barrier Reef, extending over 1,200 miles, is considered the largest of its type. Finally, if the reef sinks below the ocean surface, it can be considered an atoll, and surrounds a lagoon.

On the voyage out, Columbus had erroneously considered the appearance of sargassum a sign that he was approaching land, and he set about sounding the depths of the Atlantic only to find that he was nowhere near the shore, a mistake he did not repeat when inbound.

For more on the mesmerizing Sargasso Sea and seaweed, see Stan Ulanski, *The Gulf Stream* (2008), pages 78–81, a worthwhile popular account.

Chapter 4: "The People from the Sky"

For more on the Treaty of Alcáçovas, see Morison, *Admiral of the Ocean Sea*, pages 40 and 344.

Columbus's inadvertent return to Portugal rather than Spain remains one of the most hotly contested issues in Columbus scholarship. Partisans of his supposed Portuguese origins seized on it as an example of where his true sympathies lay. Other commentators have suggested that Columbus's return to the Iberian Peninsula indicated that he unconsciously had his heart set on returning to Portugal all along, or that he pursued a covert agenda favoring João II rather than his announced sponsors, Ferdinand and Isabella. Or even that he functioned all along as a secret agent on behalf of Portugal. Columbus did have some residual feeling for Portugal after all his years there, but in reality, João II contemplated assassinating Columbus to prevent his return to Spain, and the mariner lived to regret washing up on the

Portuguese coast in a tempest. Had the weather been better, he would have proceeded directly to Spain rather than engaging in a distracting and dangerous detour.

Had Columbus by some miracle managed to cross the Pacific Ocean and make
it to China, no Grand Khan would have greeted him as Marco Polo had once been
greeted; instead, he would have been rebuffed by the newly resurgent Ming dynasty,
whose bureaucrats had banned maritime trade and led their nation into deep iso-
lationism. How can we know? That was exactly what happened to Columbus's cousin
(on his wife's side), Rafael Perestrello. He sailed on behalf of Portugal to the Chinese
coast in 1513, the first European to accomplish that feat. Perestrello traded successfully in Guangzhou, but when a Portuguese embassy charged with opening formal
relations reached the Chinese court, the Ming emperor, Zhengde, threw them in
jail, and all dealings between the two nations ceased.

Columbus's "Letter on the First Voyage," sometimes known as "The Spanish Letter of Columbus," has a varied and intriguing history of its own. The original four-
page black-letter document, issued without a title, was probably published in
Barcelona in April 1493, based on Columbus's original manuscript, dated February
15 of that year. The Admiral called it "Columbus's Letter to Santángel," although it
was actually intended for his Sovereigns. It is possible that the conventions of the
royal court demanded that an intermediary, such as King Ferdinand's finance minister, Luís de Santángel, announce or otherwise convey a document like this to the
Sovereigns rather than their receiving it directly.

Leandro de Cosco's Latin translation, probably completed in late April of the
same year, elevated the document's stature, and went through nine editions in a
year's time. A copy can be found at the New York Public Library, although the images contained within are misleading. One portrays a figure purported to be Columbus disembarking from a large galley with oars. That, like the others, were
simply reprints from books already printed in Switzerland. Nevertheless, Columbus's "Letter on the First Voyage" ranks as the first significant American document.

Chapter 5: River of Blood

Financing the fleet for the second voyage is described in *Christopher Columbus:
Accounts and Letters*, vol. 6, part 2, *Nuova Raccolta Colombiana*.

Las Casas's remarks on the voyage are mentioned in Hugh Thomas, *Rivers of
Gold* (2003), page 304.

For a thorough discussion of Fernández de Oviedo, Las Casas, and Martyr,
among other Spanish historians who have written about Columbus, see *Oviedo on
Columbus*, vol. 9, *Repertorium Columbianum* (2000), pages 9–27. Details of Fernández de Oviedo's biography have been drawn from *Oviedo*, pages ix–xvii.

The Discoverers (1983) by Daniel Boorstin presents a concise overview of this
transformative era of exploration on pages 248–59.

Coma's description of the raucous departure from Cadiz can be found in "Syl-
lacio's Letter to the Duke of Milan 13 December 1494" in Morison, *Journals and
Other Documents on the Life and Voyages of Christopher Columbus*, pages 229–30.
The "huntress" description appears on page 231.

Animals on the ships are described in *Christopher Columbus: Accounts and Letters*, vol. 6, *Nuova Raccolta Colombiana*, page 17.

Fernández-Armesto discusses festivities in *Columbus*, page 53.

The report about Doña Beatriz de Peraza can be found in Morison's *Admiral of the Ocean Sea*, page 399.

The tale of the friar and the cannibals is related in *Admiral of the Ocean Sea*, page 405. In general, the evidence presented by Columbus and other participants in the voyages is more reliable than subsequent efforts to reinterpret their experiences. For a scholarly discussion of this fraught subject, see Myers, "Island Carib Cannibalism."

Peter Martyr is believed to have based his description of *areítos* on the observations of Santiago Cañizares, who had witnessed them. And information about Taíno music and instruments has been drawn from Lynne Guitar, "New Notes about Taíno Music and Its Influence on Contemporary Dominican Life." Peter Martyr is also known as Peter Martyr d'Anghiera.

Peter Martyr's letter to Cardinal Ascanio Sforza is in *The Discovery of the New World in the Writings of Peter Martyr of Anghiera*, vol. 2, *Nuova Raccolta Colombiana* (1992), page 229.

The remarks by Guillermo Coma are from Morison, *Journals and Other Documents on the Life and Voyages of Christopher Columbus*, page 236.

Fernández de Oviedo expounds on poison apples on page 91 of Fernández de Oviedo y Valdés, *Natural History of the West Indies*.

The term "buccaneer" derives from the French term for the rack, *boucan*, used for barbecuing meat, an early occupation of such "freebooters," another word of piratical origin, referring to plundering and booty.

Columbus's remarks about the city of La Isabela are in Kathleen Deagan and José María Cruxent, *Columbus's Outpost among the Taínos* (2002), pages 48–50, 54.

Chapter 6: Rebellion

The list of requested supplies can be found in Deagan and Cruxent, *Columbus's Outpost among the Taínos*, page 137.

Ferdinand and Isabella's kingdom of Castile was only the most recent empire to claim the endlessly contested city of Cadiz, believed to have been founded by Phoenicians as a trading center, who called it Gadir, for "walled city." In AD 711, the Moors seized it, and held it until 1262, when it was conquered by Alfonso X of Castile. Under Spanish rule, the city assumed the name Cadiz. As exploration grew, Cadiz attracted mariners from across Europe, especially Genoa. By one estimate, nearly half the city consisted of Genoese in search of opportunity, and they were about to greet one of their own.

Columbus's advice to the Sovereigns is quoted in *Christopher Columbus: Accounts and Letters*, vol. 6, part 1, *Nuova Raccolta Colombiana*, pages 13–39.

The letters of Ferdinand and Isabella beginning April 13 are quoted in Morison, *Admiral of the Ocean Sea*, page 436.

Fernández de Oviedo discusses mining for gold on pages 106–9 of Fernández de Oviedo y Valdés, *Natural History of the West Indies* (1959).

Las Casas's description of Ojeda can be found in Morison, *Admiral of the Ocean Sea*, pages 432–33.

On page 36 of Deagan and Cruxent's *Columbus's Outpost among the Taínos*, the authors write that the Indians ate, in addition to hutias, "iguanas, birds, snakes, giant beetle grubs, and insects. This versatility did not commend them to the Spaniards," who were disgusted by the practice.

Andrés Bernáldez's vivid and appealing description of the Indians of Jamaica is reproduced in Morison, *Admiral of the Ocean Sea*, pages 474–76.

Columbus's remarks about the second voyage come from *Christopher Columbus: Accounts and Letters*, vol. 6, part 1, *Nuova Raccolta Colombiana*, written February 26, 1495, pages 267–325 passim.

Chapter 7: Among the Taínos

Michele de Cuneo on La Bella Saonese is quoted in Morison, *Admiral of the Ocean Sea*, page 478. His other observations can be found in *Admiral of the Ocean Sea*, pages 482–88.

Columbus writes about converting Indians to Christianity in *Christopher Columbus: Accounts and Letters*, vol. 6, part 1, *Nuova Raccolta Colombiana*, pages 340–41. And he explains his ideas about educating Indians on page 355.

Las Casas discusses greyhounds and Indians in *Christopher Columbus: Accounts and Letters*, vol. 6, part 2, *Nuova Raccolta Colombiana*, pages 113, 152. And he explores Columbus's increasingly tormented relations with the Indians on page 492 of *Admiral of the Ocean Sea*.

In addition to Peter Martyr, Columbus himself refers to the massive number of Indian deaths in a letter to Ferdinand and Isabella dated October 15, 1495, in *Christopher Columbus: Accounts and Letters*, vol. 6, part 1, *Nuova Raccolta Colombiana*, page 337. Here he says the famine killed two-thirds of the region's 50,000 inhabitants, and "it is not over yet, nor do we know when to hope the end." For more statistics about the depopulation of the Indians, see *Admiral of the Ocean Sea*, page 493.

The Dominican Republic (1998) by Frank Moya Pons reviews the political structure of the Indians, pages 22–23.

Aguado is quoted in Deagan and Cruxent, *Columbus's Outpost among the Taínos*, pages 63–64, relying on Las Casas.

Ramon Pané and his Indian investigations receive a thorough consideration in Antonio M. Stevens-Arroyo, *Cave of the Jagua* [sic] (2006), pages 41–83.

The anecdote about the headless people at La Isabela appears in *Columbus's Outpost among the Taínos* on page 72, quoting Las Casas. I have adjusted the translation slightly for syntax.

Interlude: The Columbian Exchange

The starting point for considering the Columbian Exchange is Alfred Crosby's 1972 work, *The Columbian Exchange: Biological and Cultural Consequences of 1492* (republished in 2003). Related studies of this resonant subject include the following:

Woodrow W. Borah and Sherburne F. Cook's *The Aboriginal Population of Central Mexico on the Eve of the Spanish Conquest* (1963); Noble David Cook's *Born to Die; The Native Population of the Americas in 1492* (1992), edited by William M. Denevan; Bernal Díaz del Castillo's *Historia verdadera de la conquista de la Nueva España* (1956); William H. McNeill's *Plagues and Peoples* (1976); Elinor G. K. Melville's *A Plague of Sheep* (1994); Redcliffe N. Salaman's *The History and Social Influence of the Potato* (1993); and Russel Thornton's *American Indian Holocaust and Survival* (1987).

The following chart suggests the extent of the Columbian Exchange as it affected both the Old World and the New:

	OLD WORLD TO NEW WORLD	NEW WORLD TO OLD WORLD
Diseases	Smallpox	Syphilis?
	Measles	
	Chicken Pox	
	Malaria	
	Yellow Fever	
	Influenza	
	The Common Cold	
Animals	Horses	Turkeys
	Cattle	Llamas
	Pigs	Alpacas
	Sheep	Guinea Pigs
	Goats	
	Chickens	
Plants	Rice	Corn (Maize)
	Wheat	Potatoes
	Barley	Beans
	Oats	Tobacco
	Coffee	Peanuts
	Sugarcane	Squash
	Bananas	Peppers
	Melons	Tomatoes
	Olives	Pumpkins
	Dandelions	Pineapples
	Daisies	Cacao (chocolate)
	Clover	Chicle (chewing gum)
	Ragweed	Papayas
	Kentucky Bluegrass	Cassava (tapioca)
		Guavas
		Avocados

Chapter 8: "A Great Roaring"

Columbus's impassioned complaints about his detractors at court and the heat he endured on the third voyage can be found in *Christopher Columbus: Accounts and Letters of the Second, Third, and Fourth Voyages*, vol. 6, part 1, *Nuova Raccolta Colombiana*, pages 66–67.

For more on Columbus's flamboyant ideas concerning biblical sites, see Delno C. West, "Christopher Columbus, Lost Biblical Sites, and the Last Crusade."

The Dragon's Mouth is mentioned in *Las Casas on Columbus*, page 46. Meanwhile, references to the earthly paradise and the characteristics of the people he encountered appear in *Christopher Columbus: Accounts and Letters of the Second, Third, and Fourth Voyages*, vol. 6, part 1, *Nuova Raccolta Colombiana*, pages 87 and following.

Columbus's observation that "the world is small" appears in the Letter Rarissima, quoted in *Nuova Raccolta*, vol. 6, part 1. Columbus wrote this letter in Jamaica in July 1503.

For more about Columbus and the Guaiqueri Indians and *chicha*, see Morison and Obregón's *The Caribbean as Columbus Saw It* (1964), beginning on page 160. This work contains photographs of vistas as they might have appeared to Columbus, but five hundred years of erosion and other changes have altered the land- and seascapes. Nevertheless, this document remains an evocative view of Columbian harbors and ports.

Chapter 9: Roldán's Revolt

For full accounts of the back-and-forth between the two sides as related by Ferdinand Columbus, see Fernando Colón, *The Life of the Admiral Christopher Columbus by His Son Ferdinand* (1959) and *The History of the Life and Deeds of the Admiral Don Christopher Columbus, Attributed to His Son Fernando Colón* (2004). Also, Las Casas delivers his own stinging assessment in *Las Casas on Columbus: The Third Voyage*, vol. 11, *Repertorium Columbianum* (1999). Las Casas lamented that Roldán was never brought to justice in Spain—his lineage worked in his favor, just as Columbus's worked against him.

Chapter 10: "Send Me Back in Chains"

The letter to Doña Juana appears in Cecil Jane, *The Four Voyages of Columbus* (1988), vol. 2, page 54.

Letters from Bobadilla read aloud: *Las Casas on Columbus: The Third Voyage*, pages 24–128. Here, as in many other places, Las Casas shows his mettle as a historian when he refrains from strident editorializing and learned digressions to focus on the matter at hand.

Background about Bobadilla's inquiry is drawn from the corrective study by Consuelo Varela, *La caída de Cristóbal Colón, el juicio de Bobadilla* (2006).

In *Las Casas on Columbus: The Third Voyage*, page 136, Las Casas writes that

Vallejo was "my good friend." The letter in which Columbus avows that he has been diligent, and says "I swear," appears in the same work, page 43.

The Royal Mandate restoring Columbus's possessions is contained in Morison, *Journals and Other Documents on the Life and Voyages of Christopher Columbus*, pages 300–302.

Chapter 11: El Alto Viaje

John Noble Wilford's *The Mysterious History of Columbus* offers an absorbing discussion of the mystical *Book of Prophecies* on pages 217 and 223.

Ferdinand's extensive library emphasizes the bookish, scholarly side of the Columbus family. Although Christopher, as a mariner, is considered primarily a man of action, he was thoroughly educated in the sea, and throughout his life he was eager to absorb (if not apply) new information and lore. His brother Bartholomew was, of course, a map and book dealer, and his son a historian and bibliophile.

Ferdinand Columbus never married.

Chapter 12: Castaways in Paradise

Columbus's striking description of ascending his ship and hearing the voice of God appears in *Christopher Columbus: Accounts and Letters of the Second, Third, and Fourth Voyages*, vol. 6, part 1, *Nuova Raccolta Colombiana*, pages 143 and following. The entire letter is an extraordinary cri de coeur that would be easy to dismiss were it not so self-dramatizing and nakedly poignant.

The "Account by Diego Mendez of Certain Incidents on Christopher Columbus's Last Voyage" can be found in J. M. Cohen, *The Four Voyages of Christopher Columbus* (1969), pages 305–17.

Chapter 13: February 29, 1504

Las Casas's first crossing: quoted in David Boyle, *Toward the Setting Sun* (2008), page 264.

Details of the death of Isabella can be found in Hugh Thomas's authoritative study, *Rivers of Gold*, page 236. Thomas appears much less troubled by Columbus's humanitarian failings than other contemporary historians, and encompasses a wide swath of the age of discovery in his sturdy account.

Isabella's reputation for piety lived on after her death. A movement took shape to have her canonized for sainthood on the basis of her protection of the poor and of the Indians of the Caribbean, despite her fervent support of the Inquisition and the expulsion of the Jews from Spain in 1492, the year of Columbus's first voyage. As recently as 1974, Pope John Paul VI nominated Isabella I for beatification, the third of four steps toward canonization. A person who is beatified has been recognized by the Catholic Church to have ascended to heaven, and can intercede on behalf of the faithful who pray to her. She was survived by her husband, Ferdinand II, who lived on for another eight years, until 1512.

For a review of Columbus's numerous health issues, see Wilford, *The Mysterious History of Columbus*, pages 240 and following. And details of Columbus's burial can be found in "Burial Places of Columbus," in Silvio Bedini, *The Christopher Columbus Encyclopedia*, vol. 1, pages 77–80.

Epilogue

The dedication of the Columbus Fountain at Union Station in Washington, DC, to name one prominent example of many, occasioned a tremendous outpouring of official public recognition. The Columbus Fountain was designed by Lorado Taft, an American sculptor who enjoyed celebrity status as a speaker and educator. One hundred fifty thousand people attended the ceremony on June 8, 1912, which was sponsored by the Knights of Columbus, the world's biggest Catholic fraternal organization, founded in 1882 and named, inevitably, for Christopher Columbus. (Its knights, incidentally, do not belong to a chivalric or sovereign order such as the Knights of Malta; the organization is devoted to charitable service.) During the celebration, General Robert K. Evans, chief of military affairs, served as marshal, leading 15,000 troops, 50,000 representatives of the Knights of Columbus, horse-drawn floats, participants in so-called knightly costumes, and several thousand automobiles as President William Howard Taft watched from the stands. Among other large-scale public events was a Mass with Cardinal James Gibbons, attended by about 10,000 individuals.

❧ SELECTED BIBLIOGRAPHY ❦

Books

Abulafia, David. *The Discovery of Mankind: Atlantic Encounters in the Age of Columbus.* New Haven: Yale University Press, 2008.

Airaldi, Gabriella, et al. *Cristoforo Colombo nella Genova del suo tempo.* Torino: Edizioni RAI, 1985.

Baker, J. A. *Complete History of the Inquisition in Portugal, Spain, Italy, the East and West-Indies.* Westminster: O. Payne, 1736.

Bedini, Silvio A., ed. *The Christopher Columbus Encyclopedia.* 2 vols. New York: Simon & Schuster, 1992.

Benzoni, Girolamo. *History of the New World.* Translated and edited by W. H. Smith. London: Hakluyt Society, 1857. (Originally published 1565.)

Berggren, J. L. *Ptolemy's Geography: An Annotated Translation of the Theoretical Chapters.* Princeton: Princeton University Press, 2000.

Bergreen, Laurence. *Over the Edge of the World: Magellan's Terrifying Circumnavigation of the Globe.* New York: William Morrow, 2003.

———. *Marco Polo: From Venice to Xanadu.* New York: Alfred A. Knopf, 2007.

Birmingham, Stephen. *The Grandees: America's Sephardic Elite.* New York: Harper & Row, 1971.

The Book of Privileges Issued to Christopher Columbus by King Fernando and Queen Isabel, 1492–1502. Edited and translated by Helen Nader. Vol. 2, *Repertorium Columbianum.* Berkeley: University of California Press, 1996.

Boorstin, Daniel J. *The Discoverers.* New York: Random House, 1983.

Borah, Woodrow W., and Sherburne F. Cook. *The Aboriginal Population of Central Mexico on the Eve of the Spanish Conquest.* Berkeley: University of California Press, 1963.

Boyle, David. *Toward the Setting Sun: Columbus, Cabot, Vespucci, and the Race for America.* New York: Walker, 2008.

Bradford, Ernle. *Christopher Columbus.* New York: Viking, 1973.

Braudel, Fernand. *The Structures of Everyday Life: The Limits of the Possible.* London: Collins, 1981.

Brinton, Daniel G. *The Maya Chronicles.* New York: AMS Press, 1969. (Originally printed 1882.)

Brook, Timothy. *The Confusions of Pleasure: Commerce and Culture in Ming China.* Berkeley: University of California Press, 1998.

Brown, Lloyd A. *The Story of Maps.* New York: Dover, 1977. (Originally published 1949.)

Catz, Rebecca. *Christopher Columbus and the Portuguese, 1476–1498.* Westport, CT: Greenwood, 1993.

Cesarini, Secondo Francesco. "Nomi ricorrenti di banchieri (alcuni legati al papato) nella preparazione dell'impresa Colombiana." In *Atti e Memorie, Nuova Serie,* vol. 34–35. Savona: Società Savonese di Storia Patria, 1998–1999.

Christopher Columbus: Accounts and Letters of the Second, Third, and Fourth Voyages. Translated by Luciano F. Farina and Mark A. Beckwith. Vol. 6, part 1, *Nuova Raccolta Colombiana.* Roma: Istituto Poligrafico e Zecca dello Stato, 1994.

Christopher Columbus: Accounts and Letters of the Second, Third, and Fourth Voyages. Edited by Paolo Emilio Taviani, Consuelo Varela, Juan Gil, and Marina Conti. Translated by Luciano F. Farina and Mark A. Beckwith. Vol. 6, part 2, *Nuova Raccolta Colombiana.* Roma: Istituto Poligrafico e Zecca dello Stato, 1994.

Christopher Columbus and His Family: The Genoese and Ligurian Documents. Edited by John Dotson. Vol. 4, *Repertorium Columbianum.* Turnhout, Belgium: Brepols, 1998.

Christopher Columbus: The Journal, Account of the First Voyage and Discovery of the Indies. Translated by Marc A. Beckwith and Luciano Farina. Edited by Paolo Emilio Taviani and Consuelo Varela. Vol. 1, part 1, *Nuova Raccolta Colombiana.* Roma: Istituto Poligrafico e Zecca dello Stato, 1992.

Christopher Columbus: The Journal, Account of the First Voyage and Discovery of the Indies. Translated by Marc A. Beckwith and Luciano Farina. Edited by Paolo Emilio Taviani and Consuelo Varela. Vol. 1, part 2, *Nuova Raccolta Colombiana.* Roma: Istituto Poligrafico e Zecca dello Stato, 1992.

Christopher Columbus's Discoveries in the Testimonials of Diego Alvarez Chanca and Andrés Bernáldez. Translated by Giocchino Triolo and Luciano F. Farina. Vol. 5, *Nuova Raccolta Colombiana.* Roma: Istituto Poligrafico e Zecca dello Stato, 1992.

Clough, Cecil H., and P.E.H. Hair. *The European Outthrust and Encounter: The First Phase c. 1400–c. 1700.* Liverpool: Liverpool University Press, 1994.

Cohen, J. M., ed. and trans. *The Four Voyages of Christopher Columbus.* London: Penguin, 1969.

Colón, Cristóbal. *Textos y documentos completos: relaciones de viajes, cartas y memorials, edición, prólogo y notas de Consuelo Varela.* Madrid: Alianza, 1982.

Colón, Fernando. *The History of the Life and Deeds of the Admiral Don Christopher Columbus, Attributed to His Son Fernando Colón.* Edited by Ilaria Caraci Luzzana. Translated by Geoffrey Symcox and Blair Sullivan. Turnhout, Belgium: Brepols, 2004.

———. *The Life of the Admiral Christopher Columbus by His Son Ferdinand.* Translated by Benjamin Keen. New Brunswick, NJ: Rutgers University Press, 1959.

Columbus, Christopher. *Columbus Discovers America A.D. 1492* (letters of Christopher Columbus and of Ferdinand Columbus). Historical booklets; no. 104, n.p., n.d. Columbia University Libraries.

Columbus, Ferdinand. *Historie Concerning the Life and Deeds of the Admiral Don Christopher Columbus.* Edited by Paolo Emilio Taviani and Ilaria Luzzana Caraci. Translated by Luciano F. Farina. Vol. 4, part 1, *Nuova Raccolta Colombiana.* Roma: Istituto Poligrafico e Zecca dello Stato, 1998.

Columbus, Ferdinand. *Historie Concerning the Life and Deeds of the Admiral Don Christopher Columbus.* Translated and edited by Luciano F. Farina. Vol. 4, part 2, *Nuova Raccolta Colombiana.* Roma: Istituto Poligrafico e Zecca dello Stato, 1998.

Conti, Simonetta. *Bibliografia colombiana, 1793–1990.* Genova: Cassa di Risparmio di Genova e Imperia, 1990.

Cook, Noble David. *Born to Die: Disease and New World Conquest, 1492–1650.* Cambridge: Cambridge University Press, 1998.

Crane, Nicholas. *Mercator: The Man Who Mapped the Planet.* London: Weidenfeld & Nicolson, 2002.

Crayton, Michael, and Gail Saunders. *Islanders in the Stream: A History of the Bahamian People.* Vol. 1. Athens: University of Georgia Press, 1992.

Crosby, Alfred W., Jr. *The Columbian Exchange: Biological and Cultural Consequences of 1492.* Westport, CT: Greenwood, 1972.

Crow, John A. *Spain: The Root and the Flower.* New York: Harper & Row, 1975.

Darwin, Charles. *The Voyage of the Beagle.* Washington, DC: National Geographic Society, 2004.

Davidson, Miles H. *Columbus Then and Now: A Life Reexamined.* Norman: University of Oklahoma Press, 1997.

Deagan, Kathleen, and José María Cruxent. *Columbus's Outpost among the Taínos: Spain and America at La Isabela, 1493–1498.* New Haven: Yale University Press, 2002.

De Madariaga, Salvador. *Christopher Columbus: Being the Life of the Very Magnificent Lord Don Cristóbal Colón.* New York: Macmillan, 1940.

De Negri, Teofilo Ossian. *Storia di Genova.* Milano: Aldo Martello Editore, 1968.

Denevan, William M., ed. *The Native Population of the Americas in 1492.* 2nd ed. Madison: University of Wisconsin Press, 1992.

De Vorsey, Louis, Jr. *In the Wake of Columbus: Islands and Controversy.* Edited by John Parker. Detroit: Wayne State University Press, 1985.

Diamond, Jared. *Collapse: How Societies Choose to Fail or Succeed.* New York: Viking Penguin, 2005.

Díaz del Castillo, Bernal. *Historia verdadera de la conquista de la Nueva España.* Translated by A. P. Maudslay (*The Discovery and Conquest of Mexico, 1517–1521*). New York: Farrar, Straus, and Cudahy, 1956.

Didiez Burgos, Ramón J. *Guanahani y Mayaguain, las primeras isletas descubiertas en el Nuevo Mundo: análisis del diario de Colón.* Santo Domingo: Editora Cultural Dominicana, 1974.

The Discovery of the New World in the Writings of Peter Martyr of Anghiera. Edited by Ernesto Lunardi et al. Translated by Felix Azzola and Luciano F. Farina. Vol. 2, *Nuova Raccolta Colombiana.* Roma: Istituto Poligrafico e Zecca dello Stato, 1992.

Dor-Ner, Zvi. *Columbus and the Age of Discovery.* New York: William Morrow, 1991.

Drew, David. *The Lost Chronicles of the Maya Kings.* Berkeley: University of California Press, 1999.

Dugard, Martin. *The Last Voyage of Columbus.* New York: Little, Brown, 2005.

Ebbesmeyer, Curtis, and Eric Scigliano. *Flotsametrics and the Floating World.* New York: HarperCollins, 2009.

Epstein, Steven A. *Genoa and the Genoese, 958–1528.* Chapel Hill: University of North Carolina Press, 1996.

Fernández-Armesto, Felipe. *Amerigo: The Man Who Gave His Name to America.* New York: Random House, 2007.

———. *Columbus.* Oxford: Oxford University Press, 1991.

———. *1492: The Year the World Began.* New York: HarperCollins, 2009.

———, ed. *The Times Atlas of World Exploration: 3,000 Years of Exploring, Explorers, and Mapmaking.* New York: HarperCollins, 1991.

Fernández de Oviedo y Valdés, Gonzalo. *Natural History of the West Indies.* Translated and edited by Sterling A. Stoudemire. Chapel Hill: University of North Carolina Press, 1959.

Ferro, Gaetano. *Liguria and Genoa at the Time of Columbus.* Translated by Anne Goodrich Heck. Vol. 3, *Nuova Raccolta Colombiana.* Roma: Istituto Poligrafico e Zecca dello Stato, 1992.

Fiske, John. *The Discovery of America: With Some Account of Ancient America and the Spanish Conquest.* 2 vols. Boston: Houghton Mifflin, 1896.

Freud, Sigmund. *Totem and Taboo: Some Points of Agreement between the Mental Lives of Savages and Neurotics.* Translated by James Strachey. New York: W. W. Norton, 1950.

Frimmer, Steven. *Neverland: Fabled Places and Fabulous Voyages of History and Legend.* New York: Viking, 1976.

Frye, John. *Los Otros: Columbus and the Three Who Made His Enterprise of the Indies Succeed.* Lewistown, NY: E. Mellan, 1992.

Fuson, Robert H., trans. *The Log of Christopher Columbus.* Camden, ME: International Marine Publishing, 1987.

Gardiner, Robert, ed. *Cogs, Caravels and Galleons: The Sailing Ship, 1000–1650.* Annapolis: Naval Institute Press, 1994.

Genoa, Commissione Colombiana. *Cristoforo Colombo, documenti & prove della sua appartenenza a Genova.* Bergamo: Officine Dell' Istituto Italiano D'Arti Grafiche, 1931.

Genoa, Commissione Colombiana. *Christopher Columbus: Documents and Proofs of His Genoese Origin.* English-German edition. Bergamo: Officine Dell' Istituto Italiano D'Arti Grafiche, 1932.

Gerace, Donald T., ed. *Columbus and His World: Proceedings First San Salvador Conference.* Fort Lauderdale, FL: Station, 1987.

Gerber, Jane S. *The Jews of Spain.* New York: Free Press, 1992.

Gil, Juan. *Columbiana: Estudios sobre Cristóbal Cólon, 1984–2006.* Santo Domingo: Academia Dominicana de la Historia, 2007.

Gould, Alicia B[ache]. *Nueva lista documentada de los tripulantes de Colón en 1492.* Madrid: Academia de la Historia, 1984.

Granzotto, Gianni. *Christopher Columbus: The Dream and the Obsession.* Garden City, NY: Doubleday, 1985.

Guillen y Tato, Julio. *La parla marinera en el diario del primer viaje de Cristóbal Colón.* Madrid: Instituto Histórico de Marina, 1951.

Haliczer, Stephen. "The Expulsion of the Jews as Social Process." *The Jews of Spain and the Expulsion of 1492.* Edited by Moshe Lazar and Stephen Haliczer. Lancaster, CA: Labyrinthos, 1997.

Haring, Clarence Henry. *Trade and Navigation Between Spain and the Indies in the Time of the Hapsburgs.* Cambridge: Harvard University Press, 1918.

Harrisse, Henry. *Christophe Columbe: Son origine, sa vie, ses voyages, sa famille & ses descendents.* 2 vols. Paris: E. Leroux, 1884–5.

———. *Christopher Columbus and the Bank of St. George* (Ufficio di San Giorgio in Genoa): Two Letters Addressed to Samuel L. M. Barlow, Esquire, by Henry Harrisse. New York, 1888. (Privately printed.)

Heers, Jacques. *Christophe Colomb.* Paris: Hachette, 1981.

Henige, David. *Historical Evidence and Argument.* Madison: University of Wisconsin Press, 2005.

Hitchings, Henry. *The Secret Life of Words: How English Became English.* London: John Murray, 2008.

Houben, H. H. *Christopher Columbus: The Tragedy of a Discoverer.* Translated by John Linton. New York: E. P. Dutton, 1936.

Houston, Stephen D. *The First Writing: Script Invention as History and Process.* Cambridge: Cambridge University Press, 2004.

Houston, Stephen D., et al. "Maya Systems." *The Oxford Encyclopedia of Mesoamerican Cultures.* Edited by David Carrasco. Oxford: Oxford University Press, 2006.

Howgego, Raymond John. *Encyclopedia of Exploration, 1800 to 1850.* Sydney: Hordern House, 2004.

Irving, Washington. *The Life and Voyages of Christopher Columbus.* New York: University Society Publishers, 1828.

Italian Reports on America, 1493–1522: Accounts by Contemporary Observers. Edited by Geoffrey Symcox. Translated by Theodore Cachey Jr. and John C. McLucas. Vol. 10, *Repertorium Columbianum.* Turnhout, Belgium: Brepols, 2002.

Italian Reports on America, 1493–1522: Letters, Dispatches, and Papal Bulls. Edited by Geoffrey Symcox and Luciano Formisano. Translated by Peter D. Diehl. Vol. 12, *Repertorium Columbianum.* Turnhout, Belgium: Brepols, 2001.

Jane, Cecil, ed. and trans. *The Four Voyages of Columbus.* New York: Dover, 1988.

Keay, John. *The Spice Route: A History.* London: John Murray, 2005.

Kuhn, Thomas S. *The Structure of Scientific Revolutions,* 3rd ed. Chicago: University of Chicago Press, 1996.

Landström, Björn. *Columbus: The Story of Don Cristóbal Colón, Admiral of the Ocean, and His Four Voyages Westward to the Indies, According to Contemporary Sources.* Retold and illustrated by Björn Landström. Translated by Michael Phillips and Hugh W. Stubbs. New York: Macmillan, 1967.

Larner, John. *Marco Polo and the Discovery of the World.* New Haven: Yale University Press, 1999.

Las Casas, Bartolomé de. *A Short Account of the Destruction of the Indies.* Edited and translated by Nigel Griffin. London: Penguin, 1992, rev. 2004.

Las Casas on Columbus: Background and the Second and Fourth Voyages. Edited and translated by Nigel Griffin. Vol. 7, *Repertorium Columbianum*. Turnhout, Belgium: Brepols, 1999.

Las Casas on Columbus: The Third Voyage. Edited by Geoffrey Symcox. Vol. 11, *Repertorium Columbianum*. Turnhout, Belgium: Brepols, 2001.

Lea, Henry Charles. *A History of the Inquisition of Spain*. Vol. 3. New York: AMS Press, 1988. (Originally published 1906–1907.)

———. *Torture*. Philadelphia: University of Philadelphia Press, 1973. (Originally published 1866.)

León Guerrero, Montserrat. *Los compañeros de Don Cristóbal Colón en su segundo viaje a las Indias*. Valladolid: Instituto Interuniversitario de Estudios de Iberoamérica y Portugal, 1998.

Lester, Toby. *The Fourth Part of the World: The Race to the Ends of the Earth, and the Epic Story of the Map That Gave America Its Name*. New York: Free Press, 2009.

Lewis, Monty, and Sara Lewis. *Explorer Chartbook: Far Bahamas*. 4th ed. Ocean City, MD: Lewis Offshore, 2008.

Library of Congress. *Hispanic and Portuguese Collections: An Illustrated Guide*. Washington, DC: Library of Congress, 1996.

Limborch, Philippus van. *The History of the Inquisition*. Translated by Samuel Chandler. 2 vols. London: J. Gray, 1731.

Liss, Peggy K. *Isabel the Queen: Life and Times*. Rev. ed. Philadelphia: University of Pennsylvania Press, 2004.

Lockhart, James, ed. and trans. *We People Here: Nahuatl Accounts of the Conquest of Mexico*. Berkeley: University of California Press, 1993.

Lowney, Chris. *A Vanished World: Muslims, Christians, and Jews in Medieval Spain*. New York: Oxford University Press, 2006.

Machiavelli, Niccolò. *The Prince*. Translated and edited by Paul Sonnino. Atlantic Highlands, NJ: Humanities Press, 1996.

McNeill, William H. *Plagues and Peoples*. Garden City, NY: Anchor, 1976.

Mandeville, John. *The Travels of Sir John Mandeville*. Translated by C.W.R.D. Moseley. London: Penguin, 1983.

Mann, Charles C. *1491: New Revelations of the Americas before Columbus*. New York: Alfred A. Knopf, 2006.

Manzano Manzano, Juan. *Colón y su secreto: el predescubrimiento*. Madrid: Cultura Hispánica, 1989.

Marchant, John, et al. *A Review of the Bloody Tribunal; Or the Horrid Cruelties of the Inquisition*. Perth: G. Johnston, 1770.

Markham, Clements R., trans. and ed. *The Letters of Amerigo Vespucci and Other Documents Illustrative of His Career*. London: Hakluyt Society, 1894.

Martínez-Hidalgo, José María. *Columbus' Ships*. Edited by Howard I. Chapelle. Barre, MA: Barre Publishers, 1966.

Mascarenhas, Barreto. *"Colombo" Português: Provas Documentais*. 2 vols. Lisboa: Nova Arraniada, 1977.

Maxwell, Judith M., and Robert H. Hill. *Kaqchiqel Chronicles: The Definitive Edition*. Austin: University of Texas Press, 2006.

Melville, Elinor G. K. *A Plague of Sheep: Environmental Consequences of the Conquest of Mexico*. Cambridge: Cambridge University Press, 1994.

Michener, James. *Caribbean*. New York: Random House, 1989.

Milani, Virgil I. *The Written Language of Christopher Columbus*. Buffalo: State University of New York at Buffalo, 1973.

Milhou, Alain. *Colón y su mentalidad mesiánica en el ambiente franciscanista español*. Valladolid: Casa-Museo de Colón, Seminario Americanista de la Universidad de Valladolid, 1983.

Mocatta, Frederic David. *The Jews of Spain and Portugal and the Inquisition*. New York: Cooper Square Publishers, 1973.

Morgan, Edmund S. *American Heroes: Profiles of Men and Women Who Shaped Early America*. New York: W. W. Norton, 2009.

Morison, Samuel Eliot. *Admiral of the Ocean Sea: A Life of Christopher Columbus*. 2 vols. Boston: Little, Brown, 1942.

———. *Admiral of the Ocean Sea: A Life of Christopher Columbus*. Boston: Little, Brown, 1942. (1 vol. abridgment.)

———. *Christopher Columbus, Mariner*. New York: Meridian, 1983.

———. *The European Discovery of America: The Southern Voyages, 1492–1616*. New York: Oxford University Press, 1974.

———. *The Second Voyage of Christopher Columbus from Cadiz to Hispaniola and the Discovery of the Lesser Antilles*. Oxford: Oxford University Press, 1939.

———, ed. and trans. *Journals and Other Documents on the Life and Voyages of Christopher Columbus*. New York: Heritage, 1963.

Morison, Samuel Eliot, and Mauricio Obregón. *The Caribbean as Columbus Saw It*. Boston: Atlantic Monthly Press, 1964.

Moya Pons, Frank. *Después de Colón: Trabajo, sociedad y política en la economía del oro*. Madrid: Alianza Editorial, 1987.

———. *The Dominican Republic: A National History*. Princeton, NJ: Markus Wiener, 1998.

———. *Los Restos de Colón—Bibliografía*. Santo Domingo: Academia Dominicana de la Historia, 2006.

Munro, John H. *Textiles, Towns and Trade: Essays in the Economic History of Late-Medieval England and the Low Countries*. Brookfield, VT: Variorum, 1994.

Naipaul, V. S. "Columbus and Crusoe." In *The Writer and the World*. New York: Vintage, 2003.

Navarrete, Martín Fernández de. *Colección de los viages y descubrimientos, que hicieron por mar los Españoles desde fines del siglo XV, con varios documentos inéditos concernientes á la historia de la marina castellana y de los establecimientos españoles en Indias*. 2nd ed. 5 vols. Madrid: de Ordean de S.M. en la Imprenta Nacional, 1837–1880.

Nunn, George E. *The Columbus and Magellan Concepts of South American Geography*. Glenside, 1932. (Privately printed.)

———. *The Geographical Conceptions of Columbus: A Critical Consideration of Four Problems*. New York: American Geographical Society, 1924.

Ober, Frederick A. *Amerigo Vespucci*. New York: Harper & Brothers, 1907.

Obregón, Mauricio. *From Argonauts to Astronauts: An Unconventional History of Discovery.* New York: Harper & Row, 1980.

Oviedo on Columbus. Edited by Jesús Carillo. Translated by Diane Avalle-Arce. Vol. 9, *Repertorium Columbianum.* Turnhout, Belgium: Brepols, 2000.

Pandiani, Emilio. *Vita privata genovese nel Rinascimento.* Genova: Tipografia Nazionale di Luigi Sambolino, 1915.

———. *Vita della Repubblica di Genova nell'Etá di Cristoforo Columbo.* Genova: Pubblicazione del Civico Istituto Colombiano, Comitato Cittadino per le Celebrazioni Colombiane, 1952.

Parr, Charles McKew. *So Noble a Captain.* New York: Thomas Y. Crowell, 1953.

Parry, J. H. *The Discovery of the Sea.* Berkeley: University of California Press, 1981.

Pérez-Mallaína, Pablo E. *Spain's Men of the Sea.* Translated by Carla Rahn Phillips. Baltimore, MD: Johns Hopkins University Press, 1998.

Phillips, William D., Jr., and Carla Rahn Phillips. *The Worlds of Christopher Columbus.* Cambridge: Cambridge University Press, 1992.

Pike, Ruth. *Enterprise and Adventure: The Genoese in Seville and the Opening of the New World.* Ithaca, NY: Cornell University Press, 1966.

———. *Linajudos and Conversos in Seville.* New York: Peter Lang, 2000.

Polo, Marco. *Marco Polo: The Description of the World.* Translated by A. C. Moule and Paul Pelliot. 2 vols. New York: AMS Press, 1976.

———. *The Travels of Marco Polo, the Venetian.* Translated by W. Marsden. Revised by T. Wright and Peter Harris. New York: Alfred A. Knopf, 2008.

Provost, Foster. *Columbus: An Annotated Guide to the Scholarship on His Life and Writings, 1750–1988.* Detroit, MI: Published for the John Carter Brown Library by Omnigraphics, 1991.

———. *Columbus Dictionary.* Detroit, MI: Published for the John Carter Brown Library by Omnigraphics, 1991.

Ptak, Roderich. *China, the Portuguese, and the Nanyang: Oceans and Routes, Regions and Trades (c. 1000–1600).* Aldershot, Hampshire, UK; Burlington, VT: Ashgate/Variorum, 2004.

Qétel, Claude. *History of Syphilis.* Translated by Judith Braddock and Brian Pike. Baltimore, MD: Johns Hopkins University Press, 1990.

"The Recovery of Ptolemy's *Geography* in Renaissance Italy and Its impact in Spain and Portugal in the Period of the Discoveries." In *Geography, Cartography and Nautical Science in the Renaissance: The Impact of the Great Discoveries,* by W.G.L. Randles. Aldershot, Hampshire, UK; Burlington, VT: Ashgate/Variorum, 2000.

Rosengarten, Frederic, Jr. *The Book of Spices.* Rev. ed. New York: Pyramid, 1973.

Roth, Norman. *Conversos, Inquisition, and the Expulsion of the Jews from Spain.* Madison: University of Wisconsin Press, 1995.

Rouse, Irving. *The Tainos: Rise and Decline of the People Who Greeted Columbus.* New Haven: Yale University Press, 1992.

Rumeu de Armas, Antonio, ed., *El Libro Copiador de Cristóbal Colón,* 2 vols. Madrid: Real Academia de la Historia, 1989.

———. *Hernando Colón, historiador de descubrimiento de América.* Madrid: Instituto de Cultura Hispánica, 1973.

Salaman, Redcliffe N. *The History and Social Influence of the Potato.* Cambridge: Cambridge University Press, 1993.

Sale, Kirkpatrick. *The Conquest of Paradise: Christopher Columbus and the Columbian Legacy.* New York: Alfred A. Knopf, 1990.

Sauer, Carol Ortwin. *The Early Spanish Main.* Berkeley: University of California Press, 1966.

Smith, Bradley. *Columbus in the New World.* Garden City, NY: Doubleday, 1962.

Smith, Roger Craig. "Vanguard of Empire: 15th and 16th-Century Iberian Ship Technology in the Age of Discovery." PhD dissertation. Texas A&M University, 1989.

———. *Vanguard of Empire: Ships of Exploration in the Age of Columbus.* New York: Oxford University Press, 1993.

Soyer, François. *The Persecution of the Jews and Muslims of Portugal: King Manuel I and the End of Religious Tolerance (1496–7).* Leiden; Boston: Brill, 2007.

Stevens-Arroyo, Antonio M. *Cave of the Jagua [sic]: The Mythological World of the Tainos.* Scranton, PA: University of Scranton Press, 2006.

Taviani, Paolo Emilio. *Christopher Columbus: The Grand Design.* Translated by William Weaver. London: Orbis, 1985.

———. *Columbus: The Great Adventure.* Translated by Luciano F. Farina and Marc A. Beckwith. New York: Orion, 1991.

———. "Il ruolo di Genova e Liguria nella formazione culturale di Colombo." In *Cristoforo Colombo e l'Apertura degli Spazi.* Roma: Istituto Poligrafico e Zecca dello Stato, 1992.

Testimonies from the Columbian Lawsuits. Edited and translated by William D. Phillips, Jr. Vol. 8, *Repertorium Columbianum.* Turnhout, Belgium: Brepols, 2000.

Thacher, John Boyd. *Christopher Columbus: His Life, His Works, His Remains, As Revealed by Original Printed and Manuscript Records, Together with an Essay on Peter Martyr of Anghiera and Bartolomé de Las Casas, the First Historians of America.* 3 vols. New York; London: G. P. Putnam's Sons, 1903–4.

Thomas, David Hurst, ed. *Columbian Consequences.* Vol. 1, *Archaeological and Historical Perspectives on the Spanish Borderlands West.* Washington, DC: Smithsonian Institution Press, 1989.

———. *Columbian Consequences.* Vol. 2, *Archaeological and Historical Perspectives on the Spanish Borderlands East.* Washington, DC: Smithsonian Institution Press, 1990.

———. *Columbian Consequences.* Vol. 3, *The Spanish Borderlands in Pan-American Perspective.* Washington, DC: Smithsonian Institution Press, 1991.

Thomas, Hugh. *Rivers of Gold: The Rise of the Spanish Empire, from Columbus to Magellan.* New York: Random House, 2003.

Thornton, Russel. *American Indian Holocaust and Survival: A Population History Since 1492.* Norman: University of Oklahoma Press, 1987.

Torre y del Cerro, José de la. *Beatriz Enríquez de Harana y Cristóbal Colón: estudio y documentos.* Madrid: Compañía Iberoamericana de Publicaciones, 1933.

Ulanski, Stan. *The Gulf Stream: Tiny Plankton, Giant Bluefin, and the Amazing Story of the Powerful River in the Atlantic.* Chapel Hill: University of North Carolina Press, 2008.

Varela, Consuelo. *La caída de Cristobál Colón, el juicio de Bobadilla.* Madrid: Marcial Pons, Ediciones de Historia, 2006.

Viola, Herman J., and Carolyn Margolis. *Seeds of Change: A Quincentennial Commemoration.* Washington, DC: Smithsonian Institution Press, 1991.

Wassermann, Jakob. *Christopher Columbus: Don Quixote of the Seas.* Translated by Eric Sutton. London: M. Secker, 1930.

Wey Gómez, Nicolás. *The Tropics of Empire: Why Columbus Sailed South to the Indies.* Cambridge, MA: MIT Press, 2008.

Wiesenthal, Simon. *Sails of Hope: The Secret Mission of Christopher Columbus.* Translated by Richard and Clara Winston. New York: Macmillan, 1973.

Wilford, John Noble. *The Mapmakers.* New York: Alfred A. Knopf, 2000.

———. *The Mysterious History of Columbus.* New York: Alfred A. Knopf, 1991.

Winsor, Justin. *Christopher Columbus and How He Received and Imparted the Spirit of Discovery.* Boston: Houghton Mifflin, 1892.

———, ed. *Narrative and Critical History of America.* Vol. 2. Boston: Houghton Mifflin, 1886.

Zamora, Margarita. *Reading Columbus.* Berkeley: University of California Press, 1993.

Zhang, Tianze. *Sino-Portuguese Trade from 1514 to 1644: A Synthesis of Portuguese and Chinese Sources.* Leyden: Late E. J. Brill, 1934.

Periodicals

Cook, Noble David. "Sickness, Starvation, and Death in Early Hispaniola." *Journal of Interdisciplinary History,* vol. 32, no. 3 (Winter 2002), pp. 349–86.

Deagan, Kathleen A. "La Isabela: Europe's First Foothold in the New World." *National Geographic,* vol. 181, no. 1, pp. 40–53.

Grennes, Thomas. "The Columbian Exchange and the Reversal of Fortune." *Cato Journal,* vol. 27, no. 1 (Winter 2007).

Guitar, Lynn. "New Notes about Taíno Music and Its Influence on Contemporary Dominican Life." *Issues in Caribbean Amerindian Studies,* vol. 7, no. 1 (Dec. 2006–Dec. 2007), p. 394.

Hobbs, William Herbert. "The Track of the Columbus Caravels in 1492." *Hispanic American Historical Review,* vol. 30, no. 1 (Feb. 1950), pp. 63–73.

Judge, Joseph, and James L. Stanfield. "Where Columbus Found the New World." *National Geographic,* vol. 170, no. 5 (Nov. 1986), pp. 566–99.

Keegan, William F. "Beachhead in the Bahamas: Columbus Encounters a New World." *Archeology,* Jan./Feb. 1992, pp. 44–50.

Keith, Donald H., Toni L. Carell, and Denise C. Lakey. "The Search for Columbus' Caravel *Gallega* and the Site of Santa María de Belén." *Journal of Field Archeology,* vol. 17, no. 2 (Summer 1990), pp. 123–40.

Kingsbury, John M. "Christopher Columbus as a Botanist." *Arnoldia*, vol. 2, no. 52 (Spring 1992), pp. 11–28.

Lyon, Eugene. "15th-Century Manuscript Yields First Look at *Niña*." *National Geographic*, vol. 170, no. 5 (Nov. 1986).

———. "Search for Columbus." *National Geographic*, vol. 181, no. 1 (Jan. 1992), pp. 2–39.

———. "The *Niña*, the *Santa Cruz*, and Other Caravels as Described in the *Libro de Armadas* and Other Spanish Records." *American Neptune*, vol. 53 (1993), pp. 239–46.

Marden, Luis. "Tracking Columbus across the Atlantic." *National Geographic*, vol. 170, no. 5 (Nov. 1986).

Myers, Robert A. "Island Carib Cannibalism." *New West Indian Guide* (Leiden), vol. 58, no. 3–4 (1984), pp. 147–84.

Parodi, Giuseppe. "L'Arte dei Macherolii." *Atti della Società Ligure di Storia Patria* (Genova), *Miscellanea Storica*, vol. 53 (1926).

Rumeu de Armas, Antonio. "Cristobál Colón y Doña Beatriz de Bobadilla en las antevisperas del descubrimiento." *El Museo Canario* (Las Palmas de Gran Canaria), vols. 75–76, no. 21 (1960).

———. "Los amoríos de doña Beatriz de Bobadilla." *Anuario de Estudios Atlánticos*, no. 31 (1985), pp. 413–55.

Taylor, Paul S. "Spanish Seamen in the New World during the Colonial Period." *Hispanic American Historical Review*, vol. 5 (1922).

Torodash, Martin. "Columbus Historiography Since 1939." *Hispanic American Historical Review*, vol. 46, no. 4 (Nov. 1966), pp. 409–28.

Varela, Consuelo. "Proof That Columbus Was Born in 1451: A New Document." *American Historical Review*, vol. 12, no. 2 (Jan. 1907), pp. 270–79.

Vignaud, Henry. "Columbus a Spaniard and a Jew." *American Historical Review*, vol. 18, no. 3 (Apr. 1913), pp. 505–12.

West, Delno C. "Christopher Columbus, Lost Biblical Sites, and the Last Crusade." *Catholic Historical Review*, vol. 78, no. 4 (Oct. 1992), pp. v–vi, 519, 541.

Wilford, John Noble. "What Doomed the Maya? Maybe Warfare Run Amok." *New York Times*, March 10, 2009.

✺ INDEX ✺

ILLUSTRATION CREDITS

Insert 1

13   *Top*: Museo Galileo, Florence – Photo Franca Principe. *Bottom*: HM 177 Gonzalo Fernández de Oviedo y Valdes, Historia general y natural de las indias, 1539–1548, The Huntington Library, San Marino, CA.

14   *Top*: HM 177 Gonzalo Fernández de Oviedo y Valdes, Historia general y natural de las indias, 1539–1548, The Huntington Library, San Marino, CA. *Center*: akg – images. *Bottom*: Private Collection / The Bridgeman Art Library.

15   *Top and Bottom*: Bibliothèque nationale, Paris, France / Archives Charmet / The Bridgeman Art Library.

16   akg – images.

Insert 2

1   The Granger Collection, New York.

2   The Granger Collection, New York.

3   The Granger Collection, New York.

4–5   The Art Archive / Museo Navale Pegli / Gianni Dagli Orti.

6–7   Art Resource, NY.

8–9   Huntington Library and Art Gallery, San Marino, CA, USA / Photo © AISA / The Bridgeman Art Library.

10–11   akg – images.

12–13   Courtesy of the John Carter Brown Library at Brown University.

14–15   Courtesy of the John Carter Brown Library at Brown University.

16   *Top*: Courtesy of the John Carter Brown Library at Brown University. *Bottom*: bpk, Berlin / Staats- und Stadtbibliothek, Augsburg, Germany / Knud Petersen / Art Resource, NY.

Insert 3

1 *Top*: akg – images. *Center*: Courtesy of the John Carter Brown Library at Brown University. *Bottom*: The Granger Collection, New York.

2 Scala / Art Resource, NY.

3 *Top and Center*: akg – images. *Bottom*: Courtesy of the John Carter Brown Library at Brown University.

4 *Top and Bottom*: Courtesy of the John Carter Brown Library at Brown University.

5 *Top and Bottom*: Courtesy of the John Carter Brown Library at Brown University.

6 *Top and Bottom*: bpk, Berlin / Staats- und Stadtbibliothek, Augsburg, Germany / Knud Petersen / Art Resource, NY.

7 *Top*: akg – images. *Bottom*: Courtesy of the John Carter Brown Library at Brown University.

8–9 Library of Congress, Geography and Map Division.

10 *Top*: The Granger Collection, New York. *Bottom*: akg – images.

11 *Top*: Biblioteca Colombina, Seville, Spain / The Bridgeman Art Library. *Bottom*: Courtesy of the John Carter Brown Library at Brown University.

12 *Top*: akg – images. *Bottom*: The Art Archive / General Archive of the Indies Seville / Gianni Dagli Orti.

13 Musée des Beaux-Arts Andre Malraux, Le Havre, France / Giraudon / The Bridgeman Art Library.

14 Courtesy of the John Carter Brown Library at Brown University.

15 Erich Lessing / Art Resource, NY.

16 Erich Lessing / Art Resource, NY.